ROMAN CATHOLICISM

ROMAN CATHOLICISM

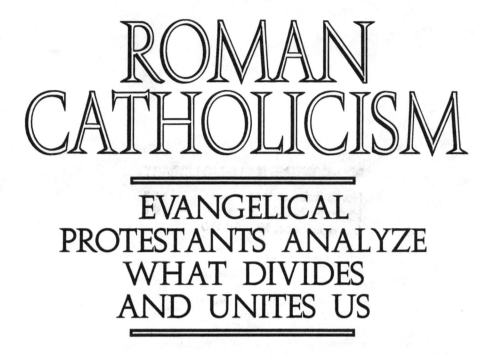

EVANGELICAL PROTESTANTS ANALYZE WHAT DIVIDES AND UNITES US

ALISTER MCGRATH
HAROLD O.J. BROWN
DONALD BLOESCH
MICHAEL HORTON
AND OTHERS
JOHN ARMSTRONG
GENERAL EDITOR

MOODY PRESS
CHICAGO

1994 by
THE MOODY BIBLE INSTITUTE
OF CHICAGO

All Scripture quotations, unless indicated, are taken from the *Holy Bible: New International Version*®. NIV®. Copyright © 1973, 1978, 1984, International Bible Society. Used by permission of Zondervan Publishing House. All rights reserved.

Scripture quotations marked (NASB) are taken from the *New American Standard Bible,* © 1960, 1962, 1963, 1968, 1971, 1972, 1973, 1975, and 1977 by The Lockman Foundation, and are used by permission.

Scripture quotations marked (KJV) are taken from the King James Version.

The use of selected references from various versions of the Bible in this publication does not necessarily imply publisher endorsement of the versions in their entirety.

ISBN: 0-8024-7181-1

1 3 5 7 9 10 8 6 4 2

Printed in the United States of America

*For the reformation of the church
and the revival of biblical Christianity
in an increasingly dark time in history,
when integrity in both life and doctrine
is the crying need of evangelical Christianity.*

*And for my late father, Dr. Thomas Armstrong,
who modeled integrity and quiet courage;
and for Mrs. Marie Armstrong,
my best intercessor and life-long Bible teacher,
a mom who still teaches me to love Christ, His church, and His Word.*

CONTENTS

CONTRIBUTORS

John H. Armstrong (B.A., M.A., Wheaton College; D.Min., Luther Rice Seminary) is founder and director of Reformation and Revival Ministries in Carol Stream, Illinois. He served as a Baptist pastor for twenty-one years before becoming a conference speaker and editor of *Reformation and Revival Journal*, a quarterly publication for church leadership. His forthcoming Moody Press book (1995) deals with ministerial moral failure and biblical concern for a faithful pastoral ministry.

Donald G. Bloesch (B.A., Elmhurst College; B.D., Ph.D., Univ. of Chicago) has done postdoctoral work at Oxford, Basel, and Tübingen. A professor of systematic theology at the University of Dubuque Theological Seminary for more than thirty years, he is the author or editor of twenty-eight books, including *Essentials of Evangelical Theology* (1978), *The Struggle of Prayer* (1980, 1988), *A Theology of Word and Spirit* (1992), and *Holy Scripture* (1994).

Harold O. J. Brown (B.D., Harvard Divinity School; A.B., Th.M., Ph.D., Harvard Univ.) holds the Franklin and Dorothy Forman Chair in Ethics in Theology at Trinity Evangelical Divinity School and is director of the Rockford Institute Center on Religion and Society. Besides pastoring at churches in Switzerland and Massachusetts, he has written several books, including *Death Before Birth* (1978), *The Reconstruction of the Republic* (1981), and *Heresies* (1988).

D. Clair Davis (B.A., M.A., Wheaton College; B.D., Westminster Theological Seminary; Th.D., Göttingen Univ.) has been professor of church history at Westminster Theological Seminary for almost thirty years and is currently chairman of that department as well as chairman of the faculty. An associate pastor at New Life Presbyterian Church in Fort Washington, Pennsylvania, he has also contributed to *John Calvin: His Influence in the Western World, Challenges to Inerrancy,* the *New Dictionary of Theology, Inerrancy and Hermeneutic,* and *Theonomy: A Reformed Critique.*

W. Robert Godfrey (A.B., M.A., Ph.D., Stanford Univ.; M.Div., Gordon-Conwell Theological Seminary) is president and professor of church history at Westminster Theological Seminary in California. The editor of *Westminster Theological Journal* for several years, he has contributed to *John Calvin: His Influence in the Western World, Reformed Theology in America, Scripture and Truth, The Agony of Deceit, Christ the Lord,* and *Discord, Dialogue and Concord.*

Michael S. Horton (B.A., Biola Univ.; M.A.R., Westminster Theological Seminary; D.Phil., Oxford Univ.) is founder and president of Christians United for Reformation (CURE). He is the editor of *The Agony of Deceit* and *Power Religion* and the author of *Mission Accomplished, Made in America, Putting Amazing Back into Grace,* and *Beyond Culture Wars.*

S. Lewis Johnson (Th.M., Th.D., Dallas Theological Seminary) has held professorships at Trinity Evangelical Divinity School and Dallas Theological Seminary. He was involved in the Scripture translation of the *New International Version* and the *Berkeley Bible* and is author of *The Old Testament in the New.*

Alister E. McGrath (M.A., B.D., D.Phil., Oxford Univ.) is presently research lecturer in theology at Oxford University, research professor of systematic theology at Regent College, and lecturer in historical and systematic theology at Wycliffe Hall, Oxford. He is author of *Reformation Thought: An Introduction, Intellectuals Don't Need God and Other Modern Myths, Spirituality in an Age of Change,* and *The Making of Modern German Christology.*

Ronald Nash (M.A., Brown Univ.; Ph.D., Syracuse Univ.) is professor of philosophy and theology at Reformed Theological Seminary. He is the author of more than twenty-five books, including *Is Jesus the Only Savior?, Faith and Reason, Worldviews in Conflict, Beyond Liberation Theology,* and *Great Divides.*

Thomas J. Nettles (M.Div., Ph.D., Southwestern Baptist Theological Seminary) serves as professor and chairman of church history at Trinity Evangelical Divinity School. He is the author of several books, including *Baptists and the Bible* and *By His Grace and For His Glory.*

Kim Riddlebarger (B.A., California State Univ., Fullerton; M.A., Simon Greenleaf Univ.; M.A.R., Westminster Theological Seminary) is a Ph.D. candidate in historical theology at Fuller Theological Seminary. He is executive vice president of Christians United for Reformation (CURE), dean of the CURE Academy, and cohost of the "White Horse Inn" radio program. He has contributed to *Power Religion* and *Christ the Lord* and is a regular contributor to *Modern Reformation* magazine.

Robert B. Strimple (B.A., Univ. of Delaware; B.D., Th.M., Westminster Theological Seminary; Th.D., Univ. of Toronto) is professor of systematic theology at Westminster Theological Seminary in California, serving as the school's first president. He is the author of the forthcoming book *The Search for the Real Jesus* and has contributed to *Christ the Lord* and *Studying the New Testament Today*.

William Webster (B.A., Southern Methodist University), a former Roman Catholic, is a businessman and director of Christian Resources, Inc., a book and tape ministry devoted to teaching and evangelism. He is the author of *Salvation, the Bible, and Roman Catholicism* and *The Christian: Following Christ as Lord*.

ACKNOWLEDGMENTS

The editor would like to thank the board of Reformation & Revival Ministries, Inc. for their support and genuine friendship in laboring with me for reformation in our generation. Each brother is a source of immense encouragement and faithful counsel.

Thanks also to Thomas N. Smith, a true friend who sticks closer than a brother and has done more to teach me to think critically and biblically than anyone in my life.

Thanks also to Dr. Donald Anderson, a faithful editor who serves me in his professional retirement in ways that this word of gratitude cannot adequately express.

A special place will always remain in my heart for the members of Trinity Baptist Church, Wheaton, Illinois, who encouraged me as their pastor for sixteen years and allowed me to read, grow, and minister with such freedom that all I now do in both writing and itinerant ministry is a part of their ongoing contribution to the larger body of Christ.

Mentors, friends, family, and even critics have helped me in far too many ways to express, but special acknowledgment is due Matthew and Stacy, two children who make my life as dad a real joy and bring continual delight to my heart.

Finally, thanks to the one person, my wife Anita, who has shared this project with me for well over a year, giving encouragement, genuine support, and much labor in reading the manuscripts and in the preparation of several important parts of the volume, especially the glossary. She always believed I could write and edit and urged me to stay with it when I might have given up!

INTRODUCTION

John H. Armstrong

A n old English proverb says, "Use soft words and hard arguments." If
anything does *not* describe the ensuing centuries of debate between the
heirs of the Protestant Reformation and Roman Catholicism it is this old proverb! Exceptions have popped up over the years and recent developments
have fostered some improvement in the tone of the debate, but very often the
landscape has been littered by heated debate, often without understanding
truly profound theological disagreements. It is almost like two historic ships
passing in the night without seeing or hearing one another. Neither side can
claim innocence in terms of the harsh manner in which issues have often
been argued. Religious tolerance and the willingness to disagree without
persecution have only recently marked the spirit of both traditions, at least in
Europe and North America. All who name the Name should approach such disagreements with a spirit of humility when they consider the history and issues
of religious disputation between Roman Catholics and Protestant evangelicals.

As the twentieth century comes to a close, the ground is moving beneath
both historic Western traditions in a manner that differs significantly from
any time since the sixteenth century. We are living through an era of rapid
change. Said one statesman some years ago, "All the certainties of the in-
dustrial society in which we live are disintegrating. We are witnessing an
erosion of ideologies, economic theories, and traditional culture."[1] Western
civilization is experiencing shifts of seismic proportions, and the Christian
church is caught up in these major movements. Let me explain.

Protestantism has been fractured in this century both by the devastating
effects of theological liberalism and by the culturally bankrupt reactions of
an increasingly sterile fundamentalism. On the one side, the old historic
denominations are scurrying about trying to find ways to stop their bleeding,
as historic churches and groups experience a slow death through the chilling
effects of a blatant denial of ancient Christian confessions. This was summed
up for me personally a few years ago when I stood in the study of a Protestant pastor who was serving a local church historically related to the Great
Awakening and the best traditions of evangelical religion. I kept trying to
"get a read" on what this pastor believed and affirmed. He kept telling me

that he stood in the Protestant *liberal* tradition, much of which he insisted was in the teaching of the Protestant Reformers. I finally asked him, "Will you affirm the Apostles' Creed with your mind and heart?" He dodged my question several times and noticeably refused to reply. I thought as I left his study that afternoon, What fellowship can I have with a man who will not ascribe honestly to the *essentials* of historic Christianity?

Virtually the opposite experience has frequently been mine as well. As I travel about in more evangelical circles I find myself talking to ministers in a more conservative tradition, who almost always consider themselves quite orthodox, yet they often don't even know the doctrines of the Apostles' Creed. The language of the Chalcedonian Creed (where the essential nature of Christ's person was carefully stated) sounds like a strange dialect unless they vaguely remember something from an old seminary course. Their understanding of the great Christological issues that faced the church in her early centuries is almost nil, and their view of the development of Christian doctrine and practice extends over the inadequate range of some twenty years

What excites these evangelical pastors is church growth, contemporary worship style, and popular music that will move the people. Far be it from these evangelicals to engage in serious discussion of historic debates that literally shaped the streams of the two great Western traditions of Christianity. (Do they even realize that there is an Eastern tradition?) For these, the term *evangelical* has become an adjective used to describe a certain methodology and conservative cultural stance. Historically the word is a noun and a virtual synonym for the theology of salvation (*sola fide, sola gratia*) as taught by the Protestant Reformers. That is, to be evangelical was to be Protestant.

In a significant book, *No Place for Truth,* Professor David Wells sums up my observations well:

> As evangelicalism has continued to grow numerically, it has seeped through its older structures and now spills out in all directions, producing a family of hybrids whose theological connections are quite baffling: evangelical Catholics, evangelicals who are Catholic evangelical liberationists, evangelical feminists, evangelical ecumenists, ecumenists who are evangelicals, young evangelicals, orthodox evangelicals, radical evangelicals, liberal evangelicals, liberals who are evangelical, and charismatic evangelicals. The word *evangelical*, precisely because it has lost its confessional dimension, has become descriptively anemic. To say that someone is an evangelical says little about what they are likely to believe (although it says more if they are older and less if they are younger). And so the term is forced to compensate for its theological weakness by borrowing meaning from adjectives the very presence of which signals the fragmentation and disintegration of the movement. What is now primary is not what is evangelical but what is adjectivally distinctive, whether Catholic, liberationist, feminist, ecumenist, young, orthodox, radical, liberal, or charismatic. It is, I believe, the dark prelude to death, when parasites have finally succeeded in bringing down their host. Amid the clamor of all these new modes of evangelical faith there is the sound of a death rattle.[2]

On the other side of the great Protestant–Roman Catholic historical divide one sees some of the same twentieth-century forces at work. Borrowing from theological liberalism and eating the poisonous fruit of post-Enlightenment modernity, much of Roman Catholic theology and practice has drifted away from its historical roots in the Christian tradition. Relativism reaches from the best Roman Catholic educational institutions all the way down to the priest and his parish committee who no longer believe the doctrines of their own church. The problems of authority have cut deeply into every aspect of Roman Catholic faith and practice. If the reader doubts this observation consider what all the surveys tell us about Catholic practice regarding the papal teaching on birth control. The tradition of the church is maintained, not because it is true but simply because it is *my* tradition. Radical feminism, critical views regarding the real Jesus, liberational social theologies—and old-fashioned syncretism dressed in new and modern clothing—all threaten to destroy the Christian foundations of Roman Catholicism. Even John Paul II leaves us with confusion when he corrects the liberals in his own church and calls upon the curia to address problem theologians like Hans Kung, while at the same time he prays with Hindus, Buddhists, and other non-Christian leaders. More than one Roman Catholic is asking, "What is going on? Why has my church left its foundations? What do we *really* believe?"

In the midst of this confusion a small, new, quite evangelistic, movement in the Roman Catholic Church has arisen that calls for the devout Catholic to understand and commit himself to all of the centuries-old doctrines of the Council of Trent. It was this council, convened during the second phase of the Protestant movement, that promulgated the anti-evangelical positions that effectively slammed the door on meaningful ecumenism in the sixteenth century. Devotion to Mary, to the saints, and to distinctively Roman Catholic sacramentalism is alive and well in these circles and is being urged as the way to a new spiritual revival and genuine Catholic reformation. Converted Protestant evangelicals are now joining ranks and urging young Catholics to remain in the fold while separated evangelicals are aggressively recruited for the church. Those who strongly question these movements are often referred to as "anti-Catholics."[3]

Notable examples of these trends and the converts made through them abound. Many evangelical radio and television outlets give or sell considerable time to this movement, only expanding their effect in many quarters. We will look at this trend and the new converts who are turning to Roman Catholicism.

And now a significant group of leading evangelical and Roman Catholic theologians, ethicists, writers, and teachers have signed a major document of agreement known as "Evangelicals & Catholics Together: The Christian Mission in the Third Millennium" (April 1994). This document, recently reported in the media and much discussed at the present moment, has raised the level of discussion between evangelicals and Roman Catholics to a whole new level, for better or for worse. What are evangelicals, concerned as they must be for the truth confessed by their theological forebearers and committed to serious evangelism in a Protestant biblical manner, to make of a document that properly cites areas of considerable agreement but at the same time urges a moratorium of sorts on overt efforts to call Roman Catholics to find confessionally sound New Testament churches where Word and sacrament are still ordered by the Bible?

Into this uniquely contemporary context this present book is directed. It is not an anti-Catholic book, as a perusal of the essays and the tone of the contributors will readily show. It is an attempt at candid consideration of where we agree and where we still disagree. Many of us count as Christian friends some who are communicant members of the Roman Catholic Church.

We are all serious evangelical Protestants who believe that our tradition reflects the very concerns of the councils of early Christianity. We think of ourselves as those who genuinely affirm the historic teachings of the Christian church. Though Roman Catholic apologists have often accused our forefathers of schism, we rather believe that the evangelicals of the sixteenth century stood on the gospel and affirmed the same view of the Scripture as that universally held by the church Fathers. We do not desire to perpetuate division or separation. We are heartened by certain changes in the twentieth century. We are disheartened by others. We do take the prayer of Jesus in John 17 quite seriously. We have no other choice since we are under the authority of the Word of God.

We hope to show where evangelicals agree with elements of Roman Catholic doctrine. We do have much in common. We affirm the same formulations regarding Christ. We affirm, with those Roman Catholics who have not taken the liberal apple of modern relativism, that Jesus is both God and Man, that He was crucified, that He died a literal death, and that He was buried and on the third day rose again. We affirm His bodily ascension and His coming again at the end of this age. In clearest distinction from the bankrupt modern theologies of both our traditions we affirm with conservative Roman Catholics that the hope of fallen man is in the person of Jesus. We both believe that fallen man needs the forgiveness of sin, that his only hope is in God's grace, and that heaven and hell are realities that must be taken with complete seriousness.

In this present age we affirm, further, that there is much that we can and should cooperate upon in the public arena. As Western nations face moral and spiritual bankruptcy and a continual slide into neopaganism, we see ourselves standing as cobelligerents against the encroaching darkness of cultural breakdown. We raise, properly, our collective voices against abortion, euthanasia, marital breakdown, the destruction of the family, and the kind of statism that destroys the national soul. In nations where the political situation is one of civil liberty and democratic ideals we can stand together against the forces of secularization.

At the same time, as Protestant evangelicals, we wish to affirm our loyalty to the gospel of Jesus Christ. We do not believe that the Protestant Reformers were errorists, or heretics, as Rome labeled them at the time, but careful scholars and courageous ministers who recovered and preached the gospel in a time of great awakening. We fear that too many of our peers have apologized for the Protestant Reformation, and, though we do not agree with all of the rhetoric or tone of the sixteenth-century debate, we stand in awe of the faithfulness of those noble souls to whom the gospel of Jesus Christ was "the power of God for the salvation of everyone who believes" (Romans 1:16). We are indebted to them in that we believe they stood solidly upon the grace of God alone, received by faith alone, mediated to believing sinners through Christ alone, and grounded in the authority of Scripture alone. It was this evangelical heritage that the Reformers gave to us, and we thank God for it to this day. We count ourselves as debtors because of their faithfulness to the centrality of the gospel.

This book is meant to be both an apologetic and a dialogue. It seeks to explain and support the Protestant evangelical heritage by looking at our history and our theology. It will also examine some of the issues that still keep us apart, though this division saddens us. It shows why the two central tenets of the Protestant Reformers, the so-called material and formal principles, are still important to us: namely, justification by grace alone through faith alone, and the sole and final authority of the written Scriptures.

This book will explore some areas often left unconsidered by this generation. It will explore the issue of spirituality and why we differ in our approach to spiritual life as we do, and it will suggest that we need to further efforts at honest dialogue, but not at the expense of the serious disagreements that we still have regarding the nature of the gospel and the authority of the Word of God.

Many issues that evangelicals and Roman Catholics have differed on—and will probably continue to differ on—are not addressed in this book. We have radically differing views regarding the canon of Scripture, the pope's authority and infallibility as the pastor of the Christian church, the mission of the church in this age, and religious liberty. Massive volumes beyond the scope of a single collection of essays by evangelical scholars would be needed to address profound concerns like these. This present book is not meant to be a final word in an ongoing discussion, but we hope it will be a word that will awaken fellow evangelicals to some of the important issues of our time.

We hope that Roman Catholic readers might sense our desire to "reason together" in a different spirit than that seen in more acrimonious times. We hope all will hear our appeals for unity where we can achieve that, but never at the expense of biblical Christianity. We also hope that these same readers will hear our argument for the gospel that reconciles sinners to God on the basis of grace alone, received through faith alone, and mediated by Christ alone. We also hope that they will understand better our arguments for the finality and sufficiency of the Word of God. No creeds, counsels, or popes have spiritual authority, except they have it under the authority of the written Word. The "priesthood of the believer" is more than an old creedal word with us. Popes and councils, ministers and denominations may err, but the Word of our God shall stand forever. God's Word does not change, and through it the Holy Spirit will always be about the work of leading the people of God to the spirit of *semper reformanda* ("always reforming").

More than anything else this book is offered at a time when a new reformation is needed, one that touches every Christian tradition very deeply and one that touches the entire thought and practice of the individual Christian and the church. This reformation needs to address both old and new concerns. It must, however, like the Protestant Reformation of the sixteenth century, begin with the recovery of the message of the Cross. We are convinced that the gospel is still the power of God unto salvation.

It was Martin Luther who saw this spiritual North Star and called the church back to this central message of the entire Bible. It was Luther who said, "The cross is the criterion of all things." And in light of 1 Corinthians 2:2 he wrote, "The cross alone is our theology." It was here, at the Cross, that Luther saw the hidden God revealed in weakness and shame, yet with the radiance of divine glory.

Alister E. McGrath, a contributor to this present volume, writes in another place,

> The theology of the cross has assumed a new significance and urgency in the present century, in the aftermath of two world wars and with the ever-increasing threat of a third. It must never be forgotten that the theology of the cross is far more than an historical idea. The increasing recognition of the shallowness and naïveté of much Christian thinking about God and man has caused many to begin to retrace the steps taken by Luther before them, and to join him as he kneels at the foot of the cross, and adores the God who is "hidden in suffering."[4]

The current absence of confidence in the gospel message itself parallels the scene in Luther's day. Can the West be turned before our Christian heritage is completely abandoned? The greatest threat to us as we stand at the beginning of a new millennium is not in the world around us, but in the church itself. Only a great outpouring of God's Spirit in the recovery of the doctrines of the gospel answers to the need of our time. My prayer is that this present volume will add to this discussion and that a careful consideration of some of these very important issues can be used by the Spirit of God to fuel the fires of a new reformation and spiritual awakening.

Soli Deo Gloria!

NOTES

1. Michel Poniatowski, Minister of Interior under former French President Valery Giscard d'Estaing, in an interview for the news magazine *Pourquoi Pas?* of Brussels, quoted in *World Press Review* 29, No. 10 (October 1982): 23; cited in *Verdict,* Essay 8 (1983), 3.

2. David Wells, *No Place for Truth* (Grand Rapids: Eerdmans, 1993), 134.

3. Karl Keating, *Catholicism and Fundamentalism: The Attack on "Romanism" By "Bible Christians"* (San Francisco: Ignatius, 1988). Keating, who is professionally trained in law, is now the director of Catholic Answers, a lay organization in San Diego, California, that seeks to defend traditional Tridentine Roman Catholicism (i.e., the dogmas articulated after the time of Luther in opposition to his recovery of grace and the sufficiency of the Scriptures) against what he calls "anti-Catholic" attackers. He helpfully points out a number of weak arguments advanced in the debate by certain "Bible Christians" but fails to deal adequately with the central issues that have divided us since the sixteenth century. Labeling important elements of confessional evangelical Protestant teaching as "anti-Catholic" is no more fair than for Protestants to revert to labels like "Papists." We can be thankful to Keating for pointing out doctrinal misrepresentations and an uncharitable spirit among some Protestants, but there are still major doctrinal divides that can't be overcome by merely restating the old doctrinal positions that have divided us for centuries. It is important for the reader to understand that Keating's work does not represent the professional and academic theology of Roman Catholicism in the American church.

4. Alister E. McGrath, *Luther's Theology of the Cross* (Oxford, Eng., and Cambridge, Mass.: Basil Blackwell, 1985), 2–3.

PART
1
THE HISTORICAL BACKGROUND

Whereas the Reformation created a distinct break with Roman Catholicism concerning salvation, religious authority, and the church, it does not follow that the Reformers' system of thought was brand new. Nor does it mean that all theological and spiritual development prior to the Reformation unilaterally confirms the position of Roman Catholicism at the time of the Reformation. The progress of doctrinal development is too complex and dynamic to encourage such confidence. The doctrines of Christ's person and work belong to all Christians, and the foundation for the Reformation's understanding of salvation was laid in patristic Christology.

The early church established its life and thought through adherence to the doctrine of the sole authority of Scripture and protected that principle vigorously against the attempts of heretics to move Christians away from biblical doctrine. The early church confession of the truth was born out of a willingness to suffer for the truth. Evangelicals have shared, and must continue to share, that stewardship.

ESSAY
1
ONE, HOLY, CATHOLIC, APOSTOLIC CHURCH

Thomas J. Nettles

It was Sanctity of Human Life Sunday at Crossroads Church, a Southern Baptist church in Libertyville, Illinois, a village about thirty-five miles north of Chicago. The church has a mixture of transplanted Southerners, Midwesterners, Northerners, and Easterners from denominational backgrounds ranging from Baptist, Lutheran, United Methodist, Presbyterian, Evangelical Free, Bible church, Mormon, and Roman Catholic.

Present to make a few informative remarks about life alternatives to abortion was an energetic, yet humble and earnest, young woman representing several organizations in Lake County. She introduced herself as "a member of St. Joseph's" (the large Roman Catholic church in town) and said, "our Scripture reading this morning was, 'Behold, I am come to do your will, O God.'" She said that, although she was naturally shy, this thought had given her courage, and she had come to our congregation with that purpose in mind. After outlining how we could use and contribute to several programs in which she was involved, she departed from her outlined speech and said with a moving sincerity, "I know that I am not supposed to be sectarian in my presentations, but I think you will understand. These problems I'm describing would not even exist if our society would simply believe and practice the commandments, 'Thou shalt not kill' and 'Thou shalt not commit adultery.'"

Though there were many things she could have said that our congregation would have disagreed with, and though several of our members formerly had been at St. Joseph's, none of us disagreed with her motive for speaking or with her theological foundation for being active in supporting the ministry of life. Personally I felt at one with her on this issue.

AN UNEASY DISHARMONY

That personal experience is a microcosm of the present evangelical–Roman Catholic coexistence. We have so much in common in a world that is increasingly post-Christian and virtually neopagan in its morality and worldview. Evangelicals often find allies among Catholics in their neighborhood

25

on many moral issues, in a belief in divine revelation, the reality of the fall of humanity and its connection with Adam, the Trinity, and the "character value" of church attendance. Catholics and Protestants alike are often more divided within their own ranks on foundational Christian issues than the conservatives in each group are against each other.

Contemporary experience gives new slant to the way evangelicals discuss Roman Catholic theological heritage. Evangelicals should recognize that some structures and current practices of local congregations give at least an implicit place of prominence to the necessity of trusting Christ alone for salvation. Within Roman Catholicism many individuals are experiencing the power of the saving grace of Christ just as surely as within evangelical protestantism.

Whenever God grants saving faith, it is the same. It always embraces God's righteousness and approves His way of justifying sinners as seen in the completed work of Christ. Peter wrote to "those who through the righteousness of our God and Savior Jesus Christ have received a faith as precious as ours" (2 Peter 1:1). Peter's faith was not superior in quality to that of the humblest saint in the churches to which he wrote. Wherever our God grants faith He does it by the righteousness of Christ, and it is of the same quality and value as apostolic faith. Saving faith for an evangelical is not different from saving faith for a Roman Catholic.

Nor would we claim that all the members of evangelical churches understand the gospel of justification or have ever experienced its reality. One of the great laments of most evangelical pastors concerns the chronic absenteeism and lack of spiritual evidences on the part of 50 percent of the congregation. Some of this exists because evangelicals have developed a superstitious ritualism in evangelism that rivals the doctrine of Penance or the use of indulgences in creating carnal and false security. On a recent trip to the Ukraine one evangelistic mission reported 3,500 professions of faith. It appears that the majority of these were tallied by counting the number of raised hands. One of the Ukrainians told the group's leader, "We did not all raise our hands, but if you would come back to teach the Bible every week I am certain that we all would."

At an evangelistic rally in Texas a young girl walked the aisle during a postsermon altar call, explaining that she was doing it on behalf of a friend. Her friend had been to the rally the year before and had became a Christian some months after that. Having recently died of cystic fibrosis, however, she was not able to attend this one. But, before she died, her friend assured her that she would would "walk down the aisle to make public her decision" in her place at the next conference. This was probably more a sentimental gesture than a superstitious ritual, but many evangelicals have "walked the aisle" thinking that simply by doing so they have ensured their salvation. These extrabiblical activities have been used as a substitute for true gospel preaching on many occasions in evangelical practice, and the results have been no less devastating than the false gospel embodied in the sacramental system of Rome.

Given that admission, we are quick to say that the errors in evangelical practice do not ameliorate the doctrinal errors of Roman Catholicism. The evangelical error generally occurs through ignorance and the lack of theological consistency; the Roman error is institutionalized and creedalized. The evangelical error comes in spite of a confessional history to the contrary; the Roman error purposefully canonized a historical aberration at the sixteenth-century Council of Trent and has maintained it since.

BUILDING UP THE BODY OF CHRIST

The scriptural pattern for this development was described by Paul in 1 Corinthians 3 and expanded in Ephesians 4. As a wise masterbuilder Paul laid a foundation. That foundation was—and is—Christ. Others built on the foundation with materials either worthy or unworthy of the majesty and strength of the foundation.

The history of the church has followed that pattern. Christians in the first centuries laid the foundation in confessional precision. The doctrine of God in particular relation to the person of Christ received intense attention and resulted in a crescendo of affirmations, unpacking in a brilliant display of theological tenacity the biblical treasures of Christ's deity and humanity and the ineffable wonder of the One God in His three-personed eternal existence. Our grasp of who He is was always tied to what He came to do. As the Creed of Nicea (A.D. 325), in harmony with Luke 19:10 and John 3:16 and 12:47, states, "on account of our salvation" the one who was essentially God was made also man. Salvation never receded from the picture in early church history, but, unlike the issue of Christology, it did not receive a clear definitive formulation. Already, on top of the foundation, worthy and unworthy materials were becoming part of the construction.

Irenaeus's development of the concept of recapitulation was powerful, and, though manageable as a part of different soteriological schemes, its dependence on Christ's human obedience clearly harmonizes with the doctrine of imputed righteousness. Tertullian's traducianism in anthropology virtually demands the monergism of reformation thought, but his soteriology was disorganized and shows little coherent development. The distinction between venial and mortal sins was prominent in his thinking. Augustine's profound understanding of sin and grace exposed and corrected several erroneous tendencies of the patristic period, which were exaggerated and systematized by Pelagius. Pelagianism, after conciliar rejection at Ephesus in A.D. 431, could not appear under its own name any longer, but it continued in disguise as a particular emphasis of Augustinianism.

The subsequent centuries of Christian thought moved in and out between these types of materials until the crisis of the Reformation began to sort out with finality the dross from the precious metal. The Reformers rediscovered Augustine; they also expanded and clarified his teaching by means of heavy exposure to biblical exposition. The soteriology that emphasized justification as a forensic, declarative, imputative act of God consistent with all aspects of the obedience of Christ emerged as a corrective to the semi-Pelagianism into which much scholastic thought had fallen.[1]

Rome refused to recognize the validity of the theological insights of the Reformers and called a council, not to discuss the issues openly but to issue a series of dogmas and anathemas. The pope served as an oracle, not as a clear exemplar of apostolic commitment to biblical doctrine. Calvin responded, "The proclamation of the Council is entitled to no more weight than the cry of an auctioneer."[2] He summarized the grave concerns of the Reformers concerning the conciliar method of treating the serious theological issues that were at stake.

> Can anyone still be so stupid as to think of seeking any alleviation of our evils from a council? We complain that the whole doctrine of godliness is adulterated by impious dogmas; that the whole worship of God is vitiated by foul and disgraceful superstitions; that the pure institution of the sacraments has been supplanted by horrible sacrilege; . . . that poor souls, which ought to have been ruled by the doctrine of Christ, are oppressed by cruel bondage; . . . that the grace of Christ not only lies half-buried, but is partly torn to pieces, partly altogether extinguished. All these complaints, which we have made for many years, and in published books, and which we make in our daily sermons, we are prepared to prove well founded, whenever a freedom of utterance is given. . . . Still, lest the Christian world might lay aside dissension, and unite in holy concord, a Council is summoned. Ought not its members to have discussed controverted points before they prejudged either themselves or others? They allow nothing of the kind. Nay, should any one have attempted to change one tittle of their customs, they hold him as already condemned.[3]

The Reformers sought to remove what they saw as wood, hay, and stubble from the foundation of Christ. The Roman response at Trent was not according to Christ or the early church. Establishing a parity of authority between oral tradition and Scripture contradicts the structure of authority and method reflected in the writings of Ignatius, Justin, Irenaeus, and others.

Wherever gold, jewels, and precious stones appear, they claim our loyalty, celebration, and embrace. Wherever dross scums the surface or chaff chokes the air, they deserve our rejection and sometimes call for our mourning. Sometimes the impurity is harmless, sometimes it is damning; sometimes it is merely an idiosyncrasy, sometimes it is heresy. Sometimes there is much of both jewels and dross in any one individual or era. The worth and beauty of Christ have no more noble expression than in the words of Bernard's "Jesus, the Very Thought of Thee." Few things, however, match the thick darkness of his (mis)understanding of the nature of Christian "mission" than that seen in his advocacy of the Second Crusade. The church is indebted to Calvin's exegetical powers and his coherent presentation of reformation thought, but it certainly must shrink from his approval of the death of Michael Servetus. All that accords with the foundation constitutes the form of the true church—that which defines what "unity in the faith" is and what the "knowledge of the Son of God" is. This is the heritage of everyone who is a Christian.

Every earnest quest for the truth, every courageous defense of the faith once delivered to the saints, every event that exposes error and strengthens one's grasp of true doctrine, every confession (individual or corporate) in which Christ is honored and the powers of this world are scorned, and every act of brotherly love done in the name of Christ—these belong to all of us. Polycarp's faithfulness to death, Ignatius's zeal for unity and truth and warnings against heretics, Justin's philosophical sophistication subdued to the truth of Jesus, Tertullian's pugnacious protection of the rule of faith, Irenaeus's pastoral alertness to the demands of biblical revelation in contrast to Gnostic speculation, Athanasius's penetrating grasp of the Incarnation, Augustine's experiential theology of grace, Anselm's devotional philosophy, and Aquinas's philosophical devotedness are all cords within the tapestry of Christian testimony in the world. Whether it is doctrine or devotion, if it is true, it claims the Christian. It inheres in the structure of the one, holy, catholic, apostolic church that is the pillar and foundation of the truth.

HOW FIRM A FOUNDATION:
CHRIST IN THE CREEDS

Evangelicals strongly affirm the creedal conclusions that extend from Nicea to Chalcedon. They are principial elements of Christianity, not because they are conciliar but because they give clear and studied affirmation of the biblical teaching on the most foundational truth of Christian faith. The confessional history of evangelicalism roars its agreement with the Christological and theological formulations of those early councils and endorses them as its own.

Nicea counteracted Arius's reductionistic Christology by affirming the "essential Unity of the Father and the Son . . . without destroying the personal distinctness."[4] The creed affirmed that God by eternal nature is Father and, therefore, out of his nature as Father, generates, not creates, the Son. The Son thus shares the same nature as the Father and can be called "true God from true God" maintaining both His deity and eternality as a separate personal subsistence. In addition, His being "made flesh" for our salvation means that He was "made man." Human nature undiminished in any of its essential properties was His.

29

A series of reactions in the following generation led alternatingly to anti-thetical heresies for over a century beyond Nicea until a balanced and biblical formula was adopted at the Council of Chalcedon in A.D. 451. The chief architect of the statement was Leo I, bishop of Rome from 440 to 461. His clarity of thought was of benefit to the whole church. His contribution is not, however, due to his claim of authoritative regulation of church affairs in the West[5] but to his insightful Christological vision. His application of the creed of Nicea and of the rule of faith, and the richness of his insights into the implication of scriptural passages concerning Christ, have become the model of clear practical thinking about the Incarnation.

After a discussion of the "common and uniform profession of faith" and the "teaching of the Scriptures," Leo opened to the Christian world one of the richest caches of verbal jewels ever to grace a Christian pen: "In this preservation, then, of the real quality of both natures, both being united in one person, lowliness was taken on by majesty, weakness by strength, mortality by the immortal."[6]

How can one construct a more profound bedrock for the doctrine of penal, substitutionary, propitiatory atonement accomplished once for all than these words of Leo: "And in order to pay the debt of our fallen state, inviolable nature was united to one capable of suffering so that (and this sort of reparation we needed) one and the same mediator between God and men, the man Jesus Christ, could die in the one nature and not die in the other."[7]

What better preparation could evangelicals have for exposing the errors of kenoticism than Leo's analysis of the nature of the union between the human and the divine?

> In the whole and perfect nature of the true man, then, the true God was born, complete in His own nature, complete in ours. But by ours we mean that which the Creator formed in us at the beginning and which He took upon Himself, to redeem it. That part which the Deceiver added and man, deceived, accepted left no traces in the Saviour. He did not share in our sins just because He undertook to share in our weaknesses. He took on the aspect of servitude without the stain of sin; He added to the humanity but did not lessen the divinity. For that putting off of self whereby He the invisible made Himself visible and as Creator and Lord of all things wished to become one of the mortals was an inclination to mercy, not a failure of power. He who keeping the form of God created man, the same was made man in an aspect of servitude. Both His natures keep their intrinsic quality without defect; and, just as the aspect of God does not remove the aspect of servitude, so also this latter does not lessen the aspect of God.[8]

Pertinent passages in this letter of Leo could be multiplied. They became immortalized in theological history when they served as the foundation for the symbol of Chalcedon in the following section:

Our Lord Jesus Christ is to us One and the same Son, the Self-same Perfect in Godhead, the Self-same Perfect in Manhood; truly God and truly Man; the Self-same of a rational soul and body; co-essential with the Father according to the Godhead, the Self-same co-essential with us according to the Manhood; like us in all things, sin apart; before the ages begotten of the Father as to the Godhead, but in these last days, the Self-same co-essential, for us and for our salvation (born) of Mary the Virgin Theotokos as to the Manhood; One and the Same Christ, Son, Lord, Only-begotten; acknowledged in Two natures unconfusedly, unchangeably, indivisibly, inseparably; the difference of the Natures being in no way removed because of the Union, but rather the property of each Nature being preserved, and (both) concurring into One Person and One Hypostasis.[9]

That evangelicals gladly embrace these truths as elements of what the Constantinopolitan Symbol called the "One, holy, catholic, apostolic church" and see them as essential for evangelicalism is demonstrated in its confessional history. Consistent with this doctrinal commitment, the *Augsburg Confession,* written by Philipp Melanchthon early in the Reformation, began, "We unanimously hold and teach, in accordance with the decree of the Council of Nicea, that there is one divine essence, which is called and which is truly God, and that there are three Persons in this one divine essence, equal in power and alike eternal." In its article on "The Son of God" Augsburg affirms Chalcedonian Christology as well as all the Christological elements of the Apostles' Creed: "It is also taught among us that God the Son became man, born of the virgin Mary, and that the two natures, divine and human, are so inseparably united in one person that there is one Christ, true God and true man, who was truly born, suffered, was crucified, died, and was buried in order to be a sacrifice not only for original sin but also for all other sins and to propitiate God's wrath."[10]

Chapter 2 of the *Westminster Confession* affirms the doctrine of the Trinity and provides an abundance of Scripture proofs along with the conciliar language: "In the unity of the Godhead there be three persons, of one substance, power, and eternity: God the Father, God the Son, and God the Holy Ghost. The Father is of none, neither begotten nor proceeding; the Son is eternally begotten of the Father; the Holy Ghost eternally proceeding from the Father and the Son." Paragraph 2 of chapter 8 combines the language of Nicea and Chalcedon in its exposition of the "Son of God." The Son "being very and eternal God, of one substance, and equal with the Father" in His incarnation took "upon him man's nature, with all the essential properties and common infirmities thereof, yet without sin." Being conceived in the womb of the Virgin Mary, He was born "of her substance" with the result that "two whole, perfect, and distinct natures, the Godhead and the manhood, were inseparably joined together in one person, without conversion, composition, or confusion." This one person is "very God and very man, yet one Christ."[11]

31

The Thirty-nine Articles of the Church of England speaks of the unity of the Godhead in "three persons, of one substance, power, and eternitie, the father, the sonne, and the holy ghost." The Son is described in the language of the creeds as "very and eternall God, of one substaunce with the Father" who also "toke man's nature in the wombe" of Mary, that is "of her substaunce: so that two whole and perfect natures, that is to say, the Godhead and manhood, were joyned together in one person, never to be divided, whereof is one Christe, very GOD and very man."[12]

When the Evangelical Alliance for the United States was founded in 1867, it adopted a nine-point doctrinal statement of the English counterpart and added the following resolution:

> Resolved, that in the same spirit we propose no new creed, but taking broad, historical, and Evangelical catholic [!] ground, we solemnly reaffirm and profess our faith in all the doctrines of the inspired word of God, and in the *consensus* of doctrines as held by all true Christians from the beginning. And we do more especially affirm our belief in the *divine-human person and atoning work of our Lord and Savior Jesus Christ* as the only and sufficient source of salvation, as the heart and soul of Christianity, and as the center of all true Christian union and fellowship.[13]

THE STRUGGLE FOR TRUTH

A COMMON BUT SEPARATING PRINCIPLE

A principle that undergirds the continuing polemic between Catholic and Protestant is this: Biblical faith can exist only in the presence of truth. For that reason, not only *may* we embrace these truths, we *must* embrace *the truth* wherever found just as surely as we must eschew error and heresy. Belief in anything but the truth is death itself; one cannot breathe in a vacuum or have one's thirst quenched by "springs without water" (2 Peter 2:17). Genuine believers may have error mixed with the truth by which they are saved, but the error contributes nothing to the vitality of faith; it only weakens it. For this reason Peter was urgent in his assurance that he had not followed cunningly devised fables but was an eyewitness of the events he set forth as the basis of faith (1:16). Even so, Luke takes care that Theophilus may know the "certainty of the things" he had been taught (Luke 1:4). The union of faith and truth is a commitment of the one, holy, catholic, apostolic church and was defended vigorously by the Fathers.

To the Fathers, faith and truth were inextricably related to each other. In his *Proof of the Apostolic Preaching* Irenaeus urges Marcianus, "We must keep strictly, without deviation, the rule of faith, and carry out the commands of God, believing in, and fearing Him, because He is Lord, and loving Him, because He is Father." He then explained further the relation of truth to faith.

Action, then, is preserved by faith, because unless you believe, says Isaias, you shall not continue; and faith is given by truth, since faith rests upon reality: for we shall believe what really is, as it is, and believing what really is, as it is for ever, keep a firm hold on our assent to it. Since, then it is faith that maintains our salvation, one must take great care of this sustenance, to have a true perception of reality.[14]

Though the Christological foundation for Romanism and evangelicalism is virtually the same, significant soteriological disagreements persist. Evangelicals contend that Roman Catholicism refused to embrace the truth of justification during the period when it was most actively and clearly discussed. Instead, Rome opted for a very strong stream of medieval thought, which isolated the efficacy of saving grace to the sacraments and included the sinner's progressive sanctification by infused grace as an essential element of their definition of justification.

This is both legalistic and antinomian, unbiblical on both counts. It is legalistic in that the sinner's obedience constitutes a part of his standing justified before God; it is antinomian in that it accepts as meritorious an obedience that falls short of the law's true demands. It creates, therefore, false issues of conscience on the one hand and false security on the other. Obedience to the truth—and the church is the "pillar and foundation of the truth"—demands that one expose as false and damaging any trust in the sacramental efficacy of the ordinances, the successful completion of penitential satisfaction, or one's own devotion or merits. These are obnoxious to the completed work of Christ whose perfect righteousness and propitiatory death compose the sole ground of the sinner's right standing before God.

In the same way, any evangelical idols that provide superstitious strongholds must be destroyed. The quest for truth cannot be a respecter of persons. Not only must evangelicals criticize Rome's failure to embrace the gospel, they must judge themselves for their failure to implement in its purity the gospel they profess.

AN ENERGETIC QUEST FOR FAITHFULNESS TO TRUTH

Just as the patristic affirmation for the unity between faith and truth is common, so is the existential quest for faithfulness to, and willingness to suffer for, that truth. The reality of our own faith and struggle demands that we go beyond the words as doctrinal abstractions and enter into at least a portion of the ante-Nicene struggle. The particular vocabulary finally creedalized culminated a dynamic process. Christological vocabulary made cameo appearances in the drama of life and death before the Nicene climax and the Constantinopolitan denouement. We are interested in being a part of not just the conclusions but the faithful stewardship of gifts that developed them. The movement toward Nicene orthodoxy fueled intensity of devotion to the gospel in personal purity, material sacrifice, and aggressive witness. The laborers who bore the toil in the most unclimatable part of the day are the brothers of all who are true believers. Our fellowship is with the truth and with all who have believed it, defended it, and suffered for it in any age.

The reality of Christ's personhood as God and man fired the devotion and purity of the Fathers. Polycarp urged young men to be "blameless in all things, caring for purity before everything," and exhorted virgins to walk in a "blameless and pure conscience" that they might be "well pleasing unto Him in the present world."[15] He commended Ignatius and others who ran "in faith and righteousness" and are in "their due places in the presence of the Lord," for they "loved not this present world, but him that died for our sakes and was raised by God for us."[16] His prayer for the "patient endurance" and "purity" of his contemporaries was with the confidence that God would Himself grant "a portion among His saints" to all who "shall believe on our Lord Jesus Christ and on His Father that raised him from the dead."[17]

His admonitions to others were not empty charades, for Polycarp himself sealed the witness that he commended so strongly in Ignatius forty-five years earlier. When asked to revile Christ to save himself Polycarp replied, "Fourscore and six years have I been His servant, and He hath done me no wrong. How then can I blaspheme my King who saved me?" When he offered his final prayer, it was in thanksgiving that his intercession for the martyrs a generation before was now an intercession for himself that he would "receive a portion among the number of martyrs in the cup of Christ unto resurrection of eternal life."[18]

On his way to Rome as a prisoner, Ignatius wrote to Polycarp and to six churches. His letters throb with energy and admonition. Interpreters may be divided over the meaning of his strong urgings for union with and obedience to the bishop in each respective congregation. "Let us be careful," he admonished the Ephesians, "not to resist the bishop, that by our submission we may give ourselves to God."[19] He had said already in a startling but cryptic exhortation that they should glorify Jesus Christ by being perfectly joined together in one submission. In this submission, which he identifies with "submitting yourselves to your bishop and presbytery," they would "be sanctified in all things."[20]

None, however, can read his letters unmoved by his zeal for Christ, a zeal manifested in purity of life and willingness to suffer for the truth. The most prominent theme of the Ignatian correspondence is *oneness*. This unity expresses itself in God Himself, in the Incarnation, and in the church. In God we see the unity of Father and Son. In the Incarnation we see the unity of Christ's person and the unified purpose of His passion and resurrection. In the church we see a unity of members with officers and members with each other. All this can be summarized as a unity in the truth.

Early in his letter to the Ephesians, Ignatius expressed his desire to write them a separate treatise in order to expound the present economy of God's plan "relating to the new man Jesus Christ."[21] Though his circumstances never allowed him to expound this in detail, it undergirds the concerns expressed in all his letters. He summarizes his formulation in the phrase, "which consisteth in faith towards Him and in love towards Him, in His passion and resurrection."[22]

While he formulated a model to enhance Christian unity and perseverance, Ignatius also anticipated the existential and doctrinal issues that developed Nicene orthodoxy. The central theme of this "new man" is reconciliation, God's creation of unity in His redeemed community. At the most basic level, the "new man" reflects the unity that exists within the Godhead. The unity of Father and Son, as well as the unity of the apostles with Christ, establishes the foundation upon which the church should strive toward unity. In fact, its unity is a mark of its truthfulness. Ignatius considered that model so compelling that he told the Magnesians that they should make no attempt even to "think anything right for yourselves apart from others," and they should "be zealous to do all things in godly concord."[23] Nothing should have power to divide them; one should no longer "regard his neighbor after the flesh" (that is, he should consider his neighbor as one with himself in the manifestation of the new man), should study conformity to God and "pay reverence one to another," and should be united "with the bishop and with them that preside over you as an ensample and a lesson of incorruptibility."[24]

In the same spirit Ignatius exhorted the Trallians to submit to their bishop: "For when ye are obedient to the bishop as to Jesus Christ, it is evident to me that ye are living not after men but after Jesus Christ, who died for us, that believing on His death ye might escape death."[25] It is as if Ignatius were saying, "Christian faith is not the creative manifestation of religious individualism, but comes by a revelation from outside of us and calls for belief, unity, and submission. We forsake our own way and move into the corporate expression in word, worship, and life of His way." Consequently,

Let there be one prayer in common, one supplication, one mind, one hope, in love and in joy unblameable, which is Jesus Christ, than whom there is nothing better. Hasten to come together all of you, as to one temple, even God; as to one altar even to one Jesus Christ, who came forth from One Father and is with One and departed unto One.[26]

An even more striking picture of God's purpose of unity in the "new man" comes from the Incarnation. The Christ is both God and man in one person. Ignatius greets the Ephesians in the name of "Jesus our God." Jesus Christ is "our inseparable life," the "only physician, of flesh and of spirit, generate and ingenerate, God in man, true Life in death, Son of Mary and Son of God."[27] The newness of His humanity is in its unity with His deity. He is "one Jesus Christ who after the flesh was of David's race, who is Son of Man and Son of God."[28] "One Jesus Christ" is a phrase I take to foreshadow the affirmation of the unity of the person of Christ. He retains undiminished all the attributes of His deity while taking into His person a full human nature. For this reason, "It is monstrous to talk of Jesus Christ and to practise Judaism" (not only because as a whole it rejected Christ's deity, but because it identified itself through racial and ceremonial exclusiveness); Jews may be included in the "one body of His church" joining the Gentiles as "His saints and faithful people," for an ensign has been set "through His resurrection."[29] Believers who formerly were Jews no longer observed sabbaths but fashioned their lives "after the Lord's day, on which our life also arose through Him and through His death."[30]

The sure demise of wickedness accompanied the Incarnation when "God appeared in the likeness of man unto newness of everlasting life." Since this has occurred, Ignatius can ask, "Wherefore do we not all walk prudently, receiving the knowledge of God which is Jesus Christ." And in imitation of Him we are zealous, "vying with each other who shall suffer the greater wrong, who shall be defrauded, who shall, be set at nought. . . . In all purity and temperance abide ye in Christ."[31]

We have true union with each other only if we have "union with Jesus and with the Father."[32] The Son, preincarnate, pre-Christ, dwelt in the full consciousness of His deity "with the Father before the worlds." He has now "appeared at the end of time," individuated as a person in a body located in time and space on earth, having come "forth from One Father." His spatialization as man diminished neither His own deity nor His union with the Father ("and is with One"); and in His ascension he reestablished that unity on a different basis now as the Christ ("departed unto One").[33] If we receive these truths, our union is with each other, with Christ, and with the Father. Our individuality is heightened and refined and maintained in its purity; yet at the same time it is submitted to other members of the body, united with Christ, and joined with the Father.

TRUTH AND THE HOPE OF SUFFERING

Christians endure persecutions so that unbelievers might be convinced that "there is one God who manifested Himself through Jesus Christ His Son, who is His Word that proceeded from silence, who in all things was well-pleasing unto Him that sent Him."[34] And seeing that He was raised from the dead and through the Spirit He is our only teacher, "How shall we be able to live apart from Him?" It would be vain, then, to forsake such a life by departing from the true teachings about His work. "Be ye fully persuaded concerning the birth and the passion and the resurrection, which took place in the time of the governorship of Pontius Pilate; for these things were truly and certainly done by Jesus Christ our hope."[35]

The reality of hope seemed to push itself into the forefront of Ignatius's correspondence to the Trallians. Having addressed them as "elect and worthy of God" and having reminded them of the "peace in flesh and spirit" that comes through the "passion of Jesus Christ," he emphasized that Christ Himself "is our hope through our resurrection unto Him."[36]

The unity between the historicity of doctrine and the comfort of personal experience is strong in this epistle. He clearly perceives the devastating implications of the Gnostic heresy and voices uncompromising exhortations concerning the church's belief in the incarnation, death, and resurrection of Christ. In fact, we learn that much of his concern about the churches' obedience to the bishop is at bottom a concern for theological integrity. "For when ye are obedient to the bishop as to Jesus Christ," he wrote, "it is evident to me that ye are living not after men but after Jesus Christ, who died for us, that believing on His death ye might escape death."[37]

The context of this urgency, however, is the necessity of maintaining apostolic teaching if we are to have any true hope in this fatal conflict with the world. This obedience, therefore, is "as to the Apostles of Jesus Christ our hope; for if we lived in Him we shall also be found in Him." This identification of the bishop with apostolic doctrine, and thus apostolic hope, is reemphasized when Ignatius warns the Trallians against those who mingle heresy with an apparent "show of honesty" as those who administer a "deadly drug with honied wine." The best guard against such men is to be "inseparable from Jesus Christ and from the bishop and from the ordinances of the Apostles." They are to be strengthened by faith (which he identifies with "the flesh of the Lord") and love (which he identifies with "the blood of Jesus Christ").[38]

THE BISHOP AND TRUTH

Ignatius believed that union with the bishop was for the eternal safety of Christ's sheep, not because sacramental efficacy exists in such union but because only in that fold may one find the truth of Christ's incarnation, passion, and resurrection. Without those truths one cannot be saved. He told the Philadelphians, therefore, "As children . . . of the truth, shun division and wrong doctrine." These two adhere to each other. Division—because it places one outside the community of revelation—naturally leads to wrong doctrine. "As many as are of God and of Jesus Christ, they are with the bishop; and as many as shall repent and enter into the unity of the Church, these also shall be of God, that they may be living after Jesus Christ." One who follows a schismatic does not inherit the kingdom of God, says Ignatius. Why so? Because the only thing that would prompt a break from the church and its bishop was disagreement with apostolic doctrine and "if any man walketh in strange doctrine, he hath no fellowship with the passion."[39]

Some of Ignatius's strongest admonitions for obedience to the bishop occur in his letter to Smyrna, where Polycarp was bishop. "Let no man do aught of things pertaining to the Church apart from the bishop," Ignatius insisted, and "He that honoreth the bishop is honoured of God; he that doeth aught without the knowledge of the bishop rendereth service to the devil."[40]

In addition, he wrote Polycarp not only that men and women should marry "with the consent of the bishop" but that he should "let nothing be done without thy consent."[41] These urgings reflect Ignatius's concept of the church as a separate society in a hostile world, an army of God encamped together always ready for battle with enemy forces, a family seeking to preserve its unity and integrity against those who would destroy it either by force or subtlety.

To this point the Smyrneans were sound in the faith and had resisted doctrinal compromise. God had given them wisdom and had established them in "faith immovable." They were, figuratively speaking, "nailed on the cross of the Lord Jesus Christ, in flesh and in spirit." The source of their love was the "blood of Christ," and they had no hesitancy in believing that "He is truly of the race of David according to the flesh, but Son of God by the Divine will and power." Jesus the Christ was truly born of a virgin, was truly baptized by John, "truly nailed up in the flesh for our sakes under Pontius Pilate and Herod the tetrarch," and was truly raised from the dead. All these things He suffered "for our sakes that we might be saved." They were established in these truths and in Ignatius's belief that Jesus Christ "was in the flesh even after the resurrection," and ate and drank with His disciples in the flesh, "though spiritually he was united with the Father." They themselves were "so minded." Nevertheless, he must warn them of the deadly craft of the deniers of Jesus' flesh.[42]

More dangerous than the physical persecution and obliteration, which loomed large in his near future, Ignatius feared the insidious activity of heretics creating division and sniping off individuals one by one. These crafty ones had been particularly active in Smyrna, and Ignatius saw greater danger in "wild beasts in human form" who would take the passion of Christ from them, more than the wild beasts of Rome who would inflict the passion of Christ on him.[43] They were persuaded neither by "the prophecies nor by the law of Moses, nay nor even to this very hour by the Gospel" that the Christ "was a bearer of flesh."[44] The Smyrneans should pray that they might repent, but Ignatius himself did not even want to recall their names "until they repent and return to the passion, which is our resurrection."[45]

The problem of docetic heresy compounded exponentially when the heretics sought to pass themselves off as Christian ministers. Ignatius therefore warns, "Let not office puff up any man," but be sure to notice their lack of faith and love. Their lack of faith is demonstrated in that they "hold strange doctrine touching the grace of Christ." Their lack of love is shown in their complete misappropriation of the ministerial office:

They have no care for love, none for the widow, none for the orphan, none for the afflicted, none for the prisoner, none for the hungry or thirsty. They abstain from eucharist and prayer, because they allow not that the eucharist is the flesh of our Saviour Jesus Christ, which flesh suffered for our sins, and which the Father of His goodness raised up.[46]

For that reason the Christians in Smyrna should avoid speaking to them in public or private. Instead, they must study the Scriptures, that is, they should "give heed to the Prophets, and especially to the Gospel, wherein the passion is shown unto us and the resurrection is accomplished."[47] Division is the "beginning of evils," since it creates isolation from the body and vulnerability to the false teachers. Their increase in faith and love, therefore, depends on their following the bishop.

The same truth stated by Ignatius in his singular focus on the bishop, Irenaeus stated by a larger focus on the apostolic tradition as a whole. Tradition, according to Irenaeus, is identical with Scripture. The power of the gospel was given to the apostles "through whom also we have known the truth."[48] This message that they proclaimed in public they "handed down to us in the Scriptures, to be the ground and pillar of our faith." The heretics reject a revelation through "written documents," however, and opt for the communication of truth *viva voce*. This oral revelation is unique to each heretic; none of their systems conforms to another or to any other system that has gone before. They perversely reject the "tradition" that lives within the apostolic churches and still resounds from the mouth of the bishops.

But if such a thing as an oral tradition of "hidden mysteries" exists, to whom would the apostles have committed it? Irenaeus answers: "They would have delivered them especially to those to whom they were also committing the churches themselves."[49]

To demonstrate the truth of this as well as the falsity of the heretics, Irenaeus points to "that tradition derived from the apostles, of the very great, the very ancient, and universally known church founded and organized at Rome by the two most glorious apostles, Peter and Paul." Irenaeus performs the task of tracing the lineage from the "blessed apostles" and the next in line, Linus, to the current bishop, Eleutherius, the twelfth from the apostles. He says, "For it is a matter of necessity that every church should agree with this church, on account of its pre-eminent authority, that is, the faithful everywhere, inasmuch as the apostolical tradition has been preserved continuously by those faithful men who exist everywhere."[50]

Irenaeus points out that the tradition could be established just as surely through Polycarp, who "always taught the things which he had learned from the apostles, and which the church has handed down, and which alone are true." All the Asiatic churches testify to that truth, including Philippi and Ephesus. The latter who had John among them until "the times of Trajan" stood with all the others including Rome as "a true witness of the tradition of the apostles."[51]

Irenaeus's argument is designed to underline the truth of Scripture and to discourage any departure from what is written. The Scripture is that which is "handed down," that is, tradition. He appeals to the authority within the churches only because it is more compelling logically and historically to look to the immediate successors, even the appointees, of the apostles to verify what is and is not "the tradition of the apostles."[52] Under the hypothetical condition that the "apostles themselves had not left us writings," it would be necessary, in that case, "to follow the course of the tradition which they handed down to those to whom they did commit the churches."[53]

Since the hypothesis has no real existence and the apostles "did also write the Gospel, in which they recorded the doctrine regarding God, pointing out that our Lord Jesus Christ is the truth, and that no lie is in Him," Irenaeus proposes that he "revert to the scriptural proof furnished by those apostles" for the exposition of true doctrine.[54]

To this clearly patristic principle of *Sola Scriptura* evangelicals gladly agree.

FAITH AND HISTORY

Both Irenaeus and Ignatius wrote as if one's union with the saving work of Christ cannot be attained without a belief in the separate parts of His historical work. This conviction gives surpassing urgency to guarding those truths. If godless persons say that He suffered "only in semblance," why was Ignatius in bonds and why did he desire to fight with wild beasts? In short, if what the heretics say is true, "I die in vain." Maintaining truth in doctrine is the only motive to suffer in this life, that one might live forever before God. So it is with Irenaeus. The relation between confession of Christ as the one who "must suffer many things" and our willingness to take up the cross and follow Christ cannot be broken.[55]

If Christ has not truly suffered, why should we? Because Christ invites us to Himself through His passion, those who will not be branches of His cross will bear no fruit—rather their fruit is deadly, and the one who eats of it dies eternally.

Be ye deaf, therefore, when any man speaketh to you apart from Jesus Christ, who was of the race of David, who was the Son of Mary, who was truly born and ate and drank, was truly persecuted under Pontius Pilate, was truly crucified and died in the sight of those in heaven and those on earth and those under the earth; who moreover was truly raised from the dead, His Father having raised Him, who in the like fashion will so raise us also who believe on Him—His Father, I say, will raise us—in Christ, apart from whom we have not true life.[56]

Ignatius spoke of his coming death as the "lot which I am eager to attain" in his letter to the Smyrneans. His willingness to suffer for the cause of Christ pulsates more strongly in the letter to the Romans than in any of the other six: "Grant me nothing more than that I be poured out a libation to God, while there is still an altar ready."[57] If they had power to intercede on his behalf, he urged them not to do so. He was quite eager that the wild beasts become his sepulchre. "It is good to die for Jesus Christ rather than to reign over the farthest bounds of the earth." Passion to be in the presence of Christ elevated his literary art to an intense irony as he contemplated what he hoped was a sure martyrdom.

> Him I seek, who died on our behalf; Him I desire, who rose again for our sake. The pangs of a new birth are upon me. Bear with me, brethren. Do not hinder me from living; do not desire my death. Bestow not on the world one who desireth to be God's. . . . Permit me to be an imitator of the passion of my God.[58]

Whereas some might discuss whether this sort of running after death should be shunned and seen as an evidence of a bit of imbalance, the wonder of Ignatius's zeal for God must not be lost. On the other hand, perhaps Ignatius here is stating the very heart of Christian faith. His certainty about his future with Christ was so clear, his submission to the passion of Christ in doctrine and experience so thorough, and his vision of the glory of Christ so rapturous that he could say in truth with Paul, "For to me, to live is Christ and to die is gain" (Philippians 1:21). That too, and maybe that only, is what it means to be one of the elect in the holy, catholic, apostolic church.

Notes

1. For a forceful exposure of this tendency, see Luther's *Disputation Against Scholastic Theology*. This was written as part of a formal procedure in the pedagogical structure of the University of Wittenberg. Evidently Luther felt that the issue was still open and could be debated with the possibility of significant alterations being made.

2. John Calvin, "Acts of the Council of Trent: With the Antidote," in *Calvin's Selected Works,* 7 vols. (Grand Rapids: Baker, 1983), 3:36.

3. Ibid., 39–40.

4. T. Herbert Bindley, *The Oecumenical Documents of the Faith,* 3d ed., rev. (London: Methuen & Co., 1925), 2.

5. Leo, *St. Leo the Great: Letters,* trans. Brother Edmund Hun (New York: Fathers of the Church, 1957), 37–47 (Letter 10). Basing his argument on Matthew 16 and John 21, Leo said, "And although the power to bind and loose was given to Peter before the others, still, in an even more special way, the pasturing of the sheep was entrusted to him. Anyone who thinks that the primacy should be denied to Peter cannot in any way lessen the Apostle's dignity; inflated with the wind of his own pride, he

buries himself in hell." Significant exegetes prior to Leo give no support to this interpretation; even granting it, Leo would have no objective means of demonstrating that Peter was bishop of Rome or, granting that, that all subsequent bishops inherit his position of authority.

6. Ibid., 95 (Letter 28).

7. Ibid.

8. Ibid., 96.

9. Bindley, *The Oecumenical Documents of the Faith*, 297.

10. Philip Schaff, *The Creeds of Christendom*, 3 vols. (reprint, Grand Rapids: Baker, 1969), 3:7, 9.

11. Ibid., 607, 608, 619, 620.

12. Ibid., 488.

13. *The New Schaff-Herzog Encyclopedia of Religious Knowledge*, ed. Samuel Macauley Jackson, s.v. "Evangelical Alliance." The exclamation point after "catholic" is added.

14. Irenaeus, *Proof of the Apostolic Preaching*, trans. Joseph P. Smith, S.J. (Westminster, Md.: Newman, 1952), 49.

15. J. B. Lightfoot and J. R. Harmer, eds., *The Apostolic Fathers* (1891; reprint, Grand Rapids: Baker, 1984), 178. This is from Polycarp's letter to the Philippians. Future references to this volume will contain only the name of the apostolic father, the writing, and the number of the paragraph.

16. Ibid., 9.

17. Ibid., 12.

18. *Martyrdom of Polycarp*, 14.

19. Ignatius, *Ephesians*, 5.

20. Ibid., 2.

21. Ibid., 20.

22. Ibid.

23. Ignatius, *Magnesians*, 6.

24. Ibid.

25. Ignatius, *Trallians*, 2.

26. Ignatius, *Magnesians*, 7.

27. Ignatius, *Ephesians*, "greeting" and 7.

28. Ibid., 20.

29. Ignatius, *Smyrna*, 6.

30. Ignatius, *Magnesians*, 9–10.

31. Ignatius, *Ephesians*, 19, 10.

32. Ignatius, *Magnesians*, 1.

33. Ibid., 7.

34. Ibid., 8.

35. Ibid., 11.

36. Ignatius, *Trallians*, "greeting."

37. Ibid., 2.

38. Ibid., 2, 6, 7, 8.

39. Ignatius, *Philadelphians*, 3.

40. Ignatius, *Smyrnaeans*, 8–9.
41. *Martyrdom of Polycarp*, 4–5.
42. Ignatius, *Smyrna*, 3.
43. Ibid., 4.
44. Ibid., 5.
45. Ibid.
46. Ibid., 6.
47. Ibid., 7.
48. Irenaeus, *Against Heresies*, trans. Rev. Alexander Roberts and Rev. W. H. Rambaut, vol. 5 of *Ante-Nicene Christian Library*, ed. Rev. Alexander Roberts and James Donaldson (Edinburgh: T. & T. Clark, 1868), III. i. 1.
49. Irenaeus, *Against Heresies*, III. iii. 1.
50. Ibid., III. iii. 2.
51. Ibid., III. iii. 4.
52. Ibid.
53. Ibid, III. iv. 1.
54. Ibid., III. v. 1.
55. Ibid., III. xviii. 4–5.
56. Ignatius, *Trallians*, 9.
57. Ignatius, *Romans*, 2.
58. Ibid., 6.

In the Middle Ages, the focus of theology was on the work of Jesus Christ and how an individual could appropriate it to himself. Anselm laid the foundation by showing how Christ made atonement by taking upon Himself God's wrath, making propitiation for our sins. But the questions of personal appropriation of that work by faith and repentance proved difficult, being complicated by philosophical questions of how the free grace of God can be understood within any explanation or structure of human thought or behavior. Grace came to be thought of as arbitrary, such that any human attempt to receive it was necessarily uncertain.

At the same time, it was believed that if one did the best he or she could to come to God, God would probably reward that effort. Is that earning salvation? The Augustinians of the late medieval period were sure that it was, so they focused attention on God's covenantal binding of Himself in His promises as the basis for confident faith. This became the foundation of the Reformation and almost all revivals ever since. That faith that receives forgiveness and justification is the faith that doesn't look to itself but looks away to the sure promises of a covenant-keeping God.

2

HOW DID THE CHURCH IN ROME BECOME ROMAN CATHOLICISM?

D. Clair Davis

The church of Jesus Christ entered the medieval world with a new beginning and a sharper focus. In the early centuries the church had moved from a persecuted minority to an very active part of the imperial cultural establishment. The church had been victorious in its struggles with a pagan religious culture, so its perception of salvation tended to become one laden with the terminology and thought of victory. Jesus Christ had won the victory over sin and death, over all the powers on earth and in hell. *Christus Victor!* became the old church's comprehensive concluding summary of the meaning of the gospel. Today on the ceiling of an Orthodox Church you still witness the cosmic Pantokrator, the exalted and reigning Jesus Christ.

Though conditioned by the church's history, this theology of the early church faithfully reflected an important aspect of the biblical teaching of salvation. It stressed redemption—how God delivers His people from their bondage into the freedom of life with Him. As God once said to the Israelites, "I will redeem you with an outstretched arm and with mighty acts of judgment" (Exodus 6:6), so throughout the Bible He emphasizes that it is by His power alone that He delivers His people.

THE MEDIEVAL CHURCH'S SHIFT OF EMPHASIS

By the beginning of the medieval period, not only had the world changed radically but so had the place of the church within it. No longer was the world a unified urban empire with an established culture. Since the fall of Rome, northern Europe had turned into a disconnected rural society, where simple literacy, to say nothing of a real knowledge of the old civilization, had become only a distant memory. Horizons had become closer, and relationships with people—and also with God—had become much more personal and direct. The extended-family values of "Germanic" tribal feudalism replaced the anonymous generalities of the old urban ways. The maintenance of friendships and the restoration of damaged alliances became the focus of ordinary life.

This way of perceiving life became the new direction for thinking about an individual's relationship to his God. More biblical understanding was needed, further recognition of what the Bible meant by salvation. The doctrine of redemption had made a compelling statement of God's overwhelming power to transform the world. It had objectified the change God accomplished in the cross and resurrection of Christ and had emphasized the all-inclusive nature of His work. But what could that mean for the individual? Though the old church's understanding of grace was comprehensive enough, it could still appear to be impersonal or even mechanical in its subjective application.

So the medieval church welcomed a shift to other, more personal, biblical expressions, such as atonement, propitiation, and justification. Sin could now be seen not just in terms of enslaving forces without, but as something within man himself for which he was personally accountable and radically guilty. God was not just the only possible Savior, but He was a person whose own character and honor had been offended by sin. Whatever cosmic dimensions sin and salvation had, there could never be a satisfying or comforting understanding of salvation without a resolution of the great personal disruption between God and mankind.

Concentrated attention needed to be given to the restoration of personal concord and fellowship between the holy God and His sinful creatures. This is first of all the question of objective atonement for sin. In the old church this had either been discussed much too vaguely in sweeping terms expressing general divine victory, or it had become bogged down in the fruitless exploration of the question, "To whom had the redemption price been paid?" If Satan was the one from whom people need to be liberated, then must not the price be paid to him? But how then could that constitute defeat for him, since he obtains Jesus Christ as his prize? In order for Satan to be both the owner of Christ and also the one defeated by Him, the only resolution appeared to be the infamous "bait" theory of the Atonement: Christ was indeed the price paid, but Satan had overreached himself by claiming that price; thereby Christ was the bait God used to catch the arrogant Satan. Ingenious this theory may have been, but it was so patently artificial and even humorous that it was unworthy of extended consideration.

Obviously only a serious, fresh start could be of any lasting help. That the medieval church did this is the greatest single contribution of the entire period. It radically rethought what the Bible meant by atonement. Today Christians wonder, "How could a doctrine of such pivotal importance for Christian thinking have been so long in emerging?" In an attempt to answer this question, historians have noticed a parallel between the arrangement of topics in a systematic theology textbook and the historical development of doctrine. In a textbook, the work of Christ is not generally touched on until after discussions of the nature of God, His creation and direction, and man in his sin. Interestingly, this is exactly the progression of doctrinal development in the church's history.

Either this means, more pessimistically, that the church never reworks what it has once considered (but just keeps tacking on supplemental material at the end of what it has done before), or it means, more optimistically, that there is something reasonable about the development of Christian doctrine—from the basic to the developed—from God to man to sin to atonement. Man's nature, his sin, and his need had been well defined in the interchanges between Pelagius and Augustine; now it was time, in the progress of dogma, for God's answer to sin to be clarified decisively. Finally, near the end of the eleventh century, the great theologians Anselm and Abelard took a fresh look at the doctrine.

THE CONTRIBUTIONS OF ANSELM AND ABELARD

Anselm, Archbishop of Canterbury, is remembered for his theological method and his conviction that we believe in order to understand. That is, we begin with Christian theological certainty and then reason backwards to determine the significance of what we already know. In his signature contribution of the "ontological argument" for the existence of God, he turned away from the old way of reasoning from the existence of a very large and very well-ordered universe to the God who must have made it—someone who must be even greater and better-ordered than the universe (though logically not infinitely great or wise). Instead, Anselm argued, we must begin with God Himself as He really is, considering Him as truly perfect in His being and character, not approximately perfect as other arguments would conclude. And if God is perfect, then He must exist, for anything less than existence would not be perfect! This "argument" is either theological sleight-of-hand or the pinnacle of profundity, and it is not surprising that philosophers and theologians have difficulty even in knowing whether they understand what Anselm was saying. Perhaps he should be understood as saying this: Unless God exists then no thought or meaning is possible; so to even think of God means to think of Him as He is—that is, as existent.

Anselm applied much the same way of thinking to the Atonement[1] and reasoned from its existence—its actuality—back to its interpretation. In his classic *Cur Deus Homo* (*Why the God-Man*), he argued from the fact of the Incarnation and the Cross to God's purpose in sending His Son. What can it mean? God would not have done this astounding thing if providing some lesser remedy for sin had been possible. The uniqueness of the Son of God must involve necessarily a unique work, a work of atonement that could not have been accomplished in any other way. From there Anselm recognized that the effects of sin include not just the cosmic distortion of creation but go deeper, into the character of God Himself. What only Christ can do is to bear the wrath of God, a holy being whose honor has been violated. For that to have been really necessary must mean that God's honor, and hence His wrath against sin, is at the very heart of the nature of the Atonement. The Atonement was directed, then, not at the cosmos or at man, but at God! It "satisfied" His offended honor or character. Only such a substantial and exceptional necessity could possibly justify God's giving over of His Son unto death.

This God-directed significance of the Atonement is what made Anselm's work new and epoch-making. It is likely the greatest legacy of the Christian church from the Middle Ages. Since then, any attempt to understand the death of Christ from the perspective of propitiation for sin, or as the foundation for justification and forgiveness, has been known as the "Anselmic" or "satisfaction" view. Without the new "Germanic" focus on a subjective or personal understanding of the Christian faith, it would have been much more difficult to recognize this biblical emphasis on the personal character of atonement. But Anselm's concentration upon Christ Himself and why only He could do what needed to be done is what provides the heart of the new breakthrough in understanding the love of God for poor sinners.

It is also possible to have a personal view of the Atonement that is not God-centered but that rather focuses on the way sinners perceive Christ's death. That was the direction taken by Anselm's great rival, Peter Abelard. For him the value of the Atonement was in the individual's personal response to what Christ had done for him. As he came to appreciate and bow in gratitude at the extent of God's love for him, he would respond in turn with his own love to the God who had loved him so much.

Was Anselm or Abelard closer to the truth? To the present day, Christians have disagreed. A liberal thinks it unworthy of God that He would require satisfaction before He could express His love to sinners. An evangelical is sure that the Cross did much more than persuade sinners that God loved them; limiting its work to that seems to be a trivializing of sin and the full dimensions of God's work of salvation. An evangelical never questions the power of the Cross to demonstrate the love of God; but to him that love is not merely a generic demonstration but is a very particular action in which God actually did take away His wrath against sinners by directing it toward Christ.

MASS AND PENANCE: AVENUES OF GRACE

The atonement theology, with its realization of the personal character of the work of Jesus Christ, made a good beginning, but it was necessary to think further about what this really means, especially in terms of how that objective work becomes mine—that is, how it becomes subjective. One can not long avoid that next question: "How can I individually lay hold on what Christ has done for me? What must I do to receive what Christ has done for me?"

That question for several centuries had been answered in terms of the grace provided in the sacraments. God Himself had given His own channels of grace, and it was only necessary that the individual make use of them. A causal chain was involved. Christ had died and presented the value of His death to His church. He had chosen its first head, the apostle Peter, and all his successors as bishop of Rome, or pope, to have the same authority He had. That centered particularly around the power of binding and loosing, qualifying and disqualifying for the grace of the sacraments. Concretely, the pope has the power to consecrate bishops, who in turn have the power to ordain priests, who then have the authority to say the Mass—to sacramentally transform the bread and wine into the body and blood of Christ, to "make the body of the Lord"—which finally is the channel of grace to the church. The theology and scriptural arguments against this understanding are carefully developed in chapter 5 by S. Lewis Johnson.

At first reflection the idea that the church had been given channels of grace by Christ would seem to settle the matter. Do not all those who are present at Mass receive the grace offered automatically (*ex opere operato*)? Much of the structure of the Mass would seem to indicate this observation when the transformed elements are raised so all can see and the bell is rung to remind all to look (observing the transformation itself may actually convey grace more obviously than the eating of the bread).

Certainly the objective character of sacramental grace is vital to its nature, but to the devout there must be more to it than that. Some sort of religious attitude of heart must be necessary on the part of the worshiper in order for him or her to receive grace worthily. Faith and repentance must be present for the sacrament to be received properly. Does that mean that salvation finally depends on the ability of a frail and sinful individual to come to God with a truly worshipful heart? Surely not, for that would mean that the chain of salvation is only as strong as its weakest link, and the human heart is a very weak and deceitful link indeed. For that reason medieval theologians spoke of a further graceful provision of a way to enable one to receive the grace of the Mass.

That indispensable way became the sacrament of Penance, in many ways the very heart of medieval religion. This new sacrament was seen to provide the means for transforming weak, inadequate, even self-deceiving faith and repentance into the sort acceptable to a holy God. As in the case of any sacrament the transformation was not empirically discernible. In the Mass, for example, the church taught that the elements still taste like bread and wine even though they no longer are; in the language of Aristotelian physics, the accidents (empirical characteristics) have not been changed but the essence has. In Penance, grudging repentance has been changed into heart-felt repentance, and superficial faith into concentrated love for God—even though no one could perceive the difference!

But even if motivations and attitudes could not be evaluated, at least Penance could be made so difficult and time-consuming that only those truly committed to pleasing God would make use of it. Earlier monastic penance had been therapeutic in character: its intention was to enable the individual to substitute godly behavior for sinful actions, for example, by directing the greedy to give to the poor, patterned on the biblical model of "put off and put on." Within an intimate monastic setting, a personalized penance could be helpful, though even there confessors began to make use of the standardized penances of the penitential manuals. But when an annual confession was required of all the people, it was hardly reasonable that an individual penance would be possible. Further standardization of penances easily led to the perception of Penance as not being intended to alter behavior but rather to serve as punishment for what had already been done.

Previously some had found life-changing significance in traveling to the site with which a great saint was associated, that he might reflect upon the life of one whose example was especially well-suited to his own sins and weaknesses. But when pilgrimages were selected to many sites at great distances and when it seemed that the only point of the expedition was to cover as many miles as possible yet still get back home while something of normal life remained, then what possible personal value could come from all that travel?

When substitute penances were devised, including the payment of money, any remaining therapeutic value could only be nebulous and fragmentary. Penance became even more abstract and meaningless when the church began to offer substitutes that involved even the removal of the penalty for future sins (indulgences). Technically, only the *temporal* penalty for sin was being dealt with (the punishment due sin this side of eternity, including that endured in purgatory), but for practical purposes that was all that any one knew about anyway. Knowledge that one's *eternal* punishment had been dealt with (the assurance of salvation) was available in any case only to those few—the saints—to whom it had been revealed by extraordinary revelation.

Hence the resolution of the most important question of all—"How can I lay hold upon the salvation given by God through the death of Christ?"—was still inaccessible. A clear answer to today's Evangelism Explosion question—"Why should God let you into His heaven?"—could not really be given by even the greatest theologian. The gap that Penance was devised to bridge was, in the end, still a great chasm: How can a weak sinner come to a holy Christ?

THE REDISCOVERY OF PREVENIENT GRACE

It was obviously time for yet another fresh look at the greatest of life's questions. Could there yet be a way of seeing the problem that was not in terms of cause and effect? Obviously the supernatural effect of eternal salvation could not come from any natural cause, not even from a life of penance. If salvation required even a slight initial action on our part, then we could never obtain it. Could a new philosophical paradigm, one that avoids causal thinking, be of help?

Throughout the history of Western thought, especially in the ancient and medieval periods, it has seemed that there were really only two options: Platonic idealism or Aristotelian empiricism. What is the better explanation of the world—seeing it in terms of nonempirical entities (those that are grasped by the human mind and not by sense experience) or the other way around? Because Christianity is concerned with supernatural reality (that which transcends what the senses can experience), it seemed to many that Platonic idealism was the most helpful way for a Christian to look at the world. But Christians also knew how harmful it was to suggest that the empirical character of the Christian faith is irrelevant; after all, that includes the incarnation, death, and resurrection of Christ, as well as His return. It is also terribly misleading to think of the nonphysical aspect of human beings as being somehow closer to God than the physical aspect, as somehow partaking of God's character in a noncreated and dependent way. Platonic idealism could easily lead to a blurring of the line between God and man and to a trivializing of the historical Jesus.

If idealism had come to have such serious weaknesses that Christians were beginning to call it into question, the obvious alternative framework for Christian theology was the empiricism of Aristotle. It already served that function for Islam, medieval Christianity's greatest competitor and field for mission. Indeed, the greatest expression of medieval contextualization, the attempt to present the gospel in a meaningful way to a non-Christian culture, is found in the *Summa Contra Gentiles* of the Aristotelian Thomas Aquinas. Thomas was as aware as any of his critics today of the difficulties of using an empirical model to present transempirical realities. Accordingly, he made use of many corrective procedures intended to preserve Christian theology from being overwhelmed by pagan methodology. He realized that an empirical approach, which argues from the finite universe to God, must be supplemented by revelation, for no amount of finite effects would ever yield an infinite God. Further, an empirical argument is designed to lead to a single cause, never the biblical Trinity. So natural theology always needs supplementary revelation to reach the God of the Bible. What can be known about God empirically only functions analogically, not directly, if the living God is to be reached.

But when all this has been recognized, Thomistic Aristotelianism by its very nature was bound to be the theology of the ecclesiastical establishment, of the church and her sacraments. Though Thomas personally was as deeply mystical as any medieval Christian, the function of his teaching was to demonstrate the way God brought salvation through the intermediate causes of the grace offered by the church. Though God's reason was not an abstraction but rather a compelling expression of his love, still the way He worked was through the institution He had placed in the world for the salvation of sinners. Empirical, causal thinking was almost inevitably ecclesiastical and sacramental.

But the issue was no longer about the effectiveness of the sacraments as such; rather it was about the new question of the personal link between them and the weak, foolish sinner. That was the weakest link in the chain of salvation, and when salvation depended on the sinner's ability, the assertion of the strength of the links of the sacraments could only be seen as meaningless.

For that reason the entire medieval edifice, with church and sacraments, all given validity by Aristotelian causality, came into serious question. The grand "medieval synthesis" was about to unravel. If ecclesiastical, causal, sacramental grace was not the answer to salvation, where could the answer be found?

Obviously a sinner cannot be saved without the grace of God. If sacramental, objective grace is insufficient, there must be some other kind of grace. That grace must be direct, not mediated by the sacraments. It must be comprehensive, not requiring any other grace to complete it. It must be there at the very beginning of the individual's turning to God, and it must enable him to lay hold upon whatever other grace that may be there for him. In a word, it must be the grace Augustine had long ago spoken of—"prevenient" grace.

Prevenient grace works in the heart of God's elect well before sacramental grace does, and it depends on nothing except the saving love of God; it is the grace of predestination and election. Augustine had spoken of the church in two different ways: as the institutional or visible church, and as the true people of God, known only to Him. That construction had become a popular medieval model and could be employed to advance almost any viewpoint. Those with a papal or sacramental agenda could bring institution and election so close together they were virtually identical—God's purpose to save and the visible church are one and the same. But reforming elements, appalled over the ignorance and corruption of the visible church, could pull election and institution so far apart that the institutional church could be seen as the enemy of the elect, the exact opposite of the true church. This was regularly depicted in the recurring visual aid of the medieval period, a three-panel cartoon. The first panel showed the destitute Christ in shabby clothing, riding on a donkey; the second an affluent bishop in jewels and furs, riding a magnificent war horse; and the third a poor monk, with apparently the same clothing and donkey as Christ had. Christ's question, was it possible for a rich man to enter heaven, had been rephrased: Could a bishop be saved? The assumed answer was, only if he renounced his office with its wealth and he became a monk. Another cartoon, this time of a ship surrounded by drowning men, featured monks on the ship attempting to pull in the lost from the water. Featured among those drowning in the water were always the clergy and the bishops.

Now approaching the end of the Middle Ages, the sacramental system had come to be preoccupied with Penance, and it in turn upon the high finance of the indulgence system. The "ordinary" means of grace had come to be seen to display the exact opposite of the values for which the true church stood. How long could Christian apologists maintain a position that implied that along with the salvation of God's people by the sacraments there inevitably came a corrupt ecclesiastical establishment? The same situation had been faced in the ancient period in the Donatist controversy, when some had maintained that only the sacraments of those persecuted for their faith had validity and those of the compromisers did not. Though the orthodox position was that the character of the priest had nothing to do with the value of the sacraments, that position was much more difficult to maintain at the end of the Middle Ages. After all, who is sure that he would not apostatize under the severe, unending torture of a period of persecution? But to voluntarily sell out to wealth and power and lust, how could that be taken as anything but a sordid betrayal of Christ?

Who else could be on the third panel but a poor monk? It could not be a monk of the older establishment orders, with their wealth and corruption. But as always in the church's history, when monasticism went to seed, there could always be a fresh start, this time with the mendicant (begging) orders of Franciscans and Dominicans. These orders had two important goals: the imitation of Christ in His poverty and servanthood, as set forth in the Sermon on the Mount; and serious study and teaching of the Bible, such that the entire church could understand what it meant to follow Christ and capture His example. It became clear that to teach about Christ as He really was would inevitably subvert the church.

But it was not easy to stay poor. Dominicans became university teachers and needed to accumulate books, the most expensive treasures of all. The imitation of Christ was much too threatening to the pope, who commanded the Franciscans to abandon the mendicant principle and to cease living from day to day; the "spiritual" (disobedient) Franciscans found it hard to survive papal persecution. But the vision and memory of the mendicants lived on. The third panel continued to sound a familiar and self-evident note. The practical bottom line was clear: the grace of the sacraments came through the local, ignorant, drunken priest with his housekeeper/mistress; but the prevenient grace that could change hearts to receive sacramental grace came through the itinerant, poor monk, who demonstrated in his life what it was to be a true Christian and who taught Bible stories about Jesus. So the sacrament did not rest on godliness or on the gospel; true grace had precious little to do with the institutional church and her sacraments. Augustine's invisible church turned out to be the only obviously godly church after all. Election, the theological backbone of the invisible church, could become the most subversive doctrine of all.

THE CONFLICT BETWEEN
MEDIATED AND CAUSAL GRACE

Philosophically, the issue between immediate causal grace (sacramental) and mediated grace (through reflection on the monk's teaching and mirroring of Christ) is closely related to the question of the suitability of Thomas's Aristotelianism as a framework for Christian thinking. If natural theology can yield only descriptions of God by listing His "attributes" but can say nothing about *who* He is, His personal being as Trinitarian Father and Son and Spirit, what kind of God is being spoken of? Is not the God of Thomism little more than an abstract scientific principle of purpose and regularity? Will not the inadequacy of this understanding of God's being lead inevitably to serious weaknesses in understanding His deeds? If God's grace is merely His plan for achieving a goal, is it still possible to see it as a expression of election, dependent upon nothing but His will and love? If by definition the grace that we need more than anything else is not sacramental, then Thomism's grand causal scheme is in the end worth very little. What was needed was a paradigm for understanding the personal, direct grace of God.

One would perhaps have anticipated a reversion from the Aristotelian experiment back to the old Platonic or neo-Platonic philosophy of Augustine. That would have also meant a return to unadulterated theological Augustinianism, with its limited or personal atonement, where all of God's grace came through Christ and His work. But too many centuries had gone by and too many theologians had been unwilling to think of grace in such a thoroughgoing way. They had preferred a milder Augustinianism, one that affirmed that sinners cannot be saved without the grace of God, but unwilling to draw Augustine's own conclusion: that the only grace there is comes through the death of Christ; that consequently those who are saved are those for whom He died. Medieval theologians considered their theology semi-Augustinianism or just Augustinianism, but a much more accurate label is the old church's designation of semi-Pelagianism. When the question is, to what extent does a miserable sinner need the crucified Christ, the halfhearted Augustinian answer yields a glass half empty, not one half full.

But if not Augustinianism, what philosophy is available as a foundation for nonsacramental, prevenient grace? What is there besides Platonism and Aristotelianism? The victor (but more by default) is nominalism.

THE RISE OF NOMINALISM

Nominalism is hardly a full-fledged world-and-life view; it is more a technical methodology for coordinating different perspectives. Much of medieval thinking, especially in its more basic phase, was concerned with the nature of language and logic. What does it mean when we say that two individual things belong to the same class of being and may have the same predicate attached to them both? (This appears to be an especially important question when much of medieval thought is patterned after Aristotelian biology, with its divisions and subdivisions of reality into genus, species, and individual.) Is the common classification the important thing, or is it the individual identity? That is, is the classification simply a convenient linguistic handle, just a name, or is it more than that, something real? Those who say "real" are called "realists," while those who say "name" are "nominalists."

Perhaps a nominalist does not inherently believe in arbitrary classification, but one who says "name" is likely to be heard as saying "just a name." Are linguistic classifications arbitrary, necessary, or something else? Nominalists wisely considered not just statements concerning the past and present but also those concerning the future, and that complicated the question considerably. Is such a statement true or false, or something else? When one is asked whether he believes a future statement, he might well say, "I don't know." Nominalists then have a three-value logic: right, wrong, and undetermined. This discussion begins to sound theoretical and impractical until one realizes that Christianity is all about future statements, which Christians call "the promises of God," or even "covenant promises." Finally the issue becomes existentially straightforward: What is the value of God's promises to me, those that promise eternal life if I do certain things, especially if I am uncertain how to do them, and how I would ever know if I had? If Nominalism can really help with those questions, it deserves serious attention.[2]

The most basic question of all—What must I do to be saved?—has come into its own. The original answer was, receive God's grace in the Mass. But if I'm not sure I'm approaching the Mass in true faith and repentance, what then? The next answer was, make use of the sacramental grace of Penance to prepare for the Mass. But if I'm not sure I'm coming to Penance with proper—even minimally proper—faith and repentance, what then? What if proper faith and repentance is not a quantitative matter, of needing more than I now have, but a question of having from the outset a qualitatively opposite—a holy kind—of faith, what should I do? And what if the right kind of faith is the kind that looks to God's glory alone and not at all to my selfish wish to avoid hell?

If, after all, what I desperately need is to receive prevenient, electing grace, how is that done? Is election not, by definition, something mysterious and ineffable, utterly out of my influence and control? Nominalism's primary answer to this final question was that, whereas there was absolutely no causal relation between what people do and God's grace and whereas no one could in any way deserve God's grace (*de condigno*), still it was only fitting or congruous (*de congruo*) that God give His grace to those who sincerely desired it and expressed that desire by seeking to please God the best they could. Though whoever does this has no certainty or assurance of salvation (which no one in the Middle Ages had anyway), at least it was probable. And, though doing the best you can does not guarantee the gift of God's grace, not doing it makes it highly unlikely that you will receive grace.

Sacramental grace was efficacious for those who sought it sincerely— efficacious because it was rooted in the objective, atoning work of Christ, mediated through His church and its sacraments. But "sincerity" was so nebulous and tantalizingly unobtainable that even the work of Christ became only theoretically efficacious. Truly effective grace consequently had nothing to do with the sacramental system—but also nothing to do with that which gave it its foundation, the saving work of Christ. Nominalist grace was so immediate and direct that it evaded not only the church, but Christ Himself. Election could not be God's purpose carried out and revealed through His Son but was instead the naked will of God who saved as He chose, with or without Christ. The Jesus Christ that the monks presented was not the God-man who made atonement. Rather, their Jesus could be meditated upon, and that meditation could be the occasion of salvation through the naked will of God. Perhaps. At bottom, the monks' preaching of the simple Jesus who showed us the loving heart of God turned out to be only a front for the unknown God.

This medieval denouement was far more than the "dissolution of the medieval synthesis"; it was simply the dissolution of the Christian faith itself. The Cross had been rejected as irrelevant to the most basic question of all: "How can I be forgiven by God?" All that remained after this was the unknown God and the value of morality. This was the religion of pre-Reformation Renaissance Christianity, which was to surface later as the religion of the Enlightenment.

PRE-REFORMATION DEVELOPMENTS

Enlightenment religion could be expressed as the Christian humanism of Erasmus: Christianity is reduced to trying to do the best one can. Theology is essentially unknowable, and it is foolish to waste time on its irrelevant puzzles. Instead, one must emphasize what can be known, the simple ethics of the Sermon on the Mount. Those who occupy themselves with organized religion are fools or scoundrels. Never again should it be taken seriously, except as it advances basic morality.

Enlightenment religion could also express itself much more directly, a humanism without Christian veneer. It affirmed that esoteric theology and philosophy had proven their worthlessness. There were much simpler guides for life—the revived practical philosophies of the declining days of the Roman empire, fitting enough for the declining days of medieval Christendom. These old philosophies were counsels of desperation and negation, of resignation and cynicism: Skepticism, Epicureanism, Stoicism. All philosophies and theologies were of equal value or lack of value. There was no absolute truth, and the role of humankind in its last days was to learn to live without striving foolishly for meaning in life. That could mean living lives either of noble suffering or of pleasure in the face of a meaningless future.

Or the call to doing the best you could with the goal of pleasing God could be taken painfully seriously. Remember Martin Luther with his perpetual confessions until finally his confessor charged him with the sin of overscrupulosity! Think of his endeavoring to please his father by studying law and to please God instead by becoming a monk, and of therefore being radically disobedient either way. Think of him at the brink of despair, and then coming to understand that the righteous never live by sincerity or by trying harder, but by faith in the God who justifies the ungodly.

But before Luther there came a revival of consistent, homogeneous Augustinianism—from the pens of the monk Gregory of Rimini and another Archbishop of Canterbury, Thomas Bradwardine. Bradwardine wrote a book with the offensive title *The Cause of God against the Pelagians,* as if his opponents really were Pelagians, in an age when all felt quite certain of their allegiance to Augustine. But he meant it nevertheless: if one relies on his own attempts to please God with the purpose of motivating God to give him grace by earning it (whether or not he thinks *de condigno* or *de congruo*), then at bottom he relies on his own efforts for salvation, which is standard Pelagianism. However piously it may be expressed, any thought of preparing oneself for grace is idolatrous trusting in the flesh.

Constructively, the new Augustinians concentrated on God's covenant promises. Later the covenant emphasis came to be thought of with a narrower focus, in terms of the continuity between Old and New Testament, between circumcision and baptism. But at the end of the medieval period the issues were more basic: When I trust in God's promises, it is His promise that is the central issue, not my trust. Further, God's election, His plan from eternity, may not be separated from His covenant, His revelation of that plan in time. Election is not a mysterious unknowable black hole that may swallow up or subvert God's revealed covenant to His people. Rather, it is the reflection of the integrity of a God who stands behind His promises.

At this point the Reformation could not be far away. The new focus on election, and the immediate grace of God, had pointed both Wycliffe and Huss away from a papal and sacramental church to a church based on the

Word—preached, heard, and followed. That biblical church committed itself to obedience, to correcting what God's people had not done, where the church described in the Bible was patently and strikingly entirely different from the church of Rome. Though the pre-Reformation forerunners did not go all the way to arrive at justification, they did prepare God's people to receive with faith whatever God's Word said; when they came to see that the Bible taught justification, they would accept it with joy and enthusiasm. With the formal principle (the sole authority of God's Word) now in place, the material principle (justification) could not be far away.[3]

Understanding justification would come inexorably, when the bankruptcy of nominalistic preparatory grace become clear. Article by article the gospel in all its richness became clear: Without the grace of God, a sinner can do nothing to save himself. He can do nothing to prepare for grace, for without it he is still just a sinner. God does not receive a foolish sinner trying to do his best but, rather, the one who knows the truth about his sin and who trusts only in the righteousness of Christ. He knows his trust is not a "virtue," to be evaluated in terms of its strength or consistency; instead its value comes only through its object, the faithful Savior Jesus Christ. To give us that Savior is not something God does piecemeal or by measure; for us to know and trust Christ is to know and trust the "whole" Christ, "in all of his offices."

The doctrine of election may sometimes seem like a peripheral dogmatic fossil from a long-distant past. In the late Middle Ages and in the Reformation, however, it meant personal relationship with God, one not dependent on the offices of the church. It meant the grace of God, resting on nothing other than His love and kindness to His people. In the midst of suffering and doubt, it meant the persistent, continuing love of the Father of Jesus Christ to His children. This is seen clearly in the organization of John Calvin's *Institutes of the Christian Religion*. There election is taken up as was usual in the older theological outlines, under the doctrine of God: God has made the world and is in complete control of it, including the actions and thoughts of people, and their relationships to Himself. But that is a comparatively brief treatment compared to the later extended discussion under how God's people receive the blessings of the Cross, particularly how they continue to trust in God in the midst of suffering and doubt. For Calvin takes up election primarily under the topic of the perseverance of the saints, following substantially the outline of Paul's letter to the Romans. There, chapters 6–8 discuss the believer's struggles with sin, temptation, persecution, and suffering; and at the end Paul asks the most basic question of all, "What shall separate us from the love of Christ?" The triumphant answer, that "nothing shall," is set within the eternal plan of God. The God who chose us from the beginning will surely continue His work in us to the end. This biblical understanding of divine election is not some dark cloud behind which the inscrutable

God hides Himself, keeping His mysterious foreboding plan to Himself, while He reveals only a tantalizing, possible salvation. Rather, it is the election revealed in Christ, who is the mirror of election.[4]

No wonder the Reformation was so exhilarating and promising. Instead of terrifying doubt, there was the sure promise of God's favor; instead of fluctuating introspection, there was a clear look at the faithful Savior Jesus Christ; instead of a life of fearful cynicism, there was a heart full of gratitude over the full forgiveness of sin.

THE LEGACY OF NOMINALISM

But major questions still remain. Was nominalism only a momentary aberration in Catholic thought? Though Luther and others were right in rejecting it, were they wrong in thinking that they were rejecting the teaching of the church? Certainly the nominalists did not carry the day forever in the church; ultimately the older Thomism was to become its official theology. But one must consider the later conclusions of the Catholic Council of Trent—its rejections of justification and assurance—well after the obvious dangers of nominalist constructions should have been seen. It is very hard to see why the Roman church would have stood so vigorously against the Reformation if it were not at least extremely sympathetic to nominalism. At that time there were hardly any real alternatives.

At least as basic is the Protestant question, how much did the children of the Reformation value their heritage, forged as it had been out of the abyss of medieval confusion and doubt? Would they ever regress, if not to the name of Rome, then to its kind of theology? One of the most astonishing developments in Protestant church history is the recurring pattern of return back to moralism and away from Christ. The accounts of historic evangelical revivals or awakenings are very instructive. The revival preacher would present the old Reformation message, that sinners are saved by trust in the work of Christ, that justification is of the ungodly by faith alone. When that gospel was clearly heard, over and over again many would came to faith in Christ, rejoicing in finally hearing a message they had never heard before. But when they spoke to their pastors about their new faith, the pastors said that they also believed in justification in the same way. "Then why didn't you ever tell us?" was the skeptical reply. Why not indeed?

The answer may be as simple as pastors thinking that every one knew it and that it could be presupposed. But it may have been more complex. The Church of England forbade local pastors or elders to exercise church discipline, since membership in the church had civil implications; they reserved that discipline for bishops or probably their lay chancellors. These men could exact fines for various offenses, but they knew nothing about the spiritual counsel that should accompany rebuke for sin. In that case it would be easy for a pastor to seek to reach the disobedient or lax in the congregation by preaching on the danger of a dead faith, or that many believe they are converted but really aren't, and the like. The outcome might well be that many had their attention diverted from the objective saving work of Christ toward the subjective quality of their faith. The rifle that church discipline should use toward specific offenders could easily turn into the shotgun that would wound those for whom it was not intended—and so attack and ultimately remove their assurance of salvation.

From a more theological point of view, one's understanding of the nature of faith has much to do with whether it is being seen from the perspective of regeneration (spiritual change) or justification (forgiveness). In older theological vocabulary, from justification's side faith is "passive" (not considering itself but instead looking to Christ); but from regeneration's side faith is "lively" (coming from a heart radically changed by the Spirit of God). In ordinary language it would be hard to think of something as both passive and lively, but what was meant was something like this: "God has so radically changed my heart that I no longer trust in myself but only in Christ." Historically not many have been able to grasp that. Either they were convinced that the sinner's great need was change and the consequent commitment to obeying Christ (seen in the "Anabaptist" lively direction) or sure that people are so inherently self-righteous that they need to be told to recognize that their forgiveness does not rest upon their changed lives, but only on Christ (the "Lutheran" passive direction).

Calvinists thought they could avoid that dilemma and be committed to both directions. They taught that Christ was to be taken as Savior and as Lord, as the fountain of both forgiveness and change. But when one looks at the history of Reformed theology, most of what he sees is the history of the tension of those who were "antinomian" (the danger of the Lutheran, passive side) or those who were "neonomian" (the danger of the Anabaptist, lively side). Is the danger to the church greater from those who are lazy and indifferent to radical obedience to Christ? Then teach them that a Christian needs much more than mere faith. Or is the danger greater from those who are consumed with doubt and unbelief, convinced that they dare not come to Christ until they have made significant change in their lives? Then teach them that salvation is only from the Lord. In a personal, pastoral or discipling relationship, counseling could be directed so that the answer would depend on the individual's need or particular idol. The Protestant church has been at its best when such individual pastoral work was practiced, either by a pastor like Richard Baxter, who constantly visited everyone in his small congregation, or more likely by elder-directed, small pastoral groups (prophesyings, conventicles, classes). When lazy people can be presented with a different biblical emphasis than fearful people, then there is no need for either neo- or antinomian overemphasis or reductionism.

Still, the neonomian option seemed to be fostered much more frequently. Though the creeds said that no one is able to prepare himself for grace, it could still be argued that it's not the "plan of salvation" that is being presented, but only the "way of salvation." That distinction is either very profound or completely unintelligible. The alleged difference is, God doesn't require that people go through a preparatory process of conviction of sin and despair over never being saved, as a kind of prerequisite for salvation. But on the other hand, that is the way almost everyone ever came to Christ. It's at least the way all the testimonies before the congregation sound: if you've heard one you've heard them all. It could be stated that since no one can control the work of the Holy Spirit, at least he can place himself where the Holy Spirit works best, in the way of grace. No one can know how the Spirit works, but he can be aware of the usual circumstances through which He works. He cannot control grace, but he can arrange to be where grace is usually to be found. More people are converted in churches than in bars, and more people are converted while praying than while getting drunk. The doctrine of the "means of grace," which was intended to describe what Christians should do in order to grow spiritually, came to be applied to how non-Christians are converted.

The nominalist three-value logic had reemerged. According to this variety of theological thought, not only were there regenerate and unregenerate people, Christians and non-Christians, but also great varieties of the people in between, falling into the general category of the quickened or awakened. The cutting edge of the gospel could be blunted, for no longer could the great alternatives of life or death, Christ or self, be maintained. Instead, preaching could be turned away from the presenting of the gospel into describing how God frequently works. The sure promise of God could be diffused into vague probabilities. Indeed, it would be hard to tell the difference between the probability God of Enlightenment moralism and Protestant neonomianism.[5]

Revivals did come—and still come—and the Reformation was recapitulated again and again, with its great signatures of justification and assurance. But, more often than not, nominalist election was confused with biblical election, and the new revivals frequently went without that great theological backbone, a theme that will be developed as the heart of John Armstrong's appeal in chapter 13 in his call for a new reformation of evangelical Christianity that understands and preaches the gospel more faithfully.

CONCLUSION

Without understanding the struggles of the medieval church it will be hard to understand the weakness of modern conservative Catholicism's interest in questions regarding personal salvation. By the same token, it will also be hard to understand the weaknesses of modern Protestantism. Its liberalism did come, after all, from the Enlightenment. Its evangelical weaknesses come from continual neonomian influences. Both Catholic and Protestant churches need to take up again a serious reevaluation of the great questions of the relation between Christ as Savior and as Lord; is it forgiveness or is it change people need? Or both? It still needs to be said to all, Don't just describe the gospel; preach it! The apostle of the cross did say, "Woe is me if I do not preach the gospel" (1 Corinthians 9:16). Without these perspectives gained from the medieval background, the pursuit of comprehending the need and state of our twentieth century churches, and thus the need of our time, will take much longer than it should. With the help gleaned from such study both Catholics and Protestants should learn more quickly what personal faith in Christ really means and how to preach the gospel more faithfully. Only this discovery will bring the reformation most needed in our time.

NOTES

1. For the significance of Anselm's understanding of the Atonement, especially as compared with other views, see B. B. Warfield, "Atonement," in *Studies in Theology* (Edinburgh: Banner of Truth, 1988), 261–80.

2. See my "Nominalism," in *New Dictionary of Theology* (Downers Grove, Ill.: Inter-Varsity, 1988), 471–72.

3. For further help on the great philosophical and theological shift at the end of the period and its significance for the Reformation, the work of Heiko Oberman is the most rewarding. In order of easiest to read to most technical, see *Forerunners of the Reformation* (New York: Holt, Rinehart & Winston, 1966); *Dawn of the Reformation* (Grand Rapids: Eerdmans, 1986), 1–154, 204–33, 269–98; *Harvest of Theology* (Grand Rapids: Eerdmans, 1967); *Archbishop Thomas Bradwardine* (Utrecht: Kemink & Zoon, 1957); *Gregor von Rimini* (Berlin: de Gruyter, 1981).

4. John Calvin, *Institutes of the Christian Religion*, Book Three, XXI–XXIV (Philadelphia: Westminster Press, 1960).

5. On preparatory grace in evangelical theology, see (in favor) W. G. T. Shedd, *Dogmatic Theology* (Grand Rapids: Zondervan, 1959), II:511–28; (balanced and cautious) Herman Bavinck, *Gereformeerde Dogmatiek* (Kampen: Kok, 1976), IV:7–13.

What were the causes of the Reformation? What were its basic concerns and theology as presented by John Calvin? Since Calvin was the most talented of the second-generation Reformers, his perspective on the key issues of the Reformation is especially helpful. In three separate treatises, Calvin explains and defends the Reformation.

In "The Reply to Sadoleto" (1539), Calvin gives a personal defense of the reform. "The Necessity of Reforming the Church" (1544) is Calvin's most comprehensive examination of the issues that divided Rome from the Protestants. "The True Method of Reforming the Church and Healing Her Divisions" (1549) is a passionate defense of the reform in the face of serious military defeats. Taken together these three treatises reveal Calvin's understanding of what was at stake in the Reformation.

ESSAY
3

WHAT REALLY CAUSED
THE GREAT DIVIDE?

W. Robert Godfrey

Why did the Reformation take place? Historians have sought to answer that question from a wide variety of perspectives. They have given attention to the political, social, and economic circumstances of the sixteenth century to understand the setting of the Reformation. They have studied the cultural and intellectual developments of the late medieval and Renaissance periods as crucial backdrop for the Reformation. But ultimately it was not these factors that divided the church. These factors may have contributed in a variety of ways to the success of the Reformation, but they were not the heart of the Reformation. The heart of the Reformation was a distinct spiritual and theological vision—quite different from the one that had dominated the medieval church.

During the Middle Ages many reformations had occurred in the life of the church. But all of them were movements for moral reform. They sought to address various moral abuses and corruptions of the personal and institutional life in the church. The great Reformation of the sixteenth century also addressed various moral problems in the church. But the essence of the Reformation was doctrinal. The Reformers were persuaded that the spiritual and moral corruption of the church stemmed from doctrinal error that needed to be reformed by the Word of God.

Martin Luther expressed his concern for doctrinal reform in many of his writings. In 1520 he wrote two of his most powerful treatises calling for reform: "The Appeal to the German Nobility" and "The Babylonian Captivity of the Church."

Philipp Melanchthon effectively summarized Protestant concerns for reform in the Augsburg Confession of 1530. Part I of the Confession in twenty-two articles stated positively the Reformation doctrine. Part II in seven detailed articles described the abuses of the old church that needed to be reformed.

John Calvin, as a second-generation Reformer, also wrote in many different ways about the need for and character of the reform of the church. His famous *Institutes of the Christian Religion* was the fullest systematic presentation of Reformation theology prepared in the sixteenth century. This chapter will examine Calvin's own understanding and defense of the Reformation by looking at three treatises in which he specifically addresses that subject. These treatises were written over a ten-year period in Calvin's life and are directed to the needs and circumstances of those years. But taken together they give a fine picture of Calvin's reforming concern. The three treatises are "The Reply to Sadoleto" (1539), "The Necessity of Reforming the Church" (1543), and "The True Method of Reforming the Church and Healing Her Divisions" (1548). By listening to Calvin speak in these works, we can hear the deepest concerns of the Reformation.

"REPLY TO SADOLETO"

The first of these writings—"The Reply to Sadoleto"[1]—was written in peculiar circumstances. In 1538 John Calvin was exiled from Geneva after less than two years of ministry there. He settled in Strassburg, where he continued to work as a pastor and to write. In 1539 Jacopo Sadoleto, a bishop and cardinal in the Roman Catholic Church, wrote to Geneva urging the city to abandon the Reformation and return to the Roman obedience. Leaders in Geneva decided that the only person who could effectively answer Sadoleto was the very John Calvin they had exiled. With good grace Calvin was willing to take up the task of replying to Sadoleto and completed the work with remarkable speed in only six days.

This "Reply" is the most personal of Calvin's defenses of the Reformation and displays most fully the deep spiritual concerns at stake in the Reformation. The personal quality of the "Reply" was unusual in Calvin's writings. Calvin was by nature a very private person, little given in his writings to saying much about himself. It has often been observed that a few paragraphs in the preface to his *Commentary on the Psalms* are the only autobiography that we have from the pen of Calvin. Yet "The Reply to Sadoleto" does have a very personal dimension to it.[2] This personal quality probably results from the personal character of Sadoleto's attack on the Reformers in his letter to the Genevans. Near the beginning of his response Calvin notes that the strategy of Sadoleto was to praise the Genevans and to lay the blame for separating the Genevans from Rome on the ministers. Sadoleto further stated that the ministers had been motivated in their opposition to Rome by a desire for worldly advancement. This personal attack evoked a quite personal response from Calvin.

Calvin begins and closes his reply by scoffing at the notion that material gain had motivated the ministers in Geneva. He argued that in every case they would have been better off materially by staying in the Roman Church. He insists that he and other ministers were motivated only by their responsibility to God to be faithful pastors. Out of his continuing pastoral concern for Geneva he takes up the pen against Sadoleto. The work of the pastors is to "edify the Church, when, besides leading docile souls to Christ placidly, as with the hand, they are also armed to repel the machinations of those who strive to impede the work of God."[3]

Although Calvin's "Reply" is intricately constructed and responds in a variety of ways to Sadoleto's work, its central concerns are three: justification, the Word of God, and the church. Calvin writes of justification as "the first and keenest subject of controversy between us."[4] As he begins his discussion of justification, he explains that the Reformation position begins with an evaluation of man's plight as a sinner:

> First, we bid a man begin by examining himself, and this not in a superficial and perfunctory manner, but to cite his conscience before the tribunal of God, and when sufficiently convinced of his iniquity, to reflect on the strictness of the sentence pronounced upon all sinners. Thus confounded and amazed at his misery, he is prostrated and humbled before God; and, casting away all self-confidence, groans as if given up to final perdition.[5]

This theme of self-examination, which must result in profound recognition of sin and liability to eternal condemnation, is not an incidental matter for Calvin. Rather it is absolutely central to Reformation theology and spirituality. The doctrines of the Reformation are born of the hopelessness and helplessness of sinners. For Calvin the complete lostness of man was not only a teaching of the Bible and all sound Augustinian theology but was also his own experience. Scattered throughout this "Reply" are indications that Calvin had personally struggled with his own sin and the terrible judgment that awaited him apart from Christ. For example, he writes, "I observe, Sadoleto, that you have too indolent a theology, as is almost always the case with those who have never had experience in serious struggles of conscience."[6] Such a statement surely implies that Calvin had experienced torments of conscience and so had not fallen into the trap of a lazy, self-indulgent theology.

At two points in the "Reply" Calvin rhetorically presents prayers that a Protestant might address to God in answer to attacks on the Reformation. A part of one such prayer states, " 'I anticipated a future resurrection, but hated to think of it, as being an event most dreadful. And this feeling not only had dominion over me in private, but was derived from the doctrine which was then uniformly delivered to the people by their Christian teachers.' " The prayer continues speaking of efforts to satisfy God with works of righteousness,

> "When, however, I had performed all these things, though I had some intervals of quiet, I was still far-off from true peace of conscience; for, whenever I descended into myself, or raised my mind to thee, extreme terror seized me—terror which no expiations nor satisfactions could cure. And the more closely I examined myself, the sharper the stings with which my conscience was pricked, so that the only solace which remained to me was to delude myself by obliviousness."[7]

Although this prayer is written in the first person, it is not strictly autobiographical. Calvin is not simply presenting his life experience. But the language is so intense and personal that it must reflect some of the experiences that Calvin had had in his own conversion only six or seven years earlier. The recognition of the desperate condition of man was foundational to Reformation truth and experience.

The struggle with the reality of sin led to a desire to know God's way of salvation. Hope was to be found only in God and His work since the work of man was utterly futile. Calvin wrote (again as part of a hypothetical prayer), " 'Being exceedingly alarmed at the misery into which I had fallen, and much more at that which threatened me in the view of eternal death, I, as in duty bound, made it my first business to betake myself to thy way, condemning my past life, not without groans and tears."[8] That way of God is the way of Christ. The second teaching related to justification is salvation in Christ: "Then we show that the only haven of safety is in the mercy of God, as manifested in Christ, in whom every part of our salvation is complete."[9]

In Christ are displayed all the promises of God concerning the Savior who would fully bear the sins of His people on the cross and impute the saving benefits of His work to them. These promises bring salvation through faith alone. Faith is the link between the Savior and the sinner: "Paul, whenever he attributed to [faith] the power of justifying, at the same time restricts it to a gratuitous promise of the divine favor, and keeps it far removed from all respect to works."[10]

The result of the justifying work of Christ, which is received by faith, is great peace and assurance for the Christian:

> There is nothing of Christ, then, in him who does not hold the elementary principle, that it is God alone who enlightens our minds to perceive His truth, who by His Spirit seals it on our hearts, and by His sure attestation to it confirms our conscience. This is, if I may so express it, that full and firm assurance commended by Paul, and which, as it leaves no room for doubt, so not only does it not hesitate and waver among human arguments as to which party it ought to adhere, but maintains its consistency though the whole world should oppose.[11]

Calvin stresses the "confident hope of salvation . . . both enjoined by thy Word, and founded upon it."[12]

A key concern for Calvin throughout this treatise is answering Sadoleto's challenge to the Reformation as to the authority on which its doctrine of justification and assurance rests. For Sadoleto, correct doctrine is found by following the teaching authority of the church, which is "the greatest authority among men."[13] He expands on the authority of the church in these terms:

> First, because the Church errs not, and even cannot err, since the Holy Spirit constantly guides her public and universal decrees and Councils. Secondly,

even if she did err, or could have erred (this, however, it is impious to say or believe), no such error would be condemned in him who should, with a mind sincere and humble toward God, have followed the faith and authority of his ancestors.[14]

Sadoleto claims the authority of the Holy Spirit, the church, the universal councils and his ancestors as the foundation of the gospel that he follows.

How does Calvin respond? He begins by recognizing the need for a certain authority that stands above anything doubtful or human: "Christian faith must not be founded on human testimony, not propped up by doubtful opinion, not reclined on human authority, but graven on our hearts by the finger of the living God, so as not to be obliterated by any coloring of error."[15]

For Calvin this certain authority can only be found in the Scriptures. He fully embraced the *sola scriptura* of the Reformation and eloquently presented it. In the Word of God alone could certain truth and clear direction for faith be found: "We hold that the Word of God alone lies beyond the sphere of our judgment." All other claims to authority must be evaluated by the Scriptures. He insists "that Fathers and Councils are of authority only in so far as they accord with the rule of the Word."[16]

Calvin does not treat the authority of Scripture as simply a sparring point with Sadoleto. Scripture is at the heart of the life and experience of the Christian community. The pastor can only nourish and develop the people of God with the Word. Calvin asks those who would call themselves pastors and teachers to examine themselves on this point: "I will only exhort these men to turn for once to themselves, and consider with what fidelity they feed the Christian people, who cannot have any other food than the Word of their God."[17]

Calvin does not dismiss Sadoleto's concern for the authority of the church in a cavalier or individualistic fashion. He makes clear that he loves the unity and harmony of the church. But that church must honor the Word of God above itself.

> Ours be the humility which, beginning with the lowest, and paying respect to each in his degree, yields the highest honor and respect to the Church, in subordination, however, to Christ the Church's head; ours the obedience which, while it disposes us to listen to our elders and superiors, tests all obedience by the Word of God; in fine, ours the Church whose supreme care it is humbly and religiously to venerate the Word of God, and submit to its authority.[18]

In this same vein, he prays, "'My conscience told me how strong the zeal was with which I burned for the unity of thy Church, provided thy truth were made the bond of concord.'"[19] The Word is the power of life and peace within the church.

Calvin acknowledges that asserting the authority of the Word is not a simple solution to all problems. The Word itself is sometimes misunderstood. But whatever the problem or difficulty, the Word is a better and clearer and safer guide than some supposed inerrancy in the church. "I only contend that so long as they insist on the Word of the Lord, they are never so caught as to be led away to destruction, while their conviction of the truth of the Word of God is so clear and certain that it cannot be overthrown by either men or angels."[20] In his prayer he expresses the conviction that the Word is the only path to peace and unity in the church: "'The only thing I asked was that all controversies should be decided by thy Word.'"[21]

For Calvin the Holy Spirit teaches the truth of justification through the Scriptures in the church. His great concern for justification, the Word of God, and the church is united and energized for Calvin by the Holy Spirit. For this reason he reacts sharply to Sadoleto's improper appeal to the Spirit as a guide for the church apart from the Word:

> The Spirit [has] been promised not to reveal a new doctrine, but to impress the truth of the gospel on our minds. . . . And you, Sadoleto, by stumbling on the very threshold, have paid the penalty of that affront which you offered to the Holy Spirit when you separated Him from the Word. . . . The Spirit goes before the Church, to enlighten her in understanding the Word, while the Word itself is like the Lydian stone, by which she tests all doctrines.[22]

In the "Reply" we can feel as well as read Calvin's passion for the cause of the Reformation. We see the deep personal struggles of conscience for Calvin that were satisfied only in the Christ of the Scriptures who justified him through faith alone.

"THE NECESSITY FOR REFORMING THE CHURCH"

Only a few years after writing the "Reply," another request came to Calvin to write on the character of and need for reform. The circumstances were quite different from those that inspired the "Reply" and enable us to see other dimensions of his defense of the Reformation. Emperor Charles V was calling the Diet of the Holy Roman Empire to meet in the city of Speyer in 1544. Martin Bucer, the great Reformer of Strassburg, appealed to Calvin to draft a statement of the doctrines of and necessity for the Reformation. The result was remarkable. Theodore Beza, Calvin's friend and successor in Geneva, called "The Necessity for Reforming the Church" the most powerful work of his time.[23]

Of the three works we are considering in this chapter, the "Necessity" is the only one that is not a reply to a previous work. In a reply much of the form and content of the work is determined by the work being answered. But in the "Necessity" Calvin was free to present the cause of the reform in the way he regarded as most balanced and effective in communicating to the emperor.

Calvin organizes the work into three large sections. The first section is devoted to the evils in the church that required reformation. The second details the particular remedies to those evils adopted by the Reformers. The third shows why reform could not be delayed but, rather, how the situation demanded "instant amendment."[24]

In each of these three sections Calvin focuses on four topics, which he calls the soul and body of the church. The soul of the church is worship and salvation. The body is sacraments and church government. The great cause of reform for Calvin centers in these topics. The evils, remedies, and necessity for prompt action all relate to worship, salvation, sacraments, and church government. The importance of these topics for Calvin is highlighted when we remember that he was not responding to attacks in these four areas but chose them himself as the most important aspects of the Reformation.

That worship is the first topic discussed by Calvin may surprise us, but he is adamant as to its importance:

> If it be inquired, then, by what things chiefly the Christian religion has a standing existence amongst us, and maintains its truth, it will be found that the following two not only occupy the principal place, but comprehend under them all the other parts, and consequently the whole substance of Christianity, viz., a knowledge, *first,* of the mode in which God is duly worshipped; and, *secondly,* of the source from which salvation is to be obtained.[25]

Proper worship is Calvin's first concern. He stresses the importance of worship because human beings so easily worship according to their own wisdom rather than God's. He insists that worship must be regulated by the Word of God alone:

> I know how difficult it is to persuade the world that God disapproves of all modes of worship not expressly sanctioned by His Word. The opposite persuasion which cleaves to them, being seated, as it were, in their very bones and marrow, is, that whatever they do has in itself a sufficient sanction, provided it exhibits some kind of zeal for the honour of God. But since God not only regards as fruitless, but also plainly abominates, whatever we undertake from zeal to His worship, if at variance with His command, what do we gain by a contrary course? The words of God are clear and distinct, "Obedience is better than sacrifice."[26]

This conviction is one of the reasons that reform was required: "Since . . . God in many passages forbids any new worship unsanctioned by His Word; since he declares that He is grievously offended with the presumption which invents such worship, and threatens it with severe punishment, it is clear that the reformation which we have introduced was demanded by a strong necessity."[27] By the standard of God's Word Calvin concludes of the Roman Catholic Church that "the whole form of divine worship in general use in the present day is nothing but mere corruption."[28]

For Calvin the worship of the medieval church had become "gross idolatry." The issue of idolatry was for him as serious as the issue of works-righteousness in justification.[29] Both represented human wisdom replacing divine revelation. Both represented a pandering to human proclivities, rather than desiring to please and obey God. Calvin insists that no unity can exist in worship with idolaters: "But it will be said, that, though the prophets and apostles dissented from wicked priests in doctrine, they still cultivated communion with them in sacrifices and prayers. I admit they did, provided they were not forced into idolatry. But which of the prophets do we read of as having ever sacrificed in Bethel?"[30]

The Reformers, like the prophets of old, needed to attack the idolatry and the "external show" of the worship of their time. The antidote to the theatrics of the church in Calvin's day was a godly simplicity of worship, as reflected in the order of service in the church of Geneva. Such simplicity encouraged worshipers to give mind as well as body to worship: "For while it is incumbent on true worshippers to give the heart and mind, men are always desirous to invent a mode of serving God of a totally different description, their object being to perform to him certain bodily observances, and keep the mind to themselves."[31]

Calvin next turns to the subject of justification. Here he grants that disagreements have been the sharpest: "There is no point which is more keenly contested, none in which our adversaries are more inveterate in their opposition, than that of justification, namely, as to whether we obtain it by faith or by works."[32] On this doctrine depends "the safety of the Church," and because of errors on this doctrine the church has incurred "a deadly wound" and "been brought to the very brink of destruction."[33]

Calvin insists that justification is by faith alone: "We maintain, that of what description soever any man's works may be, he is regarded as righteous before God, simply on the footing of gratuitous mercy; because God, without any respect to works, freely adopts him in Christ, by imputing the righteousness of Christ to him, as if it were his own."[34]

This doctrine has a profound effect on the life and experience of the Christian: "By convincing man of his poverty and powerlessness, we train him more effectually to true humility, leading him to renounce all self-confidence, and throw himself entirely upon God; and that, in like manner, we train him more effectually to gratitude, by leading him to ascribe, as in truth he ought, every good thing which he possesses to the kindness of God."[35]

Calvin's third topic is the sacraments, which he examines in detail. He complains that "ceremonies devised by men were placed in the same rank with the mysteries instituted by Christ" and that the Lord's Supper in particular had been transformed into "a theatrical exhibition."[36] Such abuse of God's sacraments is intolerable. "The first thing we complain of here is, that the people are entertained with showy ceremonies, while not a word is said of their significancy and truth. For there is no use in the sacraments unless the thing which the sign visibly represents is explained in accordance with the Word of God."[37]

Calvin laments that the simplicity of sacramental doctrine and practice that prevailed in the early church has been lost. This is most clearly seen in the Lord's Supper. Eucharistic sacrifice, transubstantiation, and the worship of the consecrated bread and wine are unbiblical and destroy the real meaning of the sacrament. "While the sacrament ought to have been a means of raising pious minds to heaven, the sacred symbols of the Supper were abused to an entirely different purpose, and men, contented with gazing upon them and worshipping them, never once thought of Christ."[38] The work of Christ is destroyed, as can be seen in the idea of eucharistic sacrifice, where "Christ was sacrificed a thousand times a-day, as if he had not done enough in once dying for us."[39]

The true meaning of the Supper is summarized by Calvin simply: "We exhort all to come with faith. . . . We . . . preach that the body and blood of Christ are both offered to us by the Lord in the Supper, and received by us. Nor do we thus teach that the bread and wine are symbols, without immediately adding that there is a truth which is conjoined with them, and which they represent."[40] Christ truly gives Himself and all His saving benefits to those who participate in the Supper by faith.

This brief overview of Calvin's discussion of the sacraments gives us only a taste of his treatment of this important subject. He devotes considerable attention to baptism as well as to refuting the Roman position that there are five additional sacraments.

Finally, Calvin turns to the subject of the government of the church. He notes that this is potentially a huge subject: "Were I to go over the faults of ecclesiastical government in detail, I should never have done."[41] He focuses on the importance of the pastoral office. The privilege and responsibility of teaching is at the heart of this office: "No man is a true pastor of the church who does not perform the office of teaching."[42] One of the great accomplishments of the Reformation is the restoration of preaching to its proper place in the life of God's people. "None of our churches is seen without the ordinary preaching of the Word."[43] The pastoral office must link holiness to teaching: "Those who preside in the Church ought to excel others, and shine by the example of a holier life."[44]

Calvin complains that instead of teaching and pursuing holiness the leadership in the Roman church exercises "a most cruel tyranny" over the souls of the people of God claiming powers and authority not given to them by God. The Reformation brought a glorious liberty from unbiblical traditions that had bound the church. "As it was, therefore, our duty to deliver the consciences of the faithful from the undue bondage in which they were held, so we have taught that they are free and unfettered by human laws, and that this freedom, which was purchased by the blood of Christ, cannot be infringed."[45]

The Roman church made much of its apostolic succession, especially for ordination. Calvin insists that reformed ordination follow the genuine teaching and practice of Christ, the apostles, and the ancient church. He observes, "No one, therefore, can lay claim to the right of ordaining, who does not, by purity of doctrine, preserve the unity of the church."[46]

Calvin concludes this treatise with a reflection on the course of reformation. He attributes the beginning to Luther who with "a gentle hand" called for reform. The response from Rome was an effort "to suppress the truth with violence and cruelty."[47] This warfare did not surprise Calvin for "the uniform fate of the gospel, from its first commencement, has been, and always will be, even unto the end, to be preached in the world amid great contention."[48]

Calvin justifies this trouble in the life of the church because of the importance of the issues in dispute. He does not permit any minimizing of the fact that the "whole substance of the Christian religion"[49] is at stake. Since the Reformers acted in obedience to the Bible, he rejects any suggestion that they are schismatic:

> The thing necessary to be attended to, first of all, is, to beware of separating the Church from Christ its Head. When I say Christ, I include the doctrine of his gospel, which he sealed with his blood. . . . Let it, therefore, be a fixed point, that a holy unity exists amongst us, when, consenting in pure doctrine, we are united in Christ alone.[50]

It is not the name *church* that provides unity, but the reality of the true church that abides in the Word of God.

Calvin then turns to the practical question of who could properly lead the cause of reform in the church. He rejects the idea that the pope could lead the church or the reform in the strongest language:

> I deny that See to be Apostolical, wherein nought is seen but a shocking apostasy —I deny him to be the vicar of Christ, who, in furiously persecuting the gospel, demonstrates by his conduct that he is Antichrist—I deny him to be the successor of Peter, who is doing his utmost to demolish every edifice that Peter built—and I deny him to be the head of the Church, who by his tyranny lacerates and dismembers the Church, after dissevering her from Christ, her true and only Head.[51]

He knows that many call for a universal council to solve the problems of the church, but he fears that such a council can never meet and that, if it does, it will be controlled by the pope.[52] Therefore, he suggests that the church should follow the practice of the ancient church and settle the matters at various local or provincial councils.[53] In any case, the cause must ultimately be left to God, who will grant what blessing He sees fit to all reform efforts: "We are, indeed, desirous, as we ought to be, that our ministry may prove salutary to the world; but to give it this effect belongs to God, not to us."[54]

"THE TRUE METHOD OF GIVING PEACE
TO CHRISTENDOM AND REFORMING THE CHURCH"

The third treatise in which Calvin defends the Reformation is written in response to the imposition of the Augsburg Interim on the Holy Roman Empire by the emperor in 1548. By a series of stunning military victories the emperor broke Protestant military resistance and imposed a religious settlement on the empire that temporarily granted some small concessions to Protestant practice as well as some liberty of private conscience, but largely required a return to Roman Catholic practice in the externals of religion.

The Interim document was officially titled "The Interim, or Declaration of Religion of His Imperial Majesty Charles V being a constitution prescribing the mode in which the states of the Holy Roman Empire should mutually conduct themselves and treat each other until the decision of a general council." It dealt with three large areas of theology and practice: justification, the church, and the sacraments. One-third of the treatise was given to justification and the church. Two-thirds were given to the sacraments.

In "The True Method of Giving Peace to Christendom and Reforming the Church," John Calvin followed the same topics and proportions as the Interim except that in the section on justification and the church he added a section on worship.

Calvin began and ended the treatise with his own evaluation of the legitimacy of submitting to the Interim. Throughout his life Calvin had insisted that there must be no compromise with idolatry or false doctrine. He sharply reiterated that passion here: "Let it be our resolute determination to listen to no terms of peace which mingle the figments of men with the pure truth of God."[55] He elaborated on his opposition to the compromise offered in the Interim with these stirring words:

> For as Christ always recommends peace to us as a primary object, so he teaches that the truth of his Gospel is the only bond of peace. Wherefore, it is of no use for those who are trying to seduce us from the pure profession of the Gospel, to gloss it over with the name of Concord. What then? Peace is indeed to be longed for and sought with the utmost zeal; but rather than it should be purchased by any loss of piety, let heaven and earth, if need be go to confusion! I am . . . here debating with . . . the contrivers of a kind of specious PACIFICA-

TION, who leave us a half Christ, but in such a manner that there is no part of his doctrine which they do not obscure or bespatter with some stain of false-hood. . . . They bargain concerning the eternal and immutable Truth of God, how far it is to prevail! They say—provided what is fundamental remains safe, the loss of other things is tolerable. They speak thus just as if Christ had given himself up to be divided at their pleasure. It is something, I admit, when the entire renewal of piety cannot all at once be obtained, to secure at least the prin-cipal heads, provided we cease not to follow after what is still wanting. But when the Son of God has given us the doctrine of his gospel to be enjoyed en-tire, to rend it by compact, in order to preserve some part for ourselves, is most sacrilegious.[56]

Calvin turns to the specifics of the disputed doctrines beginning with jus-tification. He writes with the same conviction that we have seen in the other treatises. He says that it is not enough to speak generally of justification by faith, but one must give it a "distinct explanation." The freedom of the hu-man will must be rejected and a clear distinction made between the "nature of man and the grace of God." The blind man lost in sin must be "illuminat-ed by the Spirit of God." Justification "wholly consists in the forgiveness of sins," not at all in works. Justification is by an imputed righteousness, not an infused one. "We say, therefore, that we are justified by faith, be-cause the righteousness of Christ is imputed to us."[57]

Works are indeed a necessary part of the Christian life, but their role must be understood properly. "If any one, on the other hand, objects that we are made partakers of Christ only by being renewed by his Spirit unto the obedience of law, this must be acknowledged to be true; but let Regenera-tion [Sanctification] be what it may, we deny Justification is to be placed in it."[58]

Calvin again makes clear in this treatise that the imputation of righteous-ness is the only way to true assurance and peace of conscience: "If con-science cannot rest in anything short of certain righteousness, who can doubt that the whole righteousness on which man ought to lean, is contained in the remission of sins."[59] Calvin sees this peace as a central part of biblical reli-gion: "Making no mention of works, [Paul] tells us that righteousness must be sought without [i.e., outside] us; otherwise that certainty of faith, which he everywhere so strongly urges, could never stand."[60]

For Calvin, faith is the Christian's link to the righteousness of Christ: "Faith, I say, is a firm certainty of conscience, which embraces Christ as he is offered to us by the gospel."[61] In this treatise Calvin offers a marvelous summary in five points of the role of faith in justification:

With regard, then, to the obtaining of Righteousness before God, I say that we must necessarily hold the following five points concerning Faith:—First, that it is an undoubting persuasion, by which we receive the word brought by Prophets and Apostles as truth sent from God. Secondly, that what it properly looks to in the Word of God is the free promises, and especially Christ, their pledge and foundation, so that, resting on the paternal favour of God, we can venture to entertain a confident hope of eternal salvation. Thirdly, that it is not a bare knowledge which flutters in the mind, but that it carries along with it a lively affection, which has its seat in the heart. Fourthly, that this faith does not spring from the perspicacity of the human mind, or the proper movement of the heart, but is the special work of the Holy Spirit, whose it is both to enlighten the mind and impress the heart. Lastly, that this efficacy of the Spirit is not felt by all promiscuously, but by those who are ordained to life.[62]

This doctrine of justification must be maintained and cannot be negotiated away in the Interim. Those who compromise justification "are laying deadly snares against the salvation of men. . . . Hear Christ admonishing us,—"Walk in the light." (John xii, 35.) For if we allow the least cloud to obscure the clear light darkness will overtake us sooner than we suppose."[63] Both human salvation and the divine honor are at stake: "We must, in asserting the doctrine of free Justification, give proof not only how dear our salvation, but also how precious the glory of Christ is to us."[64]

Although the topic of worship was not singled out for discussion in the Interim, Calvin shows his great concern for this subject by treating it separately: "To debate about the mode in which men obtain salvation, and say nothing of the mode in which God may be duly worshipped, is too absurd."[65]

The Interim implicitly tries to reach a compromise by saying that one may believe internally whatever one wants at worship as long as one conforms outwardly to Roman Catholic practice. Calvin will not consent to seeing true worship as only interior:

> There are two principal branches [of worship]. First, we must hold that the spiritual Worship of God does not consist either in external ceremonies, or any other kind of works whatsoever; and, secondly, that no Worship is legitimate unless it be so framed as to have for its only rule the will of him to whom it is performed.[66]

God will not tolerate any form of worship not explicitly established by His Word: "All modes of worship devised contrary to his command, he not only repudiates as void, but distinctly condemns."[67]

The next topic that Calvin takes up, following the order of the Interim, is the church. One focus of his concern again is Rome's claim of apostolic succession. He insists that doctrine, not office, is our real link to the apostles: "If the Church resides in the successors of the Apostles, let us search for successors among those only who have faithfully handed down their doctrine to posterity. . . . For we deny the title of successors of the Apostles to those who have abandoned their faith and doctrine."[68]

77

Calvin again sharply criticizes the pretensions of the pope to be the leader of the church:

> Will our mediators then have the audacity to give the name of Christ's Vicar to one who, after routing the truth of Christ, extinguishing the light of the gospel, overthrowing the salvation of men, corrupting and profaning the worship of God, and trampling down and tearing to pieces all his sacred institutions, domineers like a barbarian?[69]

Calvin's passion against the pope is entirely sincere. But he no doubt also hoped that his rhetoric might move the emperor to act against the papal tyranny.

Calvin next turns to the subject of the sacraments. This topic was the one most extensively treated in the Interim, and Calvin similarly devotes the most space to it. Calvin holds to only the two biblical sacraments and explains their meaning briefly:

> Christ instituted the Sacraments to be not only symbols of the true religion, which might distinguish the children of God from the profane, but also evidences, and therefore pledges of the divine favour toward us. In Baptism, both forgiveness of sins and the spirit of regeneration are offered us; in the Holy Supper we are invited to enjoy the life of Christ along with all his benefits.[70]

The sacraments are intended to draw us to God and lift our minds from earth to heaven: "Christ invites us to himself. As we cannot climb so high, he himself lends us his hand, and assists us with the helps which he knows to be suited to us, and even lifts us to heaven, as it is very appropriately expressed by those who compare the Sacraments to ladders."[71]

The greatest error of the Roman view of the sacraments is that they tie the Christian to earthly things rather than to Christ. This fault is especially clear in the Roman practice of worshiping the consecrated bread and wine of the Supper: "When celebrating the Supper, we shall indeed worship him as present, but with minds upraised to heaven, whither faith calls us, not fixed down on the bread, which were not less at variance with the right rule of faith, than with the glorious majesty of Christ."[72]

The Interim devotes great attention to the subject of the sacrifice of the Mass. Calvin answers that doctrine at length. He summarizes his concern when he writes, "In short, those who pretend that Christ is now offered for the salvation of souls, deny that God has been reconciled to men. Can we subscribe to the Blasphemy which transfers the proper office of Christ to a human action?"[73]

The recurring theme of this treatise is the centrality of Christ in true religion and how medieval developments have undermined the proper glory of Christ. He develops this concern as he looks at numerous ceremonies and practices of the Roman church. One example is his opposition to praying to saints: "We shall find that whosoever goes about seeking for other patrons or intercessors, is not contented with the patronage of Christ."[74] Christ must be all in all for the Christian.

At the close of the treatise Calvin reiterates his passionate concern that there be no compromise of the gospel for specious notions of peace. He knows that the victory of the emperor presents a great danger to all Protestants who will not embrace the Interim. But true faith is courageous. "Do we hope for salvation from the gospel while no man is willing to run any risk in asserting its truth?"[75] Calvin urges Christians to remember that it is always ultimately safer—whatever the appearances—to be on the side of God than on the side of His enemies. To strengthen the faithful, he writes, "And that their courage fail not, let them doubt not that it is far happier for them to cast in their lot with the Church when smitten and in distress, than by acting with excessive caution, and consulting their private tranquillity, to seek a lot apart from the children of God."[76]

He ends the treatise on a personal note of commitment: "For myself, conscious as I am of my own weakness, still, by the help of God, I trust, that when the occasion demands it, I shall be able to shew how firmly I have believed, and do believe, that 'blessed are the dead that die in the Lord.'"[77]

CONCLUSION

Our study has shown that for Calvin five prime theological concerns stood at the heart of the Reformation: (1) the Bible as the only religious authority; (2) pure worship as God has commanded; (3) justification by faith in the imputed righteousness of Christ; (4) the two biblical sacraments of baptism and the Lord's Supper; (5) the true pastoral teaching office for the church. Rome had fundamentally corrupted all five of these points and, therefore, had corrupted the spirituality and morality of the church. The great concern of the Reformation was to restore them.

Were Calvin to evaluate Rome today from the perspective of these five points, what would he conclude? He would surely conclude that Rome is worse off today than it was in the sixteenth century. The Word of God is compromised not only by church traditions but also by corrosive criticism of its reliability. Worship has become even more syncretistic. Justification still rests on human cooperation, but it is often understood in a universalistic sense. The sacraments, after Vatican II, may be administered somewhat more simply, but they continue to be understood in an idolatrous and magical manner. The church continues to insist on the authority of its pope and traditions.

Calvin would no doubt equally lament the sad state of much of Protestantism today. It too is often far from the scriptural religion that Calvin and the Reformers taught. Calvin would appeal to all to return to the Bible and submit to its teaching. His final word to us might well be:

It is the will of our Master that his gospel be preached. Let us obey his command, and follow whithersoever he calls. What the success will be it is not ours to inquire. Our only duty is to wish for what is best, and beseech it of the Lord in prayer; to strive with all zeal, solicitude, and diligence, to bring about the desired result, and, at the same time, to submit with patience to whatever that result may be.[78]

NOTES

1. Quotations of Sadoleto's letter to the Genevans and Calvin's reply are taken from *A Reformation Debate*, ed. John C. Olin (New York: Harper Torchbooks, 1966).
2. In ibid., 7 n. 1, Olin observes that several of Calvin's biographers have seen autobiographical elements in the "Reply."
3. Taken from *A Reformation Debate*, 53.
4. Ibid., 66.
5. Ibid.
6. Ibid., 78.
7. Ibid., 87, 88.
8. Ibid., 90.
9. Ibid., 66.
10. Ibid., 67.
11. Ibid., 79.
12. Ibid., 83.
13. Ibid., 37.
14. Ibid., 45.
15. Ibid., 78f.
16. Ibid., 92.
17. Ibid., 91.
18. Ibid., 75.
19. Ibid., 86.
20. Ibid., 79.
21. Ibid., 86.
22. Ibid., 61.
23. Willem F. Dankbaar, *Calvin, Sein Weg und Sein Werk*, 2d ed. (Neukirchen-Vluyn: Neukirchener Verlag, 1966), 167.
24. John Calvin, "The Necessity of Reforming the Church," in *Selected Works of John Calvin, Tracts and Letters*, ed. H. Beveridge and J. Bonnet (Grand Rapids: Baker, 1983), 1:126.
25. Ibid.
26. Ibid., 128f.
27. Ibid., 152f.
28. Ibid., 132.

29. The importance of the issue of idolatry to Calvin is discussed very well in Carlos M. N. Eire, *War Against the Idols, The Reformation of Worship from Erasmus to Calvin* (Cambridge: Cambridge Univ. Press, 1986).

30. Ibid., 213.

31. Ibid., 153.

32. Ibid., 135.

33. Ibid., 137.

34. Ibid., 161.

35. Ibid., 160.

36. Ibid., 137.

37. Ibid., 139.

38. Ibid., 166–68.

39. Ibid., 195.

40. Ibid., 169.

41. Ibid., 140.

42. Ibid.

43. Ibid., 170.

44. Ibid., 141.

45. Ibid., 176.

46. Ibid., 174.

47. Ibid., 183f.

48. Ibid., 185f.

49. Ibid., 187.

50. Ibid., 213, 215.

51. Ibid., 219f.

52. Ibid., 226.

53. Ibid., 223.

54. Ibid., 233.

55. John Calvin, "The True Method of Giving Peace to Christendom and Reforming the Church," in *Selected Works of John Calvin, Tracts and Letters,* 3:242.

56. Ibid., 240–42.

57. Ibid., 243–44.

58. Ibid., 244.

59. Ibid., 245.

60. Ibid., 247.

61. Ibid., 250.

62. Ibid.

63. Ibid., 257.

64. Ibid., 260.

65. Ibid.

66. Ibid.

67. Ibid., 261.

68. Ibid., 264f.

69. Ibid., 274.

70. Ibid.
71. Ibid., 279f.
72. Ibid., 281.
73. Ibid., 313.
74. Ibid., 320.
75. Ibid., 343.
76. Ibid.
77. Ibid.
78. Calvin, "The Necessity of Reforming the Church," 200.

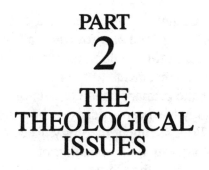

PART
2
THE
THEOLOGICAL
ISSUES

The Roman Catholic Church makes a distinction between *theology* and *magisterium*, allowing intellectual freedom for theologians but reserving authoritative pronouncements to the magisterium. For the past fifty years the primary characteristic of Roman Catholic theology has been a desire to be truly modern in terms of post-Enlightenment theology. Recent theologians have called into question the meaning of every affirmation of the historic faith of the Christian church. Thus, the debate between evangelical Protestant theologians and contemporary Roman Catholic theologians focuses on the most radically fundamental theological issues conceivable.

Many points of comparison exist between modern Catholic theology and liberal Protestant theology. Of special concern is how Roman Catholic theologians have treated the crucial issues of scriptural revelation and inspiration, as well as the relationship between Scripture and tradition. Karl Rahner, the most influential Catholic theologian of our time, embodies this new Roman Catholic theology.

ESSAY

4

ROMAN
CATHOLIC
THEOLOGY TODAY

Robert B. Strimple

Other chapters in this volume address certain themes as they are treated in Roman Catholic theology today: Mary, sacerdotalism, moral theology and public ethics, and a newer conservative ecumenism that includes the present evangelical–Roman Catholic dialogue in North America. In a generally nontheological age, evangelical laity and clergy alike are particularly unaware of the trends and direction of Roman Catholic theology in the late twentieth century. This lack of knowledge presents some significant problems when we begin to think that newer Catholicism is more evangelical in its outlook than pre-Vatican II thought. Here we shall take both a much broader look at the diversity of Roman Catholic theology today and a deeper look at some of its fundamental premises and central concerns.[1]

THEOLOGY AND MAGISTERIUM

Our focus is professional Roman Catholic *theology*; that is, our concern is with what the professors of theology in the leading Roman Catholic universities and seminaries are teaching—and particularly what they are writing. No scientific polls have been attempted to take the religious "pulse" of the "typical Roman Catholic in the pew," so to speak, or to ask what he or she is thinking theologically—although that will certainly be strongly influenced by what the parish priest has learned from his seminary professors and from the theology books he continues to read; and it is well to remember that the large majority of priests today have received their education since Vatican II (1963–1965).

Nor are we speaking here of the official teaching, or dogma, of the contemporary Roman Catholic Church. Protestants do not always appreciate sufficiently, perhaps, the significant distinction that Rome makes between the *theologians* on the one hand and the *magisterium* on the other.

The magisterium is that teaching authority committed to the church, but in a special sense to the bishops of the church, and in a most special sense to the Roman bishop, the pope. The official teaching of the magisterium is that teaching that is binding on all members of the church (although the extent of the binding chararcter of particular pronouncments is a matter of ongoing debate); and as exercised by a pope or ecumenical council it may even be infallible. On the other hand, the teaching of Catholic theologians, while instructive (it is hoped) to the magisterium, is merely the teaching of individuals—private, fallible, and nonbinding. (To emphasize this distinction is not to overlook that one may, of course, be both a bishop and a theologian.)

The reader might well conclude, therefore, that since what the theologians are saying today is not as authoritative (not binding as the documents of Vatican II are) it is not as important. True enough in a sense; but certainly it is no less interesting, and it is of great influence on the thought and practice of many of the Roman Catholic faithful. Indeed, most (Roman Catholics as well as Protestants) find reading Karl Rahner, Eduard Schillebeeckx, Gustavo Gutierrez, or Richard McBrien, much more stimulating than reading the conciliar documents because, as George Lindbeck (a Lutheran observer at Vatican II) put it in his 1970 reflection on *The Future of Roman Catholic Theology* (in terms betraying his own theological orientation): "Vatican II represents a transitional phase in a movement which began long before it was convoked and will continue to develop far into the future. . . . Its documents are often compromises between stale and tired ways of thinking and fresh and vital ones."[2] That is, the statements finally approved by Vatican II are typical consensus documents. Some of the language seems to be deliberately ambiguous, and much appears rather bland, requiring to be "fleshed out" if its significance is to be made clear.

The theologian, on the other hand, need not present a synthesis position. His statements need please no one but himself; and he can make flat-out, bald, bold, "creative," innovative statements. That is not true without exception. If the Catholic theologian steps too far out of line, particularly if he challenges Roman authority too directly, he can face official discipline—the most well-known cases since Vatican II involving Hans Küng (Germany), Leonardo Boff (Brazil), and Charles Curran (United States). But within exceedingly broad—to evangelical Protestant minds, perhaps amazingly broad— parameters it remains true that Roman Catholic theologians have free rein to express their theological conclusions.

A POST-ENLIGHTENMENT THEOLOGY

Contemporary Roman Catholicism presents a theological landscape so vast and diverse that it may seem impossible to find the forest for the trees. Indeed, the Roman church may seem to be so large, encompassing such theological variety, that the correct answer to every question along the lines of "Is such-and-such a theological position found in Roman Catholicism today?" is probably yes! Yet it does seem possible, and important, to discern one primary current in the Roman Catholic theological stream in this century; namely, the desire to bring the church's theology into harmony with the fundamental principles of the Enlightenment.

That concern first came to the fore at the beginning of the twentieth century in the writings of a diverse group of Roman Catholic theologians and biblical scholars whose work was labeled "Modernism" and was immediately and vigorously suppressed by Pope Pius X in the encyclicals *Lamentabili sane* (July 3, 1907) and *Pascendi dominici gregis* (September 8, 1907) and by the imposition of the Anti-Modernist Oath on September 1, 1910, requiring its affirmation by all priests at their ordination.[3]

The concern to produce a Christian theology that could be viewed as truly relevant to the outlook of the modern world emerged again in the 1930s and 1940s, especially among such French theologians as Marie-Dominique Chenu (the theologian of the worker-priest movement), Yves Congar (who proposed what might be called a "back to the future" approach by studying the earliest sources of the church's faith—the method of *Ressourcement*—in order to recover that purity of doctrine that the church must apply to the needs of every age), and Henri de Lubac (through whose efforts previously unpublished works by the highly influential Maurice Blondel and Teilhard de Chardin appeared).

The crucial event letting loose in Roman Catholic theology the flood tide of modern thought that had been held back for four hundred years (that is, since the Council of Trent) was Vatican II, thus fulfilling Pope John XXIII's goal of bringing the church "up-to-date" (achieving *aggiornamento*). Monika Hellwig explains the theological turmoil of the three decades since as the inevitably stormy process of assimilating the radical intellectual changes that had taken place in the world since the Reformation, particularly since the Enlightenment.[4]

The German *Aufklarung* (Enlightenment) was the philosophical product in the mid-eighteenth century of the earlier English Deism and French rationalism. Its leading figure was Immanuel Kant, whom many consider to have an even stronger claim than Descartes to be considered the father of modern philosophy. Kant defined the Enlightenment very briefly and simply as the release of man's reasoning from all external authority. The keynote of Enlightenment thought was the principle of human autonomy. At the end of the next century Ernst Troeltsch spelled out the results for historical and theological method of ultimate reliance on reason alone in terms of the principle of analogy (all historical events are in principle—in "quality"—similar; and thus "present experience and occurrence become the criteria of probability in the past"[5]) and the principle of correlation (all historical phenomena exist in a chain of cause and effect; they are mutually interrelated and interdependent, and there is no effect without an adequate and sufficient cause).

The problems raised by such philosophical presuppositions for a historical, biblical Christian faith should be evident. Those methodological premises would seem to eliminate from consideration a priori (that is, prior to any serious examination or analysis) the fundamental truth claims of Christianity—the very possibility of special divine revelation, of miracles (including the miracle of a bodily resurrection), of any direct divine activity in human history.

And yet a contemporary mainstream Roman Catholic theologian like Hellwig praises the great achievement of postconciliar theologians in making peace between the Christian faith and "modern philosophies with emphasis on reason rather than authority, on the human rather than the divine or the cosmos, on individuals rather than communities, on evolutionary rather than static conceptions of reality, on subjectivity rather than claims to be objective, and so forth."[6] J. A. DiNoia, O.P., is more critical of the direction of Roman Catholic theology today; but in an article reflecting on "American Catholic Theology at Century's End,"[7] he summarizes that direction similarly by stating that "American Catholic theology increasingly displays a typically modern profile." In such a theology "faith tailors its claim with an eye to prevailing canons of reasonability and applicability." DiNoia helpfully summarizes the characteristic concerns of such a theology as follows:

> the primacy of the category of experience—whether religious or common human experience . . . the centrality of theological anthropology; universalism in the doctrine of revelation; pluralism in the attitude to other religions; insistence on the historically conditioned nature of formulations of the faith; the ascendancy of historical-critical approaches to the study of Scripture; antipathy to doctrinal norms; the centrality of critique and dissent with reference to the tradition and magisterium.

The conservatism of the present pope and of the Sacred Congregation for the Doctrine of the Faith (formerly designated the Holy Office) headed by Joseph Cardinal Ratzinger, and the discipline exercised in recent years against a very few theologians, may have dampened the optimistic fires of progressive Roman Catholic theologians a bit; but the fundamental new direction taken by Catholic theology in the years immediately before and after Vatican II has not been diverted. The patient attitude and long-term perspective of many Catholic theologians and biblical scholars is that expressed by highly regarded Raymond E. Brown in response to a question following a public lecture at Mt. St. Mary's College, Los Angeles, in September 1990: "This pope too will pass." In 1972 David Wells asked the question: "Who speaks for Rome today? Who, then, should I read to build up a composite picture of what Catholics now believe?" And he concluded: "I have allowed progressives rather than conservatives to state contemporary belief. . . . The future is not in the hands of the conservatives."[8] I believe this assessment remains true.[9]

There continue, of course, to be Roman Catholic theologians who expound and defend a traditionalist, Tridentine, neoscholastic Catholic faith. In the United States some of these joined with other conservative Roman Catholic scholars in various fields to form the Fellowship of Catholic Scholars in 1977. (On the other hand, most of the professors of theology in the leading Roman Catholic institutions in the United States and Canada are members of The Catholic Theological Society of America, an association thoroughly committed to the kind of "progressive," "updated" theology that represents the "mainstream" in Roman Catholic theology today.) Among the Tridentine Catholics who have become best known by evangelical Protestants in recent years are Karl Keating (director of the anti-Protestant apologetics organization Catholic Answers and author of *Catholicism and Fundamentalism*[10]) and Scott Hahn (former Presbyterian Church in America pastor, now professor of theology at the Franciscan University of Steubenville, Ohio, and author of *Rome Sweet Home*[11]).

In debate with such traditionalist Catholics the most important issues to be addressed continue to be the crucial issues at the heart of the Reformation, in particular the Bible as the only infallible and absolutely authoritative rule of faith and life (*sola scriptura*) and justification by faith alone in Christ alone and on the ground of His imputed righteousness alone. (See chapter 11 by Michael Horton.)

Evangelical Protestants must recognize, however, what such conservative Roman Catholics themselves recognize: that they form the "orthodox minority" (Keating) in the Catholic church.[12] And when orthodox Protestants enter into debate with those who now form the majority of professional Catholic theologians, the issues addressed must be the even more radically fundamental ones relating to the meaning of every affirmation of the historic faith of the Christian church: that is, regarding the nature of God and of man, the understanding of a "fall" in human history and of "sin" as transgression of divinely revealed law (indeed, the very possibility of special, direct supernatural revelation of Creator to creature), the definition of "salvation" through the redemptive work of a truly unique Savior, the incarnate Son of God, and of the resurrection of the body and the life everlasting, and so on.

COMPARISON WITH MODERN PROTESTANT THEOLOGY

Establishing intellectual *rapprochement* between the Christian faith and modern (post-Kantian) thought has been the goal of many Protestant theologians ever since Friedrich Schleiermacher published his *Speeches on Religion to Its Cultured Despisers* in 1799. One way to characterize the history of Roman Catholic theology in the past fifty years is to suggest that what Catholic theologians have done in large measure is to recapitulate the meanderings of modern Protestant theology at an extremely rapid rate, condensing the developments of the last two centuries into a few decades. Since World War II (many would point specifically to 1943 and Pope Pius XII's encyclical *Divino Afflante Spiritu,* which sanctioned for the first time, though rather cautiously, the use of critical methods by Roman Catholic biblical scholars) the monolithic character of Roman Catholic theology (though always somewhat exaggerated by Protestants perhaps) has been progressively broken up, until we have now reached the point at which the Catholic theological picture presents just as much variety as the Protestant one. Theological *pluralism* (now moving increasingly toward recognition of the validity of religious pluralism) is today the clearest fact of theological life in the Roman Catholic Church.

The theological situation in the Roman Catholic Church in recent years closely parallels the situation in the Protestant churches. In Protestantism the "dialectical" or "neoorthodox" theology introduced in Europe after World War I by Karl Barth and Emil Brunner also largely won the field from the earlier Ritschlian Liberalism in the United States in the years immediately following World War II. Roman Catholicism in the past half-century has had its neoorthodox theologians also, in particular Hans Urs von Balthasar and the earlier Hans Küng.[13]

The lead in Protestant theology by the late fifties had passed to Rudolf Bultmann and his disciples, in terms of both Bultmann's form critical method of biblical criticism and his existentialist reinterpretation of theology. Form Criticism has now been practiced by an entire generation of Roman Catholic biblical scholars also;[14] and the great influence of Martin Heidegger's philosophy of existentialism, to which Bultmann was so indebted, is evident in the thinking of such leading Catholic theologians as Yves Congar, Karl Rahner, and Eduard Schillebeeckx. Indeed, Schillebeeckx has called Heidegger "the philosopher behind the whole of modern theology," even as Aristotle had been the philosopher behind the theology of Thomas Aquinas, which had earlier reigned in Catholicism for so many centuries.[15]

In the sixties the popular themes among so-called "mainstream" Protestants were the "theology of secularization" (Bishop John Robinson's *Honest to God* and Harvey Cox's *The Secular City*) and "situation ethics." Among Roman Catholics, the faculty of St. Michael's College at the University of Toronto published a symposium supporting *The New Morality,* and St. Michael's professor Leslie Dewart wrote a book on *The Future of Belief* (dubbed by conservative critics "The Future of Unbelief") that touched off a Future of Belief Debate.[16]

So also the theologies of the seventies and eighties have had not only Roman Catholic "representatives" but in some cases Roman Catholic leadership. The "theology of hope" was set forth by the Lutherans Jurgen Moltmann and Wolfhart Pannenberg; but of even more lasting significance has been the closely related "political theology" of the European Roman

Catholic theologians Johannes B. Metz and Eduard Schillebeeckx, which gave rise to the liberation theologies presented by such Latin American Roman Catholics as Gustavo Gutierrez and Juan Luis Segundo.

Catholicism has a group of theologians significantly influenced by linguistic analysis philosophy, which includes Eduard Schillebeeckx (who at one time or other has taken up the emphases of virtually every school of contemporary philosophy) and the American David Tracy.

Theologians in the Roman Catholic Church have also brought a renewed emphasis on mysticism and a growing interest in Eastern religions—the monk Thomas Merton, for example, as well as such a respected academic theologian as Eduard Schillebeeckx, whose theme for his 1986 Abraham Kuyper Lectures at the Free University of Amsterdam was the need for Christian faith to express itself in both mysticism and politics, the otherworldly interest combined with the very-much-this-worldly.

Throughout the years since Vatican II the evolutionary theology set forth by the Jesuit priest, paleontologist, and philosopher Pierre Teilhard de Chardin has continued to be of immense significance, in spite of the Vatican's attempt to silence him. Not only is Teilhard's influence evident in such a Roman Catholic venture into process theology as Eulalio Baltazar's *God Within Process* but also in the thinking of the most important Roman Catholic theologian of our time, Karl Rahner, whose theology we shall briefly introduce in the closing section of this chapter.

We have thus come to the point today where the differences between the most academically respectable theologians of the "mainline" Protestant churches and the professors of theology in the leading Roman Catholic institutions have ceased to matter very much; current theological symposia include chapters written by theologians from both the Roman Catholic and the Protestant ecclesiastical traditions, and the reader must search out the biographical information included somewhere in the volume to discover which writer is a Roman Catholic and which is a Protestant.[17]

To note this drawing together of Roman Catholic theology and Protestant theology in the past half-century is not to suggest, however, that Roman Catholic theologians have been merely imitative in these years. In fact, you will find many Protestants insisting that the most original theological work is now being done by Roman Catholics. Already at the time of Vatican II, in acknowledging his indebtedness to Karl Rahner in particular, John Macquarrie of Union Seminary (New York) noted that "the leadership in theology, which even ten years ago lay with such Protestant giants as Barth, Brunner and Tillich, has now passed to Roman Catholic thinkers."[18] In the year of his death (1984), Rahner was hailed as "arguably the most important theologian of the last half of the twentieth century."[19] And Raymond E. Brown, Roman Catholic New Testament scholar, has often been designated the premier biblical scholar in the United States today.

Fundamental to any theology, of course, is its doctrine of Scripture. In the remaining sections of this chapter, therefore, we shall consider the themes of revelation and inspiration, and the relationship between Scripture and tradition, before closing with a very brief look at the thought of the man perhaps most representative of (certainly the most influential force in) Roman Catholic theology today—Karl Rahner.

SCRIPTURE: REVELATION AND INSPIRATION

Official Roman Catholic pronouncements regarding biblical inspiration and inerrancy were rather consistently conservative from the affirmations of Trent right up to Vatican II. Trent spoke of recognizing that the "truth and instruction" that "the Son of God first promulgated with His own mouth" is "contained in the written books and in the unwritten traditions, which have been received by the apostles from the mouth of Christ Himself, or from the apostles themselves, at the dictation of the Holy Spirit." Therefore, Trent spoke of receiving and holding

> in veneration with an equal affection of piety and reverence all the books both of the Old and of the New Testament, since one God is the author (*auctor*) of both, and also the traditions themselves, those that appertain both to faith and to morals, as having been dictated either by Christ's own word of mouth, or by the Holy Spirit, and preserved in the Catholic Church by a continuous succession.[20]

The First Vatican Council (1870) strongly reasserted Trent's high view of inspiration and guarded it from certain erroneous views that had become popular. And during the entire period from Trent down to Vatican II, plenary inspiration and total scriptural inerrancy were repeatedly declared in pontifical statements. Among the most important: Pius IX's *Syllabus Errorum* in 1864; Leo XIII's *Providentissimus Deus* in 1893; Pius X's *Pascendi dominici gregis* and *Lamentabile sane* in 1907; Benedict's XV's *Spiritus Paraclitus* in 1920; and Pius XII's *Divino afflante Spiritu* in 1943, although that encyclical is now seen by many as one of the two official statements prior to Vatican II that opened the door for new methods in Roman Catholic biblical studies.

In addition to these papal decrees, a long series of very conservative pronouncements were issued by the Pontifical Biblical Commission after its founding in 1902 on such issues as the authorship of the Pentateuch, the authorship and historical trustworthiness of John's gospel, deutero-Isaiah, the character of the first eleven chapters of Genesis, the authorship and dates of the Psalms, the synoptic problem, the historical accuracy of Acts, and the authorship of several Pauline epistles and of Hebrews. So conservative had the Commission been throughout these years that its 1964 *Instruction on the Historical Truth of the Gospels,* even though that instruction can seem rather conservative by contemporary critical standards, is now frequently cited as the second decisive step "putting Roman Catholic scholars in line with the Protestant world."[21]

Vatican II's *Dogmatic Constitution on Divine Revelation (Dei Verbum)* seems to state the same high view of inspiration as the official ecclesiastical pronouncements that had preceded it.

In light of these official declarations, then, it is understandable why, as J. T. Burtchaell puts it in describing popular opinion four years after Vatican II, "it is still often put round by Catholics and Protestants alike that the official Catholic position on the authority of the Scriptures is a placid and intransigent affirmation of plenary inspiration and total inerrancy." Burtchaell goes on to note with pleasure, however, that "we are gradually being broken of the habit (common to Catholics and Protestants alike) of thinking that Catholic belief can effortlessly be ascertained by consulting papal and conciliar documents, without troubling to discover whether or not these bespeak a broad consensus."[22]

It is well to emphasize also that it is not simply a matter of how truly representative of Roman Catholic thought those pontifical (and pontifical commission) statements have been; it is also a matter of how those statements have been understood and developed and are now actually used.

In seeking to go beyond a merely superficial view of the contemporary Roman Catholic doctrine of Scripture, we might note again that the 1943 encyclical *Divino afflante Spiritu* is frequently referred to as the crucial first step in the process of "new thinking" about the Bible in the Roman Catholic Church. The papal crackdown on modernism early in this century had the effect for almost a generation of stifling interest in studying further the nature of biblical inspiration. In *Divino afflante Spiritu* Pius XII stressed for the first time the need for biblical criticism, for paying heed to the various literary genera found in the Bible, and for interpreting the Bible according to its true intent and purpose; thereby he let loose a pent-up stream of biblical study.

The first scholar to take up the doctrine of inspiration after the appearance of that encyclical was Pierre Benoit, with the publication in 1947 of *Aspects of Biblical Revelation*. Benoit wished to stand in the Dominican, neo-Thomist tradition of Marie-Joseph Lagrange, who is often hailed today as the "father" of Roman Catholic biblical criticism and who near the end of the nineteenth century put forward a view of "verbal" inspiration in opposition to the Jesuit, Molinist view of merely "content" inspiration.

When evangelical Protestants use the qualifier "verbal" to describe their view of biblical inspiration, they mean to emphasize that the words of the biblical authors are as much "God-breathed" (2 Timothy 3:16) as are the thoughts. But when Lagrange used the adjective "verbal" to describe biblical inspiration, he wished to emphasize that the thoughts were as much *man's* as were the words. Thus, in the turn-of-the-century debate in Roman Catholic theology between the advocates of "content" inspiration and the advocates of "verbal" inspiration, it is the latter who represent the more "liberal" or "modernist" position.

Benoit not only desired to stand in that tradition in teaching "verbal" inspiration, he also presented a type of "partial" inspiration, or at least partial *revelation*, insisting that everything in the Bible is inspired, but not everything is revealed. The reader must distinguish between what is merely *affirmed* in the Bible and what is *taught*. This became a most popular theory in the years immediately following *Divino afflante Spiritu*.

The second study of this doctrine that was most influential in the crucial years leading up to Vatican II was Karl Rahner's monograph *Inspiration in the Bible*.[23] As he does in so many of his studies, Rahner (1) begins by affirming, "We . . . assume the traditional teaching of the Church as binding,"[24] then (2) states that traditional teaching, and then (3) attempts to explain what that teaching can mean to us today. In the process, as his conservative critics see it, he explains that teaching away.

Rahner sums up the official ecclesiastical doctrine of inspiration in one statement, a statement repeated at Trent, at Vatican I, and at Vatican II: "The Scriptures have God as their author (*Deum habent auctorem*)." That statement, Rahner says, seems to raise a host of problems; most important (since we know that there have also been human authors of the Scriptures), how can one effect have two causes working at the same level—"in the same dimension," so to speak?

Rahner seeks, therefore, a simple thesis that will provide a basis for answering that problem and many related ones: That the Scriptures have God as their author is simply one aspect of the fact that the church, and the apostolic church in particular, had God as its "author"—that is, its founder, the one bringing it into being. He says that "in creating through his absolute will the Apostolic Church . . . and her constitutive elements . . . God wills and creates the Scriptures in such a way that he becomes their inspiring originator, their author." Rahner emphasizes that "the term authorship, therefore, used in regard to God and to man is an analogous concept only." Is this really all that the Christian church has meant in affirming that the Scriptures have God as their author: that the Bible was one primary element that God used in bringing the church into being, without implying anything more concerning the nature and authority of that Bible?

Many, both within and outside the Roman Catholic Church, have seriously questioned this. Burtchaell, for example, has said that "Rahner has never seriously dealt with the side problem of inerrancy."[25] Though Burtchaell would seem to be justified in questioning how "seriously" Rahner deals with inerrancy, Rahner does mention this matter. Rahner's "solution" to the problem of inerrancy, however, seems to be neither clear nor convincing. He says that the answer is simply "to limit closely and carefully what the writers really wanted to say."[26]

We are in a position now to underscore how the Vatican II statement on revelation stresses that same point. Before doing so, however, reference should perhaps be made to an article by Gabriel Moran, a Christian Brother teaching at Manhattan College, that appeared during the discussions of Vatican II; it well represents the important shift of interest from the nature of *inspiration* to the nature of *revelation*. The basic concept of revelation presented by Moran should be kept in mind when we come to our next section and consider contemporary Roman Catholic thinking concerning the relationship between Scripture and tradition.

Moran begins by emphasizing "the need to examine presuppositions when questions of ultimate foundations are raised," and he insists that nowhere is this more necessary in twentieth-century theology than with regard to the concept of revelation. Contrary to the popular modern Protestant insistence on the significance of the distinction between "the God who acts" and "the God who speaks," Moran stresses that revelation consists in neither words nor events, neither statements nor history.

> Man does not believe in statements or truths, nor does he believe in events; he believes in God revealed in human experience and consciousness.
>
> Certainly, there are words in the process of God's revealing, but the words spring from reflection upon the prepredicative, prereflexive experience.
>
> There was no way in which God could give "truths" to the prophets (that is, self-contained statements) that would have expressed in an even relatively adequate way what was to be communicated to man. Neither are there events or miracles in Jewish history that can be isolated and understood as "revelations" from God.

Revelation has to do with the most valuable sort of human knowledge, knowledge of a *person*; and such knowledge, whether of one's self or of another, is always "radically dependent upon the free bestowal and the free acceptance of that knowledge."[27] In his book on *The Theology of Revelation*, published immediately following Vatican II, Moran puts it this way: "Revelation in its most basic sense is neither a word coming down from heaven to which man assents nor an historical event manifesting truth. It would be better to begin by conceiving of revelation as an historical and continuing inter-subjective communion in which man's answer is part of the revelation." It is for this reason that the Christian believes that the highest revelation is that which existed in the consciousness of Christ, who is "man receiving as well as God bestowing."

> Jesus did not present himself as God speaking truths to be written down and learned by men. . . . He recapitulated man in all his levels of uniqueness [note well: *man's* uniqueness, not Christ's] and universality. He is the summation of all that was best in the religious life of mankind. . . . Christ is the first of men [note well: not the only man] whose own existence throws light on all of human existence as it is constituted by a nature that is open upward and perfected in freedom by its nearness to God.[28]

Thus, "it follows that our supernatural knowledge is a participation in the cognitive experience of Christ."[29] The essentially Hegelian nature of Moran's Christology seems clear: the divine comes to self-expression in all men and women, not uniquely in one particular historical individual. Jesus of Nazareth was merely that person who discerned with special clarity and fulness of vision the truth about divine/human identity. He was the first to know, when His disciples asked Him to show them the Father, that He could point to Himself. Thus the apostles "as apostles have no successors. . . . They possessed revelation in a fulness not to be surpassed, because they directly experienced the one who expressed what God wished to communicate to the world."

Moran emphasizes the importance of the new concept of revelation for our understanding of the development of dogma: "It may be noted here that when knowledge is equated with words or even with ideas and judgments, then it becomes impossible to understand the development of dogma in the later Church. . . . There was no set of human statements, written or oral, that could have communicated the apostolic experience of Christ."[30]

To the evangelical Christian believer this modern concept of revelation will not seem a promising presupposition from which to develop a biblical doctrine of biblical inspiration. The Bible, according to Moran, represents that original attempt at expression, communication, objectivization, that no significant human experience can avoid "as part of the process of becoming fully human." Thus, the Bible "originated from the community and was in turn formative of the community."[31]

Notice the "closed circle" presented here—typical of post-Enlightenment thought—as the church gives birth to the Bible and the Bible in turn is formative of the church, with no "breaking into" this circle by God directly "from the outside," so to speak. Such a historic concept of the "supernatural" nature of either the Bible or Christ is castigated by Moran and other progressive Roman Catholic theologians as "extrinsicism," using the disparaging label that harks back to Maurice Blondel (1861–1941), whose philosophy was such an important influence on later Roman Catholic theologians such as Karl Rahner and Bernard Lonergan in proposing "immanentism" as the true route to "transcendence."

To sum up, then, revelation, Moran insists, cannot be put into a book. It cannot be "stated." It can only be witnessed to. *How* it can be witnessed to, however, remains very much a mystery. As already noted, "there was no set of human statements, written or oral, that could have communicated the apostolic experience of Christ." The best that Moran can offer, it seems, is that revelation comes through the fulness of the church's *life*: "If one asks where this revelation continues to exist, the answer would seem to be: in the consciousness of the believers in Christ, that is, in the life and consciousness of the Church as the continuation of Christ."[32] Since the content of that consciousness cannot be expressed, however, either to others or to oneself, it would seem that an ultimate irrationalism (a modern mysticism?) lies at the root of this theology.

Turning now to the "Dogmatic Constitution on Divine Revelation" published by Vatican II, this document (as mentioned above) seems to state the same high view of inspiration as the official Roman Catholic ecclesiastical declarations that had preceded it. It is well to underscore the words "seems to," however, because (as many have noted) it is important to remember, when interpreting what is said in this document about inerrancy, that in the council debate rejecting the original draft document proposed by the Theological Commission and approving the final document several bishops spoke of the "errors" in the Bible as the reason the new draft was needed. Therefore, it seems reasonable to suggest that the statement finally approved must be understood as saying something *different* regarding inerrancy from what had been said in the first draft.

It will be helpful to quote here at some length from chapter III of the Constitution:

> Holy Mother Church, relying on the belief of the apostles, holds that the books of both the Old and New Testaments in their entirety, with all their parts, are sacred and canonical because, having been written under the inspiration of the Holy Spirit . . . they have God as their author and have been handed on as such to the Church herself. In composing the sacred books, God chose men and while employed by Him they made use of their powers and qualities, so that with Him acting in them and through them, they, as true authors, consigned to writing everything and only those things which He wanted.
>
> Therefore, since everything asserted by the inspired authors or sacred writers must be held to be asserted by the Holy Spirit, it follows that the books of Scripture must be acknowledged as teaching firmly, faithfully, and without error that truth which God wanted put into the sacred writings for the sake of our salvation. . . . However, since God speaks in sacred Scripture through men in human fashion, the interpreter of sacred Scripture, in order to see clearly what God wanted to communicate to us, should carefully investigate what meaning the sacred writers really intended, and what God wanted to manifest by means of their words.[33]

Regarding what is said here about inerrancy, R. A. F. MacKenzie, Canadian Jesuit and Old Testament scholar, in footnote 31 in the Abbott edition, draws special attention to that key clause at the end of the first sentence in the second paragraph quoted above. He understands it as limiting what in Scripture is said to be "without error" to "that truth which God wanted put into the sacred writings for the sake of our salvation":

> It is only in this respect that the veracity of God and the inerrancy of the inspired writers are engaged. This is not a quantitative distinction, as though some sections treated of salvation (and were inerrant), while others gave merely natural knowledge (and were fallible) [contrary to certain earlier doctrines of "partial inspiration," as affirmed, for example, by John Henry Cardinal Newman]. It is formal and applies to the whole text [and is thus an affirmation of "plenary," or "verbal," inspiration]. The latter is authoritative and inerrant in what it affirms about the revelation of God and the history of salvation.

Another prominent Roman Catholic biblical scholar who thinks that "at Vatican II the Catholic Church 'turned the corner' in the inerrancy question" is Raymond E. Brown.[34] Brown refers to the "real struggle" going on in Roman Catholic theology today as the struggle "between the Catholic center [where he places himself] and the Catholic far-right," both of whom accept that the Bible is the Word of God, but who differ regarding "the *meaning* of that doctrine."

Brown suggests that it is essential to a proper reading of official documents of the Roman Catholic Church to realize "that the Roman Catholic church does not change her official stance in a blunt way. Past statements are not rejected but are requoted with praise and then reinterpreted at the same time."

That would seem to be an accurate and important observation, and one not typically grasped by the average evangelical reader of modern Catholic thought. The question that remains open to debate, however, is whether or not Brown's statement here describes exactly what he himself does with regard to the declaration of Vatican II. Is Brown to be read as requoting Vatican II with praise but then reinterpreting its statements regarding Scripture and moving them further to the theological "left" than the council really intended to go?

The particular "spin" Brown puts on the understanding of the church's affirmation that the teaching of the Bible is without error to the extent that that teaching relates to God's salvific purpose is the distinction he introduces between "what the biblical word meant and what it means." Brown reads the last sentence in the section quoted above from Vatican II as drawing a *contrast* between "what meaning the sacred writers . . . intended" and "what God wanted to manifest by means of their words."

Brown says that what a particular text of Scripture *meant* is what the biblical author *intended* it to mean, but that is not what is normative (the rule for faith and life) for the church today. Critical study of the Bible "points to religious limitations and even errors" in the Bible. (Note that well: not simply historical or scientific errors.) And this, Brown says, is exactly what we should have *expected* (*a priori*) to find in the Bible as far as the original, intended teaching of its authors is concerned—error, even religious error—because "only human beings speak words," God does not write books,[35] and to err is human.

> This is no minor issue, because if God did not actually speak words (external or internal), one must admit clearly and firmly that every word pertaining to God in story of the human race, including the biblical period, is a time-conditioned word, affected by limitations of human insight and problems.

This is viewed by contemporary "centrist" Roman Catholic theologians as perhaps the most important insight of modern Roman Catholic theology: the full recognition of the "historicity," that is, the "time-conditioned" character of all human statements, including those found in the Bible—which points to the limitations, the errors, the less-than-full-and-forever adequacy of those statements.

If what the Bible *meant* is not without error and cannot be what the Bible *means* for the life and faith of the church today, where is that meaning to be found? Brown answers:

> I would contend that the way in which the Church in its life, liturgy, and theology comes to understand the Bible is constitutive of "biblical meaning," because it is chiefly in such a context that this collection is serving as the Bible for believers. . . . *It is crucial that we be aware that the church interpretation of a passage and the literal sense of that passage may be quite different.*

But if what the Bible normatively *means* for the Christian today is not what it originally *meant* (as determined by careful historico-grammatical exegesis), how can that presently normative (authoritative) biblical meaning be discovered? Brown gives the distinctively Roman Catholic answer: "For me the principle that the teaching office [the magisterium] of the Church can authentically interpret the Bible is more important now than ever before, granted the diversity and contrariety among biblical authors uncovered by historical criticism."

It is frequently alleged that the Roman Catholic Church offers its members *certainty* regarding what they are to believe to a degree that the Protestant churches can never offer. It would be theologically naive, however, to think that all our problems in the area of faith have been resolved once the Roman Catholic Church (the magisterium) has proclaimed the meaning for the church today, because while Brown insists that there can be, of course, no differences among Roman Catholics as to what the official Catholic doctrines are (all Catholics must submit to the judgment of the magisterium regarding that), he must acknowledge that "there are sharp differences in the way doctrines are understood."

And is that not the important thing after all? If it is the task of the biblical scholars to tell us what the Bible *meant* (which on Brown's principles seems to be of merely historical interest) and the task of the official magisterium of the church to tell us what the Bible *means* for the church today, it is left to the theologians to tell us how that meaning is to be *understood*. And as we have stressed earlier in this chapter, the clearest characteristic of Roman Catholic theology today is *pluralism*—with vastly different conceptions proposed for every element of the Christian faith and life. Of what value is a purely formal official statement of the "meaning" of the Christian faith without an understanding of what that meaning means? And what can determine for us which understanding is correct if the original, intended meaning of the Bible is not our criterion? What then becomes our *norma normans non normata* (to use the Reformers' phrase, "the measuring measure, itself unmeasured") if not the Bible?

And, of course, it is not only that church members, even theologians, understand official church dogma differently; it is also the case, as Brown and other modern Roman Catholics see it, that that official dogma itself is time-conditioned and severely limited as far as being without error is concerned. In that regard church dogma leaves the modern Christian with an authority no more infallible than the Bible. And Brown acknowledges this: "Even the doctrinal statements of the Church are, in a sense, time-conditioned." Brown emphasizes that *"today the centrist position is securely within the boundaries of Catholic thought loyal to the magisterium"*; but the result is that the Roman Catholic believer is left without a sure and certain "living voice of God (*viva vox dei*)."

We must remember and take to heart the answer of the *Westminster Confession of Faith* to those in the seventeenth century seeking the security of possessing the "living voice of God": "The supreme judge by which all controversies of religion are to be determined, and all decrees of councils, opinions of ancient writers, doctrines of men, and private spirits, are to be examined, and in whose sentence we are to rest, can be no other but the Holy Spirit speaking in the Scripture" (I:x). Notice the present tense ("the Holy Spirit *speaking*")—the Bible is no "dead letter"—and the affirmation of where the voice of the Spirit is to be heard ("in the Scripture").

Avery Dulles is an example of a Roman Catholic theologian who wishes to be quite contemporary and ecumenical but who continues to assert the traditional Catholic criticism of Protestantism: "Deprived of any authoritative tradition, [Protestants] have been constrained to breathe life into the dead

100

records."[36] Raymond Brown, however, has shown that the Catholic contention that the present voice of the magisterium transcends the problem of historic conditioning that allegedly plagues the Bible is a false hope. Brown insists that "fidelity to Catholic doctrine is not narrow or confining and, when understood properly, allows plenty of room to think." Our question, however, must be: Does it allow any room for true certitude and full assurance? This was the tremendous problem the Reformers had with the theology of the Roman church, and the problem continues with the same force for Rome today.

SCRIPTURE AND TRADITION

Many, both Protestants and Catholics, have viewed the question of the relationship between Scripture and tradition as no longer an issue dividing Protestants from the church of Rome.[37] Even before Vatican II, Jean Cardinal Danielou said that "a more accurate understanding on the part of Catholics of the agreement between Scripture and tradition does away with the principal Protestant objection to the Catholic position."[38] And G. C. Berkouwer was one of many Protestant observers greatly encouraged by the council's debate of this matter.[39]

What has been viewed as so significantly new in our generation is the denial by the leading Roman Catholic theologians of so-called "constitutive" tradition, which may be defined as tradition that is objective, divine, apostolic, dogmatic, but not contained in any sense in the Bible.[40] All the best-known Catholic theologians now agree that there is no doctrinal revelation that is not found (at least implicitly) in the Scriptures. There is no doctrinal revelation that has come to us for the very first time in tradition.

The question at issue here is carefully and narrowly limited and is precisely focused. The pre- and post-Vatican II debate does not address the matter of "disciplinary" tradition—that is, the whole wide area of church rituals and church practices. It has not been denied that tradition has been an *original* source for such. Nor has modern Roman Catholic theology cast any doubt upon the so-called "formal insufficiency" of Scripture—that is, the fact that the Bible is not sufficient in itself to give anyone a knowledge of God's will, because that cannot be understood apart from the Catholic church's authoritative interpretation of the Scripture. *Sola Scriptura* in the Protestant sense has not been affirmed. The discussion in the Roman Catholic Church has dealt only with the question of the *material* sufficiency or insufficiency of Scripture, the question as to whether there are revealed dogmatic truths that can be known only through tradition.

The impression has frequently been left, however, that if the Roman Catholic theologian rejects the notion of constitutive tradition (and the large majority today do), then the Protestant has no further objection on the subject of the role of tradition. This is a false conclusion. But our critique of the contemporary Roman Catholic doctrine of the relationship between Scripture and tradition cannot end there.

The key figure in the Roman Catholic debate has been Josef Rupert Geiselmann. It was Geiselmann who challenged in a definitive way (though he appealed to others who saw the primary point clearly before him, particularly among his predecessors at the University of Tübingen) the so-called "two-source" view of revelation that was the traditional Catholic view of the relationship between Scripture and tradition.

The traditional Catholic understanding of revelation was that revelation is contained partly in the Scripture and partly in tradition; that is, there are revealed dogmatic truths that can be known only through tradition. That "partly—partly" understanding came to explicit expression in the original wording proposed at the Council of Trent: "this truth is contained partly in written books, partly in unwritten traditions." Geiselmann sees it as quite significant, however, that that original construction was rejected at the Fourth Session of the Council of Trent. The two "partly"s were deleted and replaced with a simple "and" so that the statement approved was simply the affirmation that divine truth is contained in the written Scriptures and in unwritten traditions.[41] Geiselmann's conclusion is that that affirmation was a compromise formula and "nothing, absolutely nothing, was decided at the Council of Trent concerning the relation of Scripture and Tradition."[42]

Vatican II evidently chose to take the same route and not come down on one side or the other of this issue. The original draft of the "Dogmatic Constitution on Divine Revelation" contained a first chapter titled "Two Sources of Revelation." This was replaced by *two* chapters, the first on "Revelation Itself" and the second on "The Transmission of Divine Revelation." R. A. F. MacKenzie, in his "Introduction" to this constitution in the Abbott edition, is no doubt correct in concluding that Vatican II did not explicitly adopt Geiselmann's view; but that view certainly prevented the council from explicitly enunciating the "two sources" view.

When we examine Geiselmann's own doctrine of revelation, however, and his answers to his traditionalist critics, we discover that his theology is rooted so firmly in a modern, post-Kantian view of revelation that his denial that there is any revelation that comes for the first time in tradition and his affirmation that the whole of the gospel is found in Scripture—though that denial and that affirmation on the surface have seemed so encouraging to so many Protestants—are actually farther from the orthodox Protestant understanding of revelation and of Scripture than the traditional Catholic position and are calculated not to support a biblical understanding of divine revelation but to destroy it.

Geiselmann emphasizes that we must reject the fundamentalists' notion of the Scriptures as revelation, as "a gift by God of a bonus of truths."[43] Scripture is actually two levels removed from revelation. Revelation is to be seen as the fundamental reality, the "real reality," which is at the heart of our religious experience; that is, the self-communication of God. Christians speak of that as the Christ Event. That Event is God's revelation, or God's Tradition with a capital "T," God's *paradosis* of the Son (that Greek word we translate "tradition" literally means "handing over").

That Event was proclaimed in the original gospel preaching, or (to use the Greek word for "preaching" found in the New Testament) the *kerygma*. That gospel, that *kerygma*, is not itself revelation but is rather a human reflection on and an interpretation of the revelation, the Christ Event. That original gospel proclamation has later been recorded in the Scripture and in tradition, both of which are, according to Geiselmann, "modes of existence within the Church of the one Gospel of Jesus Christ."[44]

The church is Christ's continuing presence, God's continuing tradition, God's continuing handing over of His Son. Therefore, although Geiselmann speaks here of "Church, Scripture, and tradition" (note the order) forming "a coherent whole," the fact is that in his view the three are not really coordinate; the church is all.

In Geiselmann's view, the contemporary Roman Catholic view, neither Scripture nor tradition is revelation, the Word of God in the full sense and therefore absolutely authoritative. Both Scripture and tradition are the human record of and witness to revelation, and thus a guide to the church. This is precisely why I am convinced that the theological situation in the Roman Catholic Church today must be viewed as worse than it was at the time of the Reformers. (But, of course, this is also why hope has been expressed for eventual ecumenical unity between progressive Roman Catholics and modernist Protestants.) A simple diagram may prove helpful:

	Old Roman Catholic View	**New Roman Catholic View**
DIVINE REVELATION Authoritative	Scripture and Tradition	
HUMAN RECORD OF REVELATION A guide		Scripture and Tradition

The Reformers condemned the exaltation of tradition to the level of authoritative divine revelation, but we cannot praise a more modest estimate of tradition if it entails a like devaluation of the absolute authority of Scripture. We are not to distinguish between revelation and inspiration as though they were two altogether different kinds of reality. Rather, we are to see inspiration as one mode of divine authoritative revelation and, indeed, that mode "most necessary" for the church today, "those former ways of God's revealing his will unto his people being now ceased" (*Westminster Confession of Faith*, I:i).

In other words, Scripture is not simply a later pointer to or radiation from or interpretation of the history of redemption. God's giving of this authoritative written Scripture is part of the history of redemption. Our reliance upon Scripture alone is not because we see this collection of Christian writings simply as the first interpretation of the Christ Event and, therefore, as in some sense perhaps the best interpretation. (Recall our earlier consideration of Rahner's view of the Bible.) Our recognition of the unique authority of Scripture rests on the recognition that Scripture's interpretation is not simply the first or the best; it is *God's*.

Before concluding our consideration of Geiselmann, it should be noted that the major portion of his study *The Meaning of Tradition* is actually occupied with a theme that we have not touched on thus far. It is, however, a theme that reveals the truly Roman Catholic nature of Geiselmann's theology and its distance from a biblical emphasis on the uniqueness of the gospel, the exclusive character of the Christian faith and the indispensable necessity of Scripture if sinners today are to have "that knowledge of God, and of his will, which is necessary to salvation" (*Westminster Confession of Faith,* I:i).

That theme to which Geiselmann devotes greatest attention is "the nature of religious tradition as a universal human reality which attains its highest perfection in the Judeo-Christian tradition."[45] Geiselmann is in full agreement with the universalistic tendency that has always been present in Roman Catholic thought, the notion that Christianity only exemplifies at its highest what is true for all men everywhere at all times. Geiselmann says that not only Catholics but Protestants are discussing "natural tradition . . . which forms the basis of supernatural tradition. . . . Without this natural tradition rooted in the nature of man, supernatural tradition based on revelation would lack any firm point of contact in man and would, as it were, remain in the air."[46]

In such a Catholic nature/grace perspective there is no recognition of the fact that natural tradition is sinful, Creator-rejecting (Romans 1), and that scriptural revelation is necessitated by man's sin and is not simply the complement or supplement to what he has in natural tradition.

KARL RAHNER: TWENTIETH CENTURY THEOLOGIAN

One way to taste the flavor of Roman Catholic theology today is to consider how the fundamental presuppositions that have been our concern have been applied in the thought of one particularly influential theologian. Making the choice of which theologian to consider is not difficult. In the estimation of contemporary Catholics, as well as many Protestants, Karl Rahner is "arguably the most important theologian of the last half of the twentieth century."[47] Anne Carr, University of Chicago, says that "Rahner's influence on Catholic thought has been enormous."[48] The Reformed theologian,

George Vandervelde, considers this "Holy Ghost writer of the Second Vatican Council" to be "the most brilliant theologian since Thomas Aquinas" and insists that "any theologian worth the name must come to grips with his thought."[49]

Some traditionalist Roman Catholic theologians, of course, while acknowledging Rahner's influence, have lamented it as the influence of a heretic. Paul D. Molnar, St. John's University (New York), agrees with the Jesuit Martin R. Tripole that Rahner's Transcendental Thomism is actually an attempt to reduce theology to philosophy and concludes that Rahner "cannot in reality distinguish God from the world."[50] Malachi Martin is extremely caustic in his criticism: "Celebrated as the greatest Jesuit theologian in one hundred years," Rahner actually "wrote and lectured . . . with subtle logic and passionless mind to unlimber the dearest held tenets of faith in the minds of his readers and listeners."[51]

Born on March 5, 1904, Rahner entered the Society of Jesus in 1922, studied Thomism at the University of Freiburg—where he also participated in seminars led by the existentialist philosopher Martin Heidegger—in 1964 accepted the chair of Christian Worldview and Philosophy of Religion at the University of Munich, and died in Innsbruck on March 30, 1984. His more than 3,500 published items consist mainly of occasional essays, many of them collected in English translation as *Theological Investigations.*[52]

Rahner is not an easy read. Mark Schoof refers to his "inordinately long sentences" and "his almost discouraging productivity" covering an exceedingly wide range of subjects, from the deeply theological to the apparently mundane.[53] Rahner presents a Thomism understood in terms of modern German philosophy (in particular of Kant, Hegel, and Heidegger), but also under the influence of such French Transcendentalists as Maurice Blondel and Joseph Marechal. Thus, the reader needs a broad knowledge of modern philosophy in order to totally comprehend Rahner.

At the same time, contemporary Roman Catholic "moderates"[54] such as Avery Dulles and Richard McBrien view Rahner as clearly in harmony with such fundamental emphases of historic Catholicism as (1) the recognition that God's redemptive plan extends "to the whole of humanity and even to the inanimate material world"[55]—the universalistic note is one of the most dominant in Rahner's thought—and (2) "*radical openness to all truth and to every value.*"[56] Dulles reminds us that "theologically speaking, Catholicism is characterized . . . by a both/and rather than an either/or approach": nature/grace, reason/faith, law/gospel, Scripture/tradition, faith/works, authority/freedom, past/present, stability/change, unity/diversity—the *via media.*[57]

Anne Carr notes that "the texture and shape of any theology is most clearly suggested by its point of departure."[58] In *Foundations of Christian Faith,* Rahner's goal is to establish the intellectual respectability and credibility of the Christian faith. Thus, God cannot be his starting-point or pre-supposition because, as Dych puts it, "in the modern world God is not an answer but part of the problem."[59] Similarly, neither Jesus Christ nor the Bible can be the starting-point.

The question may then come: Is there any common starting-point, any "point of contact" between believer and unbeliever? Yes, Rahner answers; that starting-point is our common shared experience of what it means to be human. Therefore, Rahner continually challenges his reader to test what he presents in terms of the reader's own "existentiell" experience as a human person. The reader is continually challenged to ask, Does what Rahner writes about human existence, as a Christian theologian, "ring true" in terms of my own human existence?

Always we must remember that experiential knowledge, "unthematic" knowledge, is original, first-level knowledge. Conceptual knowledge, "thematic" knowledge, is second-level knowledge. The latter is an attempt to express, to symbolize (in language) the former; but conceptual knowledge is never identical with experiential knowledge, and the norm for its truthfulness must always be experiential knowledge.

This starting-with-the-human approach is what is referred to as Rahner's "transcendental method," and his theology is most often referred to as a "Transcendental Thomism." A *Transcendental* Thomism is a Thomism in harmony with the principle so basic to all post-Enlightenment thought, and modern Catholic theologians often refer to it as "the turn to the subject," a reorientation away from the object of knowledge and toward the knowing subject. Catholics most frequently appeal at this point to the writings of Blondel and Marechal earlier in this century; but the revolutionary epistemological "turn" took place earlier in the philosophy of Immanuel Kant.

J. J. Mueller helpfully notes that, although the term transcendental refers most basically to "the capacity to go beyond ourselves," since the time of Kant the term has also carried the technical meaning of "grasping the conditions for the possibility of."[60] Rahner stresses that it is the transcendental character of the human person—the capacity to go beyond oneself—that makes possible, conceivable, believable the central affirmations of the Christian faith. A person discovers himself or herself to be one who asks questions, not only about his world but about himself—who asks such questions continually, without end. Thus, the "horizon," the outer limit of his questioning, is infinite.

But such an infinite horizon must have a source, a ground. And that source must be Being, not Nothing, because nothingness grounds nothing. "Logically and existentielly" the questioner "cannot think that the movements of hope and the desire to reach out that he really experiences are only a charming and foolish illusion."[61] McBrien offers this definition of "transcendental": "The person is transcendental insofar as the person is oriented beyond himself or herself toward God as the source, sustainer, and final perfection of the person's existence."[62]

Rahner speaks of certain "existentials" of human experience; that is, "those characteristics or capacities of human existence which make it specifically human and distinguish it from other modes of existence."[63] Those existentials include not only transcendence (the ability always to go beyond oneself, most apparent in one's questioning) but also self-awareness, personhood and subjectivity (consciousness, freedom, responsibility), intersubjectivity (the fact that our subjectivity is always exercised in relation to other subjects), and dependence.

And to these existentials of human experience Rahner adds another, which he calls "the supernatural existential"—that is, humankind's existentiell orientation toward grace. Grace refers to the divine's continual offer of self-communication and man's continual capacity to freely accept that offer. In summarizing Rahner's thought at this point, McBrien writes, "*Every human person has this radical capacity* and many, perhaps most, have actualized it by receiving grace."[64]

> Acceptance and rejection of grace are . . . not limited to acts with visibly religious content. They take place in any true exercise of our freedom, even if the specific act seems to have nothing to do with God.
>
> Everything that is really human can be a "channel of grace," a finite mediation of our relationship to God.[65]

Rahner thus emphasizes that the only nature that exists is *graced* nature, nature that is always oriented toward God, with salvation (that is, full unity with the self-giving God) as its goal.

Rahner does attempt to take seriously human freedom and the possibility of sin—even the possibility of ultimate sin and ultimate loss—by stressing the need for a response in faith (although he also emphasizes that the primary and climactic faith-response has already been given by Jesus, the God-man). In the concluding "remarks" in the essay on "Christology Within an Evolutionary View of the World," Rahner says that "where there is freedom . . . there can also be a guilt and freedom which closes itself against God: there can also be sin and the possibility of perdition."[66]

Indeed, in harmony with traditionalist Roman Catholic teaching, Rahner insists that no one may have certitude and assurance in this life regarding his or her eternal salvation, because to make such a claim before the final challenge of accepting one's own death has been met would be to try to unveil the hiddenness of the future.

Two points, however, need to made clear here. As indicated already, when Rahner speaks of the need for a response of faith, hope, and love, he is never thinking exclusively in terms of an explicitly *Christian* faith.

Many have encountered Christ who did not know that they had. . . . God and the grace of Christ are present to the secret essence of every reality we can choose. . . . Consequently, anyone who . . . accepts his existence in patient silence . . . accepts it as the mystery which lies hidden in the mystery of eternal love and . . . is saying "yes" to Christ even if he does not know it. . . . Anyone who accepts his humanity fully, and all the more so of course the humanity of others, has accepted the Son of Man because in him God has accepted man.[67]

Probably Rahner is best known, among those who know nothing else about his theology, for the phrase "anonymous Christianity," which speaks of the fact that grace is present "wherever human life is lived authentically, no matter what words are used to define and describe it."[68]

This is now recognized to be the generally accepted view in the Roman Catholic Church. Avery Dulles writes, "Contemporary Roman Catholicism, as represented by Vatican Council II, holds that God's saving grace is operative among all peoples, even the unevangelized."[69]

Rahner would emphasize, like Eduard Schillebeeckx and other Roman Catholic theologians today, that the church is "the sacrament of the world's salvation."[70] The church is the sign of what is true of the world.

The second point to remember when reading Rahner's statements regarding the "hidden" character of the future is that Rahner often expresses the hope that very few, if any, will actually make the wrong ultimate choice. He says that the fact that God

himself becomes the world's innermost life . . . gives us the right to have the courage to believe in the fulfillment of the ascending history of the cosmos and of each individual cosmic consciousness, a fulfillment which consists in the immediate experience of God in the most real and revealing self-communication.[71]

Rahner emphasizes that it is because the center of his theology is Christology that his theology is evolutionary and hopeful. Before closing this brief introduction to Rahner's theology, therefore, we must at least sketch the essentials of his Christology.

Bruce Marshall sees Rahner as wrestling with that most basic problem for Christian faith, which has been "pervasive . . . since the Enlightenment: how can universal and ultimate significance be ascribed coherently to Jesus of Nazareth, a particular person?"[72]

In the eighteenth century Gotthold Lessing called this question the "ugly ditch" that he could never get across, no matter how earnestly he tried to make the leap: How can the accidental truths of history ever become the proof of necessary truths of reason? Marshall sees Rahner as presenting simply another version of Schleiermacher's answer; namely, that Jesus Christ is merely "the ideal perfection of the basic condition of which all persons are at least implicitly aware as their own." And though Marshall grants that

Rahner's version is "brilliantly" executed, he considers it to be "finally unsuccessful."[73]

In keeping with his transcendental method, Rahner approaches his task—showing how Jesus Christ, a particular person, can be the unique Redeemer—by identifying those conditions in human experience that make the Christian faith regarding Christ possible, believable. This part of the theologian's work Rahner refers to as "transcendental Christology."

But, of course, a demonstration that the Christian doctrines concerning Christ are "existentielly" understandable to human beings "in a deeply meaningful way" does not prove that there actually is such a savior or that that savior is Jesus Christ.[74] To show that requires a study of the actual Jesus of history and the Christ of the church's faith. This kind of study Rahner refers to as "categorical Christology." These two approaches to Christology—the "transcendental" and the "categorical"—mutually inform one another.

If a student had to choose just one of Rahner's essays to read as an introduction to his theology, that one would perhaps be the essay on "Christology Within an Evolutionary View of the World." Rahner begins that essay by noting that his concern is with "the transcendental possibility for man to take the question of a God-man seriously." He wants his reader, therefore, to understand clearly that "we are presupposing . . . the evolutionary view of the world as a given, and we are asking whether Christology is compatible or can be compatible with it, and not vice versa."[75]

Rahner then summarizes the conclusions he shall try to establish:

> We have to try to understand man as the existent in whom the basic tendency of matter to discover itself in spirit through self-transcendence reaches its definitive breakthrough [again we note the Hegelian thrust of the argument].
>
> The permanent beginning and the absolute guarantee that this ultimate self-transcendence . . . will succeed and has already begun is what we call the "hypostatic union." . . . From this perspective the Incarnation appears as the necessary and permanent beginning of the divinization of the world as a whole. . . . insofar as this definitive phase of world history has indeed already begun but is not yet complete, the further course of this phase and its result remain, of course, shrouded in mystery.[76]

The fulfillment of this original goal of all creation Rahner speaks of as "grace." Clearly for Rahner grace does not necessarily involve God's undeserved mercy to sinners. In the "remarks" that conclude this essay, Rahner acknowledges that in this study of the Incarnation he has not spoken of "guilt and redemption, i.e., liberation from sin." And he asks, "Does this mean that we have after all deviated in some unlawful way from the traditional Christology?"[77]

The Pontifical Biblical Commission in its 1984 statement on "The Bible and Christology" suggests that perhaps he has. The Commission links

Rahner's Christology with Teilhard's and asks this question: "Does the optimistic interpretation of this evolution, aimed at the 'Omega point,' allow sufficiently for *questions about evil,* and for the redemptive activity of the death of Jesus, even if account is otherwise taken of the crises that human evolution is to overcome."[78]

An interesting and instructive exercise is to follow up the reading of Rahner's influential essay by reading John Calvin's *Institutes of the Christian Religion* II:xii:1–7,[79] where Calvin deals with the central issue raised by Rahner. Calvin would conclude that Rahner has indeed "deviated" not only from "the traditional Christology" but from a biblical one. Calvin refers to the suggestion of Osiander, a Lutheran, that "Christ would still have become man even if no means of redeeming mankind had been needed"—that is, even if mankind had not disobeyed and fallen in sin—as the kind of "vague speculations that captivate the frivolous and the seekers after novelty." Calvin insists that "since all Scripture proclaims that to become our *Redeemer* he was clothed with flesh, it is too presumptuous to imagine another reason or another end. . . . Since we learn that Christ himself was divinely appointed to help miserable *sinners,* whoever leaps over these bounds too much indulges foolish curiosity" (italics added). Calvin appeals to many specific Scripture texts and then concludes again, "It is quite enough for me to say that all those who propose to inquire or seek to know more about Christ than God ordained . . . are breaking out in impious boldness to fashion some new sort of Christ."

Calvin calls the speculation that the Son of God would have become incarnate even if Adam had not sinned "this monstrous thing—which all godly men justly abominate as detestable" and argues that "if Adam's uprightness had not failed, he . . . would have been like God; and it would not have been necessary for the Son of God to become either man or angel." Rather than viewing man as evolving beyond matter into pure spirit and eventual divinization,[80] Calvin sees man being, as originally created, as much like God as he was ever intended to be! As it has often been expressed, the difference between the Roman Catholic doctrine of salvation (both in its traditional form and now in its modern, Rahnerian form) and the Reformed doctrine of salvation is the difference between an ontological concept (man as created needing some "additional" gift) and an ethical one (man's problem being his disobedience, needing forgiveness and sanctification).

Rahner is eager to explain to his modern audience the ancient Chalcedonian doctrine of the hypostatic union (Christ = one person but two natures). This doctrine means, according to Rahner, that "this saviour . . . must be at the same time *both* the absolute promise of God to spiritual creatures as a whole *and* the acceptance of this self-communication by the savior." Thus, the Savior—mark it well—becomes also the Saved: "We are saved because this man who is one of us has been saved by God, and God has thereby made his salvific will present in the world historically, really and irrevocably."[81]

Does Rahner escape the modern, post-Hegelian error of presenting a concept of the Incarnation, the hypostatic union, in which the difference between Jesus' affirmation, "I and the Father are one," and my affirmation or your affirmation of the same truth, is simply a difference in *degree* rather than a difference in *kind*? He seems to try valiantly to do so. He repeatedly stresses the "uniqueness" of Jesus Christ. He explicitly denies that the difference between Jesus' experience of divine intimacy and mine is merely one of degree. Ultimately, however, Rahner cannot maintain that the Hypostatic Union that came to historical expression in Jesus of Nazareth is truly unique. The difference between Jesus and every other human person—at least every one who does not finally reject God's offer of self-communication—is only the difference between the "already" and the "not yet." What Jesus is is what we all will be.

Bruce McDermott explains what Rahner means by Jesus' "uniqueness": "The hypostatic union happens once in human history. But its uniqueness in no way puts a ceiling, so to speak, on those who are not Jesus; rather it opens up the full plentitude of the divine mystery as the goal and beatitude of all people."[82]

In order that the reader may see the correctness of McDermott's conclusion, some direct quotations from Rahner's essay may be cited:

> But such an ultimate and absolute self-transcendence of the spirit into God is to be understood as taking place in *all* spiritual subjects.
>
> The intrinsic effect of the hypostatic union for the assumed humanity of the Logos consists precisely and in a real sense *only* in the very thing which is ascribed to all men as their goal and their fulfillment, namely the immediate vision of God which the created, human soul of Christ enjoys. . . . The prerogatives which accrue *intrinsically* to the human reality of Jesus through the hypostatic union are of the same essential nature as those which are also intended for other spiritual subjects through grace.
>
> When God brings about man's self-transcendence into God through his absolute self-communication to all men in such a way which is irrevocable and which has already reached fulfillment in one man, then we have precisely what is signified by hypostatic union.
>
> This union is distinguished from our grace not by what has been offered in it, which in both instances, including that of Jesus, is grace. It is distinguished rather by the fact that Jesus is the offer for us, and we ourselves are not once again the offer, but the recipients of God's offer to us.[83]

This last distinction must not be made too sharply, however, because Jesus Himself (Rahner emphasizes elsewhere) is also *recipient* of God's grace (as well as the *offer* of God's grace).

111

Dych suggests an illustration that is very helpful for grasping Rahner's thought:

> The history of Jesus can be understood as the fullest actualization . . . of the human potential for self-transcendence. . . . Just as the real potentialities of sound are not actual and known until a Beethoven creates his music, so too the real potentialities of human existence are not actual and known until they are actualized in a concrete, historical person. But once this truth is done and achieved and thereby known, in this event there is disclosed a new vision of all human existence, a new hope for everything human. For Christians this is what happened in the life of Jesus.[84]

Notice the words at the beginning of that last sentence: "For Christians . . . " Might "the real potentialities of human existence" be disclosed *elsewhere* for others? Rahner would answer: "Yes. Of course."

In this essay Rahner has been presenting a "transcendental" Christology. But, as we previously noted, he recognizes the need for *categorical* Christology as well, the need to make the case that this savior of the world is Jesus Christ. Hence he engages elsewhere in the study of the historical Jesus, the Christ of the New Testament, and the Christ of the earlier church.

With regard to the so-called "historical" Jesus—the "real" Jesus who actually lived, preached, and died in Palestine—Rahner has been said to accept the findings of "moderate" contemporary biblical criticism. Actually Rahner concludes that New Testament criticism allows us to have confidence regarding the historical factuality of only "what may seem to be minimal details concerning the life of Jesus."[85] He insists, however, that "we really only have to prove that two theses are historically credible in order to establish . . . the grounds of faith for orthodox Christianity's whole Christology.[86] Those two theses that must be proven to be historically credible are (1) that Jesus claimed to be the eschatological Prophet, the definitive Savior, and (2) that Jesus' claim was vindicated by His resurrection.

The Resurrection, Rahner emphasizes, is not an event in time and space, not an event leaving an empty tomb, but is rather the validation of the person and His life.

> Given the non-temporal nature of what happens in the resurrection . . . the resurrection does not mean the beginning of a new period in the life of Jesus, a further extension of time filled with new and different things. It means rather and precisely the permanent, redeemed, final, and definitive validity of the single and unique life of Jesus who achieved the permanent and final validity of his life precisely through his death in freedom and obedience.
>
> We miss the meaning of "resurrection" . . . if our original preconception is the notion of a resuscitation of a physical, material body.

Faith in his resurrection is an intrinsic element of this resurrection itself. Faith is not taking cognizance of a fact which by its nature could exist just as well without being taken cognizance of. . . . In *this* sense we not only can but must say that Jesus is risen into the faith of his disciples.

We ourselves experience the resurrection of Jesus in the "Spirit" because we experience him and his "cause" as living and victorious.[87]

CONCLUSION

In this chapter we have been emphasizing that Roman Catholic theology today is, in its leading representatives, a consciously post-Enlightenment theology, the basic presuppositions and concerns of which are the same as those that have motivated Protestant theology in modern times. We have now seen this eloquently reflected in the theology of the most influential Roman Catholic theologian of the twentieth century, Karl Rahner. Because modern Roman Catholic theology has imbibed the ethos and spirit of modernity in this century, it is imperative that evangelicals recognize the influence of this spirit and respond more accurately and faithfully to the present situation as it really is. The most significant historic theological affirmations, even those we once agreed on (as we saw in chapter 2), are no longer a basis for agreement. As we have seen in this chapter, every doctrine of our historic Christian faith has been challenged; therefore we must gird up our minds if we are to respond adequately.

NOTES

1. Some of the material in this chapter appeared in the author's very brief survey of "Roman Catholic Theology Thirty Years After Vatican II" originally published in *New Horizons* (October 1992): 3–6.

2. George A. Lindbeck, *The Future of Roman Catholic Theology* (London: SPCK, 1970), 3.

3. Malachi Martin (*The Jesuits: The Society of Jesus and the Betrayal of the Roman Catholic Church* [New York: Simon & Schuster, 1987], 328) has expressed the opinion that it was a "blind" and "foolish" act when, soon after Vatican II in 1967, Pope Paul VI "did away with a universal rule that imposed on all theologians a solemn oath to combat Modernism."

4. Monika K. Hellwig, *What are the Theologians Saying Now?* (Westminster, Md.: Christian Classics, 1992), xiv.

5. Ernst Troeltsch, "Historical and Dogmatic Method in Theology (1898)," in *Religion in History,* trans. James Luther Adams and Walter F. Bense (Minneapolis: Fortress, 1991), 55.

6. Hellwig, What are the Theologians Saying Now? xvi.

7. *The Thomist* 54 (1990), 504.

8. David F. Wells, *Revolution in Rome* (Downers Grove, Ill.: InterVarsity, 1972), 8, 10, 38.

9. Eugene Kennedy (Loyola University, Chicago) presents an interesting interpretation of the theological perspective of Roman Catholics in the United States in "this new age" (p. xiii), in *Tomorrow's Catholics, Yesterday's Church* (San Francisco: Harper & Row, 1990).

10. *Catholicism and Fundamentalism: The Attack on "Romanism" by "Bible Christians"* (San Francisco: Ignatius, 1988).

11. Scott and Kimberly Hahn, *Rome Sweet Home* (San Francisco: Ignatius, 1993). Kim Riddlebarger interacts with this book in chapter 10. The Hahns' book is of interest to evangelical Protestants, naturally, in view of their having both studied at Grove City College and at Gordon-Conwell Theological Seminary and having then served in the Presbyterian Church in America; but the book is disappointing in that it provides little by way of theological argumentation and consists exclusively of extended testimony regarding their personal experience.

12. Hahn, for example, laments the fact that when he decided to seek Roman Catholic theological training he "discovered there really were no Catholic institutions at the time where a layman like me could receive orthodox doctrinal formation in the Catholic Tradition" (*Rome Sweet Home*, 103).

13. Hans Küng is often thought by evangelical Protestants to be perhaps the most avant-garde of contemporary Roman Catholic theologians because he had the temerity to deny the infallibility of the church and the pope (as well as the Bible) in his celebrated 1967 book, *Infallible? An Inquiry*. As a result the Congregation for the Doctrine of the Faith declared that Küng "can no longer be considered a Catholic theologian or function as such in a teaching role." Actually, the Barthian cast of his theology had come to be regarded by that time as rather outdated. In 1974 (English translation, 1976), in what he referred to as his "small summa," *On Being a Christian*, Küng proposed to go beyond neoorthodoxy and get in tune with the future-oriented political and liberation theologies then so popular; but, in fact, he seems to revert in that volume to an earlier liberalism.

14. As an example of form critical dogmatism in current Roman Catholic study of the New Testament, see the lecture on "The Bible as a Source for Theology," presented at the 1988 convention of The Catholic Theological Society of America by John P. Meier of the Catholic University of America. Meier scathingly criticized such leading liberation theologians as Jon Sobrino and Juan Luis Segundo for their appeals to the historical Jesus in support of their theology, insisting that such professional theologians should know that "the real Jesus . . . is no longer accessible to us by scholarly means" (*The Catholic Theological Society of America: Proceedings of the Forty-Third Annual Convention*, ed. George Kilcourse [1988], 43:6).

15. Eduard Schillebeeckx, *God the Future of Man*, trans. N. D. Smith (New York: Sheed & Ward, 1968), 14.

16. This is the title of a book of essays in response to *The Future of Belief*, edited by Gregory Baum (then teaching at the University of Toronto and now at McGill University in Montreal, whose own book was titled *Man Becoming: God in Secular Experience*).

17. For example, *The Myth of Christian Uniqueness: Toward a Pluralistic Theology of Religions* (Maryknoll, N.Y.: Orbis, 1987) has a Roman Catholic publisher and is coedited by John Hick, Presbyterian (USA) professor at The School of Theology at Claremont, and Paul F. Knitter, Roman Catholic professor at Xavier University.

18. John Macquarrie, *Principles of Christian Theology* (New York: Scribner's, 1966), ix.

19. J. J. Mueller, *What Are They Saying About Theological Method?* (New York: Paulist, 1984), 6.

20. *The Sources of Catholic Dogma*, trans. Roy J. Deferri from the 13th ed. Henry Denzinger, *Enchiriplon Symbolorum* (St. Louis: B. Herder, 1957), 244.

21. Raymond E. Brown, lecture at Mt. St. Mary's College (Los Angeles), 22 September 1990.

22. James Tunstead Burtchaell, *Catholic Theories of Biblical Inspiration Since 1810* (Cambridge: Cambridge Univ. Press, 1969), 5.

23. It is difficult to understand why David Wells (*Revolution in Rome*, 33) has referred to Rahner's view of biblical inspiration as "less radical" than Küng's.

24. Karl Rahner, *Inspiration in the Bible*, trans. Charles H. Henkey (New York: Herder & Herder, 1961). In this discussion the passages cited from this monograph appear on pp. 9, 16, 50, and 56.

25. Burtchaell, *Catholic Theories*, 256.

26. Rahner, *Inspiration in the Bible*, 78.

27. Gabriel Moran, "What Is Revelation?" *Theological Studies* 25 (June 1964): 218, 225, 224, 225–26, 221.

28. Gabriel Moran, *The Theology of Revelation* (New York: Seabury, 1966), 50, 64, 65. In a footnote appended to the last sentence cited here, Moran refers to Karl Rahner, *Theological Investigations* (New York: Seabury, 1961–), 1:183–92.

29. Moran, "What Is Revelation?" 228.

30. Ibid., 228, 229.

31. Moran, *Theology of Revelation*, 87–88, 100.

32. Moran, "What Is Revelation?" 230.

33. *The Documents of Vatican II*, ed. Walter M. Abbott (New York: Herder & Herder, 1966), 118–20.

34. Raymond E. Brown, *The Critical Meaning of the Bible* (New York: Paulist, 1981). The passages cited from Brown appear, in order, on the following pages: pp. 3, 18, 23, 16, 14, 4, 34, 37, 84, 87.

35. Remember Karl Rahner's explanation of the metaphorical meaning of the dogmatic statement that the Scriptures have God as their "author."

36. Avery Dulles, *The Catholicity of the Church* (Oxford: Clarendon, 1985), 96.

37. In this section, material has been incorporated from the author's article "The Relationship between Scripture and Tradition in Contemporary Roman Catholic Theology," *Westminster Theological Journal* 40 (Fall 1977): 22–38. That same article may be consulted for a brief consideration of the approaches taken by John Henry Cardinal Newman, Karl Rahner, Eduard Schillebeeckx, and Gregory Baum to the important subject of the development of dogma.

38. Jean Danielou, "Scripture, Tradition and the Dialogue," *Theology Digest* 9 (1961), 42.

39. See G. C. Berkouwer, *The Second Vatican Council and the New Catholicism*, trans. Lewis B. Smedes (Grand Rapids: Eerdmans, 1965), chap. 4.

40. For a full and helpful discussion of the various kinds of tradition distinguished in traditional Roman Catholic theology, see Gabriel Moran, *Scripture and Tradition: A Survey of the Controversy* (New York: Herder & Herder, 1963).

41. Josef R. Geiselmann, "Scripture and Tradition in Catholic Theology," *Theology Digest* 6 (1958): 73–78.

42. Josef Rupert Geiselmann, "Scripture, Tradition, and the Church: An Ecumenical Problem," in *Christianity Divided: Protestant and Roman Catholic Theological*

Issues, ed. Daniel J. Callahan, Heiko A. Oberman, and Daniel J. O'Hanlon (New York: Sheed & Ward, 1964), 47–48.

43. Ibid., 52.

44. Ibid., 50.

45. Josef Rupert Geiselmann, *The Meaning of Tradition* (London: Burns & Oates, 1966), summary opposite title page.

46. Ibid., 40.

47. J. J. Mueller, *What Are They Saying About Theological Method?* (New York: Paulist, 1984), 6.

48. In *A Handbook of Christian Theologians,* ed. Dean G. Peerman and Martin E. Marty (Cambridge: Lutterworth, 1984), 542.

49. In "The Grammar of Grace: Karl Rahner as a Watershed in Contemporary Theology," *Theological Studies* 49 (1988), 445.

50. Paul D. Molnar, "Can We Know God Directly? Rahner's Solution From Experience," *Theological Studies* 46 (1985), 228, 232. Molnar's criticism comes to mind when reading such statements as these in Rahner (*Foundations of Christian Faith,* trans. William V. Dych [New York: Crossroad, 1990], 63 and 215): "God to be sure is different from the world. But . . . it is precisely the difference which establishes the ultimate unity between God and the world, and the difference becomes intelligible only in this unity"; and "God makes the world his own in such a way that this world is not only his work, a work distinct from himself, but it also becomes his own reality." Such statements are strongly reminiscent of Hegel.

51. Martin, *The Jesuits,* 22.

52. See note 28. Twenty volumes have been published to date.

53. Mark Schoof, *A Survey of Catholic Theology 1800–1970,* trans. N. D. Smith (Paramus, N.J.: Paulist Newman, 1970), 126, 129. Schoof notes Rahner's "laconic remark during an interview: 'Some days I write nothing' "!

54. Remember Raymond E. Brown's reference to the Roman Catholic "center."

55. Dulles, *The Catholicity of the Church,* 20.

56. Richard P. McBrien, *Catholicism* (Minneapolis: Winston, 1981), 1173.

57. Dulles, *The Catholicity of the Church,* 3.

58. Anne Carr, "Starting with the Human," in *A World of Grace: An Introduction to the Themes and Foundations of Karl Rahner's Theology,* ed. Leo J. O'Donovan (New York: Seabury, 1980), 18 n. 35.

59. William V. Dych, "Theology in a New Key," in ibid., 3.

60. Mueller, *What Are They Saying About Theological Method?* 6.

61. Rahner, *Foundations of Christian Faith,* 33.

62. McBrien, *Catholicism,* 129.

63. Dych, "Glossary," in *A World of Grace,* 191.

64. McBrien, *Catholicism,* 160.

65. Dych, "Theology in a New Key," 69, 14.

66. Karl Rahner, *Later Writings,* trans. Karl-H. Kruger, vol. 5 of *Theological Investigations* (New York: Seabury, 1966), 186–87. These closing "remarks" are not included in the republished form of this essay in Foundations of Christian Faith.

67. Rahner, *Foundations of Christian Faith,* 228.

68. Anne Carr, in *A Handbook of Christian Theologians,* 535.

69. Dulles, *The Catholicity of the Church*, 63.

70. Karl Rahner and Wilhelm Thousing, *A New Christology*, trans. David Smith and Verdant Green (New York: Seabury, 1980), 26.

71. Rahner, *Foundations of Christian Faith*, 191.

72. Bruce Marshall, *Christology in Conflict: The Identity of a Saviour in Rahner and Barth* (Oxford: Basil Blackwell, 1987), viii.

73. Marshall, *Christology in Conflict*, 7.

74. Ibid., 29.

75. Rahner, *Foundations of Christian Faith*, 178.

76. Ibid., 181.

77. Rahner, *Theological Investigations*, 5:424.

78. Joseph A. Fitzmyer, "The Biblical Commission and Christology," *Theological Studies* 46 (1985): 424.

79. John Calvin, *Institutes of the Christian Religion*, ed. John T. McNeill, trans. Ford Lewis Battles, vol. XX of *The Library of Christian Classics* (Philadelphia: Westminster, 1967). The citations that follow appear on pages 467, 469, 470, 471.

80. The thesis of Gregory Baum's early book, *Man Becoming: God in Secular Experience* (New York: Herder & Herder, 1970), is recognized if you simply omit the colon in the title.

81. Rahner, *Foundations of Christian Faith*, 195, 284.

82. Bruce McDermott, "Roman Catholic Christology," *Theological Studies* 41 (1980): 345–46.

83. Rahner, *Foundations of Christian Faith*, 198, 200, 201, 202.

84. Dych, "Theology in a New Key," 12.

85. J. Peter Schineller, in *A World of Grace*, 100.

86. Rahner, *Foundations of Christian Faith*, 245.

87. Ibid., 266, 267, 267–68, 275.

Whereas many important and truthful teachings are found within Roman Catholicism concerning Mary, the saints, and the sacerdotal system, evangelicals find the position of the Roman Catholic Church on Mary's Immaculate Conception and Perpetual Virginity, the claim that she is the mother of God and that she was bodily assumed into heaven, and that she is a mediator between God and man to be contrary to Scripture.

Further, the sacerdotal system, which involves forgiveness of sins conveyed through the sacraments, is an attack on the fundamental biblical message that the only source of salvation is the final and unrepeatable offering of the Son of God on the cross. Contrary to the Catholic claims that grace is conferred through the sacraments, evangelicals contend that divine justification and eternal salvation is freely given to men and women through the instrumentality of faith alone.

ESSAY
5

MARY,
THE SAINTS,
AND SACERDOTALISM

S. Lewis Johnson, Jr.

Veritatis Splendor[1] (*The Splendor of Truth*), the tenth encyclical of Pope John Paul II was published in October 1993. This lengthy encyclical of more than 150 pages has already drawn significant responses from the media, who have largely regarded it as an attack on the moral and sexual ethics seemingly championed by the mainstream of our society. The encyclical, however, is more than that. It is, in fact, an attempt to lay a biblical and philosophical foundation for a sound morality.

Veritatis Splendor begins with Scripture and the teaching of our Lord Jesus Christ as the proper ground for discussing "more fully and more deeply the issues regarding the very foundations of moral theology, foundations which are being undermined by certain present-day tendencies,"[2] and that is surely the right place to begin. Evangelicals can hardly fault that.

David Burrell and Stanley Hauerwas, teachers at the University of Notre Dame and Duke University respectively, have found the text of the encyclical "inspiring" and fresh: "What makes it new is the method employed: begin with Scripture, show how rational argument contributes to faith seeking understanding, and return to a church life and practice informed by Scripture."[3]

There are many truthful and important things said by the pope in the encyclical, and it certainly would be encouraging to evangelicals if they could have confidence in the pope's desire to seek the truth first and foremost in the Word of God. But near the end of the encyclical the pope says, "Mary is also Mother of Mercy because it is to her that Jesus entrusts his Church and all humanity," and, "Mary is the radiant sign and inviting model of the moral life. As Saint Ambrose put it, 'the life of this one person can serve as a model for everyone.'"[4] In a moment the encyclical affirms Mary's compassion for "every kind of weakness," since she has not known sin.[5] The doctrinal and theological questions, therefore, remain.

There is good reason to believe that the great rupture of the sixteenth century, the period of the Reformation, may never be healed. The gospel, as understood by the Reformers—by Luther, Calvin, and others—is not that

119

propounded by the Church of Rome. In the one, there is the atoning Cross and one Mediator, the man Christ Jesus (1 Timothy 2:5); in the other, there is the Cross, but two mediators, the man Christ Jesus and the woman, the Virgin Mary. The glory of the redeeming work of the Son of God cannot be shared by any other merely human being.

It may be that after so many years of conflict the answers to Berkouwer's questions can only be no. "Is it possible," he asks,

> to see each other in true proportions and then to engage in discussion? Can we penetrate the depth of the experience of the Mass or understand the devotion paid to Mary? And can a Roman Catholic penetrate the deep meaning of the sola fide and the sola gratia, and to the action of the Holy Ghost in the Reformed doctrine of the sacrament?[6]

The distinguished Dutch theologian is certainly on target in locating the fundamental stance of Protestant evangelical and Reformed men and women on the solidity of Scripture: "The revelation of Jesus Christ calls us back to the simplicity of faith, and is meant to be a lamp unto our feet and light unto our path."[7]

The seriousness of the struggle between the Church of Christ and the Church of Rome reaches its most intense level over the unique Son of God and His one saving offering (Hebrews 1:1–4). The Christian believer in Christ insists on His sole divine sonship and His exclusive and singular redemptive offering. The glory of the exalted Son and His priestly sacrifice must never be obscured. And it is Mary herself, the biblical picture of whom has been so distorted, who underlines this in her Magnificat when she exclaims, "My soul glorifies the Lord and my spirit rejoices [lit., has rejoiced] in God my Savior, for he has been mindful of the humble state of his servant. From now on all generations will call me blessed, for the Mighty One has done great things for me—holy is his name" (Luke 1:46–49). The Lord, she says, is her "Savior." Her state is "humble," and she will be called "blessed," for great things have been done "for me." That she calls God her Savior is an acknowledgement of the fact that she has by birth the same fallen status that all have. She claims no special prerogatives with respect to sin. She is "blessed," but by virtue of what has been done for her. Berkouwer is correct: "Mary herself is not in the least the prophetess of the Mariology of after times."[8]

THE HISTORY AND DOCTRINE OF MARIOLOGY

A. N. S. Lane of London Bible College has maintained, "The Roman Catholic doctrine of Mary is a classic example of the gradual development of doctrine."[9] It will help to review some of the developments in the Mariology of the church over the centuries.

MARY'S IMMACULATE CONCEPTION

Pope Pius IX on December, 8, 1854, in the Bull *Ineffabilis,* promulgated the doctrine of the Immaculate Conception as revealed by God. The words of the decree were, "The Most Holy Virgin Mary was, in the first moment of her conception, by a unique gift of grace and privilege of Almighty God, in view of the merits of Jesus Christ, the Redeemer of mankind, preserved free from all stain of original sin."[10] The immunity from original sin pertains to her passive conception, not to her active conception at the generative activity of her parents. She was conceived as other human beings, but at the time of God's creation of her soul and its infusion into the bodily matter from her parents she was preserved from the stain and guilt of original sin. Thus, it is contended that she never knew the physical drive of concupiscence (*stimulus concupiscentiae*). The efficient cause of the freedom is Almighty God, the meritorious cause of the freedom is the redemption of Jesus Christ, and the final cause is her motherhood of God.

There is no scriptural basis for the doctrine, and the earlier Catholic church fathers differed over the matter. Anselm held that Mary was *born* with original sin.[11] Bernard of Clairvaux contended that she was *conceived* with original sin, but purified before birth.[12] Thomas Aquinas and the Dominicans held this view, but Duns Scotus popularized the view that Mary was conceived without original sin, and his view eventually prevailed, although Pope Sixtus IV in 1485 and the Council of Trent in 1546 left the issue unresolved.

Catholics admit that the doctrine is not explicitly revealed in Scripture, although three passages—Genesis 3:15, and Luke 1:28 and 1:41—have been offered in support. In Genesis 3:15 it is contended that the seed of the woman is ultimately Mary, although the generally accepted sense is that the seed of the woman intended is Christ, the Messiah. The Bull *Ineffabilis* takes the seed of the woman, following an early interpretation from Irenaeus and Epiphanius and a few others, to be the Redeemer; therefore, Mary, His mother, stands with Him in His victorious enmity toward Satan, triumphing over Satan with Christ, crushing the head of the serpent "with her immaculate foot." The Roman Catholic theologian Ott's words reveal his own unwillingness to follow the Catholic interpretation: "The Bull does not give any authentic explanation of the passage. It must also be observed that the infallibility of the Papal doctrinal decision extends only to the dogma as such and not to the reasons given as leading up to the dogma."[13]

Luke 1:28 is no real support for an immaculate conception. The text concerns the visit of Gabriel to Mary to reveal the coming birth of our Lord. To her Gabriel said, "Greetings, you who are highly favored! The Lord is with you." The verse is rendered in the Roman Catholic English version as, "Hail, full of grace, the Lord is with you." The words "full of grace" are emphasized by Roman theologians, who argue that she would have lacked such grace if she had not been exempted from sin by an immaculate conception. The Greek word rendered by "full of grace," a perfect passive participle, is more accurately rendered by the NIV as "highly favored," and its tense and voice clearly indicate in the context that the favor that has been bestowed on Mary is the privilege of bearing a child, a son who "will be great and will be called the Son of the Most High" (v. 32).

The doctrine, it is clear, has no biblical basis and, in fact, was proclaimed, Lane contends, "on the basis of the unanimity of the *contemporary* church" and, perhaps, as a "trial run" for the doctrine of papal infallibility defined sixteen years later.[14]

MARY'S PERPETUAL VIRGINITY

According to Catholic teaching Mary was a virgin before, during, and after the birth (*ante, in, et post partum*) of our Lord. The perpetual virginity was stressed by the Lateran Synod of A.D. 649 under Pope Martin I. Evangelical believers, in the light of such passages as Isaiah 7:14, Matthew 1:18–25, and Luke 1:26–27, 34–35 have no questions regarding Mary's virginity before and during the birth of the Lord. But with reference to her virginity after the birth (*post partum*) there are. The questions arise primarily from the statement of Matthew concerning Joseph's relations with Mary after the angelic announcement to him: "But he had no union with her until she gave birth to a son. And he gave him the name Jesus" (Matthew 1:25).

The tense of the verb "had no union" (lit., was not knowing her) takes the reader to the moment of the "until she gave birth." Beyond that point Scripture is of no certain help. Brothers of our Lord are mentioned (Matthew 13:55), but it cannot be determined that they were sons of Mary. Luther, with Origen, Ambrose, Jerome, Augustine, and others, affirmed the perpetual virginity. Calvin says that beyond the birth of Jesus Scripture is silent and that "none but a contentious trouble-maker will press it all the way."[15]

MOTHER OF GOD

The term is designed to indicate that "Mary is truly the Mother of God."[16] The title was given Mary at the Council of Ephesus in A.D. 431 after the repudiation of the objections of Nestorius, who insisted that she was the Mother of Christ (*Christokos*) but not *Theotokos,* which means "God-bearing." The declaration of the Council was, "If any one does not confess that the Emmanuel (Christ) in truth is God and that on this account the Holy Virgin is the Mother of God (*Theotokos*)—since according to the flesh she brought forth the Word of God made flesh—let him be anathema." Initially the dogma was designed to support the deity of the Son. It has taught that Mary was truly a mother of Christ's human nature and that she was truly the mother of God in that she conceived and bore the Second Person, not indeed according to His divine nature but according to His assumed human nature. The origin of the description *Theotokos* is unknown, but it was used many times by Athanasius, who was, as Giovanni Miegge says, "the great promoter of the Nicene orthodoxy."[17]

"In what sense," Miegge asks, "can it be said that God was crucified or that God was born of the Virgin Mary? Here is the problem that wearied the minds of the fifth century, and the heat of the passion that accompanies the fluctuations of the doctrine makes it clear that the problem was not just an arbitrary theological abstraction but was vital to faith."[18] The answer to the question can be found only in the Definition of Chalcedon (A.D. 451), which contains the vital words on the point at issue:

> . . . of one substance [*homoousios*] with the Father as regards his Godhead, and at the same time of one substance with us as regards his manhood; like us in all respects, apart from sin; as regards his Godhead, begotten of the Father before the ages, but yet as regards his manhood begotten, for us men and for our salvation, of Mary the Virgin, the God-bearer [*Theotokos*]; one and the same Christ, Son, Lord, Only-begotten, recognized in two natures, without confusion, without change, without division, without separation; the distinction of natures being in no way annulled by the union, but rather the characteristics of each nature being preserved and coming together to form one person and subsistence [*hupostasis*], not as parted or separated into two persons, but one and the same Son and Only-begotten God the Word, Lord Jesus Christ.[19]

"None of the foregoing words can be left out," Miegge warns,

> without the sense of *Theotokos* being falsified. Mary is mother of Christ "according to the flesh," because Christ "according to the spirit" is son of God and conceived by the Holy Spirit. She is mother not by divinity in herself—a blasphemous idea—but by the hypostasis of the Logos; but not by the Logos in itself, which has no mother, but the Logos incarnated. And she is the mother of the incarnate Logos by its aspect of humanity because the properties of the two natures must be respected and what is said of Christ as God is not to be said of Christ as man. This notwithstanding, in virtue of the hypostatic union, since there is only one Christ, one can say, with all the reservations and explanations above, that the Mother of Christ is the Mother of God and that such is the paradox of the faith.[20]

THE ASSUMPTION

After an official poll of all the church's bishops concerning the possibility and desirability of the promulgation of a decree that Mary's body and soul had been assumed into heaven and having received a favorable reply, Pope Pius XII, on May 1, 1950, issued by the Apostolic Constitution "Munificentissimus Deus" as dogma revealed by God: "Mary, the immaculate perpetually Virgin Mother of God, after the completion of her earthly life, was assumed body and soul into the glory of Heaven." Miegge contends that "it marks a new and accentuated departure from the accustomed traditionalism of Catholic theology."[21] The dogma is based neither on the Word of God nor on tradition but simply, it seems, on the consensus of contemporary church opinion and theological "suitability."[22]

The time and circumstances of Mary's death are unknown, although the fact of her death is generally accepted by the Fathers;[23] however, some have contended that it was not the result of punishment for sin, since she was free from original sin and from personal sin. The simplest explanation of the lack of information concerning Mary's death is that she died before there arose the practice of venerating the martyrs and eminent saints, so her death passed with no unusual notice. "She departed life humbly and modestly as she had lived it," Miegge says, "and none remembered the place of her burial, even if a tradition toward the mid-fifth century gave her a sepulchre near Jerusalem in the garden of Gethsemane."[24]

Catholic theology in the establishment of belief as doctrine generally relies on evidence from Scripture, the consensus of tradition—especially the earliest tradition—and what might be called theological value, or speculative grounds. After consideration of the evidence compiled by Martin Jugie,[25] Miegge's conclusion is,

> That Mary has indeed shared the lot of mortality with the universality of men is the only certainty that can be drawn from the silence of the Christian tradition and from its evidences. That she was brought back to life and raised to heaven with her body glorified as the first of created beings, who wants to think this is free to do so, but it must be said that there is not a shadow of proof for it.[26]

But, if it may be granted that the tradition offers no support for the assumption of Mary's body and soul into heaven—and the absence of any support for it from Thomas Aquinas, who says nothing about the Assumption, is certainly of note—what can be said for the scriptural support? It appears to be just as bleak.

The *protevangelium* of Genesis 3:15, the first announcement of the victory of the woman's seed, whom revelation reveals to be the Messianic Son of God, over the serpent has been offered as biblical support of the dogma on the basis of the claim that Christ is inseparable from Mary. Thus, the promise is also a promise of Mary's victory over death.[27] The claim cannot be substantiated exegetically.

A second piece of biblical evidence has been offered. In the salutation of the angel to Mary (Luke 1:28) she is hailed as one "full of grace" according to the Catholic translation. We have already pointed out in the discussion of the Immaculate Conception that there is no ground for the use often made of this text.[28]

The final passage offered in support of the Assumption is Revelation 12 and its reference to the "woman clothed with the sun" (v. 1). None of the interpreters before the fourth century saw the woman as Mary. Rather, they saw the woman as the church. Ticonius, the fourth-century Donatist, who was probably the instrument of Augustine's move away from premillennialism, is the first to refer the woman to Mary. There is nothing in the context, other than motherhood, to support the reference to Mary. The context and the figures used clearly suggest that the woman is a reference to Israel, from whom our Lord did spring.

What, then, may be seen in the dogma? Probably the straightest answer is that one sees further dogmatic development apart from Scripture in the cult of Mary. "In short," Miegge concludes, "the new dogma has as its sole foundation the infallibility of the Roman Catholic Church."[29]

THE CO-REDEMPTRIX

It had been hoped at Vatican II that Mary would be proclaimed "Co-Redemptrix," but that did not happen. However, although the term was not, and is not, used, the concept is evident, for Mary plays a subsidiary role in the redemptive work of Christ.[30] She plays that role by participating and co-operating in His work. For example, "The incarnation could not occur without Mary's permission or 'fiat' (Lk. 1:38)."[31]

What, then, is the sense of the term co-redemptrix (= co-redemptress)? It signifies that the Virgin Mary "actively participated in and cooperated with Christ's work of redemption and its merits on behalf of all mankind."[32] It should be noted, however, that Mary's mediation is of a secondary character. Ott puts it this way: "Although Christ is the sole Mediator between God and man (1 Tim. 2, 5), since He alone, by His death on the Cross, fully reconciled mankind with God, this does not exclude a secondary mediatorship, subordinated to Christ."[33] Christ is the perfect mediator, but others "by preparing or serving . . . co-operate in uniting men to God."[34] Bernard of Clairvaux in an extravagant paean of praise calls Mary "the inventress of grace, the mediatrix of salvation, the restorer of the ages."[35]

In the opinion of some, this has become the theme of the Mariology of the nineteenth and twentieth centuries. From Pope Pius IX to Pius XII (1846–1954) papal declarations strengthened the theme of Marian mediation.

On what grounds biblically may it be argued that Mary is the co-redemptrix with Christ? We may dispense with the supposed parallel between the disobedience of Eve and the obedience of Mary in the Fall of man and redemption.[36] For those who wish to argue Mary's co-redemption the "two culminating moments" are the moment when Mary responded to the angel Gabriel's annunciation with, "Behold, the bondslave of the Lord; be it done to me according to your word" (Luke 1:38 NASB), and the other is the very presence of Mary at the Cross and then of our Lord's words to her and to John: "He said to His mother, 'Woman, behold your son!' Then He said to the disciple, 'Behold, your mother!'" (John 19:26–27 NASB), as if He were committing the church to its spiritual mother, Mary. It is remarkable, if this is our Lord's intent, that her name only appears once in the remainder of the New Testament, and then in no significant sense (Acts 1:14).

Catholics, however, make much of the two events, the Annunciation and the Cross. In the one, it is Mary's free choice between what Roschini calls, "a mission full of ineffable sorrows and the perdition of mankind."[37] Ott contends, "The Incarnation of the Son of God, and the Redemption of mankind by the vicarious atonement of Christ were dependent on her assent. In this significant moment in the history of Salvation Mary represented humanity."[38] But there is here no collaboration of human liberty and divine grace in Mary's response. The announcement made to her is of a sovereign divine decision to which she simply submits. She does not thereby participate and collaborate with Christ in the work of redemption.

At the Cross a similar misunderstanding appears in Catholic exegesis. There it is said that Mary is offering her Son as a meritorious gift. She stands like a priest offering a sacrifice to God for humanity. "To represent Mary in that atmosphere as a sort of Abraham sacrificing on Mount Moriah," Miegge contends, "is to substitute a quite conventional and even somewhat melodramatic vision for the dark and very human reality."[39] Berkouwer has a similar comment: "The Reformers did not object to the exalted position of Mary, her unique motherhood as the blessed one among women, but they looked upon the idea of 'cooperation' that played such an important part in the Roman view as the obfuscation of salvation and a devaluation of the divine grace in Jesus Christ."[40] Thus, the Reformers and Protestants cannot follow Vatican II in affirming that Mary "was united with [Christ] in suffering as he died on the cross" and cooperated "in the Saviour's work of restoring supernatural life to souls."[41]

MEDIATRIX

Since the practice of praying to the saints increased during the Middle Ages, it is not surprising that Mary became especially popular. Jesus came to stand for the stern, forbidding and unapproachable judge. The faithful were pointed to Mary, the compassionate mother who would act as mediator for them. The period of time from Trent to the French Revolution was preeminently the time of the defining of the compassionate mediation of Mary, principally in reaction against the Reformation, Jansenism, and eighteenth-century rationalism. A leader in the development of the sense of Mary as the compassionate mediatrix was Alphonsus Liguori, a leading Italian moral theologian, who wrote many devotional and mystical works in praise of the Sacred Heart of Jesus and of Mary as "semi-divine mediatrix."[42] In his work on the glories of Mary he said, "God wants all graces to come to us by the hand of Mary."[43]

Leo XIII in an encyclical in 1891 strongly affirmed Mary's mediation: "Nothing is bestowed on us except through Mary, as God himself wills. Therefore as no one can draw near to the supreme Father except through the Son, so also one can scarcely draw near to the Son except through his mother." Vatican II reaffirmed Mary's role as mediatrix, although warning against in any way limiting the dignity and efficacy of Christ as the one mediator.[44]

Popular piety, however, often exceeds the counsel of the more mature. For Liguori she is Noah's Ark in which sinners are saved, the city of refuge, the city of God, the treasurer of all graces. And as for her compassionate concern, "A sigh of the Blessed Virgin is more powerful than the prayers of all the saints together."[45] The extremes of this kind of piety are obvious.

MOTHER OF THE CHURCH

In Vatican II the Virgin Mary is seen as the mother of the church, a title not found in the document but used by Paul VI in the promulgation of the document in 1964.

It is hard to see how this, in spite of the protestations of many Roman Catholic theologians, does not in effect rob our Lord and the Father of the glory of their loving redeeming ministry to the church. It is the Father who is celebrated in the Scriptures for His tender compassions, and it is the Son who has loved and continues to love the church with the infinite love and tenderness of one who delivered Himself over to death for her (Galatians 2:20).

The incident recorded in Luke 11 is penetratingly clear. As our Lord was expounding the worthlessness of self-reformation, a certain woman of the crowd about Him raised her voice and said to Him, "Blessed is the mother who gave you birth and nursed you." "Blessed rather," our Lord replied, "are those who hear the word of God and obey it" (vv. 27–28). His words express no disapproval of His mother, but they do make the point that true blessedness is found in submission to Him and to the Scriptures. That, too, is the message of Mary's final spoken New Testament word. When the Son, her Son, is about to begin His ministry of Word and sign as the promised Messiah and Lord, it is she who turns away all attention and interest from herself to Him: "Do whatever he tells you" (John 2:5). It is her final word!

THE CHURCH AND THE SAINTS

The Apostles' Creed contains the expression, "the communion of saints."[46] Both the Catholics and the Reformers adopted the words as expressive of their beliefs. Was their understanding of them the same? No. For the Reformers, the communion of the saints included each and all of the believing members of the church, contending that they all partook of our Lord and "all His treasures and gifts."[47] Rome's view of the communion of saints was different. The term *saints* referred to those who were holy in a special sense, such as the martyrs and others in heaven who had lived and served in notable ways and had been canonized. The intercession of the saints is not halted by death, and the invocation of the saints is valid. Direct requests to a saint in heaven for his or her intercession or for other benefits is the reference of the expression, "the invocation of the saints." The saints can hear requests and know how to answer them.[48]

Further, the church maintains a "treasury" of merit earned by the saints for deeds going beyond God's normal requirements. The merits may be distributed to those in need of remission by the bishops of the Christian communion through their "power of the keys" (cf. Matthew 16:19).[49] These indulgences were remissions of the debt of temporal punishment after guilt had been forgiven and were granted to poor saints for money. They deeply disturbed Luther in 1515 and stirred him on in his reformatory zeal. The Reformers saw the treasury of merit, consisting of rewards for meritorious deeds of the saints, which might be conveyed to individuals as means of forgiveness of sins through indulgences paid for by money, as a denial of the sole saviorhood of the Son of God. In effect, the individuals benefited by the indulgences received remission of sins by virtue of the work of Christ and the good deeds of the martyrs, the merits of which were sold to them. Thus, their salvation came from the blood of Christ and the blood of the martyrs, the martyrs becoming partners with Christ in their salvation. The "no other name" of Peter in Acts 4:12 must be modified, and the names of the saints whose good deeds are in the treasury of merit must be added to our Lord's as the source of salvation. The martyrs have become our redeemers![50]

Thus, the church that Luther faced was a church related to and connected with both the heavenly church and the church suffering in purgatory, a church immersed in the ideas of merit before God and in the veneration of saints.[51] In 1515–1516 Luther lectured on Romans, and one can see from his comments on Romans 12:13 that his concept of the church had moved away from the Catholic concept of the saints with their indulgences, veneration, and the meritoriousness of good works. In his comments on the words, "communicating to the necessities of the saints," he writes, "Today we understand the 'saints' to be the blessed ones who have been glorified; the apostle, however, and, indeed, the whole Scripture, call 'saints' all who believe in Christ. This is perhaps the reason why nowadays one does not readily communicate to the saints; one believes that there are no longer any."[52] In the medieval church the sharing was materialistic, consisting in the administering of the merits of Christ and the distinguished saints to the few who received indulgences from the church's treasury of merit. For Luther the saints had no "merits." In the fifty-eighth of his *Ninety-five Theses* he contended,

"No saint has adequately fulfilled God's commandments in this life." One can see how the idea of grace, free grace indeed, has been lodged by the Spirit of God in his heart.

Althaus expresses it well: "Luther's understanding of God and of justification shattered the medieval catholic conception of the saints. Since our salvation depends only on God's free mercy, the transfer of merits in the heavenly bank from one account to another has lost all meaning. Merit is replaced by serving one another. No one can, in the strict sense of the word, help another in God's judgment—either through substitutionary achievement or through meritorious intercession."[53]

Thus, the creed's expression, "the communion of saints," is not exclusive but inclusive. It refers to all the believers, not simply the outstanding, and they each in possessing all of Christ possess every spiritual blessing in Him (Ephesians 1:3). A satisfaction sufficient for all sin has been made, freely conveyed to those who in grace through the Spirit believe. The Protestant Reformers rejected the invocations of the saints as the dishonoring of the sole mediator between God and men, Jesus Christ (1 Timothy 2:5), and also as dishonoring the angels and saints themselves, for they all have refused such intercession and adoration (cf. Acts 10:26; 14:15; Revelation 19:10; 22:8–9).[54]

THE SACERDOTALISM OF ROME AND THE SCRIPTURES

ASPECTS OF SACERDOTALISM IN THE CHURCH OF ROME

If sacerdotalism may be defined as "religious belief emphasizing the powers of priests as essential mediators between God and mankind,"[55] Roman Catholicism is essentially sacerdotal. The entire system revolves around the claims of mediatorial priestly authority and the sacramental system.

The sacraments of the Roman church, instituted by Christ it is claimed, are efficacious signs of grace. Contrary to the Reformers who contend that there are only two sacraments, or ordinances—baptism and the Lord's Supper—the Catholic Church celebrates seven—Baptism, Confirmation, Eucharist, Penance, Extreme Unction, Holy Order, and Matrimony. Catholic theologians acknowledge that the seven sacraments have been regarded as a truth of faith only since the middle of the twelfth century.[56]

There is a decisive difference between evangelical ordinances, or sacraments, and Catholic ordinances. In the view of Reformed and evangelical believers the ordinances of baptism and the Lord's Supper do not remove sins. The one, baptism, is the representation and confession of one's entrance into the church through faith in the Lord Jesus Christ's atoning work. The other, the Lord's Supper, is by its continual celebration a representation of one's continuation in the church.

In the case of the sacraments of Rome the situation is entirely different. The sacraments remove sins. For example, Ludwig Ott, a distinguished Catholic theologian, whom we have cited frequently, states that "supernatural life is generated by Baptism; brought to growth by Confirmation; nourished by the Eucharist; cured from the diseases of sins and from the weakness arising from these by Penance and Extreme Unction."[57] These sacraments generally (baptism and Matrimony are excepted) require a special priestly or episcopal power, conferred by Holy Orders, for valid ministration. The sacraments work *ex opere operato,* that is, by the power of the completed act, and their validity does not depend on the orthodoxy of the minister or his state of grace.

The sacrament of baptism is the means of the remission of the guilt of original sin. Anathema, so the Council of Trent contended, attaches to the denier of the doctrine. In the case of adults, baptism also is the means of the eradication of all personal, mortal, or venial sins. Even when unworthily received, baptism imprints on the soul an indelible spiritual mark, the Baptismal Character, and cannot be repeated.[58]

In the sacrament of Confirmation by the imposition of hands, unction, and prayer, a baptized person is filled with the Holy Spirit for the inner strengthening of the supernatural life and for courageous outward testimony. By this sacrament baptismal grace is perfected.

The Eucharist (the Greek word means "thanksgiving") is an early name for the Lord's Supper, or Holy Communion. The sacramental actions of eating bread and drinking wine are interpreted by our Lord as symbolic actions. The relation of the symbols to the reality became controversial as indicated by the diverging views of transubstantiation, consubstantiation, and Calvin's mediating view. The Catholic doctrine of transubstantiation, first propounded probably by Paschasius Radbertus (ca. 785–ca. 860), was defined as dogma by the Fourth Lateran Council (1215).

The second significant controversy concerning the Eucharist concerns the sacrifice of the Mass,[59] or the eucharistic sacrifice. Is the Eucharist an *offering* of Christ's body and blood? The Reformers were united in contending that the Eucharist was not an offering of His body and blood, but the institution of a sacrament, or ordinance, concerning His body and blood, which were *to be offered* on the coming cross, just as the Lord and the apostles in the Passover Feast fed on a lamb that had already been offered in the Temple court.

The eucharistic sacrifice was first defined as dogma by the Council of Trent in 1562. The Council stated that the "Same Christ" is sacrificed in an "unbloody manner, who once offered himself in a bloody manner on the altar of the cross."

That claim raises the question, "What are the effects of the Eucharist?" Among the effects are unification with Christ and the preservation and increase of supernatural life, and it is a pledge of heavenly bliss and future resurrection. As a sacrament Christ is partaken as nourishment for the soul. As a sacrifice He is offered as a sacrificial gift to God. It "makes present" Christ's sacrifice. In fact, Ott speaks of "the presenting again of the Sacrifice of the Cross."[60] But, most significantly, he goes on to say, "The purpose of the Sacrifice is the same in the Sacrifice of the Mass as in the Sacrifice of the Cross; primarily the glorification of God, secondarily atonement, thanksgiving, and appeal."[61] There we have it; the Eucharist is atoning. It is a sacrifice of "expiation and impetration," effecting the remission of sins and the punishment for sin. It is a "sacrifice of propitiation" and can be offered "not only for the living, but also for the poor souls in Purgatory."[62] It works *ex opere operato,* its effectiveness not depending on the spiritual worthiness of the sacrificing priest, nor of the co-sacrificing church member.

It will be useful to mention briefly the sacrament of Extreme Unction, although Catholics admit that evidences for this sacrament among the church Fathers are not numerous. "As Extreme Unction is a Sacrament of the Living," Ott says, "it presupposes in general the remission of grievous sins. But if a person in mortal sin is seriously ill and can no longer receive the Sacrament of Penance, or if he erroneously believes that he is free from grievous sin, Extreme Unction eradicates the grievous sins per accidens, but still by reason of Christ's Institution."[63] Only bishops and priests can administer the sacrament.

ASPECTS OF SACERDOTALISM IN THE SCRIPTURES

Does the New Testament support a form of sacerdotalism? It is not easy to answer the question affirmatively without introducing a measure of confusion, for the sacerdotalism of the Bible is largely confined to the Old Testament and the priestly code of the Law of Moses. The New Testament teaching of our Lord, the apostles, and that of the epistle to the Hebrews make clear that the Mosaic system has been done away with (see, for example, Romans 3:21–8:39; 2 Corinthians 3:1–18; Galatians 2:1–5:26; Hebrews 1:1–10:18). If one is thinking of a priestly class, plural in number, who act as essential mediators between God and mankind, as Webster defined sacerdotalism, then there is no sacerdotalism in that part of the New Testament that unfolds the fact and significance of the accomplished atonement of Jesus Christ and the establishment of the new covenant assembly of the people of God.

In a lengthy passage on the Christian ministry, Bishop Lightfoot pointed out that the apostolic church had "no sacerdotal system" and that in the New Testament teaching on ministry there is "an entire silence about priestly functions."[64]

It is well known that the sacerdotalism of the Roman church was unknown in the apostolic church and grew through the early centuries of the Christian era. It is Cyprian (A.D. 200–258) who is the key figure in the transference of the Old Testament concepts of priest and priesthood to the Christian ministry, although Clement of Rome makes a statement in his epistle[65] that suggests a parallel between officials of Christian congregations and the priests of the Old Testament. Eventually there arose the stage in Roman sacerdotalism in which the priests offered the sacrifices of the body and blood of Christ for sin. This encroachment of the Mosaic Law's Levitical system upon the church's ministry reaches its culmination in Cyprian. In Cyprian's view all the passages that refer to the privileges and duties of the Aaronic priesthood refer to the officers of the Christian church.[66]

I am reminded of an experience that Kenneth Pike had in his translation of the Scriptures into the language of a Mexican Indian tribe many years ago. Pike, regarded by many as one of the world's premier linguists, said that after finishing his translation of the epistle to the Hebrews he was reading it to an Indian congregation for their reaction with no confidence that it was a good one and also afraid that it would aid the large Catholic priestly class in view of Hebrews' heavy reference to priests and priesthood. He was living at the time in a heavily priest-ridden area. While he was reading the text, an old Indian leaned back and said, "I see it now! They're just trying to prolong their destiny!" Pike said he apologized to God in his heart that, although he felt that the epistle had been rather poorly translated into the language of the tribe, he had had so little confidence in the power of God's Word to illumine hearts, even uneducated and untaught hearts.[67]

Something very similar has happened in the bringing of the Old Testament priesthood's practices into the Christian church. The old Indian was on to something, for it appears that Rome is doing just what he said: seeking to prolong the destiny of a sacerdotalism that cannot be harmonized with the New Testament.

If, however, one thinks simply of the Lord Jesus Christ as the High Priest after the order of Melchizedek, who has offered a fully sufficient sacrifice for sinners and is now engaged in the intercession that accompanies His offering at the right hand of God the Father, then there is a unique sacerdotal system in the New Testament. There is a one-of-a-kind priest. The writer of Hebrews calls Him a High Priest (2:17; 3:1; 4:15; 5:1, 5, 10; 6:20; 7:26; 8:1; 9:11), a great Priest (10:21, Gk.), and a great High Priest (4:14). Further, the whole of the mystical body of His company—the church, the true believers—constitutes a holy priesthood, the royal priesthood (1 Peter 2:9; Revelation 1:6) of Scripture. To Him belongs the *sacerdotium,* the priestly work or priestly office, and to them in Him.[68] His priestly office consists of two works, the work of sacrifice and the work of intercession.

The work of sacrifice. The writer of Hebrews is the New Testament author who most fully expounds the priestly ministry of our Lord. He cogently and conclusively makes the point that there is only one sacrifice for sins and that Christ has offered the sacrifice, finishing the work connected with it. In the sonorous and impressive sentence opening the discourse, he states that the Son has "provided purification for sins."[69] The achievement is one impossible to any other person and stresses His unique qualifications for priestly ministry. The final clause, signifying that He has "sat down at the right hand of the Majesty in heaven," indicates that the Son's priestly sacrifice, in contrast to the Old Testament Levitical priests and, I might say, to the continually laboring priests of the Church of Rome, stands finished. The ground of the purification of God's elect people has been completed. To be a seated priest at God's right hand, as Psalm 110:1 indicates, is the destiny of the High Priest according to the order of Melchizedek. The reference to the priest at the right hand of God in the glory of a finished work is the principal theme of the letter, and other passages fill in the details.

In the fifth chapter the author sets out the qualifications for high priestly ministry. The priest must not only be human, but humane, able to deal gently with those who go astray. And, further and most important, he must be appointed by God to the office. He points out, in indicating the Son's eminent qualifications for the work, that "God said to him, 'You are my Son; today I have become your Father.' And he says in another place, 'You are a priest forever, in the order of Melchizedek'" (Hebrews 5:5–6). The two texts are used to show that the Son is God's appointed priest. It is very much to the point to emphasize this, because the words of the text clearly indicate that no mere human priests now, since the end of the Levitical system, stand in office by divine authority. The Roman priests have no divine right to their pretended office.[70]

A series of texts follow in the epistle stressing that the priestly sacrifice has been offered and that it cannot be followed by another with authority and cleansing power: "Unlike the other high priests, he does not need to offer sacrifices day after day, first for his own sins, and then for the sins of the people. He sacrificed for their sins once for all when he offered himself" (7:27). Again, "He did not enter by means of the blood of goats and calves; but he entered the Most Holy Place once for all by his own blood, having obtained eternal redemption" (9:12). An eternal redemption makes it unnecessary that one have any other than that, and believing men and women have that.

"Nor did he enter heaven to offer himself again and again, the way the high priest enters the Most Holy Place every year with blood that is not his own. Then Christ would have had to suffer many times since the creation of the world. But now he has appeared once for all at the end of the ages to do away with sin by the sacrifice of himself" (9:25–26).

Once more the note of a one-time and final sacrifice is sounded in the words, "and by that will, we have been made holy through the sacrifice of the body of Jesus Christ once for all" (10:10). The note, now a rising crescendo, is heard again: "because by one sacrifice he has made perfect forever those who are being made holy" (10:14). And this is followed in the text that is probably the final note of the author's major doctrinal argument of the one sacrifice of Christ for sins: "Then he adds: 'Their sins and lawless acts I will remember no more.' And where these have been forgiven, there is no longer any sacrifice for sin" (10:17–18). These texts indicate that there is no need and no place for claims that ordinances without biblical authentication are divinely ordained means for the forgiveness of sins. There is no longer any sacrifice for sin, the author says.

In chapter 13 the author makes the statement, "We have an altar from which those who minister at the tabernacle have no right to eat" (v. 10). "The word 'altar,'" F. F. Bruce points out, "is used by metonymy for 'sacrifice'—as when, e.g., we say that a man keeps a good *table,* meaning thereby good *food.*" Our sacrifice is that made at Calvary by the Son of God, and it is in that sacrifice that believers have redemption (cf. 8:1).

> What connection is there between this passage and the Eucharist? No direct connection at all. It is remarkable how our author avoids mentioning the Eucharist when he has every opportunity to do so; for example, it would have been easy for him to derive some eucharistic significance from the bread and wine that Melchizedek brought to Abraham when he met him "returning from the slaughter of the kings" (7:1);[71] but he does not even mention the bread and wine. . . . His failure to mention them, let alone discern some Christian meaning in them, can scarcely be accidental.[72]

The work of intercession. The intercession of the priest is not prominent in the Old Testament, but it is there (cf. Leviticus 16:13; Numbers 16:1–50). They made intercession for the same persons for whom they offered sacrifices. In fact, atonement and intercession included each other, the atonement being prolonged without suffering into the work of intercession. The two functions are coextensive. In the case of our Lord's intercession it has been called "the perpetual presentation of the 'continual burnt offering' of Calvary."[73]

Passages attribute the whole of our salvation to His sacrifice and to His intercession (Hebrews 10:14; 7:25). The same priest who ministered at the bronze altar and at the mercy seat also ministered at the golden altar of incense, and for the same people. As Martin says, "But at both altars Aaron was the type of Christ; and as an offerer both in sacrifice and intercession, Christ is the antitype of Aaron."[74] "The entire work of the priest," Hodge points out, "was one work. They sacrificed for, they interceded for, they blessed precisely the same persons and no others. Num. vi. 22–27."[75]

The antitypical reference is obvious. It is our Lord who has offered the one and only sacrifice, and it is He alone who intercedes in the Holiest in the presence of the Father for His covenant members on the ground of the value of His offering. There is no place nor need for human intercessors. One sufficient heavenly intercessor is enough. Lightfoot, referring to Hebrews, sounds the same note: "Now this Apostolic writer teaches that all sacrifices had been consummated in the one Sacrifice, all priesthoods absorbed in the one Priest. The offering had been made once for all: and, as there were no more victims, there could be no more priests."[76]

Does not the epistle, however, use sacerdotal language, speaking of sacrifices and altar (13:15, 16, 10)? Yes, it does. But the sacrifices are of praise, thanksgiving, and sharing, metaphorical uses of the terms, and the altar is used by metonymy for the cross of Christ. No reference whatever is made to an officiating minister, a priest, who performs sacerdotal acts, offering sacrifices for others. The Catholic concept of the Eucharist and Mass is unknown to the Scriptures.

Conclusion. We, thus, conclude that the one offering of Jesus Christ is *sui generis,* a single, unique, lone rock of redemption by which He took possession of the divine sanctuary, the heavenly Holy of Holies, and there reigns as Savior and Lord. And we conclude that the sacraments of the Roman church with their claims that they are necessary for the forgiveness of sins tragically and fatally compromise the principle of grace in human salvation. The sacrifice of the Son of God is unrepeatable and final, the last and only valid offering for sin with heaven's blessing.

The writer of Hebrews concludes the principal doctrinal section of his epistle with a citation from Jeremiah's prophecy of the new covenant and an observation upon its promises. By citing the beginning of the prophecy from Jeremiah and then omitting much of its central content and concluding with its final lines, he makes it evident that the final words are the important ones for him here. They are, "Their sins and lawless acts I will remember no more." The finality of them is obvious, and the author's comment upon them is, "and where these have been forgiven, there is no longer any sacrifice for sin" (10:17–18). Appropriately Westcott adds, "This is the last— the decisive—word of the argument."[77] It says it all very well. Decisively, there is no longer offering for sin with heaven's imprimatur. It is the supreme and only treasury of merit. Its benefits are available to faith alone, apart from works of any kind. The author makes that plain by his citation of Habakkuk 2:4: "But my righteous one will live by faith" (Hebrews 10:38).

As readers of Hebrews know, there are two words that frequently dot the pages of the letter. They are the words "better" and "eternal." It speaks of a better hope, a better covenant, better promises, a better country, better and lasting possessions, and a better resurrection. One might, however, reason from the word "better" that things still "better" might come along, thus

135

clouding the finality of the promises. Of course, something better than these promises would have to be marvelous, indeed, so the faithful have no reason to faint. The author, however, has another favorite word. He speaks of an eternal redemption, an eternal inheritance, and an eternal covenant. It is significant that the covenant containing the promise of the forgiveness of sins is said to be better and also eternal. Thus, for the author the better things appear also to be final things. In other words, the promises that emerge from the one final and unrepeatable sacrifice are incomparable and unsurpassable. We understand why Jesus Christ, the Son of God, is God's last word to men and why He and His atoning sacrifice are man's sole, total, and eminently satisfying hope.

I mentioned in the introduction that *Veritatis Splendor* began with Scripture. It is unfortunate, however, that its well-reasoned argument has not stayed with Scripture but concludes on a note out of harmony with Scripture, on a note centering more emphatically upon Mary than upon Jesus Christ and His unparalleled redeeming sacrifice. We still await that better note from Rome.

NOTES

1. Pope John Paul II, *The Splendor of Truth: Veritatis Splendor* (Boston: St. Paul Books & Media, 1993). The English translation is the Vatican's.

2. Ibid., 14.

3. See Richard John Neuhaus, "The Splendor of Truth: A Symposium," *First Things*, no. 39 (January 1994): 21. Burrell and Hauerwas are contributors to the symposium. A puzzling sentence occurs near the end of their contribution, puzzling particularly since Hauerwas is a Methodist, in which they refer to the Pope calling "us" away to "Mary-like truth matters" (p. 23).

4. Neuhaus, "The Splendor of Truth," 143. It must be acknowledged that near the final words there is an explicit statement that "only the Cross and the glory of the Risen Christ can grant peace to his (that is, man's) conscience and salvation to his life" (p. 144). That, however, is followed by a prayer to Mary as Mother of Mercy that she not allow the cross of Christ to "be emptied of its power." Thus the confusion.

5. Ibid., 144.

6. Gerrit C. Berkouwer, *The Conflict with Rome*, trans. under the supervision of David H. Freeman (Grand Rapids: Baker, 1958), 10.

7. Ibid.

8. Ibid., 169.

9. A. N. S. Lane, "Mary," in *New Dictionary of Theology*, 415.

10. Ludwig Ott, *Fundamentals of Catholic Dogma*, trans. Patrick Lynch and ed. James Canon Bastible (1952; reprint, Rockford: Tan, 1974), 199.

11. Anselm, *Cur Deus Homo*, 2.16.

12. Anselm, *Epistle* 174.

13. Ott, *Fundamentals of Catholic Dogma*, 200.

14. Lane, "Mary," 416.

15. John Calvin, *A Harmony of the Gospels: Matthew, Mark and Luke* (Grand Rapids: Eerdmans, 1972), I:70.

16. Ott, *Fundamentals of Catholic Dogma*, 196. The titles *Theotokos, dei para,* and *dei genetrix* are similar in meaning, each referring to the Virgin Mary as the mother of God.

17. Giovanni Miegge, *The Virgin Mary: The Roman Catholic Marian Doctrine*, trans. Waldo Smith (1950; reprint, Philadelphia: Westminster Press, 1955), 53.

18. Ibid., 54.

19. Henry Bettenson, ed., *Documents of the Christian Church* (Oxford: Oxford Univ. Press, 1963), 51–52.

20. Miegge, *The Virgin Mary*, 65–66. Perhaps the titles Mother of Christ and Mother of God really, if carefully guarded, say the same thing. She did bear by humanity a person having both humanity and divinity. Elizabeth's expression, "the mother of my Lord," points as well to the dignity of both Mary and her son (Luke 1:43).

21. Miegge, *The Virgin Mary*, 103–4.

22. Ibid., 104.

23. Ott, *Fundamentals of Catholic Dogma*, 207.

24. Miegge, *The Virgin Mary*, 85.

25. Martin Jugie, A. A., *La mort et l'Assomption de la Sainte Vierge. Etude historico doctrinale* (Vatican City, 1944). I have not seen this work.

26. Miegge, *The Virgin Mary*, 103

27. Listen to the Catholic Ott's explanation in *Fundamentals of Catholic Dogma*:

    Modern theology usually cites Gn. 3, 15 in support of the doctrine. Since by the seed of the woman it understands Christ, and by the woman, Mary, it is argued that as Mary had an intimate share in Christ's battle against Satan and in His victory over Satan and sin, she must also have participated intimately in His victory over death. It is true that the literal reference of the text is to Eve and not Mary, but already since the end of the second century (St. Justin) Tradition has seen in Mary the new Eve. (p. 209)

    Even Ott admits that Genesis 3:15 has to do with Eve, not Mary; further, I miss the "intimate share" of Mary with our Lord at the biblical accounts of His temptation and Golgotha suffering!

28. Incidentally the use made of text in the Catholic prayer, "Ave Maria," is incorrect. The angel is saluting Mary, not offering a prayer to her.

29. Miegge, *The Virgin Mary*, 106.

30. Lane, "Mary," 416.

31. Ibid.

32. Mario Colacci, *The Doctrinal Conflict between Roman Catholic and Protestant Christianity* (Minneapolis: T. S. Denison, 1965), 183.

33. Ott, *Fundamentals of Catholic Dogma*, 211.

34. Ibid.

35. Miegge, *The Virgin Mary*, 115; citing Bernard's *Epistula* 174 (172) *ad Canones Lugdunenses*.

36. Justin and Irenaeus are responsible for the parallel, the latter writing, "as by her disobedience the virgin Eve was the cause of death for herself and for the human race, so the obedient virgin became a cause of salvation (*causa facta est salutis*) for herself

137

and the human race" (*Adversus Haereses*, V.19, 1). Irenaeus overlooked the sense of Genesis 3:6–7. A careful examination of the text indicates that, when Eve ate of the fruit, nothing happened. When she gave to Adam and he ate, we read in verse 7, "*Then* [Heb., waw] the eyes of *both* of them were opened." The author regards Adam as a covenantal head of the race, and it is his action that is determinative. That is why the New Testament accurately picks up on this and speaks, not of a balancing of Eve and Mary as the causes of death and salvation, but of Adam and Christ (Romans 5:12–21; 1 Corinthians 15:22).

37. Miegge, *The Virgin Mary*, 158.

38. Ott, *Fundamentals of Catholic Dogma*, 212.

39. Ibid., 161. It is difficult to be absolutely fair to Rome, for their theologians, while citing statements that imply Mary's offering of Christ, go on to deny that she cooperated in any manner other than an indirect, remote cooperation. They affirm that Christ alone offered the atoning sacrifice on the cross and that Mary merely gave Him moral support (Ott, Fundamentals of Catholic Dogma, 213). They deny her the title *priest*, and yet speak of her offering, of entering into the sacrifice of the Son for men. In spite of their protests, it is Pius XII who says in the *encyclical Mystici Corporis* (1943) that she "offered Him on Golgotha to the Eternal Father together with the holocaust of her maternal rights and motherly love like a new Eve for all children of Adam" (ibid.). How shall we respond to this?

40. Berkouwer, *The Conflict with Rome*, 164.

41. Vatican II, Dogmatic Constitution of the Church, VIII.61.

42. Howard Sainsbury, "Liguori, Alphonsus (1696–1787)," in *New International Dictionary of Theology of the Christian Church*, 597.

43. Miegge, *The Virgin Mary*, 133; citing S. Alfonso Maria De' Liguori, *Le Glorie di Maria* (Rome: Instit. Miss. Pia Societa di S. Paolo, 1947), I:8.

44. Lane, "Mary," 415.

45. Miegge (*The Virgin Mary*) has cited many of these extravagant claims made by this moral theologian (pp. 146–50).

46. Lat., *sanctorum communionem*.

47. Berkouwer, *The Conflict with Rome*, 180.

48. R. T. Beckwith, "Saint," in *New Dictionary of Theology*, 609.

49. Ott, *Fundamentals of Catholic Dogma*, 441.

50. John Calvin speaks of the treasury of merit "as that counterfeit treasury." Cf. John Calvin, *The First Epistle of Paul the Apostle to the Corinthians*, trans. John W. Fraser and ed. David W. Torrance and Thomas F. Torrance (Grand Rapids: Eerdmans, 1960), 29.

51. Paul Althaus, *The Theology of Martin Luther*, trans. Robert C. Schultz (1963; reprint, Philadelphia: Fortress, 1966), 297. Luther called all of this "workism" (*Werkerei*).

52. Martin Luther, *Lectures on Romans*, vol. XV of The Library of Christian Classics, trans. and ed. Wilhelm Pauck (Philadelphia: Westminster Press, 1961), 350

53. Althaus, *The Theology of Martin Luther*, 300.

54. The *Belgic Confession* has a remarkable article on Christ's Intercession, which makes the same points beautifully (see Art. XXVI).

55. *Merriam-Webster's Collegiate Dictionary* (10th ed.), 1028.

56. Ott, *Fundamentals of Catholic Dogma*, 338.

57. Ibid., 339.

58. Ibid., 355.

59. The word *Mass*, derived from the Latin *missio*, meaning "dismissal," or "release," referring to the dismissal of catechumens before the Eucharist was celebrated. Ambrose is the first to use it of the Eucharist. The Catholic Mass still concludes with, "*Ite, missa est.*"

60. Ott, *Fundamentals of Catholic Dogma*, 407.

61. Ibid., 408.

62. Ibid., 412–13. Ott's proof of the propitiatory character of the Sacrifice for the Mass is Matthew 26:28: "This is my blood of the covenent, which is poured out for many for the forgiveness of sins." He suggests that the present tenses in the verbs, *didomenon* (Luke 22:19–20) and *ekchunnomenon* (Matthew 26:28; Mark 14:24; Luke 22:20) indicate that the sacrifice is consummated in the present time, although a reference to the proximate future is not excluded! The presents indicate duration not consummation. Our Lord at the time of the Last Supper is simply indicating that the work at that time is simply in process of completion, for He has not yet carried out that which is being suggested in symbol. The remainder of the New Testament, written after the completion of the work always refers to it as having been completed, as does the apostle John in John 19:30.

63. Ibid., 448.

64. J. B. Lightfoot, *Saint Paul's Epistle to the Philippians* (London: Macmillan, 1898), 181, 186. To Cyprian in the third century we are indebted for the fact that the Christian ministry came to be widely understood in terms of the Old Testament levitical priesthood. He takes the Old Testament passages referring to the duties, privileges, and sanctions of the levitical priests as applying to the officers of the Christian Church. His opponents are "profane and sacrilegious; they have passed the sentence of death on themselves by disobeying the command of the Lord in Deuteronomy to 'hear the priest'" (Deuteronomy 17:12; Lightfoot, 258).

65. 1 Clement is usually dated ca. A.D. 96.

66. Ibid., 258.

67. Pike was giving the Griffith Thomas Lectures of 1956 at Dallas Theological Seminary when he related the incident.

68. Nathaniel Dimock, a British Anglican scholar around the turn of the century, wrote a number of works bearing on the question of the claims of Rome for the Mass, namely, that her priests do have the authority to offer sacrifices in the Eucharist in the Sacrifice of the Mass (cf. Hebrews 8:3; 9:7, critical texts in support of the position). Dimock, in careful textual and historical exegesis, has demonstrated convincingly that our Lord has offered one full and final propitiatory offering for sin on the Cross. Among Dimock's works are these: *Our One Priest on High* (New York, Bombay, and Calcutta: Longmans, Green, & Co., 1910); *The Sacerdotium of Christ* (New York, Bombay, and Calcutta: Longmans, Green, & Co., 1910); *The Doctrine of the Death of Christ: in Relation to the Sin of Man, the Condemnation of the Law, and the Dominion of Satan* (London: Elliot Stock, 1903).

69. The KJV has "by himself purged our sins," underlining the personal interest in the accomplishment. The prepositional phrase is found in a very early manuscript, as well as in later ones, and may be genuine. The middle voice of the participle might express the idea found in the prepositional phrase. If the phrase is genuine, the "by himself" stresses that the work of purification is the Son's alone. In fact, one might say that this is the only Purgatory in Scripture! Cf. F. F . Bruce, *The Epistle to the Hebrews*, rev. ed. (Grand Rapids: Eerdmans, 1990), 44–45. A fuller treatment is found in G. Zuntz, *The Text of the Epistles: A Disquisition upon the Corpus Paulinum* (London: Geoffrey Cumberlege, O. U. P., 1953), 43–45.

70. Pointed are the remarks of Robert L. Dabney (*Lectures in Systematic Theology* [1878; reprint, Grand Rapids: Zondervan, 1972]) concerning the necessity of deity in the work of intercession for sin:

> None but a properly divine being could undertake Christ's priestly work. Had he been the noblest creature in heaven, his life and powers would have been the property of God, our offended Judge; and our Advocate could not have claimed, as He does, John x: 18, that He had . . . to lay down His life and take it again. Then: unless above law, He could have no imputable, active obedience. Third: unless sustained by omnipotence, unless sustained by inward omnipotence, He could never have endured the wrath of the Almighty for the sins of the world; it would have sunk Him into perdition. Fourth: had there not been a divine nature to reflect an infinite dignity upon His person, His suffering the curse of sin for a few years, would not have been a satisfaction sufficient to propitiate God for the sins of the world. After a sacrifice comes intercession. His petitioners and their wants are so numerous, that unless He were endowed with sleepless attention, and omnipresence which can never tire, an infinite understanding, omnipresence, and exhaustless kindness, He could not wisely and graciously attend to so many and multifarious calls. (pp. 200–201)

How useless are human intercessors, such as the Virgin Mary and Roman priests, for deliverance from sin!

71. Ott (*Fundamentals of Catholic Dogma*) does attempt to connect the Eucharist with the bread and wine of Melchizedek, contending that Melchizedek's "sacrifice" is the archetype of the sacrifice of the Mass (p. 403). The attempt is unconvincing.

72. Bruce, *The Epistle to the Hebrews*, 379–80.

73. Hugh Martin, *The Atonement in its Relations to the Covenant, the Priesthood, the Intercession of our Lord* (1870; reprint, Cherry Hill: Mack, n.d.), 59.

74. Ibid., 60.d

75. A. A. Hodge, *The Atonement* (Grand Rapids: Eerdmans, 1953), 155–56.

76. Lightfoot, *Saint Paul's Epistle to the Philippians*, 265.

77. Brooke Foss Westcott, *The Epistle to the Hebrews: The Greek Text with Notes and Essays* (London: Macmillan, 1892), 317.

Roman Catholics and evangelical Protestants have significantly different approaches to spirituality—that is, the way we live out our faith commitment. In evangelical perspective, our works of piety and mercy do not merit final salvation (as in the Catholic view). Rather, they bear witness to a salvation already realized and perfected in the life, death, and resurrection of Jesus Christ.

Though the Reformers rediscovered the message of salvation by free grace, their movement resulted in a rent in the Body of Christ. Today we need to build bridges wherever possible, hoping and praying that the unity we already have in Jesus Christ might be made visible to the unbelieving world.

IS SPIRITUALITY ENOUGH?
Differing Models for Living

Donald G. Bloesch

Whereas evangelical Protestantism tends to uphold a theology of the Word of God, the Catholic and Orthodox traditions have generally gravitated toward a theology of the spiritual life. Evangelicals in the Reformation tradition do not ignore spirituality but always subordinate it to God's self-revelation in Christ attested in Holy Scripture. Their emphasis is on God's unmerited grace rather than on the human response in spiritual exercises. Spirituality did, however, become an important part of the theological agenda in the spiritual movements of purification after the Reformation— Pietism and Puritanism—though the priority of God's act of redeeming grace in Christ was never lost sight of, except in radical Pietism.

Spirituality in the Christian sense is the way we live out our vocation under the cross of Christ. Its principal concern is with the Christian life (*praxis*) rather than with doctrine (*logos*). Ideally, *praxis* and *logos* are held together in a dynamic tension, but often the paradoxical unity of these dimensions of Christian existence is sundered, one side being emphasized to the detriment of the other.

TYPES OF SPIRITUALITY

The role of spirituality in Christian life and thought will become more evident when seen against the background of a comparative analysis of various types of spirituality.[1] Each type has appeared in Christian history and therefore warrants critical examination.

Primitive, or animistic, spirituality is oriented toward gaining the blessing of the gods to ensure worldly security and happiness. The sacred is reduced to an impersonal force (manna) transmitted through holy objects (fetishism) and mediated through seers or shamans that make contact with the higher spirits through ecstasy (shamanism). Magic always plays a pivotal role in the primitive worldview: the goal is to manipulate and control the divine power for one's own ends. Prayer takes the form of pleading, even cajoling the divine power or powers in order to gain special favors.

Ritualistic spirituality is a more advanced stage of spiritual development in that spiritual relationships are lived out in the context of an ordered community. Grace is regarded as an energy or fluid that can be imparted through the rites of the ecclesiastical institution.[2] Sacraments are important in ritualism because they mediate grace through visible signs that are more or less under the control of a priestly elite. Prayer is reduced to incantations that often take the form of vain repetition. The spontaneity so evident in primitive religion is superseded by officially sanctioned forms that ensure the continuity and survival of the religious tradition.

Rational, or philosophical, spirituality often indicates a reaction on the part of sophisticated intellectuals against the naïveté of direct relations with a personal god or gods. Religion is purged of anthropomorphism and made to center in transcendental ideals or ideas that can guide one in ethical living. God is no longer a personal spirit but a universal principle, like the Idea of the Good, or a distant Creator conceived of as the Architect of the Universe. Prayer is reflection on the beneficence of the world order or on the mystery and wonder of nature. We penetrate the realm of spirit by rational thought rather than through prescribed ritual or methodical discipline.

Friedrich Heiler saw the two highest types of spirituality as the mystical and the prophetic, since they enable the human spirit to ascend beyond the rituals and formulas of human contrivance to a direct relationship with the Unseen.[3] Heiler was speaking as a phenomenologist of religion, but as a theologian I too see an advance in spirituality in these two types of devotion because they resonate more fully with the biblical world-and-life view.

Mysticism is a type of religion not confined to Christianity, for it appears in all the higher world religions. Its hallmark is an immediate or direct experience of the Eternal that gives meaning and direction to human life. This experience is ineffable, eluding all attempts to conceptualize it. The God who is experienced is unnameable, for he is far greater and deeper than all our feeble attempts to define him. The God of mysticism cannot be mastered or controlled (unlike the deities in primitive and ritualistic religion). We can gain access to him, however, not by prescribed ritual or rational thought but by allowing ourselves to be grasped by the Infinite who surrounds and upholds us. Or we make contact with the divine by entering into the depths of the soul and finding the point of identity between the self and God.

Christian mysticism draws upon Platonism, Neoplatonism, and Orphism as well as upon the Bible and church tradition. The result is that biblical themes are often subordinated to Hellenistic ones. God is generally rendered suprapersonal or impersonal; prayer is no longer entreaty but now ecstatic union with the ground and abyss of all being.[4]

Prophetic religion, which inspired the great prophers of monotheistic faiths, is oriented toward a divine revelation in history and is characterized by structured spontaneity in which prayer and devotion break through all prescribed forms. Its focus is not on the human ascent to God as the pinnacle of perfection but on the descent of God to the human condition (and this is especially true of biblical religion). Prayer becomes the pouring out of the soul before God, not with the intent of imposing our will upon God (as in primitive religion) but in order to bring our will into conformity with God's. Prayer may take the form of wrestling with God, but only for the purpose of discovering His will more fully. Prophetic religion is more cerebral than mystical religion, centering on a revelation that is communicated by words and concepts, even though it can never be fully assimilated except in the power of the Spirit. In prophetic religion we meet God in a divine-human encounter (in which God takes the initiative) rather than in a state of religious ecstasy or in the awe engendered by ritual performance.

A particular challenge to prophetic spirituality on the contemporary scene is the resurgence of the ancient heresy of Gnosticism, which constituted one of the principal threats to the gospel in the early church.[5] *Gnostic spirituality* is characterized by a world-denying stance far more radical than that found in Neoplatonism. The goal is to disengage ourselves from the created or material order for the purpose of rediscovering the uncreated element within humanity that links us with the divine. We find God not by His self-condescension to our condition (as in biblical, prophetic religion) nor by the power of love that takes us beyond concepts (as in Christian mysticism) but by knowledge (*gnosis*), which is none other than self-understanding; the infinite God remains essentially unknowable.

Gnosticism might be regarded as an exaggerated or aberrant form of mysticism that highlights the discontinuity between God and the created order. Human life is portrayed as a falling away from an earlier state of perfection. Whereas mysticism tends to be monistic in its attempt to break through appearance to an all-encompassing reality, Gnosticism is dualistic, underlining the cleavage between the realm of spirit and the realm of matter. Matter does not lead to spirit (as in Platonism) but constitutes an insuperable obstacle to spirit and must therefore be overcome. In some current forms of Gnosticism the cleavage is between a diseased or oppressive society and an enlightened consciousness that can be realized only through arduous discipline, sometimes involving training under a spiritual master.

Another type of spirituality, *nomism,* focuses on obedience to moral precepts rather than witnessing to a definitive revelation in history. Nomism tends toward legalism, which often goes hand in hand with ritualism. The legalistic mentality can appear in both mystical and prophetic religion, and evangelical Christianity has generally been alert to the intrusion of this alien spirit into the ethos of the gospel.

CATHOLICISM AND HELLENISM

Both Roman Catholicism and Eastern Orthodoxy are heavily indebted to classical thought and spirituality, from which they derived the conceptual tools and creative insights to implant Christianity firmly in the soil of the ancient world. At their best they sought to baptize pagan concepts into the service of the gospel; at their worst they accommodated the biblical vision to a worldview that contradicted gospel spirituality. Reinhold Niebuhr observed that in endeavoring to relate the personal-dramatic categories of biblical faith to the ontological categories of Greek philosophy, the church fathers frequently sacrificed the former to the latter.[6] The biblical-classical synthesis, which was motivated primarily by an apologetic attempt to make the faith credible to its cultured despisers, often ended in compromising the integrity of the biblical message. Some prescient theologians in the ancient world warned against any accommodation to cultural thought in the proclamation of the gospel, but even some of the heroes of the faith—such as Tertullian and Athanasius—were unable to disengage themselves completely from the classical worldview.[7]

Catholic and Orthodox spiritualities have been shaped by an often well-meaning attempt to penetrate the mind of the ancient world by finding common ground with classical philosophy, especially Platonism and Neoplatonism. Roman Catholic scholars such as Hans Urs von Balthasar and Eastern Orthodox scholars such as John Meyendorff have duly recognized the Platonic and Stoic intrusion into the thought world of the patristic fathers and have sought to combat it.[8] It is this apologetic accommodation of faith to cultural philosophy that resulted in the imbalances in faith and practice that were partially redressed in the Protestant Reformation.

Christian mysticism has proved to be a reservoir of spiritual insight throughout Christian history and has made a lasting impact on Protestant evangelical, as well as Catholic, devotion. Yet too often its claims and goals stand in tension, if not contradiction, with those of biblical personalism. The result is that faith loses its cutting edge and the gospel is transposed into instruction for daily living or a formula for self-realization. Christ becomes the paradigm of creative spirituality rather than the Redeemer who liberates us from the compulsion to make ourselves spiritual or worthy in the sight of God. The mystical tradition in the church has highlighted the importance of manuals of devotion and exercises that strengthen one in the spiritual life, but often to the point of making them a pathway to salvation itself rather than a witness and sign of a salvation already accomplished for us by Jesus Christ in His sacrificial life and death on a cross and by His glorious resurrection from the dead.

In its attempt to come to terms with Hellenism, Catholicism was prone to sacrifice the almost anthropomorphic God of biblical religion for the impersonal or suprapersonal God of mysticism and Platonism. God was depicted as the *actus purus* (a concept derived from Aristotle)—pure actuality in which all potentiality is realized in the perfection of the fullness of being. The problem is that, if all possibilities are already realized in God, can God relate meaningfully to the changing order of creation and history?[9] For the fathers and doctors of the Catholic Church, God is ever-willing—but does not God also have the freedom not to will? In Neoplatonism God's goodness necessarily overflows from His being—but does not God have the freedom to withhold His goodness, to withdraw His presence from His creation? The fathers of the church were adamant that God creates freely, but they too readily defined God's goodness in terms of creativity or productivity rather than love for a sinful humanity.[10] Aristotle's God was the unmoved mover who moved the world toward him by the sheer force of his ineffable beauty. The biblical God is not One who transcends the world in sublime detachment but One who is actively engaged in the affairs of the world, who seeks and saves those who are lost. The God of Platonism and mysticism was the self-sufficient Absolute, the summit of all perfection, who remains unaffected by the sin and misery of the human creation. The God of the Bible is a God who freely relates Himself to His creation and condescends to share in the trials and agonies of His people. The God of mysticism is immutable and impassible; the God of biblical religion makes Himself vulnerable to the pain and lostness of His people. The God of mysticism is always at rest (*Deus semper quietus*); the God of biblical religion is ever active (*Deus semper agens*).[11]

The biblical God is indeed unchanging in the integrity of His being and in His will and purpose for humankind, but He freely chooses to alter the ways by which He realizes His purposes for His people. He is essentially independent of His creation, but He makes Himself dependent on the way in which His creation responds to His love and beneficence. He is transcendent over His creation, but He makes Himself immanent in His creation so that He can be immediately available for His people.

Though the church fathers and theologians of the medieval church spoke much of the love of God, their concept of love proved to be much closer to the eros of Hellenistic philosophy than to the agape of the New Testament. Anders Nygren has shown in his ground-breaking *Agape and Eros* that a tacit and sometimes conscious attempt was made to harmonize these two opposing concepts, and the biblical idea was consequently diluted or lost altogether.[12] Eros is the self-seeking love of human desire that aspires to union with God as the summit of perfection. Agape is the self-sacrificing, other-regarding love best epitomized in God's descent to sinful humanity in the person and work of Jesus Christ. Eros moves from poverty to riches, whereas agape moves from riches to poverty. Eros is an ascending love that leaves the world in its sin and misery behind; agape is a descending and outgoing love that glorifies God by taking us into the dereliction of our neighbor in need.

Augustine's *caritas* represented a blend of eros and agape, but eros emerged as more significant. Augustine did make a prominent place for the downward movement of God's grace to the world, but the purpose of this grace was to assist mortals in their ascent and elevation to God. A salient theme in his theology was the mystical ladder to heaven, which we ascend with the aid of grace but which is also the condition for receiving eternal glory.[13] Interestingly Luther also used ladder imagery but to illustrate or convey the means by which God descends to our level in Jesus Christ.

Among the church fathers the model of salvation was deification or divinization (*theosis*) rather than justification (as with Paul and the Reformers).[14] The purpose of the Incarnation was said to be the divinization of redeemed humanity—transfiguration in the likeness of God. Through the grace of God we are made partakers of the divine nature.[15] We have an important role in cooperating with the grace of God in order to facilitate our divinization, which is fully realized at the time of death when mortality puts on immortality. Divinization was a prominent theme of the Greek fathers, though it also entered the Latin church and has become part of the Christian mystical tradition. The idea of divinization ultimately derives from Plato and Neoplatonists, who interpreted salvation as basically the assimilation of the soul to God.[16] The church fathers made a place for grace in the divinizing process but ignored or downplayed the biblical theme of salvation by the external righteousness of God—the holiness of Jesus Christ that justifies us while we are still in our sins. Moreover, they gave insufficient recognition to the fact that our union with Christ is realized solely in the gift of faith, not at the end of a long process of spiritual purification.

The fathers and doctors of the church also adopted the classical ideal of happiness (*eudaimonia*) as the goal of human endeavor. In Plato and Aristotle *eudaimonia* is achieved through the subordination of the senses to reason, which results in wholeness in being and personality. For the fathers *eudaimonia* is possible only through union with Christ—the result of faith working through love. The well-ordered soul is the transfigured soul, the soul transformed or divinized by the grace of God. The theologians of Catholicism and Orthodoxy broke with Platonism in stressing the priority of grace in Christian experience, but they continued to accept the egocentric ideal of happiness as the goal of the Christian life. In the biblical vision happiness is a by-product or consequence of a still higher goal—to give glory to God alone through service to our neighbor in need.

Catholic theology for the most part remained true to the Bible by seeing the tragic flaw as sin, not error or ignorance (as in the classical tradition). Yet in explaining the origin of sin, theologians tended to view it in ontological terms—as a privation of being—rather than in historical terms—as a conscious and deliberate rebellion of the human creation against God. Sin becomes separation from undivided unity with God (as in Platonism and Neoplatonism) rather than willful transgression of a known law of God. Salvation becomes reunion with God rather than the unmerited forgiveness of sins. It was not a matter of either/or, since Catholic theology held to both these conceptions, but it seemed that the mystical understanding time and again overshadowed the biblical understanding.[17] Catholicism was tempted not only by mysticism but also by ritualism. The sacrament of Penance reflected a legalistic view of sin in which satisfaction of law was supremely important.[18]

In both Eastern and Western branches of the church the Christian life was by and large articulated in mystical terminology. The stages of the mystical ascent to God—purgation, illumination, union, ecstasy—were spelled out by the Neoplatonic philosopher Proclus and transmitted to the church by Dionysius, the pseudo-Areopagite (ca. 500). In this schema the gift of illumination and the final gift of contemplative union with God are contingent on the struggle of the soul to purge itself of sin and to prepare itself for the visitation of God's Spirit. In Catholic orthodoxy prevenient grace is necessary to begin the salvific process, but the whole of the Christian life is seen as a mystical ascent or return of the soul to union with God. Salvation is not God's declaration of undeserved righteousness through faith in Jesus Christ but the outcome of a long process of purification and illumination in which the soul prepares itself for final union with God. One part of the church believed that even before grace reaches us we can do what lies within our power (*facere quod in se est*) and thereby dispose ourselves to receive grace.[19] The Thomistic tradition contended for the priority of grace even at the beginning of the salvific process but held that on the basis of grace we can merit an increase of grace and finally eternal life itself. This position was formally articulated and approved by the Council of Trent (1563), which saw justification as a cooperative endeavor between God and the sinner in which we are enabled to move toward final salvation by the graces available to us in the sacraments. These graces spur us on to good deeds that have meritorious value in God's sight.[20]

Prayer in the mystical type of religion is basically meditation and contemplation. Catholic theologians, such as Augustine, also made a place for petition but regarded petition as a lower grade of prayer. Petition is for beginners in the faith; as we progress toward mystical union with God we put petition behind us in order to contemplate the infinite God in His incandescent glory. In contemplation we are emptied of self and taken up into God. Silence is necessary, especially for the higher types of prayer, since union with God requires detachment from the world of things. In silence we seek to get beyond the historical Jesus, even beyond all concepts and images, into unity with the abyss and ground of all being. Christian mystics prize mental prayer over vocal prayer. Angelus Silesius concluded, "We cannot speak of

God, He is beyond compare. And so we can adore Him best with silent prayer."[21] Indeed, "so far beyond all words is He, I know no other way than not to speak. Thus without words I pray."[22] For Plotinus prayer was "the flight of the alone to the Alone." By contrast, in evangelical, biblical spirituality prayer is calling on the name of God, who is never alone but coexists in fellowship within Himself as a holy Trinity and wills to establish fellowship with all of His people.

In fairness to the Christian mystics one should acknowledge that they were often inconsistent and that their biblical faith persisted despite the Neoplatonic terminology they drew upon to clarify their faith. While cherishing the ideal of contemplative prayer, the great saints of Catholic and Orthodox mysticism also recommended prayer in the realistic or naive sense—talking with God and asking for His aid and guidance. The contemplative state was never something permanent, and the unmediated vision of God was generally something in the future—to be attained beyond the veil of death. Similarly, whereas their goal was uninterrupted union with God, the mystics in their practical advice and in their own lives often exemplified self-giving love in their relations to other people. When critiquing the Neoplatonic framework in which they articulated their faith, we need to bear in mind that we as evangelical Protestants also necessarily draw upon some philosophical system, whether it be that of Plato, Plotinus, Aristotle, Kant, Hegel, Whitehead, or some other exemplar of cultural wisdom. The important thing to keep in mind is that the gospel must be allowed to stand as a judge over all philosophical concepts and images. Philosophy can be used as a tool of faith, but it must never become its master. Otherwise we risk falling into a new synthesis between faith and cultural thought that subverts rather than enhances the unique claims of biblical faith.

GAINS AND LOSSES
IN THE REFORMATION

The Protestant Reformation of the sixteenth century signified more than a theological correction. It was none other than a spiritual revolution, posing a direct challenge to the mystical and ritualistic spirituality pervasive in Roman Catholicism from the early centuries on. Whereas Catholic spirituality had focused on making satisfaction to pay debts incurred by sins after baptism, evangelical Protestant spirituality emphasized unconditional grace that brings us out of bondage to live a life of freedom and purpose in service to a broken and lost humanity. For the Reformers the Christian no longer needs to suffer penalties for sin, since the supreme penalty has already been borne by Jesus Christ, but we still have to undergo disciplines that equip us for kingdom service. Whereas mysticism placed the emphasis on purification leading to illumination and union, Luther and Calvin contended that faith itself unites us with Christ, and works of purification follow rather than precede faith. The right order is not purification, illumination, and then union, but faith, repentance, and then service. In place of the Catholic mystical understanding of the Christian life as the stairway of the saints or the ladder to heaven, Reformation theology stressed the descent of God to the sinful human condition. It was the difference between a spirituality based on eros, self-regarding love, and one based on agape, the sacrificial, paradoxical love of the cross. The fulcrum of spirituality in Reformation perspective was no longer desire for union with God and possession of the greatest good but readiness to serve wherever God may call, even if this entails placing our spiritual status before God in jeopardy (cf. Exodus 32:32; Romans 9:3).

The Reformers stoutly challenged the Catholic conception that sinful humanity can prepare the way for justification, though always with the assistance of grace. Late medieval theology taught that even apart from prior grace works of contrition can merit justifying grace, albeit only in a loose sense. William of Ockham and Gabriel Biel spoke of merits *de congruo,* meaning that we can do works that may induce God's favor, so long as they are done in sincerity and so long as we do what in us lies.[23] Merit in the strict sense—works that truly deserve God's favor (*de condigno*)—is not possible apart from His assisting grace. The Council of Trent held that works before justifying grace cannot merit grace, but after justifying grace we can merit final justification (i.e., eternal life) through cooperating with grace. The Protestant Reformation challenged this whole legalistic schema by contending that no Christian can merit God's favor. Base motivations always accompany godly motivations and thereby render us unworthy in the sight of God on the basis of our own goodness. We can do works that are pleasing to God when these works are inspired by faith in Christ's righteousness, which covers our sinfulness and so makes us acceptable before God.

The Protestant Reformers warned against relativizing the absolute, against confounding the finite and the infinite. The church cannot dispense grace, only receive it. It cannot guarantee the trustworthiness of the biblical revelation, only acknowledge it. The body and blood of Christ are not contained in the sacrament but mediated through the sacrament by the free action of the Spirit. The Holy Spirit is not a magical force or substance that can be controlled by the church or its clerics but the power and action of a personal, living God who disciplines and chastises a church that arrogates power to itself. Glory is to be given not to the church, not to the pope, not to the saints, not to the bread and wine in Holy Communion but only to God (*soli Deo Gloria*). The Reformation signaled the triumph of prophetic spirituality over both mystical and ritualistic spirituality.

Another emphasis of the Reformers was the primacy of Holy Scripture over both church tradition and religious experience. But this was not Scripture as a book in the power of the church but Scripture as the sword of the Spirit of God who judges and renews the church. The Reformation criterion was Scripture in its paradoxical unity with the Spirit, who inspired its words and continues to speak through its witness, calling the church to renewal and repentance.[24]

Although the mainline Reformation retained the sacraments as instruments that the Spirit uses to strengthen faith, its real sacrament was the preaching of the Word. Preaching was no longer a moral homily (often brief and only tangentially related to Scripture) introducing the sacrifice of the Mass but the faithful proclamation of the gospel and the law, convicting people of sin and driving them to repentance. The sacraments have no efficacy unless they are grounded in the Word, and the service of worship is defective unless it is centered in the Word.

In their doctrine of the priesthood of all believers, the Reformers challenged the clericalism of the church, which viewed the priest as a mediator between God and the congregation. Every Christian, they claimed, can go directly to God through Christ and can and must intercede for the whole company of the saints.[25] Moreover, every Christian is called to full-time kingdom service. Even in the midst of secular and household duties we can fulfill our holy vocation of being ambassadors and heralds of the gospel. The Reformers contradicted the prevalent Catholic conception that the religious life is a surer road to perfection than the secular life, that those who place themselves under the counsels of celibacy, poverty, and obedience exemplify the ideal of discipleship under the cross. The religious life is no more meritorious than the secular life and may actually foster the illusion that we can get closer to God through prescribed spiritual exercises than through the toil and hardship of daily life in the world. The universal call to sanctity and discipleship has been affirmed in Vatican II, a sign that the wind of the Spirit is still blowing in the ancient church of Christendom.[26]

It has been fashionable in evangelical Protestantism to regard the Reformation church as the true church of Christ and the Roman Catholic church as the false church. A more biblical stance is to see one holy and apostolic church irremediably fractured by the Reformation. Both separated churches now fall short of the fullness of truth that characterizes the invisible church—the holy catholic church that crosses all denominational lines. Jaroslav Pelikan rightly described the Reformation as a tragic necessity, and this is how we should view it today, especially in light of the continued fragmentation of Protestantism and the erosion of its biblical moorings.[27] It was necessary because the theology of works-righteousness that had permeated the life and thought of the church had to be reversed. It was tragic because it split the church in two, and the wounds left from this schism continue to fester. Augustine wisely observed that when Christians are separated from one another their perception of the truth is dimmed. The key to apprehending the truth of the mystery of divine revelation is to be found in the unity of the churches, and yet paradoxically this unity can come only on the basis of a fresh apprehension of truth given by the Spirit of God. The key to both truth and unity therefore lies in a new outpouring of the Holy Spirit upon the church. Yet we must do more than simply wait and pray. We must work actively to overcome the obstacles that divide Christendom, and we must do so in a spirit of love as well as in a spirit of zeal for the truth.

The Reformation brought about solid gains in both theology and spirituality: it highlighted themes that had fallen into partial eclipse—the absolute priority of grace over works (*sola gratia*), the centrality of the cross in accomplishing the salvation of believing humanity (*solus Christus*), and the cruciality of personal faith in receiving the grace of justification (*sola fide*). It also made the Bible central again in the lives of the laity, for whom the Bible was largely inaccessible, since the only versions generally available were in Latin.

Appreciation of these facts should not, however, prevent us from recognizing that there were also losses in the Reformation—more conspicuous in the children of the Reformation than in the Reformers themselves. One of these was the diminished perception of the divinity of the church. In the new ethos engendered by the Reformation the church came to be conceived as an assembly of like-minded individuals who gather to hear the Word and have fellowship with one another. The church as the mystical body of Christ, the mother of the faithful in whose womb we are borne into the kingdom, belonged to a discarded heritage. The sacraments were reduced to ethical ordinances, no longer means of grace. Worship came to be centered exclusively in the written and proclaimed Word, and the visible Word became an appendage to the service of worship rather than its fulfillment (as in Luther and Calvin).

The Reformers sounded the call to universal discipleship, but in the process special forms of discipleship, such as religious orders, disappeared in the life of the Reformed churches. Monasticism had to be opposed because of its infiltration by a theology of works-righteousness, but the idea of separated communities performing special services to the wider church is not in itself unbiblical and may be necessary in certain periods of the life of the church. Marriage was endorsed over celibacy, but as a result the vocation to celibacy, which is solidly based in the New Testament, was denied or downplayed.

The Reformers rightly protested against the veneration of the saints and the adoration of Mary, glaringly apparent in popular Catholic devotion, though only the worship of the Triune God was officially sanctioned by the church. At the same time, they lost sight of the biblical truth that the church always stands in need of models of holiness that can guide the Christian in the way of truth and righteousness. All Christians, to be sure, are saints, but only some become great saints—not through their own endeavors and merits but by being specially chosen by God to be public signs and witnesses of the truth of the gospel in a particular time and place. Mary as the mother of Christ was respected in Reformation theology, but Mary is no longer called blessed in every generation in the churches of the Reformation (cf. Luke 1:48).

Finally, the Reformers frowned upon ascetic disciplines chiefly because the Catholic church treated them as meritorious, but as a result the very idea of spiritual disciplines to equip us for the rigors of Christian service fell by the wayside. An interest in the disciplines of the spiritual life revived in the Pietist and Puritan movements of spiritual purification after the Reformation, but in modern evangelicalism asceticism is for the most part considered a threat to faith rather than an opportunity for service on the basis of faith.

Prophets have appeared in the Reformation churches reminding their peers of a lost spiritual heritage that should be reclaimed in a new form. Philip Spener sounded the call in the seventeenth century for regenerated pastors and laity in a time of mounting formalism and secularism.[28] Missionary societies were born out of the evangelical revivals (seventeenth to nineteenth centuries) that made a place for full-time service on the mission field both single and married people. Søren Kierkegaard in the nineteenth century pointed to the need for a new kind of monasticism as a sign of protest against creeping worldliness in the churches. In the twentieth century Dietrich Bonhoeffer pleaded for a rediscovery of discipleship as not contradicting the gift of grace but instead as fulfilling its demands.[29] We are saved by grace alone, but this grace is not cheap; it is costly. It cost God the life of his own Son, so it must also cost us our lives—in service to the world for whom Christ died.

Protestantism after the Reformation separated into rationalism on the one side and Pietism on the other.[30] Both movements betray an unwarranted confidence in human capabilities, which constitutes a deviation from the Reformation emphasis on salvation by undeserved grace. In rationalism spirituality was reduced to ethics; in Pietism it became a blend of ethics and spiritual exercises. In both movements character training was regarded as more important than the adoration of the living God. The Bible became a manual for holy living rather than a sacramental vessel through which the Spirit performs the miracle of saving grace. Revelation was equated with general principles relating to faith and conduct (as in rationalism) or with interior experiences that guide us in our daily living (as in Pietism). Agape, the love of the cross, was transmuted into humanitarian love that tries to raise the unfortunate to the level of social responsibility. The coming of the kingdom was believed to rest on human effort rather than on the latter-day outpouring of the Holy Spirit. The company of true believers constituted the human agents who bring in the kingdom rather than being signs and witnesses to what God is doing in fashioning a new social and spiritual order.

If the secularization of the church and the domestication of evangelicalism in particular are to be reversed, it is incumbent on us to rediscover the catholic heritage of the Reformation and seek to realize the ideal of the original Reformers for a reformed catholic church. But in our dialogue with our Catholic and Orthodox brethren, we must remain firm in our commitment to what is genuinely biblical and evangelical in the churches of the Reformation. The Roman Catholic church needs the correction of the Protestant Reformation in order to become truly catholic and fully biblical. Modern evangelicals need to draw upon the witness of sacred tradition in order to appreciate the wider implications of the witness of Holy Scripture.[31] The church must always be under the Word, but the Word in turn is operative and effective only in the context of a community of faith and discipleship.

ENDURING ISSUES

While earnestly seeking for Evangelical-Catholic unity, we must not close our eyes to the seemingly insurmountable issues that still divide us—and indubitably will continue to divide us for some time. It is only by thinking through and talking through the great themes of faith that we can hope to make any progress at all toward Christian unity.

The doctrine of salvation by the free grace of God alone (*sola gratia*) is still a barrier to ecumenical conversations. Catholic theology will gladly accept salvation by grace, but it is adamant that this is grace that assists human free will and therefore is not grace alone. Likewise Catholics can affirm justification by faith, but this is faith formed by love, not faith alone (*sola fide*). The Council of Trent concluded that even before coming to faith we can dispose ourselves to receive God's justifying grace. Consequently, salvation was portrayed as a cooperative endeavor between the gracious God and the human sinner, though we cannot move toward God on our own apart from His grace. In evangelical Protestantism grace does more than enable our free will; it liberates our will for faith and service. Grace does not simply bring us the possibility of a salvation yet to be realized; it brings us the reality of a salvation already accomplished. Our role is not to cooperate with God in procuring grace or justification but to celebrate and proclaim a salvation won by Christ alone (*solus Christus*). We are not agents of God's saving work but witnesses to His saving work. His grace when it first comes to us is irresistible, for it breaks down the resistance of the old nature and in effect implants within us a new nature. The decision of faith is a sign that grace is working for us and in us; it is not the condition for receiving grace.

One should recognize that modern evangelicalism is probably closer to semi-Pelagianism (which viewed salvation as partly the work of the human subject and partly the work of God) than to traditional Catholicism because of the prominent role assigned to natural human free will in the effecting of salvation. In classical Protestantism faith is not a theological virtue (and thereby meritorious) but an empty vessel that only receives what is given by Christ.

The role of merits and rewards in the Christian life is another divisive issue that must be frankly faced. Reformation Protestants are willing to speak of rewards for acts of kindness and loving service, but these rewards are blessings that God brings those who are already justified and sanctified by his grace. Justification itself must not be treated as a reward for services rendered to God or humanity, for this is an unmerited gift extended to us while we are still in our sins (cf. Romans 3:21–31; 4). Nor is final salvation a reward in the strict sense, since this too is given to the undeserving (Matthew 22:8–10; Luke 17:10). But the privilege of being allowed to perform needed services for Christ and the people of God is a special grace showing that God is pleased with those who remain true to His word, though we can do so only in the power of His Spirit. Happiness in the sense of enjoying the blessings of life in this world can be a reward for diligence and faithfulness in our calling (cf. Proverbs 25:22). Our good works will also be recognized in the life hereafter (cf. 1 Corinthians 3:14; Colossians 3:24; 2 John 8) but not as the ground or cause of our justification. The rewards we receive for faithful endeavor are always to be regarded as gifts from God that enable us to do what we can for Christ and His kingdom. We can never be truly worthy of receiving Christ's blessings, but we can be used by the Spirit to do acts of service that deepen our happiness and bring us the peace that passes all understanding.

Catholic theology, and especially Catholic mysticism, reminds us of the decisive role of spirituality in the plan of salvation. We are summoned not only to faith but also to a holy life, and this entails living under spiritual disciplines in order to make ourselves available for kingdom service. For evangelicals, however, spirituality is not enough, since it does not make us acceptable before God. Even the faithful remain sinners and stand in constant need of God's forgiveness.

Spirituality in the evangelical sense is not the precondition for salvation but its fruit and consequence. A holy life is a sign of our election by God to eternal life, but it is not a means by which we merit eternal life (as in the Catholic view). Holiness does not entitle us to heaven, but it does make us fit for heaven (John Wesley). It is not a means to salvation but the demonstration and manifestation of a salvation already realized. It is not a ladder by which we reach up to God but the way we live out our vocation of being heralds of God's saving work in Jesus Christ.

Is spirituality sufficient? Both Catholic and Protestant theologians would reply in the negative if we are thinking basically of the attainment of salvation, though both would regard it as necessary for living in the full dispensation of Christian freedom. Whereas evangelical Protestants contend that efforts toward a spiritual life do not in any way procure the grace of justification, Catholic theology tends to make a modest place for human effort in preparing the way for justification and also in meriting final justification—the culmination of the salvific process. In evangelical Protestantism the human race is dead in sin and needs to be raised to new life by the Spirit of God. In Catholic theology the human will is weakened but not immobilized by sin and can therefore be used by the Spirit in moving us toward Christ and toward grace.

Catholic and Protestant theologians might be able to agree that our calling as Christians is to holiness and not to happiness, that happiness is the result rather than the goal of Christian living. Holiness moreover does not mean moral uprightness but transparency to God—living in close communion with God. The pivotal question is motivation. Do we seek to live holy lives in order to ensure the permanence of our salvation or to gain assurance of our salvation? Or do we seek to live holy lives as a token of our gratitude to a merciful God for his redeeming work on our behalf in the person of Jesus Christ?[32] Are we motivated by the desire for rewards in heaven or by the love that seeks no reward but only the good of others and the glory of God?

In evangelical Protestantism holiness is best achieved not in the solitude of the desert (as in the Catholic monastic tradition) but in the hurly-burly of the world. The holy person is not a spiritual master removed from the pain and squalor of the world but a humble disciple of Jesus Christ who absorbs the anger and hurt of the world in his or her own person. Many of the church fathers upheld the Stoic ideal of *apatheia*—mastery of the passions—though they christianized this ideal by stressing the role of grace in realizing such mastery. The perfect Christian was said to be both impassible and imperturbable, remaining above the discord and travail that mar the world in its sin and ignominy.[33] The Reformers, on the other hand, called the Christian into deeper immersion in the world in order to counter its temptations and deceptions more effectively.

The Christian life is characterized by passive sanctity and active holiness.[34] We cannot make ourselves holy, but we can demonstrate and manifest the sanctity that the Spirit of God secretly works within us. We receive sanctity from the Spirit; we do not procure or create it. Our role is to be ambassadors and heralds of Christ, but the fulfillment of this glorious vocation is always subsequent to what is done by the Spirit for us and in us. We are to be salt and light in the world so that people might see our good works and give glory to the Father in heaven (Matthew 5:13–16). We are not co-redeemers in procuring salvation, but we are co-workers with God in spreading the good news of salvation.

In our dialogue with our brothers and sisters in the Catholic and Orthodox churches we must not simply repeat what was said in the past but try to understand anew the issues that unite and divide us. The language of faith, and this includes doctrinal and creedal formulation, is shaped by history as well as by the Spirit of God. We need to discover what is of abiding value and what is chaff that can now be discarded. In promoting dialogue we must not see the Catholic church as primarily an adversary but as a community that has kept alive the flame of faith and the integrity of the gospel even when many Protestants have sold out to the culture.

I urge my fellow evangelicals to reexamine the witness of the great saints and mystics of the Catholic and Orthodox churches, and they will doubtless be surprised at the strong defense of free grace that we find among many of these people. Hans Küng points us to some of their prayers and testimonies that illustrate their commitment to salvation by free grace.[35] Thérèse of Lisieux confessed that she had no confidence in her good works and therefore chose to enwrap herself solely in the righteousness of Christ. Challenging the spirituality of her own convent, she perceived the need for a lift to heaven instead of the traditional stairway to heaven.[36] Claude de la Colombière prayed, "Others may support themselves on the innocence of their lives, on the strictness of their penitence, on the number of their charities, or on the fervor of their prayers. Thou, O Lord, in hope alone hast established me. For me, Lord, this is all my confidence, it is my confidence itself."[37] The Reformers themselves appealed to such saints and genuinely Catholic luminaries as Augustine and Bernard of Clairvaux in support of their theology of grace. Pascal has been a source of inspiration for many modern evangelicals because of his strong appeal to Scripture as the final norm for faith and practice and his commitment to the gospel that we are saved by grace through faith.[38] Hans Urs von Balthasar, who was greatly influenced by Karl Barth, saw the heart of authentic spirituality in God's descent to our level in Jesus Christ rather than in the aspiration of the soul seeking for mystical union with God.[39]

We evangelicals should remember that the road to unity and truth does not lie in conversion to a church that is still burdened with metaphysical and spiritual baggage from the past that sometimes clouds its understanding of the mandates of God in Holy Scripture. On the other hand, we need to become painfully aware of the full extent of the penetration of both works-righteousness and cheap grace in our own communions. We are called to build bridges where bridges can be built and allow the cleavage to remain where it cannot be overcome. Wherever possible we should seek for points of convergence with our Catholic and Orthodox brothers and sisters. Final unity will come as a gift of God, but we can prepare the way for at least a higher or deeper unity by speaking the truth in love, by being willing to be corrected in our own faith understanding, by recognizing that the full perception of truth lies beyond our present human capabilities—mainly because we are divided from one another and will remain so for some time to come.

NOTES

1. For the classic work on a phenomenology of religion, see Friedrich Heiler, *Prayer,* trans. and ed. Samuel McComb (New York: Oxford Univ. Press, 1958).

2. See Thomas F. Torrance, *The Doctrine of Grace in the Apostolic Fathers* (Edinburgh: Oliver & Boyd, 1948). See esp. pp. 133–41.

3. Heiler, *Prayer,* 135–71.

4. See Donald G. Bloesch, *The Struggle of Prayer* (San Francisco: Harper & Row, 1980), 97–130.

5. See Kurt Rudolph, *Gnosis,* trans. P. W. Coxon and K.´H. Kuhn, ed. Robert McLachlan Wilson (San Francisco: Harper & Row, 1983); Giovanni Filoramo, *A History of Gnosticism,* trans. Anthony Alcock (Oxford UK: Blackwell, 1992); *The Gnostic Scriptures,* trans. and ed. Bentley Layton (New York: Doubleday, 1987); Ioan P. Couliano, *The Tree of Gnosis,* trans. H. S. Wiesner (San Francisco: Harper, 1992); and Hans Jonas, *The Gnostic Religion,* rev. ed. (Boston: Beacon, 1963).

6. Reinhold Niebuhr, *The Nature and Destiny of Man* (New York: Scribner's, 1951), 2:129–148; and Niebuhr, *The Self and the Dramas of History* (New York: Scribner's, 1955), 94–104.

7. William A. Clebsch, "Preface," in *Athanasius: The Life of Antony and the Letter to Marcellinus,* trans. and intro. Robert C. Gregg (New York: Paulist, 1980), xvi.

8. See Hans Urs von Balthasar, *Prayer,* trans. A. V. Littledale (New York: Paulist, 1961), and John Meyendorff, *St. Gregory Palamas and Orthodox Spirituality* (Crestwood, N.Y.: St. Vladimir's Seminary Press, 1974), 126.

9. I do not deny that *actus purus* can be used in a Christian sense indicating God's being not as static perfection but as unlimited act and energy (Mascall). At the same time, God must not be regarded as "the sum or essence of event, act, and life in general." See Arthur C. Cochrane, *The Existentialists and God* (Philadelphia: Westminster Press, 1956), 116. Also see Eberhard Jüngel, *The Doctrine of the Trinity: God's Being is in Becoming* (Grand Rapids: Eerdmans, 1976); and Colin Gunton, *Becoming and Being: The Doctrine of God in Charles Hartshorne and Karl Barth* (Oxford, U.K.: Oxford Univ. Press, 1978).

10. See Arthur O. Lovejoy, *The Great Chain of Being* (Cambridge, Mass.: Harvard Univ. Press, 1976), 67–98.

11. See Hans Küng, *Does God Exist?* trans. Edward Quinn (New York: Doubleday, 1980), 605–6.

12. See Anders Nygren, *Agape and Eros,* trans. Philip S. Watson (Philadelphia: Westminster Press, 1953).

13. Although Alister E. McGrath (*Iustitia Dei* [Cambridge: Cambridge Univ. Press, 1986]) sees only the early Augustine focusing on the ascent to perfection, he acknowledges the Hellenistic flavor of Augustine's final view, which identifies justification with "the restoration of the entire universe to its original order . . . an understanding not very different from the Greek doctrine of cosmic redemption" (1:36). He also recognizes that the later Augustine in his discussion of justification "frequently places the concepts of adoptive filiation and deification side by side" (1:32).

14. See William G. Rusch, "How the Eastern Fathers Understood What the Western Church Meant by Justification," in *Justification by Faith: Lutherans and Catholics in Dialogue* VII, ed. H. George Anderson, T. Austin Murphy, and Joseph A. Burgess (Minneapolis: Augsburg, 1985), 131–42.

15. In the fourteenth century Gregory of Palamas emphasized that we become partakers of the communicable energies of God but not of His essence. See Meyendorff, *St. Gregory Palamas and Orthodox Spirituality.*

16. See Rusch, "How the Eastern Fathers Understood," 135.

17. See Emil Brunner, *Man in Revolt,* trans. Olive Wyon (New York: Scribner's, 1939), 131, 137, 466, and Brunner, *The Christian Doctrine of God,* trans. Olive Wyon (Philadelphia: Westminster Press, 1974), 151–56.

18. See Gustaf Aulén, *Christus Victor,* trans. A. G. Hebert (New York: Macmillan, 1951), 81–95.

19. See Heiko Oberman, *The Harvest of Medieval Theology: Gabriel Biel and Late Medieval Nominalism* (Grand Rapids: Eerdmans, 1967).

20. See Rudolf J. Ehrlich, *Rome: Opponent or Partner?* (Philadelphia: Westminster Press, 1965), 168–89.

21. Angelus Silesius, *The Cherubinic Wanderer;* cited in David Manning White, ed., *The Search For God* (New York: Macmillan, 1983), 71.

22. *The Book of Angelus Silesius*, trans. Frederick Franck (New York: Vintage Books, 1976), 95.

23. In his *Commentary on Sentences* Thomas Aquinas also taught that the unregenerate person can merit grace *de congruo* by doing what lies within human power, but Thomas abandoned this view in his mature work. See the discussion in Alister McGrath, *Iustitia Dei*, 1:85–87.

24. See my discussion in Donald G. Bloesch, *A Theology of Word and Spirit* (Downers Grove, Ill.: InterVarsity, 1992), 12–15, 20–24.

25. See Donald G. Bloesch, *Essentials of Evangelical Theology* (San Francisco: Harper & Row, 1979), 2:104–30.

26. See "Decree on the Apostolate of the Laity," in *The Documents of Vatican II*, ed. Walter M. Abbott (Chicago: Follett, 1966), 486–525.

27. Jaroslav Pelikan, *The Riddle of Roman Catholicism* (Nashville: Abingdon, 1959), 45–57.

28. See Philip Spener, *Pia Desideria*, ed. and trans. Theodore G. Tappert (Philadelphia: Fortress, 1964).

29. See Dietrich Bonhoeffer, *The Cost of Discipleship*, trans. R. H. Fuller (London: SCM, 1959).

30. See Emil Brunner, *Truth as Encounter*, trans. Amandus W. Loos and David Cairns (Philadelphia: Westminster Press, 1964), 75–85.

31. Thomas Oden ("The Bible and Me," *Christianity Today* 37, no. 8 [19 July 1993]) advises: "Beware of the 'evangelical' who wants to read the Bible without the historic voices of the church, who is only willing to listen to his own voice or the voices of contemporaries in the dialogue. Evangelicals have usually been the losers when they have systematically neglected the saints and martyrs and consensual writers of the earliest Christian centuries" (p. 40).

32. The Heidelberg Catechism (1563) states that gratitude is the principal motivation in Christian ethics (Part 3, Q. 86). See *Reformed Confessions of the 16th Century*, ed. Arthur C. Cochrane (Philadelphia: Westminster Press, 1966), 305–31.

33. Harvey D. Egan, "Indifference," in *A Dictionary of Christian Spirituality*, ed. Gordon S. Wakefield (London: SCM, 1983), 211–13.

34. See Regin Prenter, "Holiness in the Lutheran Tradition," in *Man's Concern with Holiness*, ed. Marina Chavchavadze (London: Hodder & Stoughton, 1970), 121–44.

35. Hans Küng, *Justification* (New York: Thomas Nelson & Sons, 1964), 274.

36. See Ida Friederike Görres, *The Hidden Face*, trans. Richard and Clara Winston (New York: Pantheon Books, 1959).

37. Küng, *Justification*, 274.

38. See Emile Cailliet, *The Clue to Pascal* (Philadelphia: Westminster Press, 1943).

39. See Werner Löser, "Being interpreted as love: Reflections on the theology of Hans Urs von Balthasar," *Communio* 16, no. 3 (Fall 1989): 475–90.

PART
3
THE
COMMON
GROUND

The Protestant Reformers did not intend to separate from the Roman Catholic Church. They wanted to re-form it in the sense of bringing it back to its original purity. But the Roman church resisted this effort with vigor and, frequently, violence.

Today, nearly half a millennium after Luther posted his Ninety-Five Theses, Christians are beset on all sides by the forces of atheistic secularism, newly militant Islam, the New Age Movement, and a pluralistic multiculturalism that does not believe in truth at all. Without denying or minimizing the real differences that still separate us, Protestants and Catholics alike would do well to acknowledge and build on the substantial things we have in common.

7

UNHELPFUL ANTAGONISM AND UNHEALTHY COURTESY

Harold O. J. Brown

When old-fashioned, biblical Protestants and Roman Catholics encountered one another in past decades, it often was as the worst of enemies—each side had very clear doctrines that conflicted at important points with equally clear doctrines of the other side. When liberal Protestants and modernist Roman Catholics meet today, however, it often seems to be as the best of friends. Critics will explain that this is possible because neither side has clearly held doctrines that it deems important enough to fight for. But what happens when the modern representatives of Protestant orthodoxy (usually styled evangelicals, sometimes fundamentalists) meet Roman Catholics of what used to be the standard variety (now called "traditionalists" to distinguish them from their more "flexible" or liberal fellow-Catholics)?

What can we make of a position that says it is necessary to be subject to someone called the "man of sin" in order to be saved? What is the source of this conundrum? It is based on two statements, published by the highest authorities of the Christian churches of an earlier day. "It is absolutely necessary for every human creature for salvation to be subject to the Roman pontiff." So wrote Pope Boniface VIII in his Bull *Unam sanctam* (1302). Who calls this Roman pontiff "the man of sin and son of perdition" described in 2 Thessalonians 2:3? None other than the authors of the *Westminster Confession* (1648), long the confession of faith for English-speaking Presbyterians.

Catholics and Protestants did not take their religious differences lightly in the seventeenth century, nor were they to do so for most of the next three centuries. There had already been religious conflicts in the sixteenth century, but the seventeenth was worse. The *Westminster Confession* was written in the aftermath of religious conflict in England, at a time when the European continent was licking its wounds from one horrible war—the Thirty Years' War (1618–1648)—which devastated Germany, the heartland of the Reformation. Almost immediately afterwards another murderous conflict arose farther east, in the Polish-Lithuanian Commonwealth—which was then the largest country in land area in Europe. The Cossack rebellions and associated conflicts, which Polish history calls the Deluge, had begun when the formerly tolerant Polish monarchy attempted to force its Ukrainian and Cossack subjects to abandon Orthodoxy for union with Rome; at the same time the German-speaking Protestants in Prussia and the Lutheran Swedes attacked the Commonwealth from the northwest. It left Poland-Lithuania reduced in size and deprived of most of its Orthodox and Protestant population, with repercussions that have continued right up to the present. In other words, conflicts of doctrine, practice, and jurisdiction between confessional bodies, both claiming Christ as their Master and the Scriptures as their sole or principal source of spiritual knowledge, engaged in fratricidal warfare for several generations.

How can adherents of these radically contrasting positions, which have so often resulted in violent conflict, even be civil to one another, let alone cooperate in religious activities? We see them doing it; in fact, many of today's readers are probably involved in such cooperation. How is this possible, when one side denies to the other the possibility of salvation and the other identifies its chief adversary as a manifestation of the Antichrist? Protestants and Catholics gave up fighting each other, at least on the scale of the Thirty Years' War, partly because the warring factions had simply worn each other out. Little energy was left to continue the fighting. Additionally, the conflicting religions had managed to sort themselves out geographically, such that most people resided in territories of only one religion.

The cooling of warlike passions, in which we ought to rejoice, was inevitably accompanied by, and partly caused by, a weakening of doctrinal commitments. Because of fiercely-held dogmatic commitments, the wars had broken out between groups that both called themselves Christian. Consequently, many people drew the plausible conclusion that commitments were bad and began to take a more tolerant attitude toward doctrinal differences. The great philosopher and mathematician Leibniz, who was one of the two inventors of calculus, sought to bring the confessions into harmony, but without much success. Then the Age of Reason, the so-called "Enlightenment," began. Intellectuals claimed that man was "coming of age" (G. E. Lessing) and had outgrown the need for special divine revelation—such as the Bible claims to be and as Roman Catholics believed they had in "holy tradition"—and that religion could be found within the limits of reason alone (Immanuel Kant).

Thus, one way that civility and cooperation have been made possible is by simply overlooking the traditions—and convictions—of fellow-believers of the past. Today Roman Catholics generally disregard the papal bull of Boniface VIII. The more traditionally inclined claim that it was not an *ex cathedra* pronouncement on a matter of faith and morals, as the (first) Vatican Council of 1870 specified in order for a papal declaration to be deemed infallible. Thus, it would not belong to the "deposit of faith," which must be accepted by all Catholics. Less traditional Roman Catholics simply disregard it and all other Catholic statements that say *extra ecclesiam nulla salus*—no salvation outside the church, by which, of course, the Roman Catholic Church is meant. Curiously enough John Calvin, the father of the Reformed tradition, agreed with *extra ecclesiam nulla salus,*[1] and so do the confessional Lutherans.[2] Of course, both of them define the church differently than the Catholics.

For the Lutherans, one is saved by faith and is made a member of the invisible church, the body of Christ, by that same faith. Hence, it is impossible to be saved without at the same time being brought into the church by one's faith. Calvin taught a kind of practical necessity of belonging to the church in order to be saved, for it is within her that one hears the gospel, and it is at her breast, to use Calvin's picturesque image, that the "babe in Christ" must be nourished and taught.

THE HARD-LINE APPROACH

For centuries, relationships between Catholics and Protestants were dominated by what we may call the hard-line approach. Today, they have been transformed—partly for good reasons, partly for poor ones. Pope Boniface VIII had very good reasons—at least from his own perspective—for practicing the "hard approach," that is, telling people that everyone must submit to the Roman pontiff in order to be saved. Roman Catholics, like all Christians through the centuries, have understood that it is necessary to be "born again." However, Catholics, unlike many other Christians, tie the transformation we call the new birth directly to the sacrament of Baptism, a sacrament properly administered only under church auspices—Roman Catholic auspices, to be precise. Baptism was regarded as absolutely *necessary* for salvation, based among other things on the longer ending of the gospel of Mark: "Whoever believes and is baptized will be saved" (Mark 16:16).

But here a qualification is in order. Because it was seen as such an absolute necessity, unlike the other sacraments, even Penance (now called Reconciliation) and the Eucharist, Baptism had to be made as accessible as possible. This was accomplished in two ways: (1) broadening the number of those who could administer it, and (2) by defining as Baptism things that we might not ordinarily consider such. In the Roman Catholic view, it is not necessary that Baptism be performed by a recognized Catholic ecclesiastical authority or functionary. Virtually anyone, male or female, can baptize, provided that he or she uses the correct trinitarian formula and intends to confer Christian baptism. For this reason, even "heretical" baptism, by Lutherans, Baptists, and so on, can be accepted as valid. When a baptized Protestant enters the Roman Catholic Church, he or she will not be rebaptized, although sometimes the candidate may be baptized "conditionally," in case the prior baptism was not properly performed.

But, of course, people do die with no baptism of any kind; sometimes converts were martyred for their faith before having an opportunity to be baptized by anyone at all. Therefore, Catholic theology provided a couple of escape clauses, as it so often does: it established the concepts of "baptism of blood," which occurs when one dies for the faith without having been previously baptized, and also "baptism of desire," in which one is unbaptized but seeks God and deeply desires to do whatever God requires, if one only knew what it is. Such a person would desire to be baptized and would indeed be baptized, if he or she knew that God requires it; hence, "baptism of desire" is said to have taken place, and such an individual has the possibility of getting to heaven and entering the presence of God. Thus, the church was able to define *baptism* as absolutely necessary for salvation without automatically placing all those who had not been baptized in eternal exile from heaven.[3]

Any concession that traditional Catholicism seemed to be giving by permitting anyone to perform the sacrament of Baptism was effectually taken back by the doctrine of the necessity of other sacraments, particularly Penance and the Eucharist. Baptism cleanses the soul of sin and places the recipient in the state of grace, making salvation possible. However, if one sins seriously after Baptism, then one loses one's access to salvation. The sacrament of Penance is all but necessary to return to the state of grace. (We must write "all but necessary" because here too Catholic theology provides an escape clause—"perfect contrition," as explained below.) Baptism places an individual in the state of grace, which is a prerequisite for performing meritorious works. But even more significantly, it is a necessary prerequisite for salvation.[4] If one sins mortally after Baptism—as indeed each of us does—then one falls out of the state of grace, and if one were to die in that condition, one would be condemned to hell. But how is one to regain that state of grace? Theoretically, one could regain it by "perfect contrition," defined as an utterly selfless repentance, done because one regrets having offended the gracious God, not because one is in any way afraid of punishment in hell. Perfect contrition, however, is very hard to achieve. Who among us can say, when repenting, that he or she is not the least bit concerned about the fact that the alternative to conversion and repentance is eternal damnation?

Because perfect contrition is so hard to achieve and because one cannot really be sure that one has in fact attained it, the Roman church offers baptized believers its sacraments—which it believes were authorized and established by Jesus Christ Himself. In the sacrament of Penance, the repentant sinner is restored to the state of grace and thus once again capable of being saved. The sacrament of Holy Communion—the Eucharist—is of inestimable value as well. Both Penance and the Eucharist are administered exclusively by the Roman Catholic Church, and if one is to belong to that one true church, one must be in submission to Christ's appointed head of the church, namely, to the pope. Hence, Boniface's bull may be seen less as an expression of a papal thirst for power than an expression of concern for the salvation of all, for without a proper relationship—submission—to the pope, no one can expect to be saved. But Pope Boniface seems to have meant even more: refusal to submit to the pope demonstrated a lack of faith and an unwillingness to obey God's commands, therefore virtually guaranteeing that anyone adopting that attitude would be damned.

We should bear in mind that Catholicism, partly because of its commitment to the use of reason—which the Reformers thought was an abuse of reason—always provided an escape clause, of which "baptism of desire" is but one example. Unfortunately, such escape clauses were more difficult to find and had harder and more stringent requirements than the prescribed way of the Roman Catholic Church; they really hold good only for those who are not consciously using them, for to know about an escape clause presupposes knowing Roman Catholic doctrine, which means that one knows enough to submit to the pope and therefore has to be disqualified from resorting to the clause.

Based on these considerations and many others, Roman Catholics have traditionally considered membership in their church a virtual if not an absolute necessity for salvation. The so-called Uniate churches, which recognize the authority of the pope but adhere to rites of Eastern Orthodox type, were safe havens, and even the Eastern Orthodox churches—which do not recognize papal authority—could dispense the necessary means of grace, despite being schismatic. But when one comes to the Protestant churches, the situation deteriorates rapidly. The Church of England and the Lutheran Church of Sweden preserve, or claim to preserve, the apostolic succession of priests and bishops—priests being ordained and bishops consecrated by bishops standing in an unbroken line of succession back to the Lord's apostles. But the other "churches" did not even pretend to have it, because they had quite a different concept of the gospel ministry. Indeed, in 1896 the pope declared "Anglican orders"—ordinations and consecrations of the Church of England—invalid, and the line of apostolic succession broken, regardless of who had ordained whom, because the Anglicans did not share the Catholic understanding of the priesthood; the Anglicans did not intend to ordain sacrificing priests and, consequently, cannot be thought to have done so.

Whatever the merits of these arguments, it seems self-evident that the various Protestant groups, if they claim to be faithfully following Jesus Christ, are placed in a situation where they must deny that Catholics in the tradition of Pope Boniface are also faithfully following Christ. Indeed, this hard-line approach forced non-Catholic Christians to take the position so vigorously expressed in Article XXV of the *Westminster Confession,* calling the pope a usurper and more or less identifying the papacy with the Anti-christ. By claiming authority that Christ never conferred, or even suggested that He desired to confer, the papacy in effect set itself up against God (2 Thessalonians 2:4). There is no easy way, in fact, no way at all, out of the impasse created when one party says, "It is absolutely necessary to submit to me," and the other party calls him "the man of sin."

But today the hard line has been abandoned on both sides: the pope no longer demands submission, and Protestants—or at least most Protestants—no longer call him the man of sin. There was one advantage to the hard-line position, however, which has now been sacrificed by both parties. The claims of Boniface VIII, although they were so extreme that they embarrassed many Catholics even in his own day, follow with a certain consistency some of the basic principles of Catholic theology as it was developed over the centuries. The Protestants' counter-arguments, harsh though they sound, follow logically from the Protestant understanding of justification by faith and scriptural authority. When one abandons the conflict, it may be hard to do so without losing some of the fundamental points of belief that one had thought firmly established and on which one had come to rely.

Inasmuch as we have now abandoned the conflict in its harsh form, on both sides, both Protestants and Catholics are confronted with the problems that arise when the "sound doctrines" on which one's confidence in salvation were based, appear to have slipped. How can we be kind without being foolish? How is it possible to relinquish some of the fighting words of the past without losing the fundamental faith principles behind them?

TWO LEGAL CONSTRUCTS—OR FICTIONS

Much of the Christian world—Roman Catholic and Protestant alike—has sought to escape from this impasse by adopting two legal constructs or, as the cynically inclined might say, legal fictions. The Catholics, especially since the time of the jovial Pope John XXIII (1958–1963), developed the concept of "separated brethren." According to Pope John, Protestants who acknowledge and worship Jesus Christ as Lord and Savior must be accepted as brothers in Him, although separated from the fellowship of the true mother church that He established. Unfortunately for this theory, Vatican II (1962–1965), which Pope John convened, and during which he died, in the document *Lumen Gentium,* "The Light of the Peoples," called the Constitution on the Church, expands what it calls the circle of salvation so much that virtually everyone in the whole world is taken in, even atheists, unless they deliberately refuse to believe in God against their own knowledge and judgment.[5] Thus, Catholicism has moved from saying "no salvation outside the circle of the church" to saying, "no one outside the circle of salvation."

Protestants have their own legal fictions. If we consider liberal Protestants, most have become more or less conscious universalists. In other words, they postulate, often in a vague sort of way, that ultimately all people will be saved. Not so long ago—less than half a century—liberal Protestants regularly considered the Roman Catholic Church their enemy, regarding it as no better than fundamentalism, which of course they detested. The fault, in both cases, was exclusivism. Fundamentalists insist that conversion and a personal relationship with Christ are essential for salvation; those who refuse Him will be left out, or, to put it more forcefully, damned. Roman Catholics demand—or used to demand—membership in their church and adherence to its doctrines and practices. Those who insist on remaining outside the church in this life will be left outside of heaven forever; indeed, they put it more strongly: they will suffer eternally in hell. Now that Roman Catholicism as a whole has wavered so much in its attitude of exclusivism, however, the old hostility of the liberals has all but vanished. It resurfaces when Catholics—often including the more liberal ones—once again join ranks and resist moral evils, as in the case of abortion and sexual immorality.

The difficulty with this flexibility about salvation and with the reluctance to suggest that anyone can be damned is that they are fictions. It is true that they have reduced the old hostility between the confessions, but unfortunately, in order to hold them, as both of these groups—liberal Catholics and liberal Protestants—do, one has to ignore some of the most explicit teachings of Jesus Himself. Consider, for example, John 3:36, where we read, "Whoever rejects the Son will not see life, for God's wrath remains on him." If we are required to forget what Jesus so explicitly taught in order to have peace between confessions and denominations, it would be better to go on fighting.

TWO KINDS OF "REACTIONARIES"

We are thus faced with a problem almost as difficult as that with which we began, the impasse between "submission to the Roman pontiff" and "the man of sin." If we want to have perfect peace between the Christian confessions, we can easily have it, but at the cost of ignoring some very fundamental teachings of Jesus Himself. If we want to hold on to the reliability of the words of Jesus, and of the teachings of Scripture as a whole, we cannot altogether avoid conflicts. Both Protestantism and Catholicism have their "reactionaries," folk who insist on believing the truths as their confession used to teach them and who therefore still bump heads with one another.

Not all Roman Catholics, by any means, accept the universalistic tendencies of *Lumen Gentium*. For those who do take the warnings of Jesus Himself seriously, Vatican II's Constitution on the Church represents a grave threat. When a declaration of this sort is handed down by the *magisterium*, the highest teaching authority of the Roman Catholic Church, it places the

Catholic who thinks it wrong in a worse situation than that of the conservative Protestant who thinks that his liberal church leadership is teaching false doctrine.

The Protestant comes from a tradition where the individual is expected to stand for his own convictions regardless of what the "authorities" say, just as Martin Luther did at the Diet of Worms. "Here I stand" may not be Luther's precise words at Worms, but they certainly express the great Reformer's conviction that the believer has to stand upon the Word of God, no matter what human authorities, even church authorities, may say.

The Catholic, by contrast, and especially the loyalist or traditionalist Catholic, is used to trusting his church to remain faithful to the teachings of Christ and to be careful and precise in expounding them. For such a Catholic to have to oppose the direction his church leadership is taking is to question his own justification in remaining Catholic, since Catholicism has obedience to the church as a fundamental principle of its existence. The conservative Protestant "reactionary," if we may call him that, can take comfort in the fact that in trusting Scripture, as he understands it, rather than church authority, he is in the best tradition of Protestantism. The Catholic "reactionary," by contrast, is in the awkward situation of finding that he can hold to what he considers true only by opposing the institution that was supposed to be the guardian of truth and that by so doing he is involuntarily imitating the rebellious attitude of the Protestants he had always believed to be wrong.

The kind of Christian with which we have to do in these pages is basically the "reactionary" kind. In other words, these Christians react against the tendency of their churches and church leaders to "drift away," as Hebrews puts it, and to ignore the salvation that is offered *exclusively* to those who receive Christ and believe in His name (Hebrews 2:3; John 1:12). The term "reactionary" is generally considered a bad one. However, we all recognize that in many situations, the right reaction, and frequently a very quick right reaction, is vital for survival. Every driver knows that it is essential to have the right reaction in a tense situation on the highway. If a reactionary is one who reacts, sometimes it is important to be a reactionary; that can be true in church life as well as in other situations. However, if one is nothing but a reactionary, only reacting to challenges and threats and never going on to develop something positive, one may avoid harm but is not likely to accomplish much good. If one is to be a Roman Catholic today, it is good and necessary to be a reactionary, in the sense in which we are using the term.

The same thing might be said of being a Protestant, were it not for the fact that the term Protestant, unlike the word Catholic, has become so pale and colorless that fewer and fewer Christians in the Protestant tradition are willing to use it of themselves. From the perspective of conservative Protestantism (call it evangelicalism or fundamentalism), it is better to be a "reactionary" Catholic than a "progressive" one, for the reactionary still holds to many central truths of the Christian faith that the progressive seems to have abandoned. In a real sense, it is only the reactionary Catholic whom an evangelical Protestant can accept as a Christian brother or sister, but at the same time it is only that type of Catholic who will stand up against evangelicals and evangelicalism, attempt to refute them, and in some cases pursue policies in public life designed to thwart them and ruin their plans and hopes.

Perhaps a humorous example from recent history may be offered: Boston's Park Street Church, built in 1810, when churches did not require much office space, was renting rooms in the 1960s from an adjacent fur store for some of its office and Sunday school needs. Park Street was vigorous in its attempts to evangelize and sometimes specially targeted Catholics, who, as it happens, make up the majority of the population of Boston. The store owners had several times refused to sell the building to Park Street Church. Meanwhile, a few doors farther up Park Street, the Roman Catholic Paulist order erected a beautiful Catholic Information Center. The Paulists, be it noted, were founded in the nineteenth century for the express purpose of winning Protestants to Rome. Suddenly Park Street Church learned that the store owners were about to sell their building to the Catholics, who predictably would have dumped the Protestants' offices and Sunday schools into the street. At the last minute, after much arm-twisting, the furrier sold the building to Park Street Church. Of course, such shenanigans are a far cry from the destruction of the Thirty Years' War, but it does illustrate the persistence of Catholic-Protestant rivalry right up to the era of Vatican II.

Even within the last quarter-century, well within living memory, there have been examples of mob action or police repression of evangelical Christians incited by Catholic clergy and activists. The country of Columbia and the province of Quebec come to mind, but there are other examples as well (and the less common but equally unchristian example of Protestant ministers stirring up their people against Catholics, as has happened and continues to happen in Northern Ireland).

It is not necessary to act as though doctrine itself were the be-all and end-all of Christian faith to recognize that unless one learns and accepts the faith that certain important doctrines expound, one cannot be said to be a Christian and cannot expect to be saved. It is out of the fundamental importance of true doctrine that one kind of antagonism between Protestants and Roman Catholics arose. This is an antagonism between what we might call the "better sort" of Protestants and Catholics—the more serious ones. There has, of course, been much antagonism that is based on nothing more honorable than racially or culturally motivated mistrust and dislike. Sometimes this latter kind is easier to heal, as ordinary people are frequently willing to give up their prejudices when close contact reveals to them that those they disliked are not so different and bad after all. It is harder—and properly so—to get theologians to give up their doctrines.

ANTAGONISM AND OPPOSITION

It is important to recognize that Protestantism, like the early Christian church itself, began in an atmosphere of institutional hostility. The Jewish community in which the early church originated was hostile and created problems; indeed, it forced a number of Christians to give their lives for their faith. However, the Jews did not have a nation, and even in Palestine they lacked the authority to impose the death penalty. Consequently, antagonistic Jews stirred up government authorities against the Christians. Of course, this was only the beginning, for the imperial Roman government, alarmed at the rapid growth of a sect whose members it considered potentially or actually disloyal, began persecutions on its own in earnest.

This is rather like what happened when Protestantism arose. At first, actions were taken primarily by church authorities loyal to Rome—as had generally been the case when the established church confronted heretics in earlier centuries. But soon it became evident that the ecclesiastical authorities were not powerful enough to handle the growing Protestant rebellion. Consequently, the church began to use its influence with governments in the attempt to stamp out Protestantism. The stories of Catholic persecution of Protestants are chronicled in the classic work, *Fox's Book of Martyrs.*[6] In principle, neither the Lutherans nor the Calvinists of continental Europe sought to persecute Catholics. They were actually much harder on other Reformation movements, especially the Anabaptists and the antitrinitarians. Catholics, however, seldom scrupled to use the power of the state against Protestants.

A notable example was furnished by the Catholic daughter of Henry VIII, Queen Mary (1553–1558), called Bloody Mary for her zeal to kill Protestants. Consequently, from the time of Queen Elizabeth I, English sovereigns have been required to be members of the Church of England. James II, who converted back to Catholicism, was pushed out of power by the Glorious Revolution of 1688.

As a consequence, whenever Protestants had the civil power in their hands, they tended to try to stifle the Catholics—although seldom resorting to the kind of bloodshed that characterized the Spanish in the Netherlands, for example. The population of the American colonies at the time of Independence was almost entirely Protestant, and largely Protestant of a Calvinistic streak. Only Maryland was founded on a principle of tolerance. But because Catholics were few in number until heavy waves of immigration came early in the nineteenth century, there was little scope for anti-Catholicism.

Traditional Protestants, raised on stories of the Protestant martyrs, were apprehensive about the entry of a large group of Catholics into the United States. Images of the Inquisition and of papal tyranny were evoked. Catholic worship was conducted at peculiar hours in a foreign language and did not involve good Bible preaching and teaching. Much of the Protestant leadership in the United States in the first half of the nineteenth century was affected by the liberalism and secularism that was increasingly prominent in Europe. The suspicion and resentment of the common Protestant people across the nation were consequently reinforced rather than damaged by the supercilious disdain of the Northern intellectuals for the pope and those who followed him in his religion of obscurantism and superstition.

UNEASY COLLABORATION

During the years when Park Street Church and the neighboring Catholic Information Center could carry on a kind of semi-serious guerrilla conflict, it was apparent that both parties believed that they had the truths people need to know and accept in order to be saved. They could, and occasionally did, collaborate on issues of common concern. The abortion decision of 1973, *Roe v. Wade,* and particularly the educational efforts of the late Francis A. Schaeffer, stirred up evangelical Protestants and brought them into the political arena, where the battle for the lives of unborn children had for some time been waged almost exclusively by Catholics. However, at precisely the time the Catholics were beginning to join with Protestants in this way, Catholicism was beginning to lose its clear profile, thanks to the *aggiornamento* (modernization) launched by Pope John XXIII and Vatican II. In other words, Catholics began to seek alliances with Protestants and to join forces with them when they were no longer as serious about the truths of their faith as they had been. At least some Catholics were saying, in effect, "We can collaborate with you now, for, you know, doctrines don't matter very much."

Of course, many evangelical Protestants, especially those from churches with a lively memory of Roman Catholic oppression, were reluctant to cooperate in any way with those who had once seemed so determined to exterminate all traces of the churches that believe in justification by faith alone. Fundamentalists are by definition interested in the clear, literal meaning of Scripture, and for many of them Catholic doctrines and practices appear to be in such dramatic conflict with Scripture that it is not possible to consider Catholicism a true church through which one can learn those things necessary for salvation. Cooperation of any kind with Catholics seemed to some to compromise the gospel and to suggest to Catholics that they were on the way to salvation. Thus, some fundamentalists refused to cooperate in projects such as the March for Life because it implied being "unequally yoked together" with unbelievers. Could evangelicals accept Catholics as cobelligerents, as Francis Schaeffer urged, when these doctrinal differences remained?

Collaboration on a practical level between Roman Catholics and Protestants was possible in part because the major burden of the struggle was borne by members of the laity, the rank-and-file, not the clergy and hierarchy, especially on the Roman Catholic side. As laity, they were not necessarily well-informed on disputed points of doctrine that the hierarchy considered important. The experience of cooperation, of standing shoulder to shoulder, sometimes in literally bloody conflicts with the forces of abortion (as when Operation Rescue members suffered mistreatment and physical abuse), Catholics and Protestants alike lost some of the mutual suspicions that a theoretical knowledge of their doctrinal differences and of their historical conflicts might otherwise have kept alive.

There have been notable examples of Protestant leaders who have made a sincere and vigorous effort to collaborate with Roman Catholics on issues of mutual concern. For example, in the struggles over a "gay rights" ordinance in Chicago, Pastor Erwin Lutzer of Chicago's famous Moody Church joined the Roman Catholics in opposing the proposed legislation and defeated it in the first encounter. Unfortunately, when the ordinance was proposed a second time, Chicago's Roman Catholic archbishop, Joseph Cardinal Bernardin, abandoned the struggle and left his former ally, Pastor Lutzer, to bear the wrath of homosexual activists alone. (In a rather bizarre twist in 1993, the Cardinal was charged by a young man with having sexually abused him as a teenager. It seems that even his volte-face on the gay rights issue was not sufficient to protect Cardinal Bernardin from slander by someone from the homosexual community. The accuser subsequently dropped the charge.)

Evangelicals in the pro-life movement, too, have felt themselves abandoned and their efforts undercut by political maneuvers on the part of members of the Catholic hierarchy. The Human Life Bill, proposed in 1981 by the late Senator John East of North Carolina, appeared headed for passage until it was derailed by the lobbyists of the National Catholic Bishops' Conference. This sort of thing has made evangelicals suspicious of alliances with the Roman Catholic hierarchy, but at the same time it has strengthened their sympathetic attachments to pro-life Catholic laity, who often have felt the same way about their leaders. Probably it is the crisis of conscience among American Christians caused by *Roe v. Wade* that has, as much as any other factor, led to the growing rapprochement between Roman Catholics and evangelical Protestants. There can be no doubt that standing together on the front lines, being insulted, spat upon, arrested, and sometimes brutalized as they attempt to witness to the divinely ordained value of each human life, unborn as well as born, have brought former antagonists together.

THE BLURRING OF LINES

Once again, as for a time in the eighteenth century, cooperation between Catholics and Protestants is growing, but this time for different reasons—no longer because of battle fatigue and skepticism, but because both groups have recognized that they confront a common enemy and have come closer to seeing themselves as committed to one and the same divine Lord. As the proverb says, "There are no atheists in foxholes," and there is not much doctrinal controversy on the picket lines, especially when people are being roughed up or dragged off by the police.

From the point of view of an evangelical Christian who has himself been in the front lines in a conflict with evil, the support of courageous Catholics, whether they are evangelically inclined or old-fashioned traditionalists, is always welcomed. But some suspicion remains. When Hitler invaded the Soviet Union, Winston Churchill said that he would accept the devil himself as an ally. Once Hitler was defeated, it became apparent that the Soviet Union was no longer a comfortable table companion for her former Western allies. If the united efforts of conservative Christians—Protestants and Catholics—should succeed in defeating some of the force of evil that currently threatens to destroy everything we call Christian civilization, is there not a danger that the old differences will once again give rise to interdenominational conflicts?

Questions remain. Sharing a motel room with a Catholic pro-life leader after a fatiguing and frustrating day on the picket line, one evangelical was told, "Well, as least we are saving our souls." No evangelical believer will accept the idea that good deeds, however desirable, bring salvation, but it is hard—and not necessarily productive—to launch into a doctrinal dispute with a fellow-soldier under such circumstances. Cobelligerency, standing together against the same enemies, to use Francis Schaeffer's term, has made it hard for both evangelicals and Catholics to maintain the attitudes of hostility and suspicion that were still so common in the 1950s and 1960s.

But the common danger is not the only thing that is now bringing Catholics and Protestants closer to one another. There are also theological and, above all, sociological factors that have led to more dialogue and discussion between Catholics, Protestants, and Orthodox. In the 1960s it became evident that Schaeffer was right when he said that the foundations had been eroded and that America's apparently Christian society was really a house of cards that a little nudge would topple. The Vietnam War gave more than a little nudge, and the apparently Christian structure of the nation was suddenly revealed as rotting and near the point of collapse. As late as 1965 universities and colleges around the country separated the sexes in dormitories as a matter of course and had rather strict visitation rules. Within the space of a few years, even months, these structures toppled, and, whereas prior to the 1960s it had been hard for college students to find a way to engage in premarital sexual encounters, by the end of the decade it was hard for those who did not wish to do so to find a dormitory situation where such things were not encouraged.

A recognition that "modernity," or militant secularism, was much more of a threat to the fundamental faith and basic morality of Christians of all kinds than the doctrinal differences between them led serious Christians of various groups to interact with one another in theology and worship as well as in public protests and social action. When we say "modernity," what is really meant is the increasingly militant, increasingly anti-Christian secular culture, which is in effect determined to extirpate serious Christianity of all kinds, beginning with fundamentalism and traditional Catholicism, not omitting such trivial things as Christmas carols and creches on public property. (In Waukegan, Illinois, the local atheist gadfly has begun a campaign to remove two crosses from a century-old public cemetery.)

Modernity is a militant adversary of Christianity; yet it must be distinguished from the current movement known as postmodernism. When literature scholars and others talk of postmodernism, that should not be taken to mean that the modernity that attacked Christianity has been overcome or superseded. Modernity contends that Christian truth claims are false, but it believes that they are false because certain contradictory claims are actually true. One can argue with modernity and possibly refute it and persuade its advocates to accept the truth of Christianity, just as a Protestant controversialist would argue with a Roman Catholic and hope to persuade him or her of the truth of the evangelical position—and, of course, vice-versa. Postmodernism hardly believes that truth exists or can possibly be known. Postmodernism is therefore inimical to Christian faith.

These and other factors promoted a new and, frequently, healthy kind of ecumenism (although, as we shall see, not one that is totally without dangers). During the student rebellions of the late 1960s, a spiritual renewal began among young Roman Catholics at the University of Michigan in Ann Arbor. It had a strongly charismatic flavor and sought to reaffirm the fundamentals of the Christian faith as they have always been formally professed (but far from central) in Catholicism. It soon attracted members and clergy of mainline and independent Protestant and Eastern Orthodox churches, including noncharismatics as well as charismatics. It brought together numbers of mostly young Christians, first in Ann Arbor and subsequently in other centers, and established ties to ecumenically-inclined renewal movements in other countries, such as the Protestant *Marienschwesterschaft* (Mary Sisterhood) in Germany. Structurally, it led to the foundation of the Center for Pastoral Renewal, the journal *Faith and Renewal*, and the publishing house Servant Press. The *modus vivendi* of these collaborating Protestant, Roman Catholic, and Orthodox Christians has been to stress those central things on which they are in agreement and to leave aside those on which they continue to disagree.

SUMMING UP

The great German church historian Karl Heussi listed a number of reasons why the Christian church grew so rapidly in the Roman Empire, despite the official hostility of the government and frequent persecutions. Among others he cited the fact that the early Christian churches were flexible on the margins but firm on the central convictions of their faith, as well as in their moral and social practices. The later Roman Empire was a time of immense—but not unparalleled—social and moral degeneracy, as well as of active government opposition to biblical religion. In 1950 one could have described the later Roman Empire as a time of "immense and unparalleled social and moral degeneracy," but that cannot be said today. In modern America our social and moral degeneracy is reaching a level that would have shamed even the Romans, at least those in the smaller cities and rural regions outside the capital. Modern America has not yet attained all the features of Roman degeneracy—for example, we do not have gladiatorial games—but our mass media spread the degeneracy that we do have into every nook and cranny of our land so that there is no region, town, or locality that can be considered free of its taint.

"In my Father's house," said Jesus, "are many mansions" (John 14:2 KJV), to use the older language. Usually this is taken to refer to heaven, as is apparent from the context. But perhaps it may be permissible to allegorize a bit and think of these "mansions" as houses of worship. Evangelical Protestants have learned to work, pray, and worship in consort despite the fact that they have some substantial doctrinal differences—differences that are not likely, in human terms, to be cleared away before Christ returns. We see even greater differences with those who call themselves Catholics. But we are also seeing agreements and commonalities, especially when the fury of the anti-Christian forces around us deprives us of leisure for intra-Christian polemics. In any conflict, it is important to know one's enemies, but it is also very important to know one's friends. Perhaps the very intensity of the opposition to Christianity in our aggressively secularistic culture can be used by God to help us see that what unites us—or better, the One we call Lord—is more important than the things that divide us.

NOTES

1. John Calvin, *Institutes of the Christian Religion*, Book IV, 1:4.
2. Martin Luther, *The Larger Catechism*, Part II, Art. 3.
3. Traditional Roman Catholic theology maintained that those who remained unbaptized, no matter how flexibly one defined baptism, could not enter the presence of

God, but under certain circumstances morally good people, as well as unbaptized infants, might be admitted to a place called limbo, where they would enjoy "natural blessedness" but would not enjoy the "Beatific Vision"—that is to say, they would never see God.

4. Evangelical readers should bear in mind that salvation in the Roman Catholic understanding is something that can take place only at the end of one's life, at the Judgment Seat of Christ. That is one reason why Roman Catholics find it presumptuous when an evangelical Christians says, "I *was* saved," using the past tense, and can even give the day and the hour when that happened, "once for all," at a certain time in the past.

5. Austin Flannery, ed., *Vatican Council II*, rev. ed. Vol. 1 of *The Conciliar and Post Conciliar Documents* (Northport, N.Y.: Costello, 1988), 365–68.

6. *Fox's Book of Martyrs*, edited in 1978 by W. B. Forbush, is currently available from Zondervan Publishing House.

As the size and power of America's central government have continued to expand and as the weapons of that government have been turned against religious people, it is understandable that conservative Catholics and evangelicals have come to recognize the importance of greater cooperation. Several facets of this newly evolving evangelical-Catholic partnership have great significance.

What were some of the forces that helped bring about this growing cooperation? Who are some of the key players? Why do some evangelicals oppose it? What are some of the arguments in favor of increased partnership?

ESSAY
8

EVANGELICAL AND CATHOLIC COOPERATION IN THE PUBLIC ARENA

Ronald Nash

Cooperation between evangelicals and Roman Catholics in America's public arena continues to expand in spite of the numerous theological differences between the two groups. That warrants a look at some of the forces that helped to bring it about, at some of the people who have become players in this growing cooperation, at some of the reasons offered by evangelical critics who oppose it, and at some of the arguments that support the partnership. One of the things I find most fascinating in all this is the contrast between where America stood religiously, politically, and culturally in 1960, when Americans elected their first Roman Catholic president, and in 1993, when two very liberal Southern Baptists ascended to the American presidency and vice presidency.

During the 1960 presidential campaign, many American evangelicals and fundamentalists were gravely concerned about how John F. Kennedy's Roman Catholic beliefs might affect the way he would govern America. Now those fears appear a bit ludicrous in light of what is now known about Kennedy's indifference to both his religious and marital vows. One reason Kennedy won the 1960 election was his success in deflecting concerns about his Catholicism. His most important feat in this matter was convincing many conservative Protestants that he really did believe in an "absolute" separation of church and state. But, as evangelical author Os Guinness has noted, Kennedy's commitment to the separation of church and state was absolute for reasons that were poorly understood in 1960. Kennedy "was largely uninterested in religion. With little personal faith to relate to public life, his sense of conflict [between church and state] was minimal."[1] Repeating a joke of sorts heard from many Catholics, Guinness explains that the lesson many Catholics learned from Kennedy's presidency "was that you don't have to be Catholic to be president."[2]

Thirty-two years later, a member of a Southern Baptist church occupies the White House, and large numbers of evangelicals and Roman Catholics are appalled by what they see as his contribution to the continuing decline of morality in America. Continuing questions and alleged revelations about his character and the support that his administration has lent to various left-wing causes—including the advancement of the homosexual, pro-abortion, radical feminist, and politically correct agendas, along with the assaults his supporters have made against traditional religious and family values—makes it safe to predict that if Clinton seeks reelection in 1996, millions of the same Protestants who voted against Kennedy will welcome the opportunity to vote for a conservative Roman Catholic such as William Bennett.[3] In my judgment, this type of shift in the political thinking of America's conservative Protestants is striking, at least to anyone old enough to remember the election of 1960.

So we have two presidents who, while ostensibly representing two religious constituencies that clashed in 1960, are nonetheless similar in many ways, including some that are not discussed publicly in polite company. They stand as bookends on either side of a period in which gigantic changes have occurred.

CHANGES WITHIN THE AMERICAN CATHOLIC CHURCH BETWEEN 1960 AND 1993

Many believe that the single most important factor behind the dramatic changes within American Catholicism since 1960 was the Vatican II church council that took place between October 1962 and December 1965. Though some portrayed the council as an attempt by the Roman Catholic Church to face up to the problems of modernity, theologically liberal and politically radical Catholics interpreted the results of the council in ways that created enormous confusion within Catholic circles and helped encourage movement toward more liberal political and theological beliefs and practices.

Roman Catholic author Kevin Perrotta is understandably reluctant to place too much blame for his church's recent problems upon a Catholic church council. Nonetheless, he admits that Roman Catholicism has been much more open to change since 1965, including changes that have hardly been praiseworthy for Christendom. In Perrotta's mind, the growing elasticity of Catholic belief and practice after Vatican II must also be traced to significant changes in American culture:

> Catholics let down their guard just at the moment when family life was losing its honored place in American culture, the sexual revolution was entering a more radical phase, selfism was being proclaimed more blatantly, the secular feminist movement was being launched, and the tone of public life was becoming more hostile than ever before to Christian values. Entering the mainstream, many Catholics were carried along by these powerful anti-Christian currents.[4]

During the sixties, Perrotta reports, Catholic attendance at Sunday services dropped from 75 percent of total members to 50 percent. Between

1966 and 1978, some ten thousand priests resigned from the priesthood. The number of religious sisters declined between 1965 and 1985 by some seventy thousand, effecting a major crisis in Roman Catholic school systems. Enrollment in Catholic schools declined by more than a third between 1965 and 1983.[5] By the middle of the eighties,

> The percentage of Catholics attending church had stabilized at a level much lower than before [Vatican II]. The exodus of priests and sisters had slowed, but the number of applicants remained below replacement level of those retiring. Some religious congregations of these groups seemed bound for extinction. Thus, while the number of Americans who identify themselves as Catholics was larger than ever, their degree of commitment, as evidenced in faithfulness to corporate worship and willingness to leave all to serve the Kingdom of God, was much less than it was before the council.[6]

Among Roman Catholics, the rate of both divorce and sexual activity outside marriage jumped dramatically. Equally disturbing for Perrotta, "A national organization of Catholics promoting abortion appeared, as did two national organizations of Catholic homosexuals which did not regard the Christian prohibition of homosexual practice as an absolute."[7] Large numbers of American Catholics now reject the moral and social teaching of their church.[8] Many Catholics simply ignore what their church teaches about birth control, abortion, homosexuality, and sexual chastity outside of marriage.

During the three decades under review, Roman Catholicism has also changed theologically. Conservative Protestants and Catholics used to share a common worldview that saw the world as the creation of an Almighty God who has the power and the will to act supernaturally within His creation. Roman Catholics and evangelicals used to share a common commitment to many essential Christian beliefs, including the Trinity, the deity of Christ, the Virgin Birth, the resurrection of Christ, and the final judgment that would separate humans into saved and lost. But this too has changed. In the last few decades, large numbers of Catholic professors, priests, and sisters have adopted ideas from various forms of Protestant liberalism. This has led many Catholic thinkers to adopt a hostile biblical criticism that has compromised the inspiration and authority of Scripture along with an antisupernaturalism that rejects the essential miracles of the Christian faith. As Perrotta explains, "Ideological trends in theology—feminism, the blending of Christianity with either Marxism or classical liberalism, secular trends in Scripture study, remissive trends in moral teaching—all represent serious and historically novel departures from Christian orthodoxy."[9]

This loss of faith is now apparent on the campuses of most of the best-known Catholic universities.

Recent Catholic theologians who have questioned the teaching authority of the pope and traditional Catholic formulations of Christian faith have generally advocated reinterpretations of Christianity which are essentially similar to those of secularizing Protestant theologians. Thus many Catholic and Protestant theologians find the supernatural aspects of Christian teaching implausible for modern men and women, are uncomfortable with the exclusive claims of historic Christianity,[10] see the Scriptures as basically human and culture-bound religious documents, downplay the effects of the fall of man and the need for personal faith in Christ, and recast the Christian message in terms of feminism or leftist revolution.[11]

Consequently, "Many Catholic institutions of higher learning do not accept any responsibility for offering Catholic teaching in their doctrinal and moral courses."[12] Such Catholic schools, Perrotta warns, have become de facto secularized schools.

It is the battle over this kind of unbelief that is the real issue in the dispute between radical and liberal Catholics and the pope. Richard John Neuhaus was correct when he pointed out that John Paul II "is exercised *not about dissent but about apostasy.*"[13] "It conveys a feeling of relief," Neuhaus continues,

that at last somebody, John Paul, is calling the [Catholic] church to order, is seizing a few unruly adolescents by the scruffs of their necks and knocking some sense into their heads. In short, there is a sense of being fed up, of having had enough, of refusing to take it anymore. No doubt many Catholics, along with church authorities, feel they have been subjected to extreme provocations. When, for example, at the end of the 1970s the Vatican finally withdrew from the European theologian Hans Küng the license to represent himself as a Roman Catholic theologian, the response of many Roman Catholics was to wonder why it took so long.[14]

Though this chapter does not have these kinds of religious developments as its major focus, the theological tensions within Catholicism have helped to create a climate in which Catholic and Protestant conservatives have become more aware of the important common ground they share. Although evangelicals and traditional Roman Catholics are far apart on many doctrinal issues, as several chapters in the present volume attempt to show, their common commitment to tenets of the historic Christian creeds means they are much closer to each other on those matters than they are either to Protestant or Catholic liberals. That fact is not without relevance in the growing evangelical-Catholic partnership on political and social issues.

American Catholicism has also changed politically during the last three decades. Evangelicals who were concerned about John F. Kennedy's liberalism greatly underestimated the conservatism of America's Catholics. During the fifties and sixties, one writer reports, conservative Catholics "wore their religious identity as a badge of honor."[15] What the author means is that many Americans thirty years ago were social conservatives precisely because they were Catholic. One way to get a sense of this is to go back and study old issues of William F. Buckley, Jr.'s, *National Review.* Conservative Catholics ranked among this country's strongest opponents of Communism. They were thoughtful enemies of secularism, humanism, and the liberal welfare state.[16] When pollsters began to test public opinion on the abortion issue in the early sixties, Roman Catholic opposition was far greater than that found among Protestants.[17]

But during the last three decades, large cracks have appeared within the political and social thinking of educated Catholics as various ideologies such as neo-Marxism, the New Left, and democratic socialism began to have a greater impact in Catholic circles.[18] The 1985 Pastoral Letter on the American economy published by the Catholic bishops of America was one indication of how things were going within the hierarchy of the American church. The letter was essentially a neo-Marxist critique of capitalism coupled with a plea for an expansion of the liberal welfare state and continued redistribution of wealth.

After interviewing a number of the bishops who supported the letter, Catholic writer Dinesh D'Souza published an article revealing that the typical bishop whose authority was being used to support highly questionable economic policies knew less about economics than a college freshman in the third week of a basic economics course. The title of D'Souza's article, "The Bishop of Pawns," was his way of suggesting that the real force behind the drafts of the pastoral letter were a few radical churchmen and intellectuals who had used the bishops' goodwill and general economic illiteracy to score a public relations victory for their left-wing agenda. Whereas many Catholic laypeople may have thought the pastoral letter reflected the bishops' detailed grasp of the issues, it turned out—D'Souza discovered—that the bishops themselves had no idea what they were talking about.[19]

Growing Catholic support for more hard-core Marxist views has been apparent in the unexpectedly rapid spread of liberation theology within important segments of Catholic (and Protestant) thinking. Put in the simplest possible terms, liberation theology is a movement that downplays the historic, doctrinal side of Christianity and emphasizes instead the importance of Christian action on behalf of poor and oppressed people. Liberation theology can appear attractive to dedicated Christians who find it easy to identify with the underdogs of the world. And what group of underdogs deserves compassion and help more than the poor and oppressed?

One thing that liberationists have tried to cover over is that their position has brought many of them to the brink of theological heresy. Many Catholic liberationists have been condemned by the Vatican for denying the Christian church's historic understanding of such essential beliefs as the Atonement and Resurrection. Many Protestant liberationists are heretical in similar ways.

Supporters of liberation theology want people to overlook the heavy Marxist presence in their system. They want people to think that liberation theology is simply a product of conscientious and compassionate Christians demonstrating their love and concern for the poor and oppressed. In truth, however, liberationists appear to care only about the poor and oppressed people who interest them; they never had anything to say about poor and oppressed people in Marxist countries. Liberationist efforts to address the issue of poverty have always done so from an unabashed and unrepentant Marxist perspective. What finally produced the collapse of liberation thought outside the U.S. and Western Europe was the set of incredible events that some now call "the revolutions of 1989." The sudden sweeping changes that affected Eastern Europe and that now have stabbed deeply into the heart of the former Soviet Union have unveiled once and for all what many economists and social theorists have argued for years: the bankruptcy of socialism. It helped neither the reputation nor the morale of the advocates of liberation theology that the revolutions of 1989 and the new Russian revolution of 1991 repudiated the very ideas they held dear.

Many better-known Latin American liberationists are now distancing themselves from their former beliefs and embracing, however tentatively, an idea once deemed unthinkable: that capitalism just might have something to offer the world's poor after all.

North American liberationists, however, are more intractable in their fanatical attachment to socialism. Those who dominate the mainline Protestant denominations and their left-wing allies within Roman Catholicism are not especially happy these days. They and their institutions may well be the last vestiges of the now discredited version of liberation theology. Their type of liberation theology supported means that were counterproductive because they impeded genuine and lasting progress toward the desired goal of genuine liberation. Liberationists understood little of how the poor may be delivered from economic oppression, opting only for repeatedly smaller pieces of an economic pie that, they insisted, could never grow larger. They were disturbingly complacent about democracy and noticeably lax about how the Christian faith deals with the most important kind of liberation— liberation from sin.[20]

Interestingly, the first shots in the Catholic battle over liberation theology were fired by John Paul II in his address to the General Conference of Latin American Bishops at Puebla, Mexico, in early 1979. The pope criticized efforts to politicize the gospel. He warned about people who

depict Jesus as a political activist, as a fighter against Roman domination and the authorities, and even as someone involved in the class struggle. This conception of Christ as a political figure, a revolutionary, as the subversive from Nazareth, does not tally with the church's catechesis. . . . [Jesus] unequivocally rejects recourse to violence. He opens his message to conversion to all. . . . His mission . . . has to do with complete and integral salvation through a love that brings transformation, peace, pardon, and reconciliation.[21]

Throughout the 1980s, Catholic supporters of liberation theology did everything they could to counter obvious Vatican opposition to their movement. The details of this debate are presented in my book, *Beyond Liberation Theology,* with coauthor Humberto Belli, a Nicaraguan Roman Catholic who is now minister of education in the Latin American nation that saw the Marxist Sandinistas use liberation theology as a tool in the perpetuation of their power.[22] But any doubts about where the pope stood on these matters was removed completely in his 1991 encyclical *Centesimus Annus*[23] and the 1992 "Catechism of the Catholic Church." As Robert Sirico, a Paulist priest and president of the Acton Institute in Grand Rapids, Michigan, observes, the new Catechism instructs Catholics that "they must take account of their pastors' belief that economic systems ordered around the idea of individual liberty and limited government also tend to promote the kind of moral virtues and social relationships that the church is interested in advancing."[24] As Sirico explains, "The Catechism makes clear that there will be no turning back from the developments of church social teaching made by *Centesimus Annus,* the 1991 encyclical that excited controversy by its explicit rejection of a third way between capitalism and socialism."[25]

To summarize this section, the influx of theological liberalism into the Catholic church has helped American Catholics realize the important common theological ground they have with biblically minded evangelicals. The growing support of many priests, bishops, and professors for left-wing political theories has helped to produce a similar appreciation of Catholic conservatives for their cultural soul mates within evangelicalism. In this second case, however, something new has been added. Because evangelical social thought has tended to lag far behind the social and cultural writings of conservative Catholics, a number of conservative Catholic writers have occasionally functioned as mentors to a growing number of conservative evangelical social activists. A short list of such Catholic thinkers would have to include Russell Kirk, William F. Buckley, Jr., Frank Meyer, Michael Novak, Richard John Neuhaus, and George Weigel.[26]

CHANGES WITHIN AMERICAN EVANGELICALISM BETWEEN 1960 AND 1993

The changes in Roman Catholicism just noted are matched by equally dramatic alterations within conservative Protestantism. Some of these changes are more relevant to a different kind of writing and must therefore be passed over quickly. In 1960, evangelicals and fundamentalists were still carrying on a civil war of sorts. Evangelical thinkers like Carl Henry, editor of *Christianity Today,* were pressing a scholarly assault against liberalism and neoorthodoxy. Some fundamentalist leaders acted as though every evangelical was a closet-liberal of some type. Some evangelicals responded as though the fundamentalist leaders were undereducated bigots with chips on their shoulders. It was not a happy time for conservative Protestantism in America.[27]

Thirty years later there really are some people around who insist on calling themselves evangelicals when their view of Scripture or some important Christian doctrines fall short of the evangelical test. Disciples of the "fighting fundamentalists" of three or four decades ago have not changed; they have simply shifted their hostility toward dissenting fundamentalists like Jerry Falwell, whom some describe as "the most dangerous man in America."[28] The evangelicals and fundamentalists who are in the middle of these two extremes continue to move closer together, both theologically and politically. The mention of Jerry Falwell serves as a reminder that in 1960, almost no one outside of Lynchburg had ever heard of the pastor of Thomas Road Baptist Church. The same was true of Pat Robertson, Francis Schaeffer, and a host of other evangelical pacesetters of today. The first notice a young lawyer named Charles Colson would receive occurred when people began to think of him as Richard Nixon's White House hatchet man. Still another indication of how far we've come in thirty years is that back in 1960 the explosive influence of the charismatic movement still lay in the future.

Although it is important to remember such things, these particular points of information are not especially relevant to the concerns of this chapter. One difference between sixties-style evangelicalism and our situation in 1993 is the contemporary abandonment of the political and cultural apathy of earlier evangelicals.

Within the lifetime of many readers of this book, evangelicals and fundamentalists regarded many of America's social problems as unworthy of their attention. This widespread disinterest in culture, society, and politics could be traced to a variety of causes. For some, it was a function of eschatological beliefs that taught that Christ's return for the church at the Rapture could occur at any moment, an event that would plunge the remaining world into the horrors of the tribulation period.[29] Since the best of human culture could come to naught in the next seven years, why waste one's time trying to improve it or save it? But a more significant reason for evangelical apathy in such matters seems to have been the lack of any widespread grounding of such Christians in the kind of worldview thinking encouraged so successfully in the ministry of Francis Schaeffer.[30]

Of course, evangelical social apathy thirty years ago existed in a world that was much different from today. Christian parents were concerned about a sexual and moral permissiveness that seems tame compared to today's moral climate. Three decades ago, schools did what they were supposed to do—namely, teach the content of essential subjects. Any teacher found distributing condoms or describing homosexual acts as a valid alternative to heterosexual marriage would have been fired on the spot.

Once Christians recognized their obligation to become social and political activists, something surprising began to happen: some evangelicals began to align themselves with the very liberal forces in America responsible for the disintegration of American society. The disintegration of the African-American family in America and the massive deterioration of the quality of life of America's poor is a direct, even if unintended, consequence of the misguided "compassion" of America's social liberals.[31]

Many socially active Christians lack a solid understanding of the social, political, philosophical, and economic issues that underlie effective public policy. It is one thing to care about the poor and to desire to help them in meaningful ways. But if we misunderstand the foundational issues, we risk supporting policies that will result in more harm being done to the poor.

It is bad enough that evangelicalism has been polarized by the continuing leftward drift of people who describe themselves as descendants of the Old Testament prophets. But unlike the biblical prophets of old, these evangelical leftists have aligned themselves with the very liberal statist establishment that is helping to destroy America economically and culturally. I will have more to say about this point shortly. For now, I must be content simply to note the parallels between the leftward movement of evangelicals and proponents of identical views within the Roman Catholic church. Even those who might dispute my analysis must concur that both evangelicalism and Catholicism today are in the midst of serious conflicts over important economic, political, and social issues.[32]

Unfortunately, the misadventures of contemporary Roman Catholic theology have their parallel within evangelicalism. Evangelicalism must now do battle with liberalizing tendencies within the broader evangelical movement. This can be seen in a diluted view of Scriptural authority as evangelical professors experiment with positions that deny or compromise biblical inerrancy and indulge a fascination with a neoliberal view of divine, special revelation that denies God any ability to communicate true propositions to human beings.[33] Occasionally, one encounters evangelical professors who promote variants of the finite god of process theology[34] or the Marxist god of liberation theology[35] or the pantheistic "god" of feminist theology.[36] Outside of evangelical education institutions, evangelical relief and development organizations often do a fine job of providing material assistance to needy people around the world but regrettably fail to accompany this material help with the gospel.[37] It seems clear that evangelicalism has acquired some theological baggage that few of us anticipated back in 1960.

But evangelicalism also surprised everyone, including its enemies, by returning to the focus of national attention. As Kenneth Wald explains,

> Of all the shifts and surprises in contemporary political life, perhaps none was so wholly unexpected as the political resurgence of evangelical Protestantism in the 1970s. Modernization theory had led many observers to treat traditional religion as a spent force in the United States and to discount its influence in the real world of national politics. Like other predictions associated with modernization theory, this assessment was rudely challenged by evidence that evangelical Christianity had achieved new strength and was ready to assert that power in political activity. The nomination of Jimmy Carter in 1976, the rise to national notice of organizations such as "Moral Majority," the restoration of spirited public debate about certain "moral" issues—all these signs of evangelical political awakening marked the return to national prominence of a force that knowledgeable observers had long ago written off.[38]

Dean Curry, a professor of government at Messiah College, expresses his own astonishment over this phenomenon:

> One of the most significant religious and sociological phenomena of the past twenty-five years is the emergence of theologically conservative Christianity as a cultural force in America. For over half a century, theologically conservative Christians—fundamentalists and evangelicals—lived in self-imposed exile on the periphery of public life. During this time, these conservative Christians wandered in a wilderness of cultural irrelevance, believing that this was the price to be paid for protecting the fundamentals of the faith against the onslaught of theological as well as secular modernism.[39]

Equally surprising to many is the extent to which Roman Catholics and other nonevangelicals have risen to the defense of evangelical activity in the public arena. Not surprisingly, it is *conservative* evangelicals who have been attacked for their political activity. Because evangelical and Catholic political liberals act in such harmony with their allies in the dominant liberal media and the major power structure in the Democratically controlled Congress and White House and the predominantly left-wing faculty on college campuses, they do not worry about such attacks.

Of special note is the openly displayed anger, fear, hatred, and bigotry exhibited toward evangelical conservatism from the far-left hierarchies of America's so-called mainline Protestant denominations. Not too long ago, these religious liberals were busy trying to get the federal government's help for causes and programs they supported. Reveling in their easy access to the citadels of power, these mainline liberals enjoyed chiding conservative Protestants for their supposed indifference to social issues—for ignoring what is called the social dimension of the gospel, which is simply a more polite label for the old social gospel. "All those guys ever do," the liberals pouted, "is preach what they call the gospel; they ignore everything else." Suddenly the shoe is on the other foot. Religious conservatives have discovered the social dimension of the gospel, something that for them is quite different from the old social gospel. Now the liberals wish that conservatives would go back to their churches and forget the political arena. Now the liberals tell us that evangelical political activity poses a threat to "civil liberties, to a healthy diversity of opinion, and to the hope that we can conduct public affairs free of the divisiveness of religious factionalism."[40]

Catholic defenders of evangelical conservatives dismiss such claims as rubbish. Religious conservatives, they counter, are doing essentially the same sorts of things that scores of other good American organizations have been doing for decades.[41] Evangelicalism's supporters in the Roman Catholic Church maintain that evangelicals have as much right to attempt to influence public society as other organizations. After all, that is precisely what theologically and politically liberal Christians have been doing for decades.

Many people think evangelicals have been getting unfair treatment from the media, the entertainment industry, and the academic world. As Richard John Neuhaus points out, "The pattern in the media and elsewhere is to use the term 'Fundamentalist' in a careless way that refers to anything we deem religiously bizarre or fanatical. . . . This pattern reflects intellectual laziness mixed with an unseemly measure of bigotry."[42]

According to Nathan Glazer, recent evangelical activity in the public arena should be understood as defensive, not offensive. This activity does not represent a sudden assault on a passive and tolerant society. Rather, it is a reaction to what religious conservatives see as an attack upon them and their values: "It is the great successes of secular and liberal forces principally operating through the specific agency of the courts, that have in large measure created the issues on which the Fundamentalists [and evangelicals] have managed to achieve what influence they have."[43] Glazer provides several examples to back up his claim:

Abortion did *not* become an issue because Fundamentalists [and evangelicals] wanted to *strengthen* prohibitions against abortion, but because liberals wanted to abolish them. . . . Pornography in the 1980s did *not* become an issue because Fundamentalists [and evangelicals] wanted to *ban* D. H. Lawrence, James Joyce, or even Henry Miller, but because in the 1960s and 1970s, under-the-table pornography moved to the top of the newsstands. Prayer in the schools did *not* become an issue because Fundamentalists [and evangelicals] wanted to *introduce* new prayers or sectarian prayers, but because the Supreme Court ruled against all prayers. Freedom for religious schools became an issue *not* because of any legal effort to *expand* their scope, but because the Internal Revenue Service and various state authorities tried to impose restrictions on them that private schools had not faced before.[44]

Perhaps the issue of who started these fights is now irrelevant. But it is helpful to remember that

> dominant power—measured by money, access to the major media, influence, the opinion of our educated, moneyed and powerful elites—still rests with the secular and liberal forces that created, through court action, the changes that have aroused Fundamentalists [and evangelicals]. What we are seeing is a defensive reaction of the conservative heartland, rather than an offensive that intends to or is capable of really upsetting the balance, or of driving the United States back to the nineteenth century or early twentieth century.[45]

Liberals have been so successful in getting their agenda adopted that it is easy for them to forget that "America is a many-cultured society, and that religion is an important component of many U.S. subcultures as well as of the larger culture."[46] Evangelicals are simply fighting back in an attempt to restore some balance and to regain some lost respect for beliefs and values that are important to them and have played an important role in the history of our nation.

To summarize this section, evangelicalism has undergone changes that mirror the growing split between political and theological liberals and conservatives in the Roman Catholic Church. But educated Catholic conservatives had never retreated into a religious ghetto, had never isolated themselves from America's public arena the way evangelicals did. Convincing people to leave a ghetto has often been difficult. After many fitful starts, the evangelical genie is out of the bottle and has no intention of turning back. Roman Catholic support for this new evangelical social activism has been an important factor in the growing maturity of evangelical social action.

As Richard John Neuhaus explains, "The public resurgence of [evangelical] Christianity is good both for Christianity and for America, because it returns to the national discourse a huge bloc of citizens previously estranged from . . . 'the public square.' "[47] Surely, Neuhaus continues, it is incumbent on nonevangelicals, "especially those who claim to understand our society, to do more in response to this ascendence of [evangelicalism] . . . than to sound an increasingly hysterical and increasingly hollow alarm."[48] It would be nice to think that some day perhaps America's militant secularists and religious liberals will take heed to Neuhaus's words.

It is important to observe that the size and power of the central government has continued to expand and as the weapons of that government have increasingly been turned against religious people, it is understandable that conservative Catholics and evangelicals have come to recognize the importance of greater cooperation. The time has come to examine a few arguments for and against this cooperation.

THE DEBATE OVER
EVANGELICAL-CATHOLIC COOPERATION

A few days ago, I opened a large envelope in my mail and found a sample copy of a new, privately published newsletter. The headline for that month's issue grabbed my attention: "Christianity [meaning evangelicalism] and Catholicism—An Unholy Alliance."[49]

The article began by attacking evangelicals such as Charles Colson, Randall Terry, James Kennedy, and Pat Robertson for their efforts to promote an alliance between evangelicals and Roman Catholics in America's cultural and political arena. All but a few sentences in the very long piece focused on the theological differences between evangelicals and Catholics, coupled with the insinuation that any cooperative effort would involve evangelicals in a serious compromise of their religious beliefs. I mention this publication to illustrate the strong feelings one can still encounter in some pockets of fundamentalism.

A year or so ago, a friend who was pastoring a church in the Northeast told me how his efforts to get his fundamentalist church involved in fighting abortion met with powerful resistance from a faction that argued that standing in a long line of people to show support for the pro-life position might result in some folks in the church standing next to and even holding hands with a Catholic. The leadership in my friend's church found that an unthinkable act. The pastor decided that what was truly unthinkable in his situation was continuing to minister to folks like that; he resigned and moved to a different church.

About the same time the aforementioned newsletter reached my mail box, I chanced upon a 1989 article in the Catholic monthly *Crisis,* written by the distinguished constitutional attorney William Bentley Ball. (Ball incidentally has often come to the legal aid of Protestant institutions threatened by people interested in using the power of the state to curtail the legitimate rights of Christian schools and churches.) In his article "We'd Better Hang Together," Ball argues that conservative Protestants and Catholics had better begin to recognize the importance of working together. As his subtitle indicated, "It's Time for a New Alliance Between Catholics and Evangelicals."

Ball began his article by paying tribute to evangelicals, describing them as "the most dynamic force in American Protestantism today."[50] Evangelicals, Ball went on to say, "are building schools throughout the land, amassing in their churches converts from other faiths, playing a highly visible role in the pro-life movement, and preaching what they hold to be Biblical principles for a moral public order."[51] These born-again Christians, he continued, stress "the need for separation, in family and social life, from a 'pagan' culture, take in their stride accusations that they are fanatical, self-righteous, negative, and censorious. In spite of persistent battering by the national media, they are growing in number and strength."[52]

Ball notes the occasional, often sporadic cooperation between evangelicals and Catholics in the past, usually occurring during presidential elections or more typically in pro-life causes. When the Moral Majority was still active, he reminds us, one-third of Jerry Falwell's organization was Roman Catholic.

Naturally, Ball is aware of the serious disagreements between Catholics and evangelicals. But, he argues, "While the orthodox Catholic and the traditional Protestant [evangelical] differ on historic issues such as the papacy, tradition, and the sacraments, these issues do not have direct consequence in terms of public issues in the United States today. Too often forgotten by both evangelicals and Catholics are areas of doctrine which both share." Because of our common commitment to a shared orthodoxy expressed in the historic creeds of the church, he continues, Catholics and evangelicals insist "upon certain moral principles which are at once vital to the public order and gravely threatened, [and] it is important for the common good that Catholics and evangelicals join minds and hands for the promoting of these principles."[53]

Imagine that we are walking along one of Florida's seaside beaches when we hear a man screaming that his younger daughter is caught in a riptide and is being dragged into deeper water. "Please help my daughter," he shouts. "I cannot swim, and she's going to drown!"

Rushing to the man's side, a lifeguard asks for the direction of his daughter. Suppose the father then pauses, looks at the lifeguard, and says, "Before you save my daughter's life, I am compelled to ask you one question. What church do you attend?"

I can only assume that the author of the newsletter I mentioned would applaud the father's action. I can only assume that he would object if his house caught fire and he discovered a Roman Catholic and evangelical working together to save his family. How, I am compelled to ask, can there be any religious scandal or offense in such cooperation? After all, as Ball points out, "Not a syllable of doctrine or conviction is put on the negotiating table when fully cooperative action takes place between conservative evangelicals and Catholics on issues on which they not only doctrinally agree but on which they are morally bound to act."[54]

Attorney Ball wins this debate hands down. It is time for fundamentalists to recognize that if we do not hang together we most surely will hang separately. The time for evangelical-Catholic cooperation within the public arena has come.

NOTES

1. Os Guinness, *The American Hour* (New York: The Free Press, 1993), 170.

2. Ibid., 171.

3. Bennett's name appears here only as an example of the kind of potential Catholic candidate with whom evangelicals and fundamentalists would be comfortable.

4. Kevin Perrotta, "The U.S. Catholic Church," in *Evangelical Renewal in the Mainline Churches,* ed. Ronald Nash (Westchester, Ill.: Crossway, 1987), 143–44.

5. See ibid., 144.

6. Ibid., 144–45.

7. Ibid., 145.

8. Ibid., 146.

9. Ibid., 155.

10. See Ronald Nash, *Is Jesus the Only Savior?* (Grand Rapids: Zondervan, 1994).

11. Perrotta, "The U.S. Catholic Church," 147–48.

12. Ibid., 155.

13. Richard John Neuhaus, *The Catholic Moment* (San Francisco: Harper & Row, 1987), 99.

14. Ibid., 99.

15. Paul Gottfried, *The Conservative Movement,* rev. ed. (New York: Twanye, 1993), 34.

16. See ibid., 36.

17. See ibid., 35.

18. For discussions of these ideologies, see Ronald Nash, *Poverty and Wealth* (Dallas: Probe, 1992) and *Social Justice and the Christian Church* (Lanham, Md.: University Press of America, 1992). Perhaps the best-known purveyor of neo-Marxism was the philosopher Herbert Marcuse.

19. See Dinesh D'Souza, "The Bishops as Pawns," *Policy Review,* no. 34 (Fall 1985): 50–56.

20. For more on liberation theology, including a detailed account of its historical development among both Catholic and Protestant ideologues, see Humberto Belli and Ronald Nash, *Beyond Liberation Theology* (Grand Rapids: Baker, 1992).

21. John Paul II, "Opening Address at Puebla," in *The Pope and Revolution: John Paul II Confronts Liberation Theology*, ed. Quentin L. Quade (Washington, D.C.: Ethics and Public Policy Center, 1982), 53–54.

22. See Humberto Belli, *Breaking Faith* (Westchester, Ill.: Crossway, 1985).

23. See Belli and Nash, *Beyond Liberation Theology,* 53–54, 190–94.

24. See Robert Sirico, "Embracing the Market Economy, In Good Faith," *Wallstreet Journal,* 23 December 1992. Sirico's article does a good job of summarizing important economic and political emphases in the Catechism.

25. Ibid.

26. Two of Russell Kirk's books that illustrate what one can learn from him are *The Conservative Mind,* 7th rev. ed. (Washington, D.C.: Regnery Gateway, 1986), and *The Root of American Order* (Washington D.C.: Regnery Gateway, 1991). Buckley's many books include *Up From Liberalism* (Lanham, Md.: Madison, 1985). Frank Meyer's most important book was *In Defense of Freedom* (South Bend, Ind.:

Regnery/Gateway, 1962). For an extended analysis of Meyer's contributions, see Ronald Nash, *Freedom, Justice and the State* (Lanham, Md.: University Press of America, 1980), chaps. 1 and 4. Novak's books include the following: *The Spirit of Democratic Capitalism* (New York: Simon & Schuster, 1982), *Will It Liberate? Questions About Liberation Theology* (Mahwah, N.J.: Paulist, 1986), and *The Catholic Ethic and the Spirit of Capitalism* (New York: The Free Press, 1993). Two examples of Richard John Neuhaus's writings are *The Naked Public Square* (Grand Rapids: Eerdmans, 1986) and *Doing Well and Doing Good* (New York: Doubleday, 1992). George Weigel's important books are *Tranquillitas Ordinis: The Present Failure and Future Promise of American Catholic Thought on War and Peace* (New York: Oxford Univ., 1987) and *Catholicism and the Renewal of American Democracy* (Mahwah, N.J.: Paulist, 1989).

27. For one account of those days, see Ronald Nash, *The New Evangelicalism* (Grand Rapids: Zondervan, 1963).

28. For a discussion of the old and new branches of fundamentalism, see Ronald Nash, *Evangelicals in America* (Nashville: Abingdon, 1987), chap. 8. For discussions of Francis Schaeffer, Jerry Falwell, and Pat Robertson, see chap. 7 of the same book.

29. For a critical analysis of this position, see Ronald Nash, *Great Divides* (Colorado Springs: NavPress, 1993), chap. 10.

30. For an account of worldview thinking that extends Schaeffer's approach to new limits, see Ronald Nash, *Worldviews in Conflict* (Grand Rapids: Zondervan, 1992).

31. For a defense of this claim, see Nash, *Poverty and Wealth*, chap. 16. See also Charles Murray, *Losing Ground: American Social Policy 1950–1980* (New York: Basic Books, 1984).

32. See Nash, *Great Divides,* chaps. 1, 3 and 7.

33. See Ronald Nash, *The Word of God and the Mind of Man* (Phillipsburg, N.J.: Presb. & Ref., 1992) and also chap. 11 of Ronald Nash, *The Closing of the American Heart: What's Really Wrong with America's Schools* (Dallas: Probe, 1990).

34. See Ronald Nash, *The Concept of God* (Grand Rapids: Zondervan, 1983) and *Is Jesus the Only Savior*, chaps. 8 and 10.

35. See my books *Beyond Liberation Theology*, already cited, or *Liberation Theology* (Grand Rapids: Baker, 1987).

36. See my book, *Great Divides*, chap. 3.

37. See the following: Amy Sherman, "Where You Lead I Will Follow," *First Things* (February 1993), 5–6; Thomas Guterbock, "What Do Christians Expect from Christian Relief and Development," *Stewardship Journal* 2 (Summer/Fall 1992), 23ff.; and Nash, *Is Jesus the Only Savior?* chap. 12.

38. Kenneth D. Wald, *Religion and Politics in the United States* (New York: St. Martin's, 1987), 182–83.

39. Dean C. Curry, "Biblical Politics and Foreign Policy," in *Evangelicals and Foreign Policy,* ed. Michael Cromartie (Washington, D.C.: Ethics and Public Policy Center, 1989), 43.

40. Nathan Glazer, "Fundamentalism: A Defensive Offensive," in *Piety and Politics,* ed. Richard John Neuhaus and Michael Cromartie (Washington, D.C.: Ethics and Public Center, 1987), 247.

41. See Clifford G. Kossel, "The Moral Majority and Christian Politics," *Communio* (1982), 340.

42. Richard John Neuhaus, "What the Fundamentalists Want," in *Piety and Politics,* 12. Even though Neuhaus's move from Lutheranism to Roman Catholicism occurred after he wrote these words, there has been no shift in his position.

43. Glazer, "Fundamentalism: A Defensive Offensive," 250.

44. Ibid.

45. Ibid., 251.

46. Ibid., 245.

47. Neuhaus, "What the Fundamentalists Want," 3.

48. Ibid., 18.

49. The name of the publication is *A Layman's Perspective*. The issue in question had no date but was simply labeled No. 4.

50. William Bentley Ball, "We'd Better Hang Together," *Crisis* (October 1989): 17. The article appears on pp. 17–21.

51. Ibid., 17.

52. Ibid.

53. Ibid., 20.

54. Ibid.

Ecumenism has done much to foster increased understanding between evangelicals and Roman Catholics, allowing them to work together in a number of important areas, especially concerning personal and social ethics. However, some fundamental differences remain, the doctrine of justification being the most important. Some of these differences have stemmed from misunderstandings, others from genuine disagreements.

What is the relation between the official teachings of the Roman Catholic Church and the private views of individual Roman Catholics? How will this affect the form future relations between evangelicals and Roman Catholics will take? The long-term implications are considered.

ESSAY
9

WHAT SHALL
WE MAKE OF
ECUMENISM?

Alister McGrath

Following World War II, the word *ecumenism* achieved saturation coverage in the Christian media and beyond. The agenda of the mainline Christian churches was dominated by the need for denominations to come back together after the disruptions of the war.[1] The World Council of Churches (WCC) emerged as a focus for these endeavors. Ecumenism attracted attention for some time, being widely seen as the most important item on the mainline Protestant agenda; now it is receding into the background as other more pressing issues come to the fore. "Ecumenism," a colleague remarked to me a few years ago, "has become the last refuge of the theological bore." Whether he was right or not is open to debate, but he certainly identified a widespread feeling of weariness over the ecumenical agenda in recent years. In part, this disillusionment is due to the totally unrealistic attitude of those who were convinced that Christian unity was just around the corner. Doctrinal differences could be swept to one side in a euphoric drive to come together.

An excellent example of this can be provided from the English scene. On September 18, 1964, the First British Conference on Faith and Order surprised itself by declaring that it would work for the union of all the British churches "not later than Easter Day, 1980."[2] That date has long since passed, as have the hopes of those who so naively believed that reunion could be achieved without addressing the deep doctrinal issues that divided the churches in the first place. Too often, ecumenism appears to rest on a doctrine of "cheap grace," refusing to address the real issues in order to achieve a cheap ecumenical fix in which a paper-thin and artificial "unity" is gained at the price of ignoring or sidestepping the questions that really matter. "Unity at any price" seemed to be the philosophy underlying some of the more irresponsible projects of that era.

The issue of doctrinal divergence is of special importance to the relationship between Protestant and Roman Catholic churches. Such dialogues have discovered that the agenda of the Reformation obstinately refuses to go away and that the central questions of scriptural authority, the role of Mary, and the assurance of salvation remain controversial today. There is thus a new atmosphere of realism: only by facing theological issues honestly can any progress toward Christian unity be made. The agenda of the Reformation cannot be ignored by any who hope to bring Protestants and Roman Catholics closer together. This point is stressed in an important recent essay by Don Carson (Trinity Evangelical Divinity School).[3] While noting substantial points of agreement between evangelicalism and Roman Catholicism, he rightly points out that issues of major importance remain to be addressed and resolved—such as the locus of revelation, the means of grace, the nature of the church, and the significance of Mary. The agenda of the Reformation remains on the ecumenical table today.

Despite these reservations, however, there is clearly a growing feeling among some sections of evangelicalism that increased collaboration between evangelicals and Roman Catholics, at least on some issues and at some levels, is going to be of increasing importance in the future. If Western culture continues to slide into an increasingly secular outlook, should not those who believe in, for example, the divinity of Christ and the reality of the Resurrection join forces, despite their differences on other matters, in order to ensure that the Christian voice is heard on these vital issues? Again, given that evangelicals and Roman Catholics share a common concern for the unborn, should they not join forces to form a coalition on this issue? To work together on such issues does not imply agreement on a larger scale but a willingness to work together in those limited areas where agreement on ideas or values makes it possible.

Many evangelicals have sensed hostility toward theological liberalism in Roman Catholic circles and welcomed this as an antidote to liberal trends within historic Protestantism, which they believe, with justification, to be destroying those former bulwarks of evangelicalism. Thus, where the WCC has tended to dismiss evangelism as "Christian imperialism," Pope John Paul II has stressed the importance of evangelism for the church as it seeks to make the good news of Jesus Christ known to the world. In his encyclical letter *Redemptoris Missio,* John Paul II stressed that "proclamation is the permanent priority of mission. The Church cannot elude Christ's explicit mandate, nor deprive men and women of the 'Good News' about their being loved and saved by God."[4] The encyclical speaks movingly of the full riches of the gospel in terms with which most evangelicals can sympathize:

> The subject of proclamation is Christ who was crucified, died and is risen: through him is accomplished our full and authentic liberation from evil, sin and death; through him God bestows "new life" that is divine and eternal. This is the "Good News" which changes humanity and their history, and which all peoples have a right to hear.[5]

It is no accident that some evangelicals have chosen to become Roman Catholics, sensing that there is an institutionalized orthodoxy over a series of vital issues that the mainline Protestant churches have betrayed.[6] A further issue is that of "evangelical catholicity," a theme classically associated with the Mercersburg theology but which has begun to reemerge as significant for some evangelicals.[7]

In the light of these developments, a real need exists to reappraise the ecumenical endeavor, especially to identify its positive and negative potential for evangelicals. In what follows, I shall explore the issue with special reference to one doctrine of fundamental importance: justification by faith. My reason for doing so is simple: it is the doctrine with which I am most familiar and which allows us insights into both the European Reformation of the sixteenth century, and the ecumenical discussions of the twentieth.

JUSTIFICATION BY FAITH:
A CASE STUDY

In recent years, a number of ecumenical discussions have focused on the doctrine of justification by faith. On September 30, 1983, the U.S. Lutheran –Roman Catholic dialogue group released a 24,000-word document that represented the fruit of six years of discussions on the doctrine of justification. This document, entitled *Justification by Faith,* is by far the most important ecumenical document to deal with the theme of justification to date and represents a landmark in ecumenical discussions. This has been followed by the report of the Second Anglican–Roman Catholic International Commission (ARCIC II) titled *Salvation and the Church,* published on January 22, 1987. In this section, I propose to examine some difficulties in the modern discussion of justification, with particular reference to these documents.[8]

The European Reformation of the sixteenth century saw the battle lines drawn between Roman Catholics and Protestants over the doctrine of justification by faith alone. For the Protestant Reformers, the doctrine of justification was the "article by which the church stands or falls."[9] The Roman Catholic Church, in their view, had fallen over this doctrine and thus lost its credibility as a genuinely Christian church. For the Reformers, this more than adequately justified breaking away from the medieval church in order to return to the authentic teaching of Scripture. The Reformers, by reclaiming the insights of the New Testament and Augustine of Hippo, were able to assert that they had recovered the biblical doctrine of justification by faith.[10]

But what were the differences between Roman Catholic and Protestant teachings on justification in the sixteenth century? We may make an immediate distinction between two types of differences: those that were actually *misunderstandings* (where both sides were saying more or less the same thing but misunderstood each other); and those that were *disagreements* (where both sides understood precisely what the other was saying and regarded it as unacceptable).

SIXTEENTH-CENTURY MISUNDERSTANDINGS

It is clear that both Protestants and Roman Catholics agreed on the following (although their discussion of them was confused by some difficulties that we shall note below):

1 We cannot take the initiative in beginning the Christian life—it is God who moves first. Original sin prevents our finding our way back to God unaided by grace. Popular Catholic religion in the later Middle Ages was obsessed with the doctrine of justification by works, however, pointing to a radical divergence between what theologians taught and what the common people believed. Although some evangelicals continue to insist that the Roman Catholic Church officially teaches justification by works, that is not the case.[11]

2 The foundation of the Christian life is the work of Christ and not anything we ourselves can do. Once more, popular Catholic piety tended to lay considerable emphasis upon merit and showed an obsessive interest in the various ways in which this merit could be gained and stored, rather like funds in a bank account.

3 Although the Christian life is not begun on the basis of good works, good works are the natural result of and expression of genuine Christian faith.

4 The Christian life takes place at the communal, not just the individual, level. By beginning the Christian life, the believer finds himself within a community of faith.

None of these points was the subject of dispute between responsible informed theologians in the sixteenth century; the difficulties arose primarily in relation to how these points were expressed.

An excellent example of these difficulties is provided by the term *justification* itself. Following Augustine of Hippo, the Council of Trent defined justification in terms of "making righteous." Trent's comprehensive definition of justification makes clear that "justification" includes both the initiation and the subsequent development of the Christian life, as the believer grows in holiness and righteousness. Augustine's interpretation of the postclassical Latin term *iustificare* as *iustum facere* reveals his celebrated etymological shortcomings, although the importance of this point would not be appreciated until the sixteenth century.[12]

On the basis of the new advances in philology associated with the Renaissance, and especially the new interest in the Hebrew text of the Old Testament, both Lutheran and Reformed theologians recognized that the verb *to justify* was forensic, meaning "to declare or pronounce to be righteous," and not "to make righteous."[13] Although the Reformers had a great respect for Augustine, they had no hesitation in criticizing him when the direct study of the Hebrew and Greek texts of Scripture showed him to be wrong. Augustine's definition of what justification itself actually was came to be recognized as a classical case of an error arising from the use of the Latin version of Scripture, rather than Scripture in its original language.

The Reformers, therefore, rejected the tradition hitherto predominant within the Western church concerning the meaning of the term *justification* and, by doing so, added considerably to the difficulties of the sixteenth-century debates on justification. For the simple fact was that Protestants and Roman Catholics used the term *justification* to mean rather different things. For the Protestant, justification refers to the external pronouncement on the part of God that the sinner is regarded as righteous in His sight (*coram Deo*), thus marking the beginning of the Christian life. For the Roman Catholic—who, in this matter, continues the common teaching of the Western church, deriving from Augustine—*justification* means both the *event* by which the Christian life is initiated and the *process* by which the believer is regenerated. In other words, Trent understands by justification what the Protestant understands by justification *and sanctification (or regeneration) taken together.* This semantic difference led to enormous confusion at the time, as it still does to this day.

To illustrate this point, consider the following two statements.

1. We are justified by faith alone.
2. We are justified by faith and by holiness of life.

In terms of popular polemics, the former is generally identified as the Protestant position and the latter as the Roman Catholic position. To the Protestant, the first statement stipulates that the Christian life is begun through faith alone, which is obviously right, in that it corresponds to the New Testament teaching on the matter. To the Roman Catholic, however, the same statement implies that the Christian life is begun through faith alone *and continued* in faith alone, which is obviously a travesty of the New Testament teaching on the matter, which makes explicit reference to the Christian life being continued in holiness, obedience, and good works.

Now consider the second statement. To the Roman Catholic, this would naturally mean that the Christian life is *begun* through faith and *continued* in holiness of life, which is obviously an excellent summary of the New Testament teaching on the matter. To the Protestant, however, the same statement means something very different: that the Christian life is begun through faith and holiness of life, which is virtually Pelagian and a gross distortion of the New Testament teaching on the matter. In fact, it will be obvious that the first statement (understood in the Protestant sense) and the second (understood in the Roman Catholic sense) are actually saying more or less the same thing, but the convergence is obscured by the different understandings of the term *justification.*

It will be obvious that Protestant theologians were not for one moment suggesting that it was possible to be justified without being sanctified: they were simply insisting upon a *notional distinction* between the two concepts, distinguishing *at the conceptual level* two ideas that had hitherto been regarded as essentially the same thing. On the basis of their new and more reliable knowledge of Hebrew philology, the new understanding of justification was totally justified, making correction of Augustine on this point both necessary and acceptable. Although the Reformers vigorously upheld Augustine's ideas on grace, they felt perfectly free to correct his interpretation of Scripture where it was based on bad Hebrew.

SIXTEENTH-CENTURY DISAGREEMENTS

As we noted in the previous section, there was an important degree of agreement between Protestants and Roman Catholics on the doctrine of justification in the sixteenth century. Perhaps we could summarize the situation by suggesting that both were committed to anti-Pelagian Christocentric theologies of justification. Nevertheless, alongside this real, if obscured, agreement was genuine disagreement, where each side understood perfectly well what the other was saying, and took exception to it. It is here that the real focus of the Reformation controversies is to be found. Two matters regarded as being of central importance at the time were:

1. The nature of justifying righteousness (sometimes also referred to in the period 1575–1700 as the "formal cause of justification").
2. The question of assurance (which is closely linked with the nature of justifying righteousness).

We have space to consider only the first of these two issues, although their organic connection should be noted.

Luther insisted that justifying righteousness was *iustitia aliena Christi*, a righteousness extrinsic to believers, covering them protectively in much the same way a mother hen might cover her chicks with her wing.[14] Substantially the same position was taken up by both Lutheran and Reformed theologians, who held that justifying righteousness is not a righteousness inherent to believers but one outside us. God effects our justification from outside us, prior to effecting our renewal within us. The righteousness of justification is perfect and imputed, whereas that of sanctification is imperfect and inherent. The point the Reformers wished to emphasize was that the righteousness of the saints was permanently imperfect and therefore could not function as the basis of the divine verdict of justification. We are accepted on the basis of a perfect righteousness—the righteousness of Christ.[15]

The Council of Trent, however, meeting in 1546–1547 to formulate the Roman Catholic response to the Reformation doctrines of justification, insisted that the single formal cause of justification was an inherent righteousness, a righteousness within the believer. Although stressing that this righteousness was provided by God, Trent equally insisted that it was located within the believer as part of his person. The Reformers found this idea inconsistent: if God's verdict of justification was not to be a legal fiction, it would have to be based on a perfect righteousness, and if this righteousness was inherent to believers, how could Trent speak of believers *growing* in righteousness when they already possessed a perfect righteousness? It seemed to the Reformers that any inherent righteousness was, by its very nature, imperfect and in need of supplementation—and the imputation of the alien righteousness of Christ dealt with this difficulty.

For the Reformers, it was necessary to know that one was a Christian, that the Christian life had indeed begun, that one had been forgiven and accepted by God, and, on the basis of this conviction, the living of the Christian life (with all its opportunities, responsibilities, and challenges) could proceed. Being justified on the basis of the external righteousness of Christ meant that all that needed to be done for an individual's justification had been done by God. So the believer could rest assured that he *had* been accepted and forgiven. The Reformers could not see how Trent ensured that individual believers were accepted, despite being sinners. For if believers possessed the perfect righteousness that ensured their justification, they could no longer be sinners—yet experience (as well as the penitential system of the Catholic Church!) suggested that believers continually sinned. For the Reformers, the Tridentine doctrine of justification was profoundly inadequate in that it could not account for the fact that believers were really accepted before God while still remaining sinners. The Reformers were convinced that Trent taught a profoundly inadequate doctrine of sin, with an equally inadequate doctrine of justification as a result. The famous phrase, due to Luther, sums up this precious insight with brilliance and verbal economy: *simul iustus et peccator*—"righteous and a sinner at one and the same time." Luther is one of the few theologians ever to have grasped and articulated the simple fact that God loves and accepts us just as we are—not as we *might* be, or *will* be, but as he finds us.

As the Tridentine debates on justification make clear, Trent recognized exactly what Protestant theologians were saying on this matter—and explicitly rejected it. Although a number of theologians present at Trent clearly sympathized with the Protestant position, they were outnumbered and out-maneuvered by their colleagues.[16] This was no misunderstanding but a deliberate, weighed, and explicit rejection of the Protestant position.

Here, then, is an area where there was genuine and apparently insuper-able disagreement between Trent and the Reformers in the sixteenth century. As even the most superficial survey of Protestant and Roman Catholic polemical writings from 1550 on makes clear, it is in relation to these two questions—the nature of justifying righteousness and the question of assurance—that the real divisions were perceived to lie. It is thus of some considerable interest to note that it was precisely these two questions (originally not on Trent's agenda, incidentally; they had to be added later, when it was obvious that they could not be avoided) that caused the long delay in the formulation of the decree on justification. (Indeed, at one point it seemed that Trent would not be able to say *anything* about the question of assurance, so difficult was it proving to reach agreement).

It will therefore be clear that any attempt to engage with the *real* differences between Protestants and Roman Catholics over the doctrine of justification must be addressed to these two questions, which *historically* were regarded as central. There is little to be gained from recapitulating what was agreed in the sixteenth century (although that agreement was, of course, obscured by polemics and terminological differences), unless it can be shown that these two issues are no longer of any importance.

JUSTIFYING RIGHTEOUSNESS IN THE LUTHERAN–ROMAN CATHOLIC DISCUSSIONS

The U.S. Lutheran–Roman Catholic dialogue group report noted above, *Justification by Faith*,[17] represents a landmark in ecumenical discussions. Earlier, I pointed out how sixteenth-century controversies on justification were of two types: those that rested upon *misunderstandings,* and those that reflected genuine *disagreements.* This document addresses both. Misunderstandings are resolved along the following lines:[18]

1 Christians have no hope of final salvation and basis for justification before God other than through God's free gift of grace in Christ, offered to them through the Holy Spirit. Our entire hope of justification and salvation rests on the promises of God and the saving work of Jesus Christ, expressed in the gospel.

2 As a result of original sin, all human beings—whoever they are and whenever and wherever they live—stand in need of justification.

3 Justification is a completely free act of God's grace, and nothing we can do can be said to be the basis or ground of our own justification. Even faith itself must be recognized as a divine gift and work within us. We can-

not turn to God unless God turns us first. The priority of God's redeeming will and action over our own actions in bringing about our salvation is expressed (and its mystery safeguarded) by the doctrine of predestination.

4 In justification we are declared righteous before God, and the process of making us righteous in His sight through the renewing action of the Holy Spirit is begun. In that justification, we receive by faith the effects of the death and resurrection of Jesus Christ as we respond personally to the gospel (the power of God for salvation), as we encounter the gospel through Scripture (the proclamation of the Word of God) and the sacraments, and as it initially awakens and subsequently strengthens faith in us.

5 Whoever is justified is subsequently renewed by the Holy Spirit and motivated and enabled to perform good works. That is not to say that individuals may rely on these works for their salvation, because eternal life remains a gift offered to us through the grace and mercy of God.

The document goes further than this, however, by dealing at some length with real questions of disagreement, and it is to be applauded for doing so, instead of attempting to marginalize or ignore them. It is the willingness to engage with these genuine points of difference that earns this document its abiding place in the ecumenical discussion of justification. The question of the nature of justifying righteousness is dealt with in detail (e.g., §§ 98–104), and no attempt is made to disguise the fact that real differences between the churches remain on this issue. It is recognized that the concepts of justification by an extrinsic and intrinsic righteousness are totally different: although neither excludes the other, they are not identical. The dialogue group expresses the hope that they may be *complementary,* but the gross error of suggesting that they are substantially the same, reflecting only verbal differences, is avoided. The fact that there are "remaining differences" (§§ 88, 154, 157) between the two churches on a number of important aspects of the doctrine is explicitly acknowledged; this is interpreted, however, in terms of *complementary* rather than *contradictory* approaches to the doctrine. In this way, the document recognizes the quite distinct approaches to the doctrine associated with the two churches, arguing that they are complementary and convergent, rather than contradictory and divergent.

This elimination or resolution of misunderstandings and disagreements allows the dialogue group to make the following affirmation, in which the tension between the two ways of understanding justification is maintained:

Our entire hope of justification and salvation rests on Jesus Christ and on the gospel whereby the good news of God's merciful action in Christ is made known; we do not place our ultimate trust in anything other than God's promise and saving work in Christ. Such as [sic] affirmation is not fully equivalent to the Reformation teaching on justification according to which God accepts sinners as righteous for Christ's sake on the basis of faith alone; but by its insistence that reliance for salvation should be placed entirely on God, it expresses a central concern of that doctrine. Yet it does not exclude the traditional Catholic position that the grace-wrought transformation of sinners is a necessary preparation for final salvation.[19]

The document thus affirms that the quite distinct ideas of forensic justification and justification by inherent righteousness are two ways of conceptualizing essentially the same theological principle:

It must be emphasized that our common affirmation that it is God in Christ alone whom believers ultimately trust does not necessitate any one particular way of conceptualizing or picturing God's saving work. That work can be expressed in the imagery of God as judge who pronounces sinners innocent and righteous . . . , and also in a transformist view that emphasizes the change wrought in sinners by infused grace.[20]

The crucial question of the formal cause of justification—the *real* crux of division in the sixteenth century—is thus resolved by suggesting that both positions (justification by an alien or extrinsic righteousness, and justification by an intrinsic righteousness) are appropriate (but not *identical*) ways of conceptualizing the ultimate foundation of our justification in the action of God in Jesus Christ. The document recognizes that this is no mere difference of words—it amounts to quite distinct theological frameworks, vocabularies, hermeneutics, emphases, and manners of conceptualizing the divine action. The fundamental point the document wishes to affirm is that both positions are legitimate ways of attempting to safeguard the same crucial insight.

THE ISSUE OF INDULGENCES

The doctrine of justification is not a purely theoretical affair, touching the minds of theologians but not the practices of the church. The early sixteenth century witnessed the culmination of a number of highly questionable trends in popular piety. Salvation was widely regarded as something that could be earned through good works. The confused and vague theology of indulgences lent weight to the suggestion that it was possible to buy either or both the remission of sins and the remission of purgatorial penalties, whereas the practice of paying for masses for the dead seemed to suggest that it was possible to buy salvation, or at least a diminished period of residence in purgatory.

Though such practices and beliefs may have at times been in conflict with the teachings of the more responsible schools of Catholic theology, the fact remains that no serious attempt was made to criticize or suppress them. In fact, the evidence suggests that they were tolerated to the point of being unofficially incorporated into the structures of the church in that the power and income of the ecclesiastical establishment was linked with the continuance of such practices and beliefs. Thus, in the early sixteenth century indulgences were a major source of papal revenue, and the practice of paying for masses for the dead provided a welcomed supplementation to clerical income. In an era in which ecclesiastical offices were frequently purchased, the buyer generally felt justified in at least looking for an appropriate return on his investment. As study after study of the late medieval church confirms, the idea that an individual could, for certain monetary considerations, ensure his salvation (and facilitate its progress) was of central importance to the financing of the ecclesiastical establishment.

The doctrine of justification by faith, with the associated idea of the "priesthood of all believers," thus assumed an importance that far transcended the sphere of academic theology. The doctrine effectively cut the ground from under the vested interests of these groups, threatening the basis of the practices and beliefs that secured their income and power. It is quite impossible to treat the doctrine of justification as if it were of purely academic interest, ignoring its obvious relevance to church life and practice, including such sixteenth-century practices as the selling of indulgences or beliefs such as purgatorial penalties upon which certain practices were based—because the doctrine calls such sixteenth-century practices and beliefs, *as well as their modern-day equivalents,* into question. Thus, Tommaso de Vio (Cardinal Cajetan) feared that Luther's emphasis upon the righteousness of Christ in justification would minimize the role of the church in mediating forgiveness to sinners. In treating the doctrine of justification as *articulus stantis et cadentis ecclesiae* ("the article by which the church stands or falls"), Luther stipulated that the doctrine of justification was the criterion by which the doctrine, structures, and practices of the church were to be evaluated, with a view to reforming them. This insight, it must be added, is incorporated into the chief confessional writings of Lutheranism, including the *Augsburg Confession* and the *Schmalkaldic Articles.*

The role of indulgences was thus of major importance at the time of the Reformation. But what role do indulgences play in Roman Catholicism today? In a final section, the Anglican–Roman Catholic document *Salvation and the Church* moves on to deal with "The Church and Salvation." This is by far the weakest section of the document. The entire discussion of the bearing of the doctrine of justification upon the life of the church—in other words, the *practical* questions that so aroused the Reformers—is abstract and unfocused. It is in this section that we have every right to look for, and find, a discussion of indulgences. After all, the historical origins of the Lutheran Reformation are linked with this practice, and there appears to be some degree of confusion within modern Catholic theology as to what the role of indulgences actually is. It is therefore of considerable importance that we have a *magisterial* pronouncement on indulgences, not just the views of some individual Roman Catholic theologians (the reliability of which varies considerably), but an authoritative statement by the teaching office of the Roman Catholic Church as to what the function of indulgences actually is. ARCIC II cannot flee from history: attention must be given to the question of what was actually at stake in the indulgences controversy of the sixteenth century and how such differences may be, or have been, re-solved.

As John Frith, the greatest of the neglected English Reformers, pointed out, the doctrine of justification by faith necessarily called the doctrine of purgatory into question. Indulgences, purgatory, and prayer for the dead (which *Salvation and the Church* apparently brings into the debate at § 22 for reasons that are not clear)—all these ideas and practices, brought into the discussion on account of the broadening of the theme from "justification" to "salvation and the church," point to areas of continuing divergence. As one leading Lutheran ecumenist points out, the question of how the doctrine of purgatory may be reinterpreted or revised in the modern period is an ine-vitable part of any genuine engagement with the doctrine of justification. "Catholic interpretations of purgatory leave Lutherans with nagging ques-tions: was Christ's work insufficient, and do our works somehow have mer-it?" Paul VI may have refined Trent's stipulations on indulgences, but the basic framework it presupposes (purgatory and purgatorial penalties, for in-stance) remains as unacceptable to Protestants, whether Anglican or other-wise, as it has always been.

Once more, the wisdom of *Justification by Faith* must be noted. In dis-cussing the question of how an individual may be said to apply the satisfac-tion of Christ, this document noted:

> Further study will be needed to determine whether and how far Lutherans and Catholics can agree on these points, which have far-reaching ramifications for traditionally disputed doctrines such as the sacrament of penance, Masses for special intentions, indulgences and purgatory. These questions demand more thorough exploration than they have yet received in this or other dialogues.

It is a pity that ARCIC II did not seize this opportunity to pursue this study, with a view to clarifying the bearing of the doctrine of justification on these beliefs and practices. For the indulgence question remains of impor-tance. It is at this point that the interaction of theology (the doctrine of justi-fication) and the life of the church (for example, the practices of praying for the dead, the obtaining of indulgences, and so forth) becomes clear, indicat-ing that the doctrine of justification cannot be discussed in a purely theoreti-cal manner. It must be grounded in the life and practice of the church.

The simple fact of the matter is that indulgences are not some obscure and antiquated sixteenth-century practice that can be dismissed as no longer of any importance or relevance in ecumenical discussion. The modern Roman Catholic teaching on indulgences has been stated and clarified in three documents, dating from 1967 (*Indulgentiarum doctrina*, of Paul VI), 1968 (The new *Enchiridion of Indulgences,* issued by the Sacred Apostolic Penitentiary), and 1983 (the new Code of Canon Law of the Roman Catholic Church). This last, it must be noted, was not taken into account by the U.S. Lutheran–Roman Catholic Dialogue Group, simply because it had not appeared by the time their deliberations on justification were complete. Let me quote two sections from this new code of canon law.

> 992. An indulgence is the remission before God of the temporal punishment due for sins already forgiven as far as their guilt is concerned. This remission the faithful, with the proper dispositions and under certain determined conditions, acquire through the intervention of the church which, as minister of the redemption, authoritatively dispenses and applies the treasury of the satisfaction won by Christ and the saints.

> 994. The faithful can gain partial or plenary indulgences for themselves or apply them for the dead by way of suffrage.

The casual reader of ARCIC II's report might gain the impression that the sixteenth century debate in indulgences had led to the matter being resolved. Yet here we have the same basic ideas being restated in substantially the same form within the last ten years. How, one wonders, can agreement be reached when this matter is so obviously outstanding?

It seems to me that there is only one answer to this question, and that it rests on a single phrase in § 32. "We believe that our two communions are agreed on *the essential aspects of the doctrine of salvation.*" This phrase "the essential aspects of the doctrine of salvation" seems to hold the key to ARCIC II's approach to the sixteenth-century debate on justification: indulgences are not to be regarded as an essential *aspect* of the doctrine of salvation. I think we must ask ARCIC II to be honest on this point and ask this very specific question to which we have a right to a very specific answer: Are the 1983 canons on indulgences an essential aspect of the Roman Catholic doctrine of salvation? I think ARCIC II would be obliged to say no. But as a historian, I have to say that the sixteenth-century answer given by the representatives of the Roman Catholic Church to its Protestant critics, in England and elsewhere, was rather different. After all, John Frith was burned at Smithfield in 1533 for denying that purgatory was a necessary dogma! There are clearly some difficult questions that need to be addressed here.

THE NEW UNOFFICIAL ECUMENISM:
THE SHAPE OF THE FUTURE?

In the above analysis, I have indicated reasons for suggesting that there are deep issues that remain unresolved within Protestant–Roman Catholic ecumenical discussions. I have limited my analysis to the doctrine of justification; had I extended this analysis to include, for example, the issue of the authority of Scripture, the role of Mary in salvation, or the theology of the sacraments, similar concerns would have emerged along a much wider front. For this reason, it is necessary to express a certain degree of skepticism concerning the future of such official discussions between the Protestant churches and the Roman Catholic Church. They have gotten as far as they can.

Yet there is a flaw in my analysis, and it is possible that the identification of the flaw in question may help us understand why there is growing collaboration between individual Roman Catholics and evangelicals. My analysis thus far rests on the assumption that individual Roman Catholics accept the authority of the official teachings of their church. The empirical evidence available suggests that large numbers of them do not. The widespread refusal to obey the Vatican's explicit teachings on artificial methods of birth control is simply one symptom of something much deeper: a tendency to value the Roman Catholic ethos, at least in part, while being selective concerning those aspects of its teaching that are appropriated.[21] The result is that many Roman Catholics, especially in the United States, remain outwardly and publicly loyal to their church, while inwardly and privately embracing some of the leading ideas of evangelicalism. (This contrasts sharply with the situation in Latin America, where a growing sympathy with evangelicalism has led to a public rejection of Roman Catholicism and an equally public embrace of the theological ideas and styles of worship of various forms of evangelicalism.)[22]

This observation is of major importance, as it relates directly to the conditions under which evangelicalism became of significance in the early sixteenth century. The term *evangelical* originally dates from the sixteenth century and was used to refer to Catholic writers wishing to revert to more biblical beliefs and practices than those associated with the late medieval church. Writers such as Barry Collett (University of Melbourne) have shown how evangelical attitudes toward the personal appropriation of salvation and the spiritual importance of the reading of Scripture emerged during Italian Benedictine monasteries in the late fifteenth century. The attitudes and approaches he describes parallel directly those of modern evangelicalism.[23] Similarly, E. M. Jung and other scholars of the later Italian Renaissance have identified a major spiritual movement—which becomes particularly important among the Italian aristocratic laity in the 1520s—

placing an emphasis on a personally-appropriated salvation.[24] Through an obvious lack of familiarity with Christian spirituality, Jung used the term *evangelism* to refer to this movement. It is clear that it is simply a form of evangelicalism, which can be paralleled throughout Europe during this period. In short, as Clair Davis has shown in chapter 2, there is now ample historical evidence to the effect that evangelical attitudes were espoused, whether privately or publicly, by leading figures of the Catholic Church in the late Middle Ages.

One of the most important features of the late Renaissance is the growth of lay religion, and the increased demands on the part of a Christian laity throughout Western Europe for a form of Christian spirituality that was of direct relevance to their personal spiritual concerns. It must be remembered that much medieval spirituality was developed by monastic writers and intended to be read within a monastic context. There was an urgent need for the evolution of forms of the Christian faith that related to the spiritual needs and concerns of an increasingly demanding laity.[25] Martin Luther's doctrine of justification, with its emphasis upon the faith and assurance of the individual, proved to be what they were looking for.

It can be shown without difficulty that such evangelical attitudes were not initially regarded as a threat by ecclesiastical authorities; indeed, they were even welcomed in some areas as making an overdue and positive contribution to the renewal of the spiritual vitality of a tired church. The Italian church in particular was deeply and positively affected by the emergence of evangelicalism during the 1530s. Several cardinals of the period were profoundly influenced by evangelical attitudes, which they did not regard as inconsistent with their senior positions within the church. It was only in the mid-1540s, when an increasingly anxious church, alert to the growing threat posed by northern European Lutheranism, condemned such attitudes as destabilizing, that evangelicalism went off-limits. The reason for this development? The church authorities had become convinced that to be an *evangelical* was to be a *Lutheran* and, hence, to be anti-Catholic.

The term *evangelical* is especially associated with the 1520s, when the French term *évangélique* and the German *evangelisch* began to feature prominently in the controversial writings of the early Reformation. In the 1530s, the term *Protestant* came to become more significant; increasingly, this came to be understood simply as anti-Catholic. However, it must be appreciated that this term was imposed upon evangelicals by their Catholic opponents and was not one of their own choosing. The term *Protestant* referred originally to the "protest" of the six princes and fourteen south German cities at the second Diet of Speyer (1529) against the rescinding of the guarantee of religious freedom set out by the *first* Diet of Speyer, three years earlier. In the German language, for historical reasons, the term *evangelisch* has now become more or less equivalent to Protestant and has lost its original meaning; this has not happened in English, on account of the deliberate decision to prevent this confusion from taking place. (Since the 1940s there has been a determined, and largely successful, effort on the part of the English-speaking heirs of the Reformation to recover the older term, and rehabilitate it, evident in the formation of the National Association of Evangelicals in 1942).

Evangelical is thus the term chosen by evangelicals to refer to themselves, representing most adequately the central concern of the movement for the safeguarding and articulation of the *Evangel*—the good news of God, which has been made known and made possible in Jesus Christ. The term *Protestant* too easily implies an obsession with some system of church government (such as presbyterianism), which can come to overshadow more important concerns relating to the gospel itself. Evangelicalism refuses to allow any matter of church government to take precedence over the gospel itself; the term *evangelical,* by placing emphasis upon this gospel, conveys both the emphasis and the substance of the movement. All else is deliberately subordinated, as a matter of principle, to this central theme.

Evangelicals generally are aware of the need for a well-informed biblical model of the church; they remain generally unpersuaded, however, that the New Testament intended to lay down *precise* details of church polity. A corporate conception of the Christian life is not understood to be specifically linked with any one denominational understanding of the nature of the church. In one sense, this is a "minimalist" ecclesiology; in another, it represents an admission that the New Testament itself does not stipulate with precision any single form of church government that can be made binding upon all Christians. Those who accuse evangelicals of having "immature" or "underdeveloped" theories of the church might care to ask themselves whether they might not have hopelessly overdeveloped theories. More recently, even Roman Catholic biblical scholarship—traditionally wedded to static and highly authoritarian concepts of the church—has recognized that the New Testament portrays the church in dynamic and evolving terms, using a variety of images to represent it.[26]

And it is for these reasons that many Roman Catholics appear to be attracted to evangelicalism. They sense that its concern for the gospel overshadows the lesser issue of church order. A disinclination to obey blindly each and every aspect of their church's official teaching allows them to embrace privately many of the ideas and values of evangelicalism, while retaining at least the vestiges of an outward loyalty to their church. (Interestingly, the term "Nicodemism" was used in the sixteenth century to refer to Roman Catholics, especially in France, who were outwardly loyal to their church, while privately admiring and responding to the writings of John Calvin.)

If this analysis is correct, it follows that evangelicalism can expect to gain a growing hearing within Roman Catholicism in the next decade. It will do so, not on account of any official institutional sympathy for the movement, but on account of a growing interest in and admiration for the movement on the part of individual Roman Catholics.

CONCLUSION

So what are we to make of ecumenism? I am convinced that talking to Christians of different persuasions is of major importance. We must acknowledge that there is a real danger of misunderstanding and misrepresentation; talking with others is one way of ensuring that we do others the justice that we would like them to do us. It helps clear up those misunderstandings and allows us to see how different terminologies can sometimes conceal at least some degree of agreement. In the past, evangelicals have misrepresented Roman Catholicism (not, I think maliciously; more out of confusion over the terminology used by the Council of Trent); ecumenical dialogue has sometimes helped us see them in their true light. We owe it to Roman Catholics to take the trouble to get them right, instead of perpetuating, whether by accident or design, inaccurate stereotypes of their beliefs.

Yet I have indicated that there are limits to how far *official* ecumenism will take us. For there comes a point at which misunderstandings are removed and a hard core of *real disagreements* over issues of major substance still remains unresolved. The radical agenda of the Reformation remains on the table, with Luther's Wittenberg hammer-blows still resounding throughout the church. Although there are theoretical models available to allow Roman Catholicism to take on board the Reformation agenda without significant loss of face,[27] I do not expect these to be taken up in the near future. The official dialogue between Protestantism and Roman Catholicism has probably gone as far as it can go, and it would be unrealistic to look to it for further progress.

But what I do expect to happen is this: an "unofficial" ecumenism will grow in both its extent and influence, with individual evangelicals exploring the attractions of Roman Catholicism (as shown by Kim Riddlebarger) and increasing numbers of individual Roman Catholics being drawn to evangelicalism *while generally remaining publicly loyal to their church.* In the short term, this will probably lead to a growing warmth between individual evangelicals and Roman Catholics, despite the substantial official doctrinal divide between them. I would expect this to be catalyzed by a growing sense that Christianity as a whole needs to stand up at every level against an increasingly militant secular culture, with local collaboration being seen as a legitimate way for Christians to come together and fight for their mutual rights. It is not my intention to defend or criticize this trend; I am simply reporting it and assessing its basis and potential impact. It is something that evangelicalism needs to be aware of.

I may be wrong. Ecumenism is yesterday's idea and is widely seen as a spent force. But the kind of ecumenism that seems to be emerging at street level is of a very different kind. It could well be a major force in the shaping of America's religious future in general and the evangelical future in particular. It is imperative that we understand this new ecumenism if our evangelical churches are to retain their theological distinctives in a healthy way.

NOTES

1. See Ruth Rouse and Stephen C. Neill, *A History of the Ecumenical Movement, 1517–1948* (London: SPCK, 1954).

2. For an eyewitness account, see John Wenham, *The Renewal and Unity of the Church in England* (London: SPCK, 1972), 10–12.

3. Donald A. Carson, "Evangelicals, Ecumenism and the Church," in K. S. Kantzer and C. F. H. Henry, eds., *Evangelical Affirmations* (Grand Rapids: Zondervan, 1990), 347–85.

4. *Redemptoris Missio: Encyclical Letter of the Supreme Pontiff John Paul II on the Permanent Validity of the Church's Missionary Mandate* (London: Catholic Truth Society, 1991), par. 44.

5. Ibid. I have altered the translation at one point to allow for inclusive language.

6. It must be noted, however, that other issues are involved. Many evangelicals feel that evangelicalism has a deficient sense of history, a limited appreciation of the role of liturgy in public worship, and no awareness of the importance of the sacraments, and believe that these deficiencies are corrected by Roman Catholicism. Anglicanism is proving attractive to some evangelicals for such reasons, especially on account of the growing evangelical presence within its ranks: see Robert E. Webber, *Evangelicals on the Canterbury Trail* (Waco, Tex.: Word, 1985); Alister E. McGrath, *The Renewal of Anglicanism* (Wilton, Conn.: Morehouse, 1993).

7. See Linden J. De Bie, "Saving Evangelical Catholicism Today," *New Mercersburg Review* 6 (1989): 11–21; Gabriel Fackre, "Evangelical Catholicity," *New Mercersburg Review* 8 (1990): 41–50. Donald Bloesch describes "catholic evangelicalism" in *Future of Evangelical Christianity* (Garden City, N.Y.: Doubleday, 1983).

8. "Justification by Faith," *Origins: NC Documentary Service* 13/17 (1983): 277–304; *Salvation and the Church: An Agreed Statement* (London: Church House Publishing/ Catholic Truth Society, 1987).

9. On this, see Alister E. McGrath, "The Article by which the Church stands or falls," *Evangelical Quarterly* 58 (1986): 207–28. I also explore the centrality of this doctrine in "Karl Barth and the *articulus iustificationis*. The Significance of His Critique of Ernst Wolf within the Context of His Theological Method," *Theologische Zeitschrift* 39 (1983): 349–61, and "Der articulus iustificationis als axiomatischer Grundsatz des christlichen Glaubens," *Zeitschrift für Theologie und Kirche* 81 (1984): 383–94.

10. The historical development of the doctrine of justification is exceptionally complex. See Alister E. McGrath, *Iustitia Dei: A History of the Christian Doctrine of Justification,* 2 vols. (Cambridge: Cambridge Univ. Press, 1986).

11. The origins of this evangelical belief are difficult to trace. As Peter Toon (*Evangelical Theology 1833–1856: A Response to Tractarianism* [London: Marshall, Morgan

and Scott, 1979], 141–70) has shown, it is certainly present in English evangelical polemics of the first half of the nineteenth century.

12. See McGrath, *Iustitia Dei,* 1:40–51; 2:1–3.

13. See ibid., 2:23–6, 31–2, 68–72.

14. See ibid., 2:10–13.

15. For a full analysis, see Alister E. McGrath, *Luther's Theology of the Cross: Martin Luther's Theological Breakthrough* (Oxford/Cambridge, Mass.: Blackwell, 1985).

16. Cardinal Reginald Pole is an excellent example: see Dermot E. Fenlon, *Heresy and Obedience in Tridentine Italy* (Cambridge: Cambridge Univ. Press, 1972).

17. "Justification by Faith," *Origins: NC Documentary Service* 13/17 (1983): 277–304.

18. Ibid., §156, pp. 297–98, which I have paraphrased at this point.

19. Ibid., §157, p. 298.

20. Ibid., §158, p. 298.

21. For a witty literary exploration of such themes by a leading English Roman Catholic novelist, see David Lodge, *How Far Can You Go?* (Harmondsworth: Penguin, 1980). (American edition published under the title *Souls and Bodies.*)

22. See David Martin, *Tongues of Fire: The Explosion of Protestantism in Latin America* (Oxford: Blackwell, 1990); David Stoll, *Is Latin America Turning Protestant?* (Berkeley: Univ. of California Press, 1991). For an excellent assessment of still more recent developments, see Karl-Wilhelm Westmeier, "Themes of Pentecostal Expansion in Latin America," *International Bulletin of Missionary Research* 17 (1993): 72–78.

23. Barry Collett, *Italian Benedictine Scholars and the Reformation* (Oxford: Clarendon, 1985).

24. E. M. Jung, "On the Nature of Evangelism in Sixteenth-Century Italy," *Journal of the History of Ideas* 14 (1953): 511–27.

25. For the emergence of Reformation spirituality and an assessment of its distinctive features, see Alister E. McGrath, *Roots that Refresh: A Celebration of Reformation Spirituality* (London: Hodder & Stoughton, 1992). A revised version of this book appeared under a different title in the United States in 1994 (Zondervan).

26. See Avery Dulles, *Models of the Church: A Critical Assessment of the Church in All Its Aspects* (Garden City, N.Y.: Doubleday, 1974).

27. Such as that set out in Alister E. McGrath, *The Genesis of Doctrine* (Oxford/Cambridge, Mass.: Blackwell, 1990).

PART
4
THE
WAY
AHEAD

A number of noted evangelicals have recently converted to the Roman Catholic Church. Why is this happening? The reasons fall into two categories.

The first is exemplified by Thomas Howard, who perceived an "incompleteness" about evangelicalism and a lack of stress upon history, liturgy, the sacraments, and aesthetics. The second category is represented by former Presbyterian minister and current Catholic apologist Scott Hahn, whose conversion involved many of the historic theological differences that characterize the nearly five hundred years of division between Protestants and Roman Catholics.

10

NO PLACE LIKE ROME?
Why *Are* Evangelicals
Joining the Catholic Church?

Kim Riddlebarger

There are undoubtedly as many reasons evangelicals become Roman Catholics as there are individuals who convert to Roman Catholicism. Those who have left their Protestant and evangelical heritage for the Roman church do so for a variety of reasons. Many who have converted describe intense personal struggles and painful crises of conscience associated with every step of their journey. It is not an easy pilgrimage from Wheaton to Rome. And each evangelical who converts to Roman Catholicism, it seems, has a compelling story to tell and a list of diverse reasons underlying the experience. There are, however, several common factors identified by recent converts that help answer the question, Why are evangelicals joining the Roman Catholic Church?

After developing some necessary background information and then identifying general theological trends that set the context for answering this key question, I will attempt to identify and evaluate the primary reasons given by several recent converts to justify their conversion. Two primary categories of reasons are given. The first centers on a perceived incompleteness or insufficiency of evangelicalism, which is often related to a misconception that basic evangelical beliefs and Roman Catholic dogma are not necessarily at odds. However, the reasons given by converts falling into this category are often connected to the second category, which is composed of theological objections to Protestantism that are in many cases characteristic of the 450-year-old division between Protestants and Catholics.

Scott Hahn, a former Presbyterian minister (PCA) who is now a professor at the College of Steubenville, a Roman Catholic school in Steubenville, Ohio, converted from historic Protestantism to Roman Catholicism. Hahn is an outspoken apologist and articulate advocate for Tridentine Catholicism. He is convinced that what we are presently seeing in terms of the numbers of evangelicals making their way to Rome is but the tip of an emerging iceberg. Citing the perceived similarities between this burgeoning movement and the beginnings of the Oxford Movement more than 150 years ago, Hahn notes that, unlike the Oxford Movement, which culminated in the conversion of the highly respected and brilliant Anglican John Henry Newman, this new movement does not center so much on a single prestigious convert as it does in a number of well-known evangelical Protestants, all of whom have recently joined the Roman church. He argues that since this new movement is more diversified it is perhaps more significant.[1] There are no accurate figures available quantifying the number of evangelicals who have converted to Roman Catholicism, but it appears that there are a number of significant and noted individuals involved. Cataloging a veritable *Who's Who* of fellow converts, Hahn points out that noted former Protestants such as Peter Kreeft, Richard John Neuhaus, Malcom Muggeridge, William Farmer, Thomas Howard, as well as Hahn's friend and fellow Presbyterian pastor turned Catholic apologist, Gerry Matatics, have all recently converted to Catholicism. Hahn contends that the quality and reputation of the individuals involved demonstrates that this trend is something more substantial than any other such movement.[2]

Before proceeding further, it is important to point out that I am sympathetic to some of the reasons these men have given for their conversion to Roman Catholicism. I too was raised in evangelical fundamentalism, and I too struggled during my own conversion to orthodox Calvinism and historic Protestantism from a nonconfessional, nonliturgical, and Arminian theology, typical of much of fundamentalism. It was a painful and difficult journey. I have asked many of the same questions and spent many sleepless nights wrestling with God, as have many who have made the journey to Rome. I certainly empathize with their struggle, and I have more respect for someone who follows the road to truth as they see it than I do for those who never think to question the reasons underlying their particular doctrinal positions. But I also need to point out that the answers I have found in the Scriptures are *diametrically opposed* to the arguments raised by those who have converted to Catholicism. I unashamedly side with the Protestant Reformers generally, and with confessional Calvinism specifically, on all of the issues central to this debate.

It must also be candidly admitted, as David Wells, James Davidson Hunter, Carl F. H. Henry, Harold Lindsell, and Michael Horton have all recently pointed out,[3] that evangelicalism as a movement has reached an important crossroads, if not an outright theological crisis. At such an important and critical moment of definition for evangelicals, undoubtedly there will be those who have had enough of secularism under the guise of "evangelical" religion and who will jump ship for reasons of expediency or because of reasons of conscience. The converts listed by Scott Hahn are best viewed as indicative of the latter. Indeed, one can argue that much of what lies at the root of this turmoil can be located in the fact that as evangelicalism becomes increasingly secularized and continues to move away from its biblical and historic roots, in some cases abandoning outright its Protestant heritage and theological convictions, there will be many who sense that the only lasting solution to such an ideological vacuum is to turn to one of Western civilization's most visible and stalwart pillars against such secularization, the Roman Catholic Church. As evangelicalism as a movement begins to show signs of stress fracture and possible impending collapse, we should not be surprised that men of conscience would become Roman Catholics even for what many of us do not deem sufficient or proper reasons. In the midst of such upheaval, if evangelical leaders do not give those within their sphere of influence sufficient reasons to remain Protestants, and in many cases openly forsake their own Protestant heritage, why should we be surprised if many who are tired of our double-mindedness and lack of theological integrity now find Roman Catholicism to be a viable option? I can surely empathize with many of these converts, even if I cannot agree with their reasons. But I am still one of those Protestants who feels a twinge of sorrow when I hear of someone leaving an evangelical church to join the Catholic Church.

Despite the contentions of Scott Hahn and others that the objections that can be raised against Protestantism are sufficient to convince any honest inquirer that Roman Catholicism is the true expression of the Christian religion, not only have many of the issues been hotly debated since the time of the Protestant Reformation, but Protestants have effectively answered the arguments that Catholic polemicists raise against historic Protestantism. In many cases, former Protestants simply do not like the answers they receive. For others, the theological arguments ultimately do not matter anyway—Roman Catholicism fills some need or offers something that is beyond argument and debate. In some cases, weak or nonexistent answers from evangelical leaders expected to know better are treated as "the official Protestant position." What may appear to be formidable arguments for Roman Catholicism on the surface, do not fare as well when it is pointed out that the Protestant foil in the argument is often a straw man, who is easy to knock down but who does not represent either the authentic or the best of historic Protestantism. It is also easy to take the garish extremes of theologically illiterate televangelists and reactionary fundamentalists as representative of true Protestant conviction,[4] even though televangelists and fundamentalists have at times blatantly misrepresented the intentions and doctrines of the Roman church.[5] Further complicating matters, Karl Keating, noted Catholic lay apologist, laments that not only have Roman views been misrepresented by evangelical opponents, but Catholic laity are themselves often insufficiently catechized and actually contribute to this doctrinal confusion since they are frequently unable to articulate their faith accurately.[6] And unfortunately, in the resulting confusion, the spirit of argument has dropped below the belt on many occasions.

Not only are these issues not new, neither is the ethos underlying this new movement. A few, such as Hahn, express their conversion primarily in intellectual terms. These converts find the Roman arguments against key Protestant doctrines such as *sola fide* or *sola scriptura* to be compelling. They tend to be the most militant of the converts. Others who have converted to Roman Catholicism, it seems, possess a form of idealism bordering on Romanticism, which at times reflects the Victorian sentiment of the earlier Oxford Movement that often serves as a model and source of inspiration for these former Protestants. Many recent converts see the Roman Catholic Church as the sole source of the fulfillment of subjective longings that transcend a mere intellectual conversion to Roman Catholic theology. Such people find the beauty of the liturgy, the sense of history, the focus on the sacraments, and the stress on transcendence and mystery found in Romanism to be important reasons for leaving evangelicalism.

In an uncertain and irrational age, when the best biblical and theological arguments may not necessarily carry the day, the promise of an infallible church, a worldwide community of the faithful complete with magnificent cathedrals and beautiful liturgy, specialized religious orders, and effective and compassionate social concerns, just might. Though many evangelicals dismiss this important, if subjective, aspect of conversion to Catholicism, as simply a desire for "smells and bells," that opinion ignores important issues worthy of discussion. Subjective reasons are still reasons nonetheless and need to be evaluated accordingly. It is here, then, with concerns that evangelicalism is not a complete or sufficient expression of Christianity, that we will begin to evaluate the arguments given by those evangelicals who have converted to Catholicism.

THE ROMANTIC MOTIVATION

The one book that perhaps captures this romantic idealism and the subjective aspects of the attraction to Catholicism more thoughtfully than any other is Thomas Howard's *Evangelical Is Not Enough*.[7] Howard, a noted evangelical author and brother of Elisabeth Elliot, has perhaps correctly diagnosed that a major weakness of evangelicalism and fundamentalism is a lack of the sense of God's transcendence in Christian experience. *Evangelical Is Not Enough* is more, however, than a testimonial about one man's spiritual journey. It is a powerful apologetic against a uniquely American form of Protestantism, fundamentalism—a form of Christianity that Howard contends has virtually abandoned any emphasis upon community, history, liturgy, creeds, sacraments, and beauty. These contentions are not completely without merit. They are, ironically, important themes in much of historic Protestantism, though unimportant to many fundamentalists.

Howard begins the book by describing his journey away from his fundamentalist and evangelical roots: "My pilgrimage has led me to ancient forms of Christian worship and discipline that find little place in ordinary Reformational piety and vision."[8] Since the evangelicalism (actually the fundamentalist variety) of Howard's upbringing was dominated by parachurch organizations, interdenominational activities, and nondenominational churches, "we cited texts from the New Testament and nothing else. We never said, 'the church teaches so and so.'"[9] There was little sense of any historical identity that Christianity as an ancient faith has with its past. So Howard concludes, "The flavor of Evangelicalism is very different from that of the traditional church."[10] Thus, much of *Evangelical Is Not Enough* is a narrative of the author's search for a sense of the history and symbolism of the ancient church.

This revived quest to recover our Christian roots is one of the most important reasons evangelicals are suddenly finding themselves attracted to Catholicism. Since much of American life in general is rather ahistorical, fundamentalism and evangelicalism (to the degree to which these traditions are influenced by popular culture) often reflect a strange sense that Christianity *really* began with our own conversion or with that of our leaders. In those circles where there is *some* sense of historical identity, it is not uncommon to hear evangelicals and fundamentalists speak as if New Testament Christianity were somehow recovered via the efforts of some nineteenth-century evangelist. So when evangelicals begin to investigate their own Christian roots, they may find to their chagrin that the historic Christian faith is at many points quite different from fundamentalist and evangelical practice and teaching.

Christian history is important. Protestants contend, however, that the Reformation was an important correction of many of the teachings and practices of the medieval Roman church, which in many cases had buried the apostolic faith under such an accretion of superstition and unbiblical practice that the gospel was virtually obscured from the life of the church. Since we Protestants must first of all strive to be *biblical,* we nevertheless should also have a strong sense of historical identity that dates in one degree or another forward from the New Testament era—through Augustine, Anselm, and Thomas—up to the Reformation. Furthermore, we should have no trouble tracing our own Protestant heritage from the Reformation to the present day. Protestants have always identified with the Augustinian and Anselmic theological tradition. In a profound sense, it can be argued that the Reformation was an extension and amplification of that ancient tradition. The Reformers themselves were thoroughly conversant with the church Fathers and medieval doctors. Their children, the Protestant scholastics of both the Lutheran and Reformed variety, clearly availed themselves of the Thomistic theological methodology they inherited.

However, it is here, perhaps, that we see one of the most important places where historic Protestants and many of their evangelical and fundamentalist descendants will part ways. The Lutheran, Anglican, and Reformed traditions have a much stronger historical sense than do their American fundamentalist stepchildren, who tend not to be as confessionally or historically bound. But the key issue here is that the church should always be in the process of reform according to the Word of God. Yes, new is not always better, and yes, historically speaking, the ancient church looks and sounds different from much of American evangelicalism. But the question is really one of what the true church should look like according to the Word of God, and not what the actual church looks like in a fallen world. Not all the historical practices of the ancient church are supported by Scripture. And not all of the historical practices of the church are even supported by all the Christian tradition. Even a cursory reading of the ante-Nicene and post-Nicene church Fathers reveals a divergence of opinion in many areas. Ultimately, this boils down to the relationship between the authority of tradition and the authority of Scripture, and also the relationship of the church to that authority, a point discussed below.

On the issue of authority, Thomas Howard points out that as a fundamentalist he was taught to distrust the "Roman Catholic and Eastern Orthodox emphasis on the church as the guardian and teacher of Scripture"[11] because of the Protestant notion of *sola scriptura*. According to Howard, the "stress on the Bible alone calls for a complicated vocabulary of 'inerrancy' and 'verbal inspiration' that has never marked Catholic and Orthodox theology," because, in the Roman and Eastern traditions, believers "would look to the magisterium of the church, or to Holy Tradition, to keep the ancient faith intact."[12]

Here, then, is another reason many evangelicals are being drawn to Roman Catholicism. Many evangelicals have rejected the concept of *sola scriptura* in principle, either through the acceptance of the Roman Catholic/Eastern Orthodox conception of a "sacred tradition" as an equal authority with Scripture, or because of the charismatic movement, wherein many evangelicals are becoming increasingly open to the concept of God speaking to them directly (immediately) through "prophets" or popular "gurus," apart from the written Word of God. Thomas Howard argues that "sacred" tradition and "official" teachings of the church are of equal authority with Scripture. Many evangelicals appear to be comfortable with the concept of the bible *plus* something else as constituting authority for faith and practice.

Because Howard sees inerrancy as a complicated concept and therefore problematic, he now accepts the Roman magisterium as a source of infallible interpretation of the Bible, as though simply affirming such infallibility made it so. If the problem with the inerrancy of Scripture, according to Howard, is its complicated nature, what about the perennial problem of explaining just how it is that the Roman church champions doctrines that are not taught anywhere in Scripture and are often in direct contradiction to it (i.e., the Immaculate Conception of Mary, her bodily assumption into heaven, and her supposed role as our co-redemptrix)? What should we do if at least one stream of Christian tradition has always taught *sola scriptura*?[13] Why is *that* tradition not infallible?

One of Thomas Howard's primary concerns in *Evangelical Is Not Enough* is with Christian symbols and their use. After sneaking a peek into a neighborhood church as a youth, Howard recalls the accoutrements that adorned the church: stained glass, candlesticks, and an altar. He remembers, "I was filled with awe, and even something like rapture, at how beautiful, how august, everything was."[14] It was clearly a defining moment for Thomas Howard. Over the years Howard's interest in symbols came to fruition in his belief that the incarnation of our Lord forever reversed the idea that the secular could be separated from the spiritual, since in the Incarnation, "The Eternal Word became flesh. God became man. The spiritual became physical."[15] As Howard laments, "the Evangelicalism of my childhood church taught me true doctrine about the Incarnation. It taught me about Creation and about Eden and about the Fall. But somehow it never, at least in its piety, put Humpty-Dumpty back together again."[16] According to Howard, this puts the evangelical in a serious predicament. "By avoiding the dangers of magic and idolatry on the one hand, Evangelicalism runs itself very near the shoals of Manichaeanism on the other—the view that is that pits the spiritual against the physical."[17] This is, as Howard sees it, because evangelicals sought to locate religion solely in the heart, rather than in the whole realm of life, including symbols. This tendency to avoid symbols can "most readily be observed at a glance in [evangelicalism's] church buildings." The messages that evangelicals send by denying the validity of such symbols gives a "Manichaean hue to the faith."[18]

Thomas Howard is not the only one who feels this way. Franky Schaeffer, son of the late Presbyterian apologist Francis, and who has also recently departed from his own fundamentalist heritage for Eastern Orthodoxy, similarly laments the aesthetics of much of evangelicalism. Never known for letting his brethren off easily nor tactfully, Franky describes what this absence of transcendence has done to many an American "worship center," as symbols and beauty are lost as aspects of worship.

> Most contemporary American church buildings are symbolically ugly, accurately reflecting the taste of pastor and people alike. . . . The profound ugliness of these churches is not the result of budget priorities. These buildings are expensive; studied ugliness does not come cheap. Many of these church buildings seem to express the same sense of aesthetics as that of the living-room/kitchen set from the old "Dick Van Dyke Show." They constitute an assault on the senses: a nightmare of red velvet and prefab ceiling "tile," StainWare carpet in pastel shades from hell and the Easter Bunny, a Mt. Everest of canned sweet corn and lime Jell-O.[19]

Schaeffer's comments, though acrid in tone, raise an important issue. Transcendence and beauty have been lost in much of evangelicalism. Therefore someone who comes from such a sterile environment, without sufficient understanding of why it is that Protestants have been careful to avail themselves only of those symbols found explicitly in, or directly supported by Scripture, and who then enters a magnificent cathedral for the first time, can easily be overwhelmed by the sheer awe of how certain types of architecture, religious symbols, and beauty can indeed communicate a sense of transcendence. It was such an experience that apparently changed Thomas Howard's life and planted the seed that germinated years later in his conversion to Catholicism.

But what exactly is it that moves a Protestant like Thomas Howard away from Protestantism to Roman Catholicism? When Howard wrote *Evangelical Is Not Enough* he was an Episcopalian, but soon after he completed the book he joined the Roman Catholic Church. This raises an important question in my mind. If all that Thomas Howard was really seeking was a stronger sense of community, a deeper appreciation of Christian history, a liturgical form of worship, a central role for the ecumenical creeds, a significant role for sacraments, and an appreciation of beauty, why did he leave the Anglican Communion, which identifies with all of these elements in greater measure than any other Protestant tradition? Much of what Howard writes is a personal testimony about his quest for transcendence, but there are significant theological issues that surface as well—issues that amount to a self-conscious rejection of historic Protestantism. When asked by *Christianity Today* to identify the principal reasons for deciding to convert to Catholicism, Howard gave overtly theological reasons justifying his conversion.

> The question of the unity between Christ and his church is the fundamental one. A close corollary to that, if not virtually synonymous with it, is the question of authority, which immediately turns into the question of the magisterium—the teaching authority of the Catholic church. There is no magisterium in Protestantism. Also important for me was the sacramental understanding of the nature of reality, the nature of God, the world, revelation, the gospel, and the Incarnation.[20]

Despite the focus upon aesthetical issues in *Evangelical Is Not Enough,* when he was pressed by *Christianity Today* to give the rationale for joining the Roman church, Howard clearly rejected Protestantism as a system of doctrine, and pledged allegiance to the Council of Trent's declaration on the doctrine of justification, an overtly anti-Protestant document.[21] Ultimately, there is much more involved in converting to Roman Catholicism than merely a search for a sense of history, beauty, and symbol.

It is my contention that one cannot simultaneously be an evangelical (in the historical sense of the term) and a Roman Catholic. This is historically the position of most Protestant and Roman theologians. Recently, however, there has been a marked tendency on both sides to downplay the real differences between these traditions in order to foster mutual understanding and encourage joint ministry opportunities in the face of secularism, which now threatens both. No doubt, this trend is motivated by the biblical concern for Christians from differing historical and denominational backgrounds to work together in an age of uncertainty and unbelief. Though we must always be willing *in principle* to seek unity with our Christian brothers and sisters (and yes, many of them are Roman Catholics!), we must ask ourselves if real unity is best attained by pretending that substantial doctrinal differences do not exist or by redefining our doctrines so as to forge common ground at the expense of giving up critical doctrinal distinctives that have historically characterized our own traditions. Is it not better to acknowledge the real theological differences between evangelicals and Catholics and then, if possible, declare a "truce," agreeing to work together on matters of mutual concern despite our differences? Many, it seems, are opting for the former alternative.

Acknowledging the novelty of the concept, evangelical leaders such as Chuck Colson have begun to commend the terminology, "Evangelical Catholic."[22] One Roman Catholic writer, Keith A. Fournier, whose work *Evangelical Catholics* (1990) has been warmly endorsed by Colson, attempts to demonstrate that the word *evangelical* is actually an adjective rather than a noun. Fournier argues that the meaning of *evangelical* is best understood in terms of form rather than content. Being "evangelistic" and having a definite personal conversion experience is what constitutes being an evangelical. Fournier contends that the older understanding of "evangelical" as a synonym for "Protestant" was too confining: "It is time for a radical redefinition of the word."[23] Since Fournier professes to believe and practice the "Evangel," as does any true evangelical, he concludes, "So in the truest sense of the term, I am an evangelical Christian. And since I am also Catholic, I am an evangelical Catholic Christian—without contradiction in terms, logic, theology, or history."[24]

Evangelical Catholics is irenic, profitable reading and tries to avoid "a false nondenominationalism which denies distinctives of doctrine or practice,"[25] but there is an underlying agenda as well. Undoubtedly committed to the "great commission"[26] and personal conversion to Jesus Christ on the one hand,[27] Fournier rejects the Protestant conception of *sola scriptura* and affirms the Roman dogmas of the Eucharist, the magisterium, and the papacy as Christian essentials on the other.[28] Attempting to demonstrate how it is possible to synthesize aspects of these two traditions, he adds, "I invite you on a journey that will lead us home," i.e., to Roman Catholicism.[29] If we subject the word *evangelical* to such redefinition and contend that the term is somehow compatible with Tridentine Roman Catholicism, we inevitably make it that much easier for evangelicals to convert to Catholicism. Potential converts no longer have to leave anything behind. They simply add Roman doctrines to previously held evangelical beliefs.

Critical to this discussion is the definition of the word *evangelical*. Is evangelical only an adjective? What does it mean to be an evangelical? Thomas Howard's journey to Rome serves as an effective illustration of this tension. This can be clearly seen by the fact that the title of Howard's book, *Evangelical Is Not Enough*, indicates that there is much more in view than a series of personal aesthetic preferences or a desire for a certain "form" of Christian expression. For Howard, being an evangelical is not OK; it is not enough! Evangelicalism is incomplete. And apparently, like Keith Fournier, Howard sees little problem in attempting to embrace the Roman church while referring to himself as evangelical. If being an evangelical consists in a particular style of Christian piety or in the notion that one who professes to "be born again" is an evangelical or even in the idea that evangelistic zeal is what makes one an evangelical (i.e., as an adjective), rather than by defining *evangelical* in terms of a commitment to a specific doctrinal understanding of the Christian faith that necessarily embraces Protestant distinctives at odds with Catholic dogma (i.e., as a noun), then someone like Thomas Howard can change forms of Christian expression and practice without really changing much of the basic content of his faith. As Howard understands it, one makes their evangelical heritage complete by becoming a Roman Catholic. If one can be an evangelical without affirming doctrines seen as essential to historic Protestantism (i.e., *sola fide, sola scriptura,* and the doctrine of forensic justification, defined exclusively in terms of an imputed righteousness rather than an infused righteousness), then certainly one can be a professed evangelical and join the Roman Catholic Church for reasons of aesthetics or liturgical preference.

Protestants reject this notion, however, seeing the mixing of contradictory doctrines more in terms of an unworkable Hegelian synthesis than as a logical outworking of the biblical faith. Historically defined, "evangelical" was a virtual synonym for "Protestant," and, by definition, being an evangelical included adherence to all Protestant distinctives. I for one am quite unwilling to let Keith Fournier "radically" redefine the term for me!

There are several points, then, that Protestants will find troubling about Howard's book. Admittedly, Howard's own fundamentalist upbringing was somewhat different from that of many historic Protestants, since his own fundamentalist version of Protestantism stands firmly within the pietist (a reactionary movement against sterile Protestantism) and Wesleyan traditions, which placed much more emphasis upon such things as private devotions and inward piety than do other children of the Reformation. Thus, an important concern is that as Howard describes the spiritual climate of his fundamentalist upbringing he is indeed accurately describing a pietistic form of spirituality, which does not characterize all of historic Protestant piety.

Family altar and Bible reading, hymn sings, and so forth are indeed typical evangelical practices. Protestants have historically believed in the importance of Bible reading, prayer, and catechism in the home and have encouraged their practice. However, with the stress in historic Protestantism on the doctrine of calling, there was also significant emphasis placed on Christ's lordship over all areas of life, including work, leisure, family, and so on. All of life was spiritual in a sense, since all of life was to be lived to the glory of God. Historic Protestant piety was often more broadly conceived than that of pietism. Thus, as Howard describes his experience of these fundamentalist devotional activities, it appears they took on a rigid form of "spiritual exercise" characteristic of much of pietism. Ironically Howard has, in effect, exchanged the fundamentalist piety of Ira Sankey hymnody and Keswick conferences stressing victorious Christian living for something akin to the spiritual exercises of Ignatius Loyola. When Christian piety takes on such a rigid and privatized expression, as is the case in those forms of American evangelicalism influenced by pietism, it is natural to begin seeking some historical precedent for such practices. And Rome offers a much more refined, historical, and comprehensive variety of such exercises than does the pietism of fundamentalism. In some senses it is a natural and logical progression from pietism to Roman Catholicism.

Another concern is that Howard begins *Evangelical Is Not Enough* by telling the reader how much Roman Catholics and evangelicals have in common. This is a theme throughout Fournier's work as well. Howard then catalogues a number of "catholic," or universal, doctrines that all Christian traditions have in common, especially the Virgin Birth, the second coming of Christ, the Trinity, the deity of Christ, and belief in an inspired Scripture. What Howard fails to mention is any doctrine that is uniquely Protestant, except for the doctrine of the inerrancy of Scripture, of which he is vaguely critical. Howard contends that "the supreme hallmark of Evangelicalism [is] its extremely tender conscience." Being an evangelical, then, is to be understood primarily in terms of a distinct moral lifestyle rather than in an affirmation of a distinct set of theological beliefs. This is further demonstrated by Howard's apparent confusion about how Protestants have historically understood the gospel. He contends that "the purity of the heart the gospel asks of us"[30] is characteristic of evangelicalism. Yet he fails to understand that purity of heart is not something that the *gospel* asks of us. Instead, total purity of heart in thought, word, and deed is something that the *law of God* demands of us! In the gospel a complete forgiveness for all our impurity of heart, as well as the perfect righteousness of Christ to cover our lack of purity, is freely offered to all of us who know that our hearts, even as Christians, are still quite impure. It is only confusion, redefinition, or compromise about these basic points of Protestant conviction that allows one to identify both as an evangelical *and* as a Roman Catholic simultaneously. Actually, many evangelicals are also confused on this matter, so why should we be surprised if many of those in our churches find it easy to head for Rome or Antioch.[31]

It is important to make a distinction between "form" and "content." If one already holds to similar doctrinal content (i.e., the semi-Pelagianism of Wesleyan pietism and historic Tridentine Catholicism—since it is argued by both that salvation is a synergistic process in which God contributes grace and man contributes the energy of an act of the will), it is then much easier to change forms of Christian practice (from pietism to Roman Catholicism) for reasons of preference (i.e., aesthetics). Thomas Howard is now a Roman Catholic, and yet still considers himself evangelical because, on this issue, he apparently never embraced the historic Protestant doctrine. Keith Fournier is able to call himself an Evangelical Catholic because he has redefined what it means to be an evangelical. In both cases, neither is a Protestant, and so it is impossible to see how either can be an evangelical in any historic sense of the term. Therefore, evangelicals must be careful to maintain both the biblical meaning of the Evangel itself (wherein all saving activity is assigned to God alone), as well as their own historical identity, which is necessarily Protestant.

THE THEOLOGICAL MOTIVATION

The second main category of those who have converted to Roman Catholicism is primarily theological. Here, we will find those who have become convinced that Protestantism is an erroneous rebellion and that the Roman Church is and always was the true church. The tone of converts in this category is much more strident since the issues are much clearer and more sharply defined because they are unashamedly doctrinal and historical. Scott Hahn, who describes himself as a "Luther in reverse,"[32] is representative of such converts. Another such convert, Gerry Matatics, Hahn's friend and a former Presbyterian minister, speaks in jest of these issues, describing his own conversion in Pauline-like terms.

> I too was circumcised (by the new birth) on the eighth day, of the People of Protestantism, of the tribe of Evangelicalism, a Calvinist of Calvinists: in regard to the law, a theonomist: as for zeal, persecuting the (Roman) Church: as to reconstructionist righteousness and Van Tillian virtue flawless (Phil 3:5–6 [New Ironic Version]).[33]

Hahn and Matatics are well-educated, conscientious, skilled debaters and perhaps are known to many readers as a result of their willingness to dialogue on these issues with evangelical leaders. Ironically, they have not only contributed a great deal to the Roman cause by effectively debating the issues from the Roman perspective, but they remind evangelicals that, ultimately, Roman Catholicism and evangelicalism are mutually exclusive doctrinal systems that are the logical outworking of basic theological starting points. For the Protestant, the starting point is the Word of God. For the

Roman Catholic, it is the Word of God and sacred tradition. As a Protestant, I would contend that in practice, however, Rome views sacred tradition as its ultimate authority, since in those areas where so-called "sacred" tradition and Scripture are in conflict, the Roman church resolves any tension by opting for sacred tradition over Scripture. Clear biblical doctrines are redefined and unbiblical doctrines and practices are justified solely on the basis of this "sacred" and supposedly infallible tradition. The issues raised by Hahn and Matatics will make this point clear.

Scott Hahn describes himself as having been militantly anti-Catholic and committed to Reformed orthodoxy during his seminary days.[34] But several issues raised major doubts in his mind about Protestantism. The first was Hahn's wife Kimberley's conviction that birth control was not supported by Scripture. This led Hahn to read a Roman Catholic writer, John Kippley, who argued that marriage was not a contract but a covenant. As a result of working through Kippley's understanding of the covenant, Hahn began moving away from the traditional Reformed understanding of covenant theology seen in federal/legal terms toward a more familial model based on kinship.[35] As Hahn puts it,

> Luther and Calvin explained [the covenant] exclusively in terms of courtroom language. But I was beginning to see that, far more than simply being a judge, God was our Father. Far more than simply being criminals, we were runaways. Far more [than] being made in a courtroom, [the covenant] was fashioned by God in a family room.[36]

These changes in views regarding the covenant led to a second issue: the doctrine of *sola fide*. If the doctrine of the covenant cannot be understood in legal terms, justification cannot be based on the imputation of the guilt of a sinner's sin to Christ and Christ's righteousness to the believer. This means that justification cannot be based upon faith *alone*. Instead, justification must be based on faith and works, the historic position of Tridentine Catholicism.[37] Hahn was working through these related issues in seminary when he encountered the work of Norman Shepherd, who had just been removed from Westminster Theological Seminary for teaching what Hahn describes as "the same view of justification that I was expounding."[38] Hahn declares, "I discovered that nowhere did Saint Paul ever teach that we were justified by faith *alone*. *Sola fide* was unscriptural!"[39] This led Hahn to conclude,

> Luther and Calvin often said that this was the article on which the church stood or fell. That was why, for them, the Catholic church fell and Protestantism rose up from the ashes. *Sola fide* was the material principle of the Reformation, and I was coming to the conviction that Saint Paul never taught it. . . . This was a traumatic transformation for me to say that on this point I now thought Luther was fundamentally wrong. For seven years, Luther had been my main source of

inspiration and powerful proclamation of the word. And this doctrine had been the rationale behind the whole Protestant Reformation.[40]

The next theological domino to fall was *sola scriptura*. While Hahn was teaching a course on the gospel of John (during which time he became convinced of the real presence of Christ in the Eucharist),[41] a student asked Hahn to demonstrate where the Bible itself taught sola scriptura. Feeling as though he was unable to satisfactorily answer the question, Hahn lamented, "'Lord what's happening? Where does Scripture teach sola scriptura?' There were two pillars on which Protestants based their revolt against Rome—one had already fallen, the other was shaking. I was scared."[42]

Hahn and his friend Gerry Matatics then arranged a meeting with John Gerstner, a distinguished dean of Reformed theologians. After discussing the relevant issues with Gerstner, the one issue that seemed to convince Hahn of the truth of the Roman conception of Scripture plus tradition came during the discussion of the closure of the canon of Scripture. Hahn asked Gerstner, "How can we be sure about the twenty-seven books of the New Testament themselves being the infallible Word of God, since fallible Church councils and Popes are the ones who made up the list?" Gerstner's answer, Hahn contends, pushed him over the edge. "I will never forget his response," recalls Hahn: "Scott, that simply means that all we can have is a fallible collection of infallible documents." Hahn recounts asking, "Is that really the best historic Protestant Christianity can do?" To which Gerstner replied, "Yes, Scott, all we can do is make probable judgements from historic evidence. We have no infallible authority but Scripture." Hahn remembers thinking, "I felt very unsatisfied with his answers, though I knew he was representing the Protestant position faithfully."[43] Uncertain what to do, Hahn resigned from his pastorate and pursued answers to his questions through additional graduate instruction. On Easter 1986, Scott and Kimberly Hahn joined the Roman Catholic Church, as did Gerry Matatics and his wife—two former Presbyterian minsters, now apologists for the Roman Catholic Church.

Hahn's doctrinal pilgrimage is important to examine, because it does raise important issues that merit response. However, the issues raised are complex and require in-depth response—something beyond the scope of this essay. Therefore, I will be limiting my brief response to Hahn's rejection of *sola scriptura*.[44]

This dilemma illustrates one of the primary reasons someone like Hahn is effective as a Catholic apologist. Whereas Karl Keating laments the theological illiteracy of the Roman Catholic laity, there is every indication that evangelicalism now experiences the same plight. Evangelical laity are often not interested in doctrinal matters, and neither are many of her key preachers and theologians. This is especially true in matters of controversy. Unity has become an idol of sorts, and in many evangelical circles there is more willingness to sacrifice doctrinal distinctives, so long as the peace is kept, than there should be. We should never expend any of our precious energy looking to pick doctrinal fights with anyone. Yet it is irresponsible to look the other way when the foundations of our faith are challenged. So it is lamentable how difficult it is to find church leaders and theologians willing to address contemporary doctrinal matters, such as the current debates between Protestants and Catholic apologists. Hence, the evangelical community is slow to respond to people like Scott Hahn.

Evangelical pastors and leaders need to devote much more time and energy to doctrinal matters than they do at present. Too often this burden is left at the feet of various parachurch research organizations that differ widely in doctrinal perspectives, ability, and resources. Many of our historic Protestant denominations have little stomach for such matters. When historic Protestant denominations and seminaries do respond, the answer is often, "Oh, we dealt with that in the sixteenth and seventeenth centuries." And, indeed, some excellent work was done in defense of *sola fide* and *sola scriptura* in response to the Council of Trent.[45] But what about some kind of contemporary response from those who do have the biblical and historic answers? Usually there is far too little response, and what responses are forthcoming are often too late to contribute anything of use to the debate at the key moment of battle. It is difficult to find well-written but popular historic Protestant (Lutheran or Reformed) works on any of the subjects germane to this debate. Much of the reason for the success of Catholic apologists is that they simply go unchallenged by the best and brightest of the historic Protestant traditions.

Hahn rejects the concept of Scripture alone because, supposedly, Scripture itself does not teach it.[46] How can *sola scriptura* be true, asks Hahn, if Scripture itself does not state that Scripture alone is our only authority? An additional element of this argument is that since Scripture does refer elsewhere to an "oral tradition" (i.e., 2 Thessalonians 2:15; 2 Timothy 2:2) this renders *sola scriptura* unbiblical because the existence of a distinct oral tradition, not inscripturated, must mean that oral tradition is an additional authority. Hence, Scripture and tradition constitute a kind of dual authority. Therefore, *sola scriptura* is in error.

There are two primary issues here. The first is, Does Scripture itself teach *sola scriptura*? and the second, What is the relationship between the authority of tradition and the church in relation to the authority of Scripture?

It is clear that *sola scriptura* is a biblical doctrine even if there is no one single text that expressly states, "Scripture is the only authority for faith and practice." First, we are told by Paul that "all Scripture is God-breathed" (2 Timothy 3:16; cf. also 2 Peter 1:20–21), indicating that the Old Testament was the product of God's breathing forth an inspired biblical text through the agency of human authors. Paul states that the Old Testament is profitable for teaching, rebuking, correcting, and training in righteousness so that believers may be thoroughly equipped. The ramifications of this declaration that Scripture is inspired are very important in establishing Scripture as the only authoritative source for faith and practice.

Though this affirmation about the inspiration of the Old Testament does not rule out the existence of an infallible tradition per se, the fact is that there is no mention anywhere else in Scripture of an "inspired tradition" existing as an authority equal to Scripture. In fact, based on other biblical evidence, it is clear that Scripture alone is regarded as the only infallible source of authority by the biblical writers (see below). Paul clearly says that the Old Testament is "God-breathed" and is therefore an infallible source for Christian doctrine and practice. This means that the burden of proof rests with the Roman Catholic to demonstrate that tradition (as defined by Rome) is likewise so authoritative. To argue that because the Bible refers to a "tradition" and that this is somehow the basis for Roman "sacred" tradition (which often conflicts with that same Scripture) completely begs the question.

A related point is that Scripture also clearly contains all that a Christian needs to know about the will of God and how to be saved, since both the law of God and the gospel are revealed *only* in Scripture. Therefore, Protestants have argued that Scripture *alone* is a sufficient basis for authority in all matters of doctrine and practice, since the Bible declares itself inspired and therefore infallible. The Word of God *alone* contains all that a Christian needs to know to be saved. If Scripture contains all such knowledge, what, then, is the purpose of tradition? How can tradition add anything necessary to the law and the gospel? Are the law and the gospel as found in Scripture somehow incomplete? Since the answer to these questions is no, Protestants contend that Scripture alone is sufficient, meaning that "no human tradition not firmly grounded on Scripture can be necessary to salvation."[47]

If true, this forces us to conclude that "the Word of God is both temporally and regulatively prior to the church,"[48] no small point in such discussions. An important argument raised by Protestants based on the clear biblical statements about the inspiration of Scripture, and therefore the priority of the Word of God, is that the Holy Spirit moved the biblical writers, not the church (not even the "Spirit-led" church), to produce holy Scripture. Inspired Scripture, then, is the basis for the authority of the church, but only as the church is faithful to that inspired Word. This is because "Scripture is the Word of God given as a rule to the church, [and] the authority of doctrine and of the church comes from God . . . by way of the Scriptures. Indeed, it is the Scriptures that, as the Word of God 'bring faith and authority to the church.' "[49] The church has no authority apart from the prior written Word and no authority at all apart from a faithful proclamation of that Word—a standard that I as a Protestant would argue Rome cannot meet!

A second line of argumentation against Hahn's contention that the Bible does not teach *sola scriptura* is to point out that there are numerous biblical texts supporting the concept. Since Scripture itself, being inspired, warns us against adding to or taking away from its clear declarations (Deuteronomy 4:2; 12:32), Scripture must be complete in itself. The Psalmist echoes this, stating that "the law of the Lord is perfect" (19:7), that His statutes are "trustworthy" (v. 7), and that His precepts are "right" (v. 8). Why would "sacred" tradition be needed as a dual authority if Scripture is perfect in itself?

Elsewhere, Paul tells us that "everything that was written in the past was written to teach us, so that through endurance and the encouragement of the Scriptures we might have hope" (Romans 15:4). As in 2 Timothy 3:16, there is no appeal to an infallible tradition, nor to an infallible church, but only to the Old Testament, the written Word of God for the apostolic church. In Ephesians 5:24 Paul states that the church is to "submit to Christ," which, as we learn in Colossians 3:16, is through the means of the "word of Christ." At the time of Paul's writing of these epistles, this "word of Christ" existed in oral form, but it was subsequently inscripturated in the gospels. In these passages, Paul appeals to the Old Testament (i.e., to "psalms" and "hymns"; see Ephesians 5:19, Colossians 3:16). In Ephesians 2:20, Paul writes that the church is "built on the foundation of the apostles and the prophets, with Christ Jesus himself as the chief cornerstone," a reference to the fact that the church is built on the apostolic gospel subsequently inscripturated.[50]

Scripture refers to itself as the "rule" for the Christian (Galatians 6:16), and "Scripture not only, therefore, demands obedience to God alone (Deut. 12:32; Matt. 15:9), it also clearly condemns other allegiances and is alone designated by God as a rule (2 Tim. 3:16; 2 Peter 1:21)."[51] We are to anathematize anyone who comes preaching a different gospel, for such is really no gospel at all (Galatians 1:6–9). What is that gospel according to Paul? It is the doctrine of justification by grace, through faith, on account of Christ! It is a gospel based on the finished work of Christ and received through faith *alone* (Galatians 3).

The biblical case for *sola scriptura* becomes even stronger when one looks to the words of our Lord on the subject. When tempted by the devil (Matthew 4:1–11), our Lord responded three times to Satan, "It is written." "'Here,' Jesus was saying, 'is the permanent, unchangeable witness of the eternal God, committed to writing for our instruction.'"[52] Thus, at the very height of His struggle with the devil, Jesus appeals to the authority of Scripture. There is no higher court of appeal. Jesus states that "the Scripture cannot be broken" (John 10:35) and that He came not to abolish the Word of God but to fulfill it (Matthew 5:18; Luke 6:17). Jesus instructs us to obey the Old Testament (Matthew 23:3) and tells us that the Law, the Prophets, and the Psalms bear witness of Him (Luke 24:44). Is the Old Testament incomplete in this regard, requiring a "sacred" tradition to complement it? On the contrary, Jesus declares that the Old Testament alone is authoritative in matters of doctrine when He states, "They have Moses and the Prophets; let them listen to them" (Luke 16:29). Jesus confirms this priority of Scripture when He tells the Sadducees, "You are in error because you do not know the Scriptures or the power of God" (Matthew 22:29). In fact, in the only reference to tradition mentioned by our Lord, He expressly tells us that unless such tradition conforms to the prior norm of Scripture it has no authority and is nothing but "rules taught by men" (Matthew 15:2–9).

There is no hint, therefore, in any of these texts, that the biblical writers viewed anything other than the written Word of God (the Old Testament) as the only infallible guide or authoritative source for the faith and practice of the church. This brief treatment of the biblical data certainly confirms the Protestant understanding of *sola scriptura*. As one writer put it, "Hence, even a cursory review of the teachings of Christ and the apostles suggest that, just like the Old Testament, the New Testament is saturated with the teaching of *sola scriptura*."[53]

A third issue needing to be addressed is the role and authority of tradition. Historic Protestants do not reject tradition altogether. In fact, tradition plays an important role in the life of the church. Generally speaking, Protestants have seen tradition as occupying a *ministerial* rather than a *magisterial* function.[54] Tradition has only a derivative authority (based on its faithfulness to the prior authority of the Scriptures) rather than an intrinsic authority (wherein tradition has an authority equal to Scripture in its own right). Tradition, then, has a regulative function and value, but only as a particular tradition faithfully reflects the prior authority of the Word of God. John Murray contends,

> Tradition . . . has the greatest potency and, if of the proper kind, the greatest value. But one thing must be appreciated, namely, that tradition even when it is the best, has no *intrinsic* authority. Tradition is always subject to the scrutiny and test of Scripture. Its rightness or value is always determined by its conformity to Scripture. This is just saying that it is never proper to appeal to tradition as having an intrinsic authority in matters of faith and morals. Tradition when right and true and good always flows from the Scripture and is simply God's will as revealed in Scripture coming to expression in thought and life. Tradition when right is always derived; it is never original and primary.[55]

Protestants have seen the value of creeds and confessions as serving a regulative function, by preserving church order and doctrinal clarity. Indeed, one significant difference between historic Protestants and many of their evangelical descendants is that historic Protestants are bound to both the so-called ecumenical creeds and to a series of Reformation era confessions and catechisms. Whereas a church body has the authority to demand subscription to a particular creed, the creed can never have divine authority since the church's own authority is itself only ecclesiastical and, therefore, derivative. Thus, "a creed or any other ecclesiastical pronouncement derives its whole authority from its consonance with Scripture."[56] So whereas Protestants do not reject tradition or the importance of being "confessional," they must be careful not to set up a scenario in which tradition challenges the only source of divine authority, the Word of God. For this is the primary error of Roman Catholicism.

A final area of concern regards the perennial question debated by Protestants and Catholics: Which came first, the church or the canon? Is Scott Hahn correct in rejecting Gerstner's thoroughly Protestant understanding of the closure of the canon? Does the closure of the canon demonstrate that the church has an infallible authority equal to that of Holy Scripture, thereby proving that the *Roman* church possesses that infallible authority today? Here we must keep clearly in view the fact that the divine authority of inspired Scripture serves as the foundation for the authority of the church, whose own authority is derivative and ecclesiastical. God the Holy Spirit inspired the Scripture, and God the Holy Spirit bears witness to which written books are Scripture.

Thus, Protestants have argued from "the theological principle [of inspiration] to the logical and empirical proofs" of inspiration and canonicity.[57] Therefore, while the church is a witness to, and a guardian of, the inspired Word of God, the declaration of canonicity by the church is only a pronouncement about an already existing state of affairs. Through the providential activity of God and through the guidance and power of the Holy Spirit, the church is certainly able to discern and declare which written books are Scripture. But such a declaration by the church does not give to the Scripture any authority it does not already possess by virtue of its prior inspiration.[58] As Richard Muller contends, "The question of the canon was a question of authority and, given the prior authority of Scripture, the question had to be answered theologically rather than ecclesially."[59]

It is God, the author of Scripture, who bears witness through them of their divine authority. It is to this authority of God that the church bears witness as far as the collection of canonical writings is concerned. It is to this same authority that the church must appeal if she is to have any derivative authority to make such pronouncements. Such an act of bearing witness to Scripture, while in effect, closing the canon and eliminating noninspired writings from inclusion, does not render Scripture something other than what it already is, the written Word of God, the only divine authority for all matters of faith and practice. Thus, Hahn's contention that the issue of canonicity requires an infallible church and that that infallible church is the Roman church is based solely upon his prior rejection of *sola scriptura;* it is simply a totally unsubstantiated claim to authority. If the Protestant conception of *sola scriptura* is indeed true, then the Roman conception of the canon becomes untenable. Simply declaring that the Roman church has such authority does not make it so. Hence, Gerstner's point stands.

CONCLUSION

So why are evangelicals joining the Catholic Church? In many cases it is because we have not given them good enough reasons to stay. In other cases converts have become convinced that evangelicals simply do not have the answers to Catholic objections. But in either case, unless evangelicals recall and defend their own Protestant heritage and recover the true understanding of what it means to be an evangelical in the first place, they should not expect this trend to reverse itself anytime soon.

NOTES

1. Scott Hahn, "The New Converts," Audio Cassette (San Diego: Catholic Answers).
2. Ibid. According to a recent *Newsweek* article (August 9, 1993), the latest statistics seem to indicate that membership in mainline Protestant denominations is rapidly declining, while that of evangelical churches is growing significantly. Over the last thirty years, the United Church of Christ, as but one example of mainline decline, has managed to halve itself numerically. Statistics indicate that mainline Protestant denominations decline as they become more liberal in their theological orientation. Certainly, a number of those leaving mainline Protestant churches move to evangelical churches, which oddly enough are themselves becoming less theological and more "seeker centered," in many cases downplaying their own Protestant distinctives. The vitality and longevity of this "new" evangelicalism is an open question. There are also no exact figures demonstrating how many Roman Catholics have converted to evangelicalism during the same period, though it is popularly contended that the number is significant. The point must be made, however, that, while evangelicalism is growing numerically, apparently there are not as many notable Roman Catholics becoming evangelicals as vice-versa.
3. The departure of much of evangelicalism as a movement from its historic Protestant theological foundation has been spelled out in several significant recent works: Carl F. H. Henry, *Twilight of a Great Civilization: The Drift Toward Neo-Paganism* (Westchester: Crossway, 1988); Michael S. Horton, *Made in America: The Shaping of Modern American Culture* (Grand Rapids: Baker, 1991); James Davidson Hunter, *Evangelicalism: The Coming Generation* (Chicago: Univ. of Chicago Press, 1987); Harold Lindsell, *The New Paganism: Understanding American Culture and the Role of the Church* (San Francisco: Harper & Row, 1987); and David F. Wells, *No Place for Truth: Or Whatever Happened to Evangelical Theology* (Grand Rapids: Eerdmans, 1993).
4. Catholic lay apologist Karl Keating's lengthy critique of Jimmy Swaggart and others is an example of this. Swaggart represents a crude form of Pelagianism that is rejected not only by Roman Catholics but by all historic Protestant confessions and catechisms as well. See Karl Keating, *Catholicism and Fundamentalism* (San Francisco: Ignatius, 1988), esp. 86–120.

5. One thinks of the infamous *Alberto* comic book/tract produced under the auspices of Chick Publications.

6. Karl Keating, "Dave Hunt & Karl Keating Debate 'What Catholics Believe'," Audio Cassette (Clearwater: Action Sixties Television Ministries, 1993).

7. Thomas Howard, *Evangelical Is Not Enough* (San Francisco: Ignatius, 1984).

8. Ibid., 1.

9. Ibid., 3.

10. Ibid., 4.

11. Ibid.

12. Ibid., 5.

13. See the illuminating discussion on this point in Richard A. Muller, *Holy Scripture: The Cognitive Foundation of Theology,* vol. 2 of *Post-Reformation Reformed Dogmatics* (Grand Rapids: Baker, 1993), 37ff. For a discussion of the development of two distinct understandings of the role of tradition in the medieval church, see Heiko Oberman, *Forerunners of the Reformation* (Philadelphia: Fortress, 1981), 53–66.

14. Howard, *Evangelical Is Not Enough,* 22.

15. Ibid., 29.

16. Ibid., 34.

17. Ibid., 35.

18. Ibid., 34–35.

19. Franky Schaeffer, *Sham Pearls for Real Swine* (Brentwood, Tenn.: Wolgemuth & Hyatt, 1990), 6–7.

20. Thomas Howard and John D. Woodbridge, "Why Did Thomas Howard Become a Roman Catholic?" *Christianity Today,* 17 May 1985, 48.

21. Ibid., 57.

22. Chuck Colson, "Forward," in Keith A. Fournier, *Evangelical Catholics* (Nashville: Nelson, 1990), v–vi. Colson is clearly motivated by the need for both traditions to join forces in the face of rising secularism. "When the barbarians are scaling the walls, there is no time for petty quarreling in the camp." While I for one would shout "Amen" at the thought of historic Protestants and Roman Catholics joining forces to oppose the rising tide of secularism, I simply do not agree with Colson when he describes those things that have historically divided Protestants and Catholics as "petty differences." I am much more comfortable with Roman Catholics and Protestants acknowledging that they have significant differences that are important to preserve and then declaring a temporary "truce" in the face of a mutual enemy. Is not a major aspect of a secular world-and-life view the conception that truth can be relativized? Whereas we may need to work with Roman Catholics against our common secularist opponents, if we redefine what it means to be an evangelical in order to do it, we may have already bought the secularist farm!

23. Keith A. Fournier, *Evangelical Catholics,* 21.

24. Ibid.

25. Ibid., 16.

26. Ibid., 11–12.

27. Ibid., 18.

28. Ibid., 17.

29. Ibid., 23.

30. Howard, *Evangelical Is Not Enough,* 1.

31. Witness the recent attempt by much of the evangelical leadership to get a handle on such doctrinal hemorrhaging, in Kenneth A. Kantzer and Carl F. H. Henry, *Evangelical Affirmations* (Grand Rapids: Zondervan, 1990), esp. 27–38.

32. Scott and Kimberly Hahn, *Rome Sweet Home: Our Journey to Catholicism* (San Francisco: Ignatius, 1993), 48.

33. Gerald Matatics, "The Word of God Is the Supreme Norm, but According to Scripture Itself, God's Word Is Not Entirely Contained Within Scripture Alone," *Antithesis* 1, no. 5 (September/October 1990): 50. For an account of Matatics's conversion, consult Gerry Matatics, "From Anti-Catholic to Catholic," Audio Cassette (San Diego: Catholic Answers).

34. Hahn, *Rome Sweet Home*, 25ff.

35. Ibid., 25–33.

36. Ibid., 30. Evangelical leaders such as Clark Pinnock support Hahn's contention and also seek to shift the evangelical movement away from its historic Protestant roots. See, for example, Clark Pinnock, "The New Model Explained," in *The Megashift Conference*, Audio Cassette Series (Anaheim: Christians United for Reformation, 1991).

37. See, for example, Henry Denzinger, "Systematic Index," in *The Sources of Catholic Dogma* (St. Louis: Herder, 1957), [26]; for a contemporary statement, see John A. Hardon, *The Catholic Catechism* (New York: Image, 1981), 191–93.

38. Hahn, *Rome Sweet Home*, 31.

39. Ibid.

40. Ibid., 32.

41. Hahn does not spell out whether or not his understanding of the Eucharist was Roman. The historic Reformed and Lutheran traditions have doctrines of a "real" presence that are quite different from the Roman dogma of transubstantiation.

42. Hahn, *Rome Sweet Home*, 52.

43. Ibid., 70–76. Hahn mentions that Gerstner asserted that tradition, popes, and ecumenical councils all taught contrary to Scripture on numerous occasions. This argument is simply dismissed by Hahn without dealing with the questions raised by an errant "infallible" tradition because of Hahn's contention that the church's closure of the canon must render the church infallible (pp. 74–75).

44. For an excellent discussion of the contemporary issues surrounding the doctrine of justification and *sola fide*, see D. A. Carson, ed., *Right With God: Justification and the Bible in the Modern World* (Grand Rapids: Baker, 1992).

45. Take for example, John Calvin's examination of the "Canons and Decrees of the Council of Trent, with the Antidote," in *Selected Works of John Calvin*, vol. 3, ed. Henry Beveridge and Jules Bonnet (Grand Rapids: Baker, 1983); Martin Chemnitz, *Examination of the Council of Trent, Part 1*, trans. Fred Kramer (St. Louis: Concordia, 1971); and Francis Turretin, *Institutes of Elenctic Theology*, trans. George Musgrave Giger., ed. James T. Dennison (Phillipsburg: Presb. & Ref., 1992), esp. 1:55–167. For an important discussion of the development of the Reformed doctrine of Scripture during this period, see Muller, *Holy Scripture*.

46. Hahn, *Rome Sweet Home*, 51–55. Also, Gerry Matatics, "The Bible and the Catholic Church," Audio Cassette (San Diego: Catholic Answers).

47. Muller, *Holy Scripture*, 367.

48. Ibid., 373.

49. Ibid., 366.

50. Andrew T. Lincoln, *Ephesians*, vol. 42 of Word Biblical Commentary (Dallas: Word, 1990), 152. Gerry Matatics argues that 1 Timothy 3:15 throws a different

light on this text, since Paul tells us that the church, rather than the Word of God, is the "pillar and foundation of the truth." This means, according to Matatics, that the church (specifically the Roman church) is the foundation of the truth (cf. Gerry Matatics, "The Bible and the Catholic Church"). However, in his outstanding commentary (*A Commentary on the Pastoral Epistles* [Grand Rapids: Baker, 1981], 88), J. N. D. Kelly writes, "We should note (a) that **buttress** is probably a more accurate rendering of the Greek hedraioma (nowhere else found) than 'foundation' or 'ground' (AV), and (b) that the local church is described as a **pillar**, etc., not 'the pillar, etc.', because there are many local churches throughout the world performing this role." Clearly, then, the passage does not support Matatics' contention.

51. Muller, *Holy Scripture*, 377.

52. John W. Wenham, "Christ's View of Scripture," in Norman Geisler, ed., *Inerrancy* (Grand Rapids: Zondervan, 1980), 15.

53. Douglas Jones, "Scripture Teaches That the Word of God is the Supreme Norm," *Antithesis* 1, no. 5 (September/October 1990), 48.

54. Turretin, *Institutes of Elenctic Theology*, 90.

55. John Murray, "Tradition: Romish and Protestant," in *Studies in Theology*, vol. 4 of *Collected Writings of John Murray* (Carlilse: Banner of Truth, 1982), 271.

56. Ibid., 272.

57. Muller, *Holy Scripture*, 399.

58. Turretin, *Institutes of Elenctic Theology*, 92.

59. Muller, *Holy Scripture*, 398.

After five hundred years, have Protestants and Roman Catholics achieved closer agreement? Has there been a legitimate advance, or is the current spirit of ecumenical agreement due more to a lack of doctrinal clarity and awareness of one's own doctrinal distinctives? Is it even possible for Rome to change its theological positions with regard to the condemnations of the Reformation era and subsequent declarations?

The two traditions are still—and ought to remain—divided in the hope that eventually genuine doctrinal accord may be achieved upon the most essential and divisive issues. A number of the issues that many conservative Protestants find objectionable in Rome are not necessarily the issues that actually divided the two groups in the Reformation. What are those issues, and can they be settled any time soon?

ESSAY
11

WHAT
STILL KEEPS
US APART?

Michael S. Horton

Finally, there it was in all its grandeur. I had patiently waited for this moment ever since arriving with college friends, and now here it stood before me: St. Peter's, in Rome. Center of Latin Christendom's historical consciousness, it seemed as if this mythic Renaissance edifice was part of a dream. But it wasn't. And I was overtaken with a sense of Rome's magnificence.

It is at moments such as these that one wishes this could be part of a shared history: our St. Peter's, our Rome. It is the same feeling one has (and a surely justified sense of shared history) when reading Augustine, Anselm, and Aquinas—or Bonaventure, Bernard, or Gregory the Great. Against the dull, colorless, ragged backdrop of the twentieth century, these rich golden threads capture the eye, the imagination, mind, and heart, and God rewards those who diligently seek Him through their work. It was to the bishop of Rome that many brother-bishops turned in the earliest days of the church, when heresy and schism threatened the faithful. It was Rome that stood up to the Montanists, Manicheans, Donatists, Pelagians, Cathari, Albigensians, Arians, and Monophysites, and that still stands up to so many other spurious movements plaguing a modern Protestantism that cannot seem to remember anything that happened in the church before last Tuesday.

The Roman church speaks out so unanimously and clearly (comparatively speaking) on matters such as abortion and concern for the poor that evangelicals feel a sense of camaraderie in contrast to the limits of their own public witness, driven it seems more by charismatic political personalities, coalitions, and political action committees than by a well-conceived theology of social ethics. And who can deny the commitment of the Roman Catholic Church to the arts? While Protestants closer to the Reformation have much for which to be grateful to God in this area, modern evangelicals do not seem to foster an appreciation for the aesthetic and cultural life; all too often the assumption seems to be that ugliness is next to godliness.

Fundamentalists and evangelicals, I think, find Rome attractive when the pressures of modernity weigh heavily on their shoulders. The search for certainty, ballast, and hope in the midst of relativism, weightlessness, and cynicism is more than "antimodern" sentiment; it is the very real experience of millions of conservative Protestants and Catholics. Against the backdrop of the cold, urban skyscrapers and the sprawling shopping malls, the memory of St. Peter's on a misty summer morning lingers and, one could even say, haunts the joyless modern soul.

Furthermore, the renewal movement seems to have attracted many Roman Catholics to the Scriptures, and it is not uncommon for a Roman Catholic neighbor to invite an unchurched Protestant to a Bible study. For all these reasons, and more, many (this writer included) have felt drawn to the Roman Catholic Church on more than one occasion. At least when we talk about the Incarnation, we both know what—and who—we're talking about.

So what keeps us apart after four and a half centuries? The plea for greater spiritual unity has not been limited to the ecumenical movement within mainline denominations; it has been the recent and growing cry of many traditional Protestant evangelicals as well. In his warm-hearted and thoughtful appeal, Keith A. Fournier, formerly dean of evangelism at the Franciscan College of Steubenville, Ohio, asks, "Evangelical Catholic: contradiction in terms?"—to which he answers in the negative.[1] It will be my task in this chapter to interact with this question in an effort to discern whether there is sufficient reason to warrant continued separation of Protestantism and Rome.

ARE EVANGELICALS CATHOLIC?

Before we address the question, "Can Catholics be evangelicals?" we ought to ask, "Can evangelicals be Catholics?"

The same Protestant confessions of faith that fingered the pope as the *verum antichristum* (the very Antichrist) also affirm that Protestants are indeed members of the catholic church. *Catholic* means "universal," but it means much more than that. In its historical context, it refers to those who side with orthodoxy against the sects and heresies that have challenged the clear biblical teaching concerning God (the Trinity, divine omnipotence, omniscience, omnipresence, eternity, simplicity, etc.), Christ (His eternal Sonship, virgin birth and incarnation, two natures in one person, bodily resurrection and ascension), salvation (original sin, substitutionary atonement, the necessity and priority of prevenient grace), and eschatology (the return of Christ in judgment and salvation at the end of history). These are not merely *evangelical* essentials; they are the sum and substance of our common *catholic* witness. Furthermore, the Protestant Reformers and Puritans agreed with catholic Christians of all ages that the church is Christ's ordained institution, "out of which there is no ordinary possibility of salvation," as the *Westminster Confession* (chapter 25) puts it. To stray from these cardinal claims is to forfeit the title "catholic."

As has been argued in previous chapters, the Protestant doctrine of the church distinguishes between the visible and the invisible church, the former including any congregation or collection of congregations where the Word is rightly preached and the sacraments are rightly administered. As Augustine put it, "There are many sheep without and many wolves within" this visible church. It consists of all baptized Christians and their children who profess the name of Christ, but it is assumed by Protestants that there are many in this visible church who are like the seed that fell on rocky ground or that were choked by weeds. In other words, not everyone who professes the name of Christ has exercised true saving faith. By contrast, the invisible church consists of the full number of the elect of all ages, none of whom may be lost.

The Roman church, however, has at least historically regarded "the Church universal" as synonymous with itself. In other words, to be a full member of the "Catholic Church" is to be in full communion with the Church of Rome, with the pope as the head. It must be noted, however, that ever since the Second Vatican Council (1963–65), the Roman church has regarded Protestants, like Eastern Orthodox believers, as "separated brethren." In other words, the Protestant distinction between a universal, invisible church and a visible church is admitted. The difference is that, whereas Protestants would regard Rome as one denomination within Christendom (many indeed denying its status even as a visible church), Rome still regards herself as *the* true church and other communions as more or less part of that true communion of saints to the degree that they conform to the sacramental and ecclesiastical character of the Roman church. As the warmth of the sun is felt in varying degrees, so the full radiance of communion with Christ is experienced only in full communion with the Church of Rome, and yet it is possible to be warmed and enlightened apart from that full communion. "But even in spite of" the obstacles to full *visible* union, declares the *Decree on Ecumenism,* "it remains true that all who have been justified by faith in baptism are incorporated into Christ; they therefore have a right to be called Christians, and with good reason are accepted as brothers by the children of the Catholic Church."[2] Therefore, a distinction is made between the visible and invisible church, and, even in cases where a particular congregation or denomination does not possess the full marks of the Roman church, it is necessary to regard all who confess faith in Christ and have some fellowship with the catholic (i.e., historic) church as members of the communion of saints.

In the documents of Vatican II, one definitely senses an ambiguity about how to deal with Protestants (indeed, even atheists are now admitted into eternal life); nevertheless, there is an attempt to square with modern realities the historic Roman doctrine of the church, which admits no separation from the Roman See and regards such as an act of apostasy.

Luther, Zwingli, Calvin, and the later Reformers, including the Puritans, insisted that they were not merely "catholic" in the sense that they had some historic link to Rome—"the Catholic Church"—but that they were in fact truly catholic in the sense that they were simply purging the church of its accumulated errors. Seeing themselves in continuity with the historic catholic church, the Reformers did not regard themselves as revolutionaries or sectarians wanting to overthrow the church and disregard the historic reflections of the great Christian thinkers but employed that very tradition in defense of their rediscoveries. By expelling the Protestants, the Church of Rome was believed to be excommunicating itself from the catholic church, falling under the apostolic anathema for embracing another gospel (Galatians 1:8–9). One need only scan the tracts, catechisms, confessions, and letters of the Reformation to be impressed with the volume of appeals to the church Fathers.

ARE CATHOLICS EVANGELICALS?

Having concluded that evangelicals are catholics—eschewing the heresies of the past two thousand years, which have challenged the biblical doctrine of God, rent Christ's humanity from His deity, denied one or the other, and denied human sinfulness and the need for saving grace, the question arises whether Roman Catholics can be described as "evangelicals."

In all fairness, Fournier argues that "evangelical" is an adjective, not a noun and that it can therefore be used in its most etymological sense. Taken from the Greek word from which we get "gospel," an evangelical is simply one who is concerned with the gospel: its content and its dissemination throughout the world. However, what Fournier evidences is all too typical of evangelicals themselves when he claims title to "evangelical"—namely, a heavy emphasis on "evangelical" as a style or mission. Doctrine seems these days to take a back seat to zeal; the "Evangel" is often left undefined in the pursuit of evangelism. As the pressures of secularism become increasingly burdensome and religious conviction is increasingly marginalized in society, great are the temptations to overcome four and a half centuries of separation and embrace each other in a common struggle to win the world for Christ. And I, for one, would be all too happy if just that sort of outcome were achieved.

There is only one thing standing in the way: The gospel itself.

I do not say this in a cavalier or cynical fashion. It is the serious conclusion after much reflection on the biblical message—and not only my reflection in this time and place but the considered reflection of classical Protestantism. If we do not get the Evangel right, how much excitement can there be over combining resources and energies in promoting it? That was Paul's point, indirectly, in Romans 10, where he applauds his fellow Israelites for their zeal for God but laments that it is a zeal "not based on knowledge." The specific knowledge he has in mind is the doctrine of justification by grace alone through faith alone—the gospel: "Since they did not know the righteousness that comes from God and sought to establish their own, they did not submit to God's righteousness. Christ is the end of the law so that there may be righteousness for everyone who believes" (Romans 10:2–4). If Paul concluded that his own brothers by flesh and blood, whom he dearly loved and commended for their zeal, were excluded from the kingdom of God by denying the righteousness that is a gift in an attempt to establish their own works-righteousness, surely we can be no more generous in the seriousness with which God takes His gospel.

To that end, we have to be perfectly clear about our terms. In his foreword to Fournier's book, the respected evangelical leader Charles Colson writes, "If you are an orthodox Catholic, you may find you are truly part of the evangelical camp."[3] My heart wants to agree with Colson on this point, but we cannot accept this conclusion without radically redefining the very foundations of evangelical commitment. If you are an orthodox Catholic, you are *not* part of the evangelical camp. You may indeed *feel at home* in an evangelicalism that no longer takes evangelical doctrine seriously when compared to Christian activities and social, moral, cultural, and political pursuits. But the contemporary *condition* of evangelicalism is to be distinguished from evangelical *theology*. To do this, we must first of all define *evangelical*.

WHAT IS AN EVANGELICAL?

Fournier turns to *The Westminster Dictionary of Christian Spirituality* for his definition of *evangelical*, especially since the article describes the piety of William Wilberforce:

> The main ingredients of evangelical spirituality have always been early rising, prayer, and Bible study. Wilberforce spent two hours each day, before breakfast, praying and studying the Bible, rebuked himself when the time became shortened. . . . Evangelicals kept a diary, not as a means of recording events, but of self-examination of the recent past and adjustment of the future; it was the evangelical equivalent of the confessional.[4]

Thus, Fournier can conclude, understandably, "I am that kind of Christian, and I hope to become even more so in the years I have left."[5] Indeed, we could all hope for such a high commitment to daily prayer and Bible reading. Nevertheless, I think Fournier is quite right to see no discrepancy between this description and traditional Catholic piety, but as a description of evangelical beliefs it is quite unhelpful. Fournier should probably have turned instead to *The Westminster Dictionary of Christian Theology*, where one reads, "Derived from *euangelion* (evangel, gospel, good news), the term came into use at the Reformation to identify Protestants, especially as they held to the belief in justification by grace through faith and the supreme authority of scripture (often considered the material and formal principles of Reformation teaching)."[6] But Fournier rejects this doctrinal definition of *evangelical* (p. 19), and many evangelicals, it seems, are all too happy to surrender to the same compromise. Even though well-informed evangelicals like Colson affirm their commitment to evangelical doctrine, whenever it is no longer essential to the very label itself, we begin to define our faith by spirituality instead of by the gospel, and this is tantamount to saying that the issues of the Reformation were really not significant to that soul-saving message. In 1975, a plea similar to Fournier's came from a Roman Catholic "evangelical," Paul W. Witte, who also argued that *evangelical* referred to a spiritual and missionary identity rather than to a particular doctrinal system.[7] But it is theology, not spirituality, that best defines a church and marks its distinctives. But again, we must remind ourselves that Paul's commendation of Jewish zeal (that is, spirituality) did not mean that his zealous friends and relatives were included in the camp of Christ, since they had denied that which was essential to that gospel message. Furthermore, if this shift in defining evangelical in terms of spirituality rather than doctrine is legitimate, it is surely of recent origin, since every encyclopedic reference or theological dictionary defines the word in terms of its association with the Reformation message.

If, then, *evangelical* carries a specific historical reference and well-defined dogmatic core, what is it, and can a Roman Catholic embrace it without repudiating his or her own church's teachings?

First, it is essential for us to realize that the Reformers did not believe that they were doing anything new. Rather, they were part of a general cultural trend to look backward to the classical world. For many Renaissance humanists, the "Golden Age" of Greece and Rome became the focal point; for Protestants, it was the apostles and church Fathers who needed to be recovered from the hair-splitting academics who had turned the Bible and Christian theology into a species of secret magic that could only be comprehended by the professionals. To that end, they did not want "Lutherans," "Zwinglians," and "Calvinists" populating the landscape; therefore, "evangelical" was a favored term, although we can see how poorly successive generations followed their counsel. The Reformers really believed that the gospel had been so obscured and its chief claims so consistently denied that "in the place of Christianity is substituted a dreadful profanation," as Calvin put it in the preface to his commentary on Hebrews. Luther argued in a sermon on John 14:23–31, "People say that our teaching is contrary to the old, traditional faith. To what sort of faith do they refer? To what the pope together with his priests and monks believes. How old is this faith? Two or three hundred years!" Our evangelical forebears, therefore, believed that the Roman church had substituted novelties for the apostolic faith. At this point, the concern of the evangelical Reformers must be sharply distinguished from many popular misconceptions.

First are the misconceptions of a good number of secular historians. Many secular historians of this century have been incapable of comprehending the schism of the sixteenth century in spiritual or theological terms, so they have appealed to that which is most familiar to them: secular motivations. For instance, Marxists have reduced the Reformation to a struggle for economic and social liberation. Meanwhile, political and constitutional historians such as G. E. Elton have seen the Reformation primarily as an evolution of society from feudalism to constitutional republicanism. The more psychologically inclined, like Erik Erickson, have explained the movement in terms of Luther's relationship with his father and his sexual drive, which picks up on some unhappy and unscholarly caricatures of nineteenth-century Roman Catholic hagiography.

But Protestants have had their own tradition of hagiography, and that brings me to the second group of misconceptions as to why the Reformation happened. Victorian Protestants (and this would include American Protestants from approximately 1800 to 1950) were fond of caricaturing Romanism as a political and social menace and inculcated irrational suspicion of Roman Catholics as subverters of liberty and practitioners of a secret society in which cultlike rituals were conducted. As a result, when describing the differences between Protestantism and Rome, the accent often fell upon such subjects as Mary, the intercession of the saints, the veneration of statues, superstition, calling the priest "father," going to confession. In other words, it fell on practice rather than on doctrine.

It is not that these issues do not matter but that they are of secondary importance. Luther himself declared in his debate with Erasmus over free will and grace that if the pope would simply discard his gospel of free will and merit, he would gladly cut his losses and begin negotiations on the rest. That, of course, is a paraphrase, and surely the other matters cannot be severed from the misunderstanding of the gospel. But Luther's point was that the debate over how a person is accepted before God was the whole issue of the Reformation. Everything else was derivative.

Having said all this, what were the central concerns in this question of salvation? And does one have to embrace the conclusions of the Reformation in order to be considered "evangelical"?

THE FORMAL PRINCIPLE
OF THE REFORMATION

Because it is the thing that forms, shapes, and determines what we believe as Christians, the Scriptures were singled out as the *sole* and *sufficient* source for faith and practice. "Only Scripture" (*sola scriptura*) was the phrase, and it meant that the church could not preach, teach, command, or practice anything contrary to Scripture, even for very good reasons. The church had no divine authority except to pass on what was written by the prophets and apostles. What it did not mean (but, too often, has come to mean in Protestantism) is that individuals could decide for themselves what to believe, for the individual is obligated to Scripture every bit as much as when one was obligated to the church. Furthermore, it did not mean that every Christian had the right to interpret the Bible for himself or herself, even if that meant contradicting the consensus of the Christian community. Luther reflected that this would simply mean that "each man could go to hell in his own way."

As already mentioned, Luther and Calvin certainly did not argue that they had seen something in Scripture that somehow missed the attention of every other thinker for one and a half millennia; they called upon the Fathers, and especially Augustine, for support. Thus, they demonstrated that their message was not something new but a recovery of something old—something that had been lost by a corrupt curia. It was not a brand-new insight but the recovery of a message that had been taught by the Catholic Church during its best days. Then they formed congregations based on a common confession of faith and immediately drew up catechisms (teaching guides) for the instruction of the faithful. One will notice that in every one of the Protestant confessions and catechisms, each assertion is given a scriptural reference, indicating that Scripture is the final authority and that these distillations are merely authoritative in a derivative sense (in that they are faithful to Scripture), not in an infallible sense (as though they were equal to Scripture in their freedom from the possibility of error). The shared consensus of the churches was not infallible for the Protestants, as it was for Rome, but it was certainly essential, and renegade teachers had to demonstrate to the satisfaction of the whole communion that they understood a certain point in the Bible better than everybody else before it would be accepted.

The Roman church, by the Middle Ages, had begun to argue that tradition was also a source of revelation, since God continued to speak to His church through its magestirium (teaching office), with the pope as its chief shepherd under Christ. Against both the Roman claim to continued revelation apart from Scripture and the similar claims of Anabaptist "enthusiasts," with their alleged revelations, the Reformers asserted the sufficiency of Scripture.

But, granting the infallibility of Scripture, how on earth could an infallible Word be understood and interpreted correctly without an infallible teacher? In answering this understandable objection, the Reformers simply followed many of their fellow Catholic humanists in pointing to the contradictory claims of popes and councils in the Middle Ages. History simply proved that the church was not infallible, so long as the law of noncontradiction applied. The best way to guard a true interpretation of Scripture, the Reformers insisted, was neither to naively embrace the infallibility of tradition, nor the infallibility of the individual, but to recognize the *communal* interpretation of Scripture. The best way to ensure faithfulness to the text is to read it together, not only with the churches of our own time and place, but with the wider "communion of saints" down through the ages. The community may err, but "there is much wisdom in many counselors," and we are most likely to be faithful to the text when we recognize that it is infallible but we are not.

A summary of the Protestant "formal principle" would not be complete without a discussion of the "perspicuity (clarity) of Scripture." At the bottom of Rome's suspicions lay the belief that the Bible was unclear. Obviously, if this is the case, giving the Bible to the laity would invite schism, heresy, and sectarianism. The last two centuries of Protestantism, especially in America, seem only to confirm Rome's greatest fears. Nevertheless, the Reformers were convinced that the Bible was clear, so long as the teachers, pastors, and theologians were not busying themselves with turning the straightforward statements of Scripture into puzzles. That is not to say that it is equally clear about everything. Surely the Bible is clearer in its declarations of Christ's divinity than in its apocalyptic language concerning endtime events, and there must be a distinction between the clear, essential, cardinal truths upon which all Christians must agree (and, for nearly two thousand years, have), and those convictions—perhaps even strongly felt and maintained as clearly scriptural—that are not as obvious and straightforwardly articulated in the text.

The question that keeps popping up, from Genesis to Revelation, is "How are we saved and reconciled to God?" That was Israel's longing, as it looked to God for salvation through the coming Messiah, foreshadowed in the temple, sacrifices, priesthood, kings, and prophets, and it is the oft-repeated question of those who hear the apostles' message: "What must I do to be saved?" It is answered so many times, so clearly, that this is surely in the category of things that are unmistakably clear in the text itself. To deny the doctrine of justification by grace alone through faith alone, therefore, when Paul so plainly declares, "To the man who does not work but trusts God who justifies the wicked, his faith is credited as righteousness" (Romans 4:5), which is so clearly and emphatically spelled out in many parallel passages, is to miss the whole point of the Evangel. This leads us to the second rule of the Reformation: the material principle.

THE MATERIAL PRINCIPLE
OF THE REFORMATION

It is the *articulus ecclesiae stantis et cadentis,* the "article by which the church stands and falls," the Reformers declared of the doctrine of justification. "As long as a person is unaware of this doctrine" and the distinction between the law and the gospel, Luther insisted, "he is no different than a Jew, a Turk [Moslem] or a Heathen." In other words, what distinguishes the Christian message from all others is that salvation is not a project in which God helps humans save themselves, but a rescue operation from start to finish.

First, in order to get to the root of the division on this point, we have to be clear about where the agreement lay. Just as Rome never denied the infallibility of Scripture, it never denied the necessity of grace. In the fourth century, a British monk named Pelagius disturbed the peace of the church with a pernicious teaching that his disciples developed even further. Pelagianism denied the doctrine of original sin, which teaches that we are born in sin (Psalm 51:5; Isaiah 64:6; Romans 3:9–18; Ephesians 2:1–5; 1 Corinthians 2:14; etc.). People are born into the world neutral, said Pelagius. If they exercise their free will in the direction of righteousness, following Christ's example, they will be saved; if they exercise their free will in the direction of sinfulness, following Adam's example, they will be judged. Augustine defended the biblical doctrine of original sin by insisting that we are not only sinners because we sin, following Adam's example, but we sin because we are sinners, inheriting Adam's guilt and corruption. Therefore, what we need in a Second Adam, too, is something more than an example. We need a Savior. We need someone to rescue us by His own grace, since we cannot even respond to Him of our own free will, corrupted as it is by our sinful affections. The accent, therefore, fell on God's grace in the atonement, conversion, and the gift of saving and persevering faith.

In the eleventh century, Anselm refined this Augustinian doctrine of grace on the subject of the Atonement. Jesus Christ had to be God because the debt we owed was infinite and no finite creature could pay it. And yet, He had to be man because the debt was something owed by sinful humanity. In this way, Christ performed the office of a peace-making substitute. Throughout the Middle Ages, questions about grace and works and predestination and free will were fiercely debated, but everyone knew that one rule of the game was that Pelagianism was not allowed, although many theologians came as close as they could to the edges of that heresy.[8]

So if Rome, on the eve of the Reformation, affirmed that salvation was by grace and that no one could be saved without grace first making a change, why did Luther and his associates attack the Roman church for denying that very doctrine?

It was not enough for the Reformers to say that we were saved by grace. Nor, indeed, was it even enough to say that we were saved by grace alone. Thus far they would not have said anything that a typical Augustinian would not have affirmed in his day. What Luther and the other Reformers insisted on was grace alone through faith alone. In medieval doctrine, justification was considered what evangelicals call "regeneration" or the new birth. In baptism, the child received his or her "first justification," and this began the process of sanctification. Thus, justification was seen as the beginning of moral change, and only at the end of the process—assuming one made proper use of the sacraments, confessed one's sins verbally to a priest, and died without having committed a mortal sin—could one hope to be justified. In fact, the process actually continued beyond the grave, in purgatory, where the remaining corruptions and transgressions were purged. The whole process may indeed be ascribed to "grace alone," and yet the way one received this "grace" was, in effect, by meriting it.[9]

When Luther realized, through his study of the Psalms, Romans, and Galatians in particular, that justification is a declaration based on the righteousness of Christ *imputed* to the believer through faith alone, while the sinner remained a sinner—rather than a process based on the righteousness of Christ *infused* into the believer through faith, the sacraments, love, charity, and obedience—he said it was as if the windows of heaven were "flung open and I was born again." The Latin Vulgate, the version of the Bible produced by Jerome, which had been used by the medieval scholars, was an inferior translation. This was what the classical humanists within Rome were beginning to say, and even Erasmus, the brilliant Renaissance humanist who never fully joined the Reformation, nevertheless was the first to point out that the Greek word meaning "to declare righteous" had actually been mistranslated by Jerome as "to make righteous." Though Erasmus was not willing to follow this through to its theological conclusion, his scholarship opened the door through which the Reformers would pass.

Is such a distinction just playing with words? Surely not. The difference between "to declare righteous" and "to make righteous" is the difference between a definitive, once-and-for-all verdict and a gradual progression. If we are justified by a declaration, through faith alone, then the very moment we believe that Christ is our salvation we are declared righteous in Christ. If we are justified by a process of sanctification, which is never complete in this life, there is not a sufficient basis for God to ever accept us. After all, God does not grade on the curve; He requires absolute, perfect obedience, and anything short of it is sin. A holy God will not—cannot—violate one aspect of His own character (justice and holiness) for the sake of another (love and mercy).

Just as the Jews, in spite of their zeal, had forfeited salvation because they sought to justify themselves by their own obedience and would not accept the imputation of Christ's righteousness freely given through faith alone (Rom. 10:1–11), so the Reformers believed that the Church of Rome had abandoned the gospel and substituted for it that age-old confidence in self. That was the difference between the two gospels, between life and death, heaven and hell, justification and judgment. To suggest that we are accepted by God on the basis of Christ's righteousness *and* our own cooperation—be it free will, obedience, love, charity, prayer, a good heart, whatever—is to deny the gospel.

WHAT STILL KEEPS US APART?

1. The doctrine of justification, together with its implications for theology, church life, piety, and worship.

Even as the curia began sitting in Rome to draft a conciliar response to the Reformation, there was hope of reconciliation. A number of cardinals who had gathered at the Council of Trent were convinced of one or more of the Reformers' objections to the popular teaching of the day, and the popular rejection of the gospel by the pope and the monks had not yet been solidified. Since at this stage popes were not regarded as infallible (that was not declared until Vatican I, 1869–70) the door was open to the full reformation of Western Christendom until the Council of Trent (1545–63) finally closed it with its devastating canons against the gospel. Things that had been left to debate in the universities were now closed to discussion as the Council issued what it considered infallible pronouncements on the doctrine of justification and related truths. Now, issues upon which men and women of goodwill could differ were given a single answer: tradition is equal to Scripture in authority; the interpretation of Scripture and the elements of Holy Communion are to be denied to the laity; the Mass is a repetition of Christ's sacrifice and each Mass atones for the people; transubstantiation was officially affirmed, as was the belief in purgatory.

However, the most important decree was also the longest, *Concerning Justification*. The decree begins by affirming, against any Pelagianism, the traditional Augustinian insistence on original sin and the need for grace. Human beings cannot even believe until grace first enables them. In fact, "It is furthermore declared that in adults the beginning of that justification must proceed from the predisposing grace of God through Jesus Christ, that is, from his vocation, whereby, without any merits on their part, they are called"—then the good news ends and the Roman error begins—"that they who by sin had been cut off from God may be disposed through his quickening and helping grace to convert themselves to their own justification by freely assenting to and cooperating with that grace." So, while a person is not "able by his own free will and without the grace of God to move himself to justice in his sight," he can and must cooperate with grace. Justification is defined as "not only a remission of sins but also the sanctification and renewal of the inward man through the voluntary reception of the grace and gifts whereby an unjust man becomes just."

The Protestants never denied the sanctification and renewal of the inward man, but this was identified in Scripture as *sanctification,* not as *justification.* Rome simply combined the two concepts into one: God justifies us through the process of our moving, by the power of God's Spirit at work in our lives, from being unjust to becoming just. This, however, rejects Paul's whole point in Romans 4:1–5, that justification comes only to those who (a) are wicked and (b) stop working for it. God justifies the wicked *as* wicked, the sinner *as* sinner. That is the good news of the gospel, and the scandal of the Cross!

The most relevant canons are the following:

> *Canon 9.* If anyone says that the sinner is justified by faith alone (*supra,* chapters 7–8), meaning that nothing else is required to cooperate in order to obtain the grace of justification, and that it is not in any way necessary that he be prepared and disposed by the action of his own will, let him be anathema.
>
> *Canon 11.* If anyone says that men are justified either by the sole imputation of the justice of Christ or by the sole remission of sins, to the exclusion of the grace and the charity which is poured forth in their hearts by the Holy Ghost (Rom. 5:5), and remains in them, or also that the grace by which we are justified is only the good will of God, let him be anathema.
>
> *Canon 12.* If anyone says that justifying faith is nothing else than confidence in divine mercy (*supra,* chapter 9), which remits sins for Christ's sake, or that it is this confidence alone that justifies us, let him be anathema.
>
> *Canon 24.* If anyone says that the justice received is not preserved and also not increased before God through good works (ibid., chapter 10), but that those works are merely the fruits and signs of justification obtained, but not the cause of the increase, let him be anathema.
>
> *Canon 30.* If anyone says that after the reception of the grace of justification the guilt is so remitted and the debt of eternal punishment so blotted out to every repentant sinner, that no debt of temporal punishment remains to be discharged either in this world or in purgatory before the gates of heaven can be opened, let him be anathema.
>
> *Canon 32.* If anyone says that the good works of the one justified are in such manner the gifts of God that they are not also the good merits of him justified; or that the one justified by the good works that he performs by the grace of God and the merit of Jesus Christ, whose living member he is, does not truly merit an increase of grace, eternal life, and in case he dies in grace the attainment of eternal life itself and also an increase of glory, let him be anathema.

In other words, men and women are accepted before God on the basis of their cooperation with God's grace over the course of their lives, rather than on the basis of Christ's finished work alone, received through faith alone, to the glory of God alone. There are indeed two fundamentally different answers to that recurring biblical question, "How can I be saved?" and, therefore, two fundamentally different gospels.

2. The doctrine of the church as expounded by the Roman church, which requires sound, orthodox Roman Catholics to regard the gospel, as understood by evangelicals, as heresy.

We must remember that it is not we who anathematized Rome, but Rome that anathematized the gospel and thereby anathematized itself. The issue is not even really the condemnation of Protestants (those wounds are easy to heal) but the anathema against the gospel. The evangelicals who remain authentic witnesses to the gospel of grace alone through faith alone, therefore, are carrying on the Catholic faith. Just prior to the Council of Trent, there were many—including cardinals—who accepted the material principle (that is, the gospel) as the Reformation restated it. In fact, there was still much hope on both sides that a unity could be achieved. But when the Council of Trent repeatedly declared that those who believed that their only hope for salvation was faith in Christ now fell under the church's ban. Rome became a schismatic body. It divided itself from historic Christianity by denying, in unmistakable language, that which we as evangelical believers insist upon as "the gospel." This, of course, does not mean that there are not many justified souls in the Church of Rome. As Calvin said, "There is still a church among her," but she herself is not a true visible church. She has denied those marks that are essential to the being of a church: the preaching of the true gospel and the true administration of the sacraments. Apart from these marks, there can be no true visible congregation and, indeed, no formal communion.

This is a very sad business and difficult to accept, much less to defend. It is difficult because of the many personal sympathies I have with my Roman Catholic brothers and sisters. We must not confuse Rome's general apostasy from the visible church with the apostasy of individual Roman Catholic believers. We may have fellowship with Roman Catholics who affirm the gospel, even though we may not have fellowship with the Church of Rome. In spite of the ecumenical aspirations we all share, there is a higher authority to which one must answer. Better for the church to have peace in the next life than in this one. Better to proclaim the true gospel, with earthly divisions, than to abandon the gospel for spurious, humanly crafted unity.

In recent decades, many Roman Catholic theologians have done much to promote understanding between the two traditions, and some have even confessed agreement with the Reformation doctrine. In that case, then, they are "evangelical." But in order to be sound evangelicals they cannot be sound Roman Catholics, for two simple realities: the Council of Trent regards the doctrine of justification by grace alone through faith alone as "damnable" and condemns to everlasting judgment anyone who embraces it; and the Council of Trent is as binding as Holy Scripture for Roman Catholics. That is what we have to comprehend. In Protestantism, a theologian may disagree with Luther or Calvin in principle, but in Roman Catholicism a Council is considered infallible and irrevocable. Post–Vatican II Roman Catholic theologians may irenically and zealously attempt to harmonize Vatican II with Trent; indeed, some will even reject Trent altogether, but they cannot speak on behalf of the church, so long as the Roman church retains in the very warp and woof of its ecclesiology the claim to infallibility for those councils and papal decisions.[10] As long as Rome is officially committed to its notion of an infallible tradition and unerring councils, there can be absolutely no hope for a visible restored union, for there can be no hope of its repentance for having rejected the gospel in such clear and dogmatic terms. It is not because, after all, so many martyrs spilled their blood over this matter and, therefore, we owe it to their memory to carry a grudge. If the gospel is transcendent and eternally true, *it* defines the identity of a true visible church.

Here I would like to digress briefly, to consider one recent argument made by Wolfhart Pannenberg, the distinguished German Protestant theologian.[11] This discussion is illustrative of the numerous exchanges that take place today in ecumenical circles. In the early 1980s, Bishop Lohse of the Protestant church of Germany openly published to Cardinal Ratzinger, then Archbishop of Munich, his intention "that it was now time for the churches affected to establish, not merely in personal dialogue but to declare in binding form, that the condemnatory pronouncements formulated in the sixteenth century about the doctrine, form, and practice of the Roman Catholic Church are no longer applicable to today's partner." In other words, it was Lohse's belief that the Roman church that Luther and Calvin regarded as a false congregation is no longer that same organization. Ratzinger met Lohse's olive branch by declaring that "a corresponding reexamination of the doctrinal decisions of the Council of Trent was also necessary."

It seems on the surface that Cardinal Ratzinger, now in charge of doctrinal concerns for the entire Roman Catholic Church, was much more on target than the Protestant bishop in recognizing the real impasse. Whereas Lohse was interested in establishing a commission to determine "that new realities have come into being, and that the old massive dissensus to all intents and purposes no longer exists," Ratzinger realized that the real issue was Trent. What can possibly be achieved by an attempt either to say that the Reformers did not really mean what they said they meant or to deny that Rome's anathemas are unambiguous? For those who believe that the Reformation doctrine of justification *sola fide* (that is, the declaration of a sinner to be right solely because of the righteousness of Christ imputed through the mere reception of the gift in faith) is equivalent to the New Testament doctrine of justification, the issue is not over what was said in the sixteenth century but whether Protestants and Catholics believe that this is what is still binding on the churches today.

That is surely not to say that research, debate, and dialogue on the historical understanding of particular issues in the Reformation are useless. After all, as Alister McGrath has clearly demonstrated in chapter 9, on a number of issues it may be argued that both sides exaggerated the views of their opponents in the heat of polemical warfare. Hyperbole must be distinguished from reality. Nevertheless, there are certain areas where the divisions are clear, and this, unfortunately, is where they come to a head: the Council of Trent. Here there is no ambiguity. That is why it is important to realize that the issue concerning us is not Rome's condemnation of Protestants. These, indeed, can easily be retracted or softened. But harsh words are not really at issue. The main concern is not, Does the church of Rome still condemn the Protestants? (After all, that was answered negatively at Vatican II.) The real issue is, Does the church of Rome still condemn the gospel? In other words, are those anathemas still binding on the faithful who are in communion with the Roman See? Therefore, I think Lohse missed the point, along with his ecumenical commission, and Ratzinger hit the mark. If Rome were to reverse the decisions of the Council of Trent, or even indicate an official openness to that possibility, the door would be wide open for meaningful ecumenical dialogue.

The problems, however, come into sharp focus on the Protestant side when theologians such as Pannenberg endorse this Protestant commission of Bishop Lohse when it declares that the reason such denunciations are no longer binding is that the doctrine of either side is no longer "determined by the error which the condemnation wished to avert." In other words, Roman Catholics no longer really stand where Trent stands and Protestants are realizing that they need to reevaluate New Testament teaching because of more recent studies that seem to have weakened or contradicted the Reformers' dogmatic judgments. Pannenberg implies this when he writes that "one would expect that the Protestant side be prepared at least in principle to admit certain difficulties in the form of the Reformation doctrine on justification as compared to the biblical witnesses." He adds further, "For example, the Pauline phrase about the love of God being poured out into our hearts by the Holy Spirit (Rom. 5:5)" suggests difficulties with the Reformation formulation of justification.[12] But it is not as if this passage suddenly appeared in the twentieth century; it is thoroughly exegeted by Luther, Calvin, and other Reformers in painstaking detail. They did not ignore it; they included it in the category of sanctification rather than justification. If Paul had said, "We are justified by the love of God being poured out into our hearts by the Holy Spirit," that would present difficulties, but the Reformers never denied or even downplayed the reality that both actions of God take place in a person's salvation: justification by a righteousness external to us, and sanctification by the Holy Spirit's transforming work within us.

Pannenberg's remarks point up the recurring problem with Protestant ecumenism, and that is the tendency to say that the Reformers got justification wrong. It is an understandable response if one is in a discussion with partners where a consensus is sought. In any resolution of conflict, should not both sides be willing to give up certain territory? And if Rome is kind enough to be open to taking a fresh look at Trent, should we not also be open to the possibility that the Reformers did not have it all right? Surely Protestants do not believe that the Reformers cannot be contradicted in principle (unlike the traditional Roman Catholic position on councils); nevertheless, are we actually prepared to say that the New Testament does not clearly teach justification by grace alone through faith alone? For those of us who still believe that the Reformers at least got this point correct, it is impossible to reach a consensus that falls short of endorsing it as the gospel.

One further note must be added to the discussion of Rome's official (and, therefore, binding) pronouncements. Prior to Vatican II, a devout Catholic and Protestant in America would happily work side by side but would not even dream of attending an event sponsored by the other person's church. But the Council radically changed the ethos of parish life for Catholics. The Mass was now conducted in English, the charismatic movement brought Catholics into closer proximity to evangelicals, and Bible studies were encouraged. Protestants began to exult that Rome was going through the Reformation after five centuries of rejection. Upon closer inspection, however, Vatican II appears to have sown the seeds of its own destruction, and that is attested to by many Catholic theologians who, after three decades, are wondering if the Council unleashed Protestant liberalism in the Catholic Church.

Vatican II not only did not contradict previous dogmas and decrees; it is itself even more seriously flawed at key points than Trent. The universalism of Karl Rahner, Hans Küng, and Hans Urs Von Balthasar found its way into the Council's official pronouncements. (See chapter 4 for more on this.) It is not an overstatement to say that whereas Trent avoided the Pelagian heresy, though condemning justification by faith alone, Vatican II embraced the naturalistic perspective.

By making peace with modernity, Rome embraced the Enlightenment, not the Reformation, and that means that conservative Catholics who are suspicious of the affects of Vatican II are actually closer to evangelicals than to their own theologians. Rome may appear to be moving closer to Protestantism, but those who are guided by the historic evangelical convictions must regard the change as negative rather than positive, especially for Roman Catholics, if liberal Protestantism is the partner.

It is often said that "time heals all wounds." It may indeed heal many, but one wound time can never heal is error. A wrong understanding of the way in which God justifies sinners in the sixteenth century is still a wrong understanding in the twentieth. This chapter—probably this entire volume—will be regarded by some, both Roman Catholics and Protestants, who frequently attach to the word *doctrine* some negative adjective, as a rather anachronistic, if charming, naïveté considering the ecumenical strides of the last half-century. How can we sweep away the achievements of the theological negotiators from Vatican II to ARCIC II? It is surely not because these great attempts have gone unnoticed or without sympathy from orthodox Protestant theologians; rather it is due to our conviction that the fundamental disagreement still centers on the teaching of the Council of Trent. However clever the attempts at "denying" that which is not allowed to be denied, genuine unity requires a common affirmation of a shared faith, and we simply cannot exclude from a shared faith our confidence in the very gospel that still stands officially condemned by Rome. Time has not changed either the truth of that gospel or the judgment of Rome.

But that does not mean, of course, that there is no spiritual unity between Roman Catholics and Protestants, provided both are not found to deny the gospel. There are many Roman Catholics who either do not understand enough of their church's position to deny justification or who embrace it in spite of the church's having gone on record against it. Either from ignorance, or from rebellion, there are many Roman Catholics who are surely numbered among Christ's flock and universal church. As orthodox evangelicals, we long and pray for the day when Rome repudiates her own repudiation of the gospel at Trent and related declarations so that we can once again be united in a visible demonstration to the world of the power of that gospel to not only liberate individuals and restore them to a right relationship with God but to establish peace and unity among the people of God. But if in that process of work, ministry, and prayer, we are found to have established our unity on some other foundation, on some other rock, it will be a unity built on sand, which, when the waves of God's judgment crash at the Son's appearing, will be washed out to sea.

NO PLACE FOR SELF-RIGHTEOUSNESS

In conclusion, I would be remiss not to point out how inconsistent (perhaps even hypocritical) it is of evangelicals to criticize Roman Catholics while they themselves are ignorant of, or even reject, the very Evangel they claim to protect. Very often evangelical preachers and laypeople speak of being saved by "being born again," and this expression, much less the emphasis, conveys the same impression we find explicit in the Council of Trent: that justification (that is, being made right with God) is identical to the new birth and sanctification rather than specifically linked to faith in Christ and imputation.

Earlier, I mentioned the Pelagian heresy and the stand the Roman church took (with Augustine) against this destructive teaching. Denying original sin, Pelagianism argues that human nature is not corrupted by the Fall; we sin by following Adam's poor example but not because we have inherited a corrupt nature. Therefore, all the human race needs is just enough grace to get us going in the right direction so that we will follow the right example, Jesus Christ. In this way we can get back on track (that is, be "saved"). This heresy, repudiated regularly and consistently by the Roman church, is nevertheless embraced by such noteworthy evangelicals in this country as the nineteenth-century revivalist Charles Finney and by a growing flank of evangelical thinkers in the twentieth. It is gaining a wider hearing in evangelical circles today, just as it had in the earlier part of this century, as the optimistic core of the modernist gospel.[13]

Though Rome may not maintain an official commitment to the gospel in its insistence on justification by grace alone through faith alone, surely, judging by history, it has been no less faithful than Protestants in the last two centuries in defending the doctrine of grace in general. Entire denominations that were committed confessionally to the doctrine of justification have ended up adopting, in actual practice, a Pelagian message. When evangelicals deny human depravity and inability, affirm that human beings cooperate in their own conversion by the use of their free will, and view salvation as a project of moral improvement (especially when that affirms a notion of entire sanctification), they are further afield from the gospel than Rome has ever been.

When it comes to the evangelical doctrine itself, where is the emphasis on the objective work of Christ outside of us, in history? It has taken a back seat, it seems, to spirituality, piety, morality, social and political crusades, inner healing, and psychologized inwardness. No longer are we saved from sin by grace; we are now healed from neuroses by therapy. No longer is condemnation by God for our sins our greatest fear but condemnation by ourselves for our negative self-image. No medieval theologian or mystic could improve on the inwardness of evangelical spirituality in our day. The interior experiences of the Christ within are heralded, while the objective, external work of Christ on the cross, dying for our sins and being raised for our justification, is largely ignored.

My own experience has led me to conclude that most of our people cannot even define justification. In fact, 84 percent of the evangelicals surveyed said that in the matter of salvation, "God helps those who help themselves," and well over half even thought it was a biblical quotation. Seventy-seven percent of "evangelical" Christians believe that human beings are basically good.[14] This means that 77 percent of evangelicals are Pelagian, well beyond the ranks even of traditional Roman Catholic understanding.

These things must be said because I am convinced that we need a second Reformation, but it will not be a reformation in which insults and caricatures will be hurled from Protestants who wonder why Catholics still have not gotten the message; it will be just as heated a debate within Protestantism because of unprecedented unfaithfulness to the Word of God. Who can deny that Protestants have led the way in the twentieth century away from a high view of Scripture and God's grace in Christ? Which branch of the church has done more to lower the doctrine of Christ to a mere moral example? Which church has gone so far as to deny original sin and affirm the goodness of human nature? Which tradition has done so much to deny not only the *sufficiency,* but even the *reliability* of the Word of God? In short, which branch of Christendom has so carelessly capitulated to the spirit of the age?

For these reasons and more, many conservative Protestants correctly perceive in Rome a degree of faithfulness—at least in its official declarations. (One must beware of the degree to which Roman Catholic theologians are now carriers of the modern Protestant virus, as Robert Strimple points out in chapter 4.) The temptation is to abandon an uncertain, confused Protestantism—and even an evangelicalism that is, in James Hunter's words, "a tradition in disarray"—in order to be part of something that, though it may not have it all right, looks better on a scale of 1–10. I know these temptations and have experienced them myself. Nevertheless, here is where we must constantly remind ourselves of the difference: In Protestantism, an unreformed church—regardless of how unfaithful—may, in principle, be reformed. The Roman Catholic Church, by contrast, will never repudiate its own condemnation of the Evangel until it repudiates the infallibility of the Council of Trent and the popes who have endorsed it. This is the issue upon which authentic ecumenical dialogue must turn. I do not suggest that we should give up trying to seek visible unity, nor that we refuse to dialogue with Roman Catholic laypeople and theologians, many of whom may be our brothers and sisters.

To conclude by returning to the opening query, "What still keeps us apart?" my own reply at the end of a century of Protestant "truth decay" (as Os Guinness has expressed it) is, "Nothing." Absolutely nothing keeps evangelicals and Catholics apart if evangelicals abandon the distinctive convictions that have made the past divisions so painfully necessary. We need to seek a reformation of both of our traditions.

That will require, on the part of Protestants, a return to Scripture and its Evangel and, for Rome, a repudiation of its anathema on the gospel. Though we may not agree with the total package, mark well the words of the Roman Catholic theologian Johann Baptist Metz:

> To speak about the Reformation and make it, not just an object of remembrance, but an object of hope, indeed an incentive to change—change for all of us, including myself as a Catholic—means one thing: we must bring that question and that awareness which inspired the Reformation into a relationship with the present age. . . . Many theologians writing about the Reformation assure us nowadays that Luther's famous fundamental question regarding a gracious God can scarcely be made intelligible to people today, let alone communicated as relevant to their lives. This question is said to belong to another, noncontemporary world. I do not share this position at all. The heart of the Reformation's question—How can we attain to grace?—is absolutely central to our most pressing concerns. . . . The second Reformation concerns all Christians, is coming upon all of us, upon the two great churches of our Christianity.[15]

Is this beyond the sovereignty of God's Spirit to accomplish? With Christ, in His reply to the disciples, we prayerfully answer, "With man this is impossible, but with God all things are possible" (Matthew 19:26).

NOTES

1. Keith A. Fournier, *Evangelical Catholics: A Call for Christian Cooperation* (Nashville: Nelson, 1990). I certainly do not take issue with a call for Christian cooperation, especially in the interest of a shared sense of values. My only concern here is that *evangelical* is no longer being defined theologically, in order to accommodate nonevangelicals. Why should we not simply say that there should be cooperation with nonevangelicals on matters of common interest?

2. Austin Flannery, O.P., editor, *Vatican Council II: The Conciliar and Post Conciliar Documents* (Northport, N.Y.: Costello, 1981), 455.

3. Charles Colson, in the introduction to Fournier, *Evangelical Catholics*, vi.

4. Gordon S. Wakefield, ed., *The Westminster Dictionary of Christian Spirituality* (Philadelphia: Westminster/John Knox, 1983),138.

5. Colson, in the introduction to Fournier, *Evangelical Catholics*, 22.

6. Alan Richardson and John Bowden, *The Westminster Dictionary of Christian Theology* (London: SCM, 1983), 191.

7. Paul W. Witte, *On Common Ground: Protestant & Catholic Evangelicals* (Waco, Tex.: Word, 1975).

8. Thomas Bradwardine, thirteenth-century Archbishop of Canterbury, wrote a treatise titled *The Cause of God Against the New Pelagians*, raising concern over the "Pelagian flood," sweeping many into a denial of predestination, the necessity of grace, and the unmerited nature of that grace. Johann von Staupitz also wrote in defense of the classical Augustinian doctrine of grace in his *Eternal Predestination and Its Execution in Time*. An Augustinian abbot, he argued that faith was the sole condition of

God's acceptance of the believing sinner. Staupitz was Luther's mentor, superior, and close friend to whom Luther acknowledged a tremendous debt. Many similar examples could be offered of the fluid nature of the discussion prior to Trent.

9. Here, the Roman church distinguished between *condign* merit, which is an outright payment for that which was truly earned, and *congruent* merit, which is not really earned in the truest sense of the term, but which God graciously accepts "as if" it had been merited truly.

10. Karl Barth, for instance, introducing the controversial Roman Catholic theologian Hans Küng's work on justification, concluded that the theologian had understood him correctly, but that by assuming that Barth's doctrine was the same as Trent's, Küng was perceived as doing a bit too much reconstructive surgery on the tradition. Eduard Schillebeeckx and Michael Schmaus have also attempted reconstructions, including the mild reworking in the latter's work, *Dogma 6: Justification and the Last Things* (London: Sheed & Ward, 1977). See also the important works of George Tavard, *Justification: An Ecumenical Study* (Ramsey, N.J.: Paulist, 1983), and Jared Wicks, S. J., ed., *Catholic Scholars Dialogue with Luther* (Chicago: Loyola Univ. Press, 1970). Remarkably, Richard P. McBrien (*Catholicisim: Study Edition* [New York: Harper & Row, 1981]), the Notre Dame theologian, in his glossary defines justification and sanctification as two distinct things and leaves the definition so loose that a Protestant would easily be able to navigate within its waters. Luther's *simul iustus et peccator* appears to have ecclesiastical approval in McBrien's definition, McBrien merely adding, "Catholic doctrine insists that *justification* leads to *sanctification*," but this is the Protestant doctrine. However, if Trent defines Catholic doctrine, justification *is* sanctification! McBrien returns to the traditional view, however, in the text of the book: "The *process* of passing from the *condition* of sin as a child of the first Adam to a *condition* of adopted sonship in Christ is called justification" (p. 309, emphasis mine).

11. Wolfhart Pannenberg, "Must the Churches Continue to Condemn Each Other?" *Pro Ecclesia: A Journal of Catholic and Evangelical Theology* 2, no. 4 (fall 1993): 404–23.

12. Ibid.

13. Charles Finney denied original sin, the substitutionary atonement, the necessity of supernatural grace in the new birth, and argued that the doctrine "of justification by an imputed righteousness is another gospel." See the abridged edition of his *Systematic Theology* (Minneapolis: Bethany, 1976). For modern parallels, see Clark Pinnock, *A Wideness In God's Mercy* (Grand Rapids: Zondervan, 1992). Denials of the evangelical doctrine of justification abound today, even among self-styled evangelical scholars. Russell Spittler (*Christian Spirituality: Five Views of Sanctification*, ed. Donald L. Alexander [Downers Grove, Ill.: InterVarsity, 1988]) writes, "But can it really be true—saint and sinner simultaneously? I wish it were true. . . . Is this correct: 'I don't need to work at "becoming." I'm already declared to be holy? No sweat needed?' Still, I'm grateful for Luther's phrase [*simul iustus et peccator*, simultaneously justified and sinful] and for his descendants. Their earthiness has called me away from my superspirituality. But simul iustus et peccator? I hope it's true! I simply fear it's not" (pp. 42–43). In that same book, the Wesleyan representative, Laurence W. Wood, defines justification as "freedom from the acts of sin" and "an infusion of divine love" (pp. 37–38).

14. George Barna, *What Americans Believe* (Ventura: Regal, 1993), 89.

15. Johann Baptist Metz, *The Emergent Church* (New York: Crossroad, 1986), 48–50.

One of the fundamental claims of the Roman Catholic Church is that it is the one true Church established by the Lord Jesus Christ. It states that its teachings can be traced back two thousand years in an unbroken succession to the apostles and that these teachings are necessary to be believed for salvation. Therefore, is not the Protestant church a schismatic and heretical sect that has cut itself off from the one source of salvation?

Quite the contrary, the claims of the Church of Rome are not justified in light of a careful study of church history. It is the Roman Catholic Church, not the Protestant, that has departed from the faith once delivered to the saints.

DID I REALLY LEAVE THE HOLY CATHOLIC CHURCH?
The Journey into Evangelical Faith and Church Experience

William Webster

S ince Vatican II the Roman Catholic Church has liberalized its attitude toward evangelicals. In spite of this, there has been a considerable exodus of Roman Catholics into evangelical churches. This is due in part to aggressive evangelism by evangelicals, exposure to Scripture through involvement in Bible studies and the witness of friends and family who were former Roman Catholics. Karl Keating himself admits that the figure approaches hundreds of thousands who have left Rome for evangelical or fundamental Protestantism.[1]

I have been a part of that movement. I was born and raised Roman Catholic, attending parochial schools and a Benedictine monastery in high school. I was thoroughly catechized in Roman Catholic theology. I was an altar boy in the days when the Latin Mass was still used. I used to pray earnestly for souls in purgatory and was thoroughly devoted to Mary. But as a teen I followed in the path of many young people in turning from the church to a life of sin and rebellion. By the time I was nineteen years old I was a disillusioned alcoholic. At twenty-four, through the witness of evangelical Protestants, I was converted to Jesus Christ. I joined a Protestant church, not because of an anti-Catholic attitude, but because it was through this church I had come to know Christ, and now I had a deep desire to know more of God's Word. I was completely ignorant of major differences between Roman Catholicism and Protestantism. Over a number of years, exposure to God's Word deepened my understanding of salvation and fueled a desire to share it with others, particularly Roman Catholic friends. Eventually, I studied Roman Catholic teaching carefully, finally writing a book on the subject.

TRUTH: THE DEFINING ISSUE

Shortly after writing my book I read Karl Keating's *Catholicism and Fundamentalism.* Here I encountered a very aggressive Roman Catholic lay apologist attempting to validate the authority of the church and its traditions from church history, an area that most Protestants, including myself at the time, knew little about. His book underscored an issue often overlooked or misunderstood by Protestants—because of this, most contemporary Protestants do not properly understand Roman Catholics. The issue Keating raises is truth: What is it? Who has it? and How do you know? The Protestant thinks of truth as one dimensional—*sola scriptura*—ultimate truth and authority is in Scripture alone. But for many Roman Catholics truth is not so one dimensional. For the Roman Catholic, the *church* is ultimate truth and authority, not Scripture. Whereas the Roman Catholic Church affirms the full inspiration of Scripture, it is not the *only* truth or ultimate and final authority. It is this Roman Catholic position that Keating attempts to argue on historical grounds.

What we are dealing with here are basic presuppositions about authority that have direct bearing on how one approaches Scripture. From a Roman Catholic perspective, what the conflict over the interpretation of Scripture boils down to is this: the "infallible church" versus fallible individuals who have rebelled against the "ultimate authority," which was established by Christ. This point of view was highlighted in a recent letter I received from a Roman Catholic. The writer stated, "I am a Catholic because of the promises our Lord made to the Church and the authority He gave to St. Peter as stated in the gospels. I believe they are just as valid today as then. I could not in good conscience belong to any other church." Those are, no doubt, honest heartfelt convictions. Whether or not the facts that form the foundation for those convictions are true is another matter altogether, but this writer's sentiments clearly articulate the Roman Catholic presupposition regarding the authority of the church. Keating, Hahn, Matatics, and others (see chapter 10) attempt with earnest evangelistic zeal to defend this position through historical apologetics.

Keating's book became for me a personal challenge to study church history carefully. What does history really say regarding Scripture, authority, and tradition? Was the Protestant Reformation truly justified, or did the Reformers forsake the faith of the early church and introduce novel doctrines? It is important to note that the Reformers advanced their arguments as diligently on historical grounds as on theological. They knew church history, the church Fathers, and the major theologians of the church throughout the Middle Ages. An example of what I mean can be seen in John Calvin. In his *Institutes,* he quotes from no less than thirty-seven major church Fathers of the Patristic Age, not to mention many scholastic theologians, popes, and church councils. So the historical issues Keating sets forth are by no means new.

In a recent debate Keating stated that each individual has a solemn responsibility to seek and follow truth no matter how opposed it might be to what one has been taught or what it might cost in personal terms. I cannot agree more, and that is precisely why I write this chapter. I have spent the last five years in intensive historical research. I have gone to primary source material and have read many major works of the most notable church Fathers. I have read Roman Catholic and Protestant historians and have listened to hours of taped messages by Scott Hahn and Gerry Matatics. All this is to say that I am a Protestant by conviction on the basis of the truth of both Scripture and history. I sought to honestly determine if I had left the holy catholic church when I left the fellowship of Rome.

In this chapter I state some pertinent historical facts I discovered that bear primarily upon the issue of authority and the Roman Catholic Church. I will begin by stating the Roman Catholic position in a general way and then seek to deal with specific issues in particular.

The Roman Catholic Church claims that it alone is the one true church established by Christ and boasts of a two-thousand-year consensus for its teachings. It places under anathema—that is, it condemns to hell, unless there is repentance—all who disagree with its teachings,[2] anathemas that, it is important to add, have never been repudiated. These claims are summarized in a principle implicitly enunciated by the second-century Father, Irenaeus.[3] It was explicitly taught in the fifth century by Vincent of Lerins and later affirmed and officially sanctioned by the councils of Trent and Vatican I. It is the principle known as the "unanimous consent of the Fathers." Vincent expresses the principle in these terms: Those teachings are truly catholic and apostolic that have been believed everywhere, always, and by all.[4] To claim catholicity and apostolic authority, therefore, is not simply a matter of succession but, rather, a matter of conformity to apostolic doctrine and the test of universality, antiquity, and consent. Not only does it embody doctrines, but also the interpretation of Scripture. Both Trent and Vatican I state that it is unlawful for anyone to interpret Scripture "contrary to the unanimous consent of the fathers."[5] These councils tell us that there is a test by which the teachings of the Roman Catholic Church can be judged and validated, the test of history, as expressed in the principle of unanimous consent. What do the historical facts really reveal for the claims of the Roman Catholic Church relative to its teachings on Scripture, tradition, the canon, the papacy, and Mary?

SCRIPTURE AND TRADITION

Roman Catholic dogma teaches that the doctrine of *sola scriptura* (that Scripture alone is sufficient and the ultimate authority in all matters of faith and morals) is unscriptural. This dogma is unfounded because *sola scriptura* is the express teaching of Scripture and in particular of the Lord Jesus Christ. The word *sufficient* is not found in the Word of God in an explicit sense to describe the Scriptures. But neither is the word *trinity* found in Scripture, yet the doctrine is taught plainly throughout its pages. The same is true with regard to the teaching of *sola scriptura*. It is as apparent as the teaching of the Trinity.[6] The doctrine is clearly demonstrated in the life and teaching of Christ.

Clearly Scripture was the ultimate authority for Jesus' personal life and ministry. He always appealed to the written Word of God to settle disputes, never to oral tradition. When He refers to the "Word of God" His reference is always to recorded Scripture. According to His teaching, Scripture was the final judge of all tradition. In fact, Jesus has virtually nothing positive to say about tradition (cf. Matthew 4:4; 5:17–19; 15:2–9; 22:29–32). Clearly, if the Son of God teaches that all tradition is to be judged by its conformity to the Scriptures, then tradition is subordinate to Scripture and Scripture is logically the ultimate authority.

Roman Catholic teaching claims that *sola scriptura* is unhistorical; that is, it contradicts the universal teaching of the early church. The more I have searched for the truth regarding these Roman Catholic beliefs, the more I have been compelled to conclude that the facts will not support this claim. *Sola scriptura* was the universal teaching of the church Fathers and for the church as a whole through the later Middle Ages. Cyril of Jerusalem (A.D. 315–386) is reflective of the overall view of the Fathers:

> Concerning the divine and sacred Mysteries of the Faith, we ought not to deliver even the most casual remark without the Holy Scriptures; nor be drawn aside by mere probabilities and the artifices of argument. Do not then believe me because I tell thee of these things, unless thou receive from the Holy Scriptures the proof of what is set forth: for this salvation, which is our faith, is not by ingenious reasonings, but by proof from the Holy Scriptures. . . . In these articles we comprehend the whole doctrine of faith. . . . For the articles of the Faith were not composed at the good pleasure of men, but the most important points chosen from all Scriptures, make up the one teaching of the Faith. . . . This Faith, in a few words, hath enfolded in its bosom the whole knowledge of godliness contained both in the Old and New Testaments. Behold, therefore, brethren and hold the traditions (2 Thes. 2:15) which ye now receive, and write them on the table of your hearts. . . . Now heed not any ingenious views of mine; else thou mayest be misled; but unless thou receive the witness of the prophets concerning each matter, believe not what is spoken; unless thou learn from Holy Scripture . . . receive not the witness of man.[7]

Cyril of Jerusalem was a bishop of one of the most important sees of the church and responsible for instructing catechumens in the faith. No clearer concept of *sola scriptura* could be given than that seen in these statements of Cyril. He equates the teaching he is handing on to these catechumens with tradition that he says must be proven by Scripture. Tradition is simply the teaching of the church that he is passing on orally, but that tradition must be validated by the written Scriptures. He states further that the extent of authority vested in any teacher, be he bishop or layman, is limited to Scripture. No teaching is to be received that cannot be proven from Scripture. The church does have authority, as Cyril himself acknowledges, but it is an authority grounded in fidelity to Scripture and not principally in succession. According to Cyril, the church is subject to the final authority of Scripture, and even the church is to be disregarded if it moves outside that authority in its teaching.

Cyril is a vigorous proponent of the concept of *sola scriptura*. It is a teaching he handed down to the catechumens as an implicit article of the faith. As one reads the writings of the Fathers it becomes clear that Cyril's statements are representative of the church as a whole. J. N. D. Kelly affirms this observation:

> The clearest token of the prestige enjoyed by [Scripture] is the fact that almost the entire theological effort of the Fathers, whether their aims were polemical or constructive, was expended upon what amounted to the exposition of the Bible. Further, it was everywhere taken for granted that, for any doctrine to win acceptance, it had first to establish its Scriptural basis.[8]

Therefore, the Protestant teaching of *sola scriptura* is not a heresy or a novel doctrine, but in reality it is a reaffirmation of the faith of the early church. It is both biblical and historical, yet the Roman Catholic Church continues to teach that oral tradition is a second source of divine revelation, equally as authoritative as Scripture and that this was the view held by the church Fathers. Such a claim, however, contradicts both Scripture and history. When the Fathers speak of a tradition handed down from the apostles independent of Scripture, they are referring to ecclesiastical customs and practices, never to doctrine. Tradition was always subordinate to Scripture as an authority, and the Word of God itself never teaches that tradition is inspired. The Scriptures give numerous warnings against tradition,[9] and the Fathers rejected the teaching of an apostolic oral tradition independent of Scripture as a gnostic heresy. For the church Fathers apostolic tradition or teaching was embodied and preserved in Scripture. The teaching of the Fathers is this: What the apostles initially proclaimed and taught orally, they later committed to writing in the New Testament. Irenaeus succinctly states it in these words: "We have learned from none others the plan of our salvation, than from those through whom the gospel has come down to us, which they did at one time proclaim in public, and, at a later period, by the will of God, handed down to us in the Scriptures, to be the ground and pillar of our faith."[10]

How is one to know what the apostles taught orally? It has been handed down to us in the Scriptures, and they in turn are the ground and pillar of our faith. The historical circumstances that prompted Irenaeus's words are important to understand. He was writing against the Gnostics who claimed to have access to an oral tradition handed down from the apostles, which was independent of the written Word of God. Irenaeus, as well as Tertullian, explicitly repudiates such a concept. The bishops of the church were in the direct line of succession from the apostles, and they were faithful to the apostolic teaching they proclaimed orally, but that doctrine could at every point be validated by Scripture. Ellen Flesseman-Van Leer affirms this: "For Irenaeus, the church doctrine is never purely traditional; on the contrary, the thought that there could be some truth transmitted exclusively *viva voce* (orally) is a Gnostic line of thought."[11] In fact, the apostle Paul himself states that the gospel he initially preached orally could be verified by the written Scriptures.[12] The church as a whole, up to the thirteenth century, never viewed tradition to be a source of revelation. Brian Tierney affirms this:

> Before the thirteenth century, there is little trace in the works of the medieval theologians of the view that Tradition constituted a source of divine revelation separate from Scripture and little inclination to set up a distinction—still less an opposition—between scriptural revelation and church doctrine. . . . For twelfth century theologians (as for the Fathers themselves), church and Scripture "co-inhered." This seems true in the sense that the teaching of the church and the teaching of Scripture were conceived of as essentially one. "The men of the middle ages lived in the Bible and by the Bible." When twelfth century theologians observed—as they sometimes did—that many things were held by the church that were not found in Scripture they seem to have had in mind only liturgical customs or pious practices. An extra-Scriptural source of faith like the Apostles' Creed (which was commonly regarded as a work of the apostles themselves) was held to define various tenets of Christian doctrine with absolute fidelity; but it was not considered to be a body of revealed truth supplementary to sacred Scripture. Rather, the Creed could be called in the twelfth century a "summary" of the contents of Scripture. In this view Scripture recorded divine truth once and for all, and the living voice of the church, guided by the Holy Spirit, interpreted that truth and proclaimed it anew to each succeeding generation.[13]

The Scriptures do refer to Paul delivering oral tradition to the believers of Thessalonica, which they were to obey (2 Thessalonians 2:15). But the word *tradition* used here does not refer to the same thing as the tradition of Roman Catholicism. The word as used in this text simply means "teaching." Paul has given them oral instruction, and that does not necessarily concern the major doctrines of the faith. That is clear from the same epistle, where he exhorts these believers to stand firm in the tradition they had received from him: "to keep away from every brother who is idle and does not live according to the teaching [tradition KJV] you received from us" (3:6). Paul's use of the term *tradition* here does not have the meaning assigned to it by the Roman Catholic Church in two important respects: in its *concept* and in its *content*. The very concept of Roman Catholic tradition as a separate source of revelation independent of Scripture contradicts both Scripture and the teaching of the historic catholic church. The Roman Catholic Church has departed from the teaching and practice of both the early church and the Word of God itself. The early church believed in *sola scriptura*, but the Roman Catholic Church has repudiated this principle in order to elevate its tradition to a position of authority equal to the Scriptures. The heresy of Gnosticism condemned by Irenaeus and Tertullian is embraced in this error.

In addition to the concept itself, there is also the issue of the actual doctrinal content of Roman Catholic tradition, for its specific teachings not only contradict the teaching of Scripture but that of the church of the first centuries (see chapter 4). Over several centuries the Roman Catholic Church has added doctrines to the apostolic tradition that it says are dogmas of the faith, necessary to be believed for salvation. These dogmas were either never taught in the early church or were plainly repudiated by it. This is clearly seen from the following examples.

THE CANON

From my early training I learned that Catholicism claims that the church established the canon of Scripture in the fourth century and that therefore the church is the ultimate authority, not Scripture. Roman Catholic apologists often ask, "If you accept the limits of the Canon that were authoritatively established by the Roman Catholic Church, why do you reject the ultimate authority of that Church?" The simple reason is that the premise upon which that logic rests is fallacious because the specific claims the Church of Rome makes for itself regarding the canon are contradicted by the facts of history. The Roman Catholic Church did *not* authoritatively establish the limits of the canon for the church. The New Testament books were already recognized in the church prior to the Western councils of Hippo and Carthage in North Africa in the fourth century. These were provincial councils that had no authority for the church universally, and their decrees on the Apocrypha were never accepted in the church as a whole. The church adopted the views of many of the Eastern Fathers such as Origen and Athanasius and Western Fathers such as Jerome. It expressed the view that these writings were useful for reading in the churches for the purpose of edification, but they were not to be counted as part of the canon of inspired Scripture since they were not part of the Hebrew canon. Consequently, they were not to be used for the establishment of doctrine. So the inclusion of additional books in the canon of Scripture by the Roman Catholic Church troubled me. Which visible community had this right?

In commenting on the apocryphal books, Wisdom of Solomon and Ecclesiasticus, Jerome states:

As, then, the Church reads Judith, Tobit and the books of Maccabees, but does not admit them among the canonical Scriptures, so let it also read these two volumes for the edification of the people, not to give authority to doctrines of the Church. . . . I say this to show how hard it is to master the book of Daniel, which in Hebrew contains neither the history of Susanna, nor the hymn of the three youths, nor the fables of Bel and the Dragon.[14]

That the Jewish canon did not include the Apocrypha and that the Protestant Reformers followed the practice of the Jews is affirmed by the *New Catholic Encyclopedia*: "For the Old Testament, however, Protestants follow the Jewish canon; they have only the Old Testament books that are in the Hebrew Bible."[15]

That the church as a whole never accepted the apocryphal books as part of the canon of Scripture after the councils of Carthage and Hippo is seen from these comments by Pope Gregory the Great (A.D. 590–604) on the book of 1 Maccabees: "With reference to which particular we are not acting irregularly, if from the books, though not Canonical, yet brought out for the edification of the Church, we bring forward testimony. Thus Eleazar in the battle smote and brought down an elephant, but fell under the very beast that he killed (1 Macc. 6.46)."[16] This was the view that was held throughout the ensuing centuries of the history of the church. John Cosin, in his book *A Scholastical History of the Canon,* documents some fifty-two major ecclesiastical writers and theologians from the eighth to the sixteenth centuries who held to the view of Jerome. That this was the general view of the church up to as late as the sixteenth century is evidenced by these comments from Cardinal Cajetan, the great opponent of Luther in the Reformation, taken from his commentary on the Old Testament:

Here we close our commentaries on the historical books of the Old Testament. For the rest (that is, Judith, Tobit, and the books of Maccabees) are counted by St. Jerome out of the canonical books, and are placed among the Apocrypha, along with Wisdom and Ecclesiasticus, as is plain from the *Prologus Galeatus.* Nor be thou disturbed, like a raw scholar, if thou shouldest find anywhere, either in the sacred councils or the sacred doctors, these books reckoned canonical. For the words as well as of councils and of doctors are to be reduced to the correction of Jerome. Now, according to his judgment, in the epistle to the bishops Chromatius and Heliodorus, these books (and any other like books in the canon of the bible) are not canonical, that is, not in the nature of a rule for confirming matters of faith. Yet, they may be called canonical, that is, in the nature of a rule for the edification of the faithful, as being received and authorized in the canon of the bible for that purpose. By the help of this distinction thou mayest see thy way clear through that which Augustine says, and what is written in the provincial council of Carthage.[17]

The *New Catholic Encyclopedia* affirms that Jerome rejected the Apocrypha as being canonical and that the councils of Carthage and Hippo did not establish the Old Testament canon. This was not authoritatively done until the Council of Trent:

> St. Jerome distinguished between canonical books and ecclesiastical books (the apocrypha). The latter he judged were circulated by the Church as good spiritual reading but were not recognized as authoritative Scripture. . . . The situation remained unclear in the ensuing centuries. . . . According to Catholic doctrine, the proximate criterion of the biblical canon is the infallible decision of the Church. This decision was not given until rather late in the history of the Church at the Council of Trent. . . . The Council of Trent definitively settled the matter of the Old Testament Canon. That this had not been done previously is apparent from the uncertainty that persisted up to the time of Trent.[18]

In my desire to make certain that I was in fellowship with a true church, I soon learned that the first general council of the Western church to dogmatically decree the Apocrypha to be part of the canon and therefore to be accorded the status of Scripture was the Council of Trent in the mid-sixteenth century. This was done contrary to the universal practice of the Jews and the church up to that time. And Trent places under anathema all who reject this teaching.[19] I discovered to my surprise that it was the Roman Catholic Church, not the Protestant, which was responsible for the introduction of novel teachings very late in the history of the church. When one examines the related issues of Scripture, tradition, and the canon, the facts reveal that it is the Protestant teaching that is closest to both Scripture and the teaching of the truly historic catholic church.

ON THE PAPACY

Catholicism since the late Middle Ages has taught that submission to the bishop of Rome is necessary for one's salvation. This teaching was given dogmatic expression by Pope Boniface VIII in an *ex cathedra* statement in his bull *Unam Sanctam* (A.D. 1302) and was later reaffirmed by subsequent popes and councils such as Vatican I. His decree states: "Furthermore we declare, state, define, and pronounce that it is altogether necessary to salvation for every human creature to be subject to the Roman pontiff."[20] Like all baptized Catholics I knew that the Church of Rome claimed that papal primacy was validated by the teaching of Scripture in Matthew 16:18–19 in its interpretation of the rock and keys. I had also been taught that this interpretation is validated by the unanimous teaching of the Fathers. These claims cannot be substantiated by the facts. Matthew 16 does not imply papal primacy, for the passage says absolutely nothing about successors to Peter or his office. As Oscar Cullmann has stated:

He who proceeds without prejudice, on the basis of exegesis and only on this basis, cannot seriously conclude that Jesus here had in mind successors of Peter. . . . On exegetical grounds we must say that the passage does not contain a single word concerning successors of Peter. . . . The intent of Jesus leaves us no possibility of understanding Matthew 16:17ff. in the sense of a succession determined by an episcopal see.[21]

In addition to this, the unanimous consent of the Fathers opposes the Roman Catholic interpretation of Matthew 16. The Fathers generally interpret the rock in Matthew 16 as Christ or as Peter's confession of faith in Christ. Some of the Fathers do refer to Peter as the rock but only in the sense that he is the first to confess Christ to be the Son of God and is therefore representative of the entire church. The church is built, therefore, not on Peter personally (and subsequently on the bishops of Rome as his successors) but on Peter's confession of faith and ultimately, therefore, on Christ Himself. Augustine (A.D. 354–430) is typical of the Fathers in this interpretation of Matthew 16:18:

Because thou hast said unto Me, "Thou art the Christ the Son of the living God;" I also say unto thee, "Thou art Peter." For before he was called Simon. Now this name of Peter was given him by the Lord, and in a figure, that he should signify the church. For seeing that Christ is the rock (Petra), Peter is the Christian people. For the rock (Petra) is the original name. Therefore Peter is so called from the rock; not the rock from Peter; as Christ is not called Christ from the Christian, but the Christian from Christ. "Therefore," he saith, "Thou art Peter; and upon this Rock" which thou hast confessed, upon this rock which thou hast acknowledged, saying, "Thou art the Christ, the Son of the living God, will I build My Church"; that is upon Myself, the Son of the living God, "will I build My Church." I will build thee upon Me, not Myself upon thee. . . . For men who wished to be built upon men, said, "I am of Paul; and I of Apollos; and I of Cephas," who is Peter. But others who did not wish to be built upon Peter, but upon the Rock, said, "But I am of Christ." And when the Apostle Paul ascertained that he was chosen, and Christ despised, he said, "Is Christ divided? was Paul crucified for you? or were ye baptized in the name of Paul?" And, as not in the name of Paul, so neither in the name of Peter; but in the name of Christ; that Peter might be built upon the Rock, not the Rock upon Peter.[22]

Here, all agree, is the most renowned theologian of the Catholic Church. He writes after nearly five centuries of church history and gives an interpretation of Matthew 16 (the most important verse of Scripture in Rome's argument for the church's authority) that is a direct contradiction of the Roman Catholic interpretation. How are we to explain this, if, as Vatican I states, there exists a unanimous consensus of interpretation of the meaning of this passage? Why does Augustine deliberately go against such a consensus?

The answer, quite simply, is that there never was a patristic consensus on the interpretation of Matthew 16 to support that propounded by the Roman Catholic Church. John Chrysostom (ca. A.D. 344–407), one of the greatest theologians and exegetes of the Eastern church, echoes Augustine in his interpretation with these words: "And I say unto thee, Thou art Peter, and upon this rock I will build my Church; that is, on the faith of his confession."[23] The fact is, the overwhelming majority of the Fathers of the early centuries did not support the Roman Catholic interpretation of Matthew 16:18–19 as proposed by Vatican I. Johann Joseph Ignaz von Döllinger, one of the most renowned Roman Catholic historians of the last century, a teacher of church history for forty-seven years, affirmed, to my amazement, what I discovered in the church Fathers:

> Of all the Fathers who interpret these passages in the Gospels (Matt 16:18, John 21:17), not a single one applies them to the Roman bishops as Peter's successors. How many Fathers have busied themselves with these texts, yet not one of them whose commentaries we possess—Origen, Chrysostom, Hilary, Augustine, Cyril, Theodoret, and those whose interpretations are collected in catenas—has dropped the faintest hint that the primacy of Rome is the consequence of the commission and promise to Peter! Not one of them has explained the rock or foundation on which Christ would build His Church of the office given to Peter to be transmitted to his successors, but they understood by it either Christ Himself, or Peter's confession of faith in Christ; often both together. Or else they thought Peter was the foundation equally with all the other Apostles, the twelve being together the foundation-stones of the church (Apoc. xxi.14). The Fathers could the less recognize in the power of the keys, and the power of binding and loosing, any special prerogative or lordship of the Roman bishop, inasmuch as—what is obvious to any one at first sight—they did not regard the power first given to Peter, and afterwards conferred on all the Apostles, as any thing peculiar to him, or hereditary in the line of Roman bishops, and they held the symbol of the keys as meaning just the same as the figurative expression of binding and loosing.[24]

Roman Catholic apologists have consistently charged that the Protestant exegesis of Matthew 16 grew out of the Reformers' need to legitimize their opposition to the papacy. Consequently, they invented a novel interpretation that contradicted the traditional view of the church. But the facts actually reveal the opposite, as Oscar Cullmann confirms: "We thus see that the exegesis that the Reformers gave . . . was not first invented for their struggle against the papacy; it rests upon an older patristic tradition."[25] It is the Protestant and Orthodox interpretation that is endorsed by the Fathers of the early church and not the Roman Catholic, which contradicts that consensus. The Roman Catholic interpretation is, in fact, a direct contradiction of the decrees of Trent and Vatican I, which state that it is unlawful to interpret Scripture in any way contrary to the unanimous consent of the Fathers.

This is not to say that there was never a pro-papal interpretation given to Matthew 16:18–19. Beginning in the fourth century we find a papal interpretation promoted by the bishops of Rome. Leo I, in the fifth century, is the first to combine Matthew 16 with Luke 22 and John 21 to promote the theory of papal rule, but not the teaching of infallibility. From this time on the bishops of Rome began to adopt his interpretation to promote the papal office. But this papal interpretation was never the accepted exegesis of the Fathers and theologians of the church for centuries. Karlfried Froehlich affirms this in his analysis of the history of the exegesis of these passages up through the Middle Ages:

> The earlier exegetical history of Matt. 16:18–19, Luke 22:32, and John 21:15–17 was largely out of step with the primatial interpretation of these passages. . . . The mainstream of exegesis followed an agenda set by patristic precedent, especially Augustine, but also other Western Fathers. . . . The understanding of these Petrine texts by biblical exegetes in the mainstream of the tradition was universally non-primatial before Innocent III. . . . It was the innovative exegetical argumentation of this imposing pope which began to change the picture.[26]

The Church of Rome claims that papal primacy can be validated by the facts of history in that it was the universal practice of the church from the very beginning. These claims are false; the facts of history contradict them. The attitudes and practices of the Fathers and councils[27] reveal that the church never viewed the bishops of Rome as being endowed with supreme authority to rule the church universal. And there never has been a supreme human ruler in the church. This whole concept was repudiated by Pope Gregory the Great (A.D. 590–604) when he rebuked the bishop of Constantinople for attempting to arrogate to himself the title of "universal bishop." He insisted that such a position and title are unlawful in the church of Jesus Christ:

> Now I confidently say that whoever calls himself, or desires to be called, Universal Priest, is in his elation the precursor of Antichrist, because he proudly puts himself above all others. Nor is it by dissimilar pride that he is led into error; for, as that perverse one wishes to appear as God above all men, so whoever this one is who covets being called sole priest, he extols himself above all other priests. . . . Certainly Peter, the first of the apostles, himself a member of the holy and universal Church, Paul, Andrew, John—what were they but heads of particular communities? And yet all were members under one Head. And (to bind all together in a short girth of speech) the saints before the law, the saints under the law, the saints under grace, all these making up the Lord's Body, were constituted as members of the Church, and not one of them has wished himself to be called universal. Now let your holiness acknowledge to what extent you swell within yourself in desiring to be called by that name by which no one presumed to be called who was truly holy.[28]

In the Roman Catholic Church I was taught that papal infallibility can be validated from Scripture in Matthew 16:18, Luke 22:32, and John 21:15– 17. I was further taught that its interpretation of these passages was given by the unanimous consent of the Fathers and that anyone who contradicts this teaching was to be anathematized.[29] These dogmas are simply untrue. No Father, doctor, theologian, or canonist of the church for the first twelve centuries interpreted those passages in agreement with the Roman Catholic Church. They never interpreted these verses to even imply the teaching of papal infallibility. The patristic exegesis of Luke 22:32 saw Christ's prayer for Peter as a guarantee that Peter's faith will not ultimately fail, not that he would be infallible. The patristic writers viewed Peter as representative of the church, the bride whom Christ will not allow to fall away. In the patristic interpretation, this verse has nothing to do with personal infallibility but with the grace of indefectibility or final perseverance. The situation is similar when we turn to the patristic interpretation of John 21:15–17 in which Peter is representative of all who would hold positions as pastors within the church. For the Fathers of the Patristic Age, this passage had nothing to do with papal primacy or the exclusive teaching authority over the entire church that implied a gift of infallibility. The universal teaching and belief of the church was that the bishops of Rome were fallible—that they could and *did* err. Brian Tierney affirms this in these statements regarding the views of the twelfth- and thirteenth-century canonists who were the authoritative commentators of their day:

> What can be proved beyond doubt is that no public teaching affirming the infallibility of the pope was transmitted to the canonists of the twelfth and thirteenth centuries in whose works, for the first time, abundant texts for the investigation of this whole question becomes available. The commentators on Gratian's *Decretum* knew all the most important texts—forged and genuine—relating to the authority of the pope and the indefectibility of the Roman Church. They did not associate those texts with any doctrine of papal infallibility. They showed no awareness that any of their predecessors had ever associated them with such a doctrine. . . . The theologians of the thirteenth century could not possibly have taken the doctrine of papal infallibility from the canonical tradition of the church because the doctrine simply did not exist in the writings of the canonists.[30]

I knew the Roman Catholic teaching on papal infallibility. Now I knew that it could not be validated by the facts of history and the universal practice of the church. Historical reality does not support what I had been taught as a communicant Catholic. The facts reveal that popes have erred, have contradicted themselves and each other as well. They have embraced heresy, and have been condemned for heresy by "infallible" ecumenical councils, as well as by the popes themselves, thereby demonstrating that the church in its practice, and even the bishops of Rome, did not believe that popes were infallible.

Pope Honorius, as an example of this, was condemned as a heretic by the sixth ecumenical council (III Constantinople, A.D. 680–681) in his official capacity as pope,[31] on the basis of the criteria that define an *ex cathedra* teaching. This council was confirmed by Pope Leo II who likewise anathematized the heretics mentioned by the council, including Pope Honorius. His words of condemnation are interesting, for he states that Honorius was one "who did not illuminate the apostolic see by teaching the apostolic tradition but, by an act of treachery strove to subvert its immaculate faith."[32] This pope officially condemns his predecessor for actively subverting the faith by what he taught, and this judgment was confirmed by two succeeding ecumenical councils and by individual popes, who took the oath of papal office, for centuries afterward. Clearly, neither the popes nor the church at large have historically believed the doctrine of papal infallibility.

ON SCRIPTURE INTERPRETATION

Another dogma taught me as a Roman Catholic was that the church alone had authority to interpret Scripture and that it has been granted infallibility in so doing. This claim is disproved by the facts of history. How can it be an infallible interpreter of Scripture when its interpretation of Matthew 16:18, Luke 22:32, and John 21:15–17 contradicts the interpretation given by the Fathers who make up the magisterium (which, from a Roman Catholic position, is itself an infallible interpreter of Scripture).

The Roman Catholic Church, at the councils of Trent and Vatican I, has bound itself never to interpret Scripture contrary to the unanimous consent of the Fathers. It claims, amazingly, that all of its teachings can be verified by such consent. Such claims and assertions are simply false. None of the church's teachings in its tradition can claim a *unanimous* consent and much of its interpretation of Scripture, such as the papal passages, *contradicts* the unanimous interpretation given by the Fathers of the church.

ON MARY

One of the most significant aspects of Catholic faith and practice that everyone who considers leaving the Roman Catholic Church struggles with is personal devotion to Mary. The Catholic Church claims that Mary was immaculately conceived (that is, she was born free of original sin) *and* that the Fathers likewise held to this teaching. It claims that this is a dogma of the faith revealed by God that is necessary to be believed for salvation. It states that any who would dispute the teaching are judged to be completely fallen from the faith and are condemned.[33] Once again, as I made a careful study of Scripture and history, I soon discovered that these assertions were not true. This teaching should not be a dogma of the faith. It originated in the fifth century with the heretics Pelagius and Celestius[34] and was universally rejected by both Fathers and popes of the early church, as evidenced by its rejection by Augustine and Gregory the Great, and in later centuries by Anselm, Bernard of Clairveaux, and Thomas Aquinas. The Roman Catholic patristic scholar, Walter Burghardt, confirms the patristic and papal rejection of this doctrine historically:

> Post-Augustinian patristic thought on the perfection of Mary reveals two conflicting currents. There is a negative, unfavorable trend rooted in Augustine's anti-Pelagianism; it accentuates the universality of original sin and articulates the connection between inherited sin and any conception consequent upon sinful concupiscence. The root idea is summed up by Leo the Great: "Alone therefore among the sons of men the Lord Jesus was born innocent, because alone conceived without pollution of carnal concupiscence." The same concept is discoverable in St. Fulgentius, Bishop of Ruspe in Africa (d. 533), the most significant theologian of his time; in Pope Gregory the Great (d. 604) at the end of the sixth century; and a century later in Venerable Bede, a scholar renowned throughout England.[35]

Personal study revealed to me that in later centuries the dogma of the Immaculate Conception was a matter of violent dispute within the church between Franciscans and Dominicans. It also contradicts the scriptural teaching of the universality of original, as well as actual, sin.[36]

Roman Catholicism teaches the faithful that Mary was assumed body and soul into heaven. It states that this too is a dogma of the faith, a truth divinely revealed by God and necessary to be believed for salvation. It goes so far as to assert that any who would dispute this doctrine have completely fallen from the faith and are condemned.[37] Once again I had to conclude that Rome did not possess the truth of the historic church. What I found was complete silence in the writings of the Fathers regarding the end of Mary's life. For the first six centuries nothing is said on this matter. The first Father to promote the teaching of her assumption was Gregory of Tours in 590, and he based his teaching on an apocryphal gospel found in the *Transitus* literature. The assumption doctrine actually originated with this literature[38] sometime in the fourth or fifth centuries and this specific teaching—the *Transitus* assumption of Mary—was officially rejected as heretical. It was placed in the same category with such heretics as Arius, Pelagius, and Marcion and was condemned by two popes in the late fifth and early sixth centuries—Gelasius and Hormisdas. These popes place this doctrine, its authors and the contents of their writings, as well as all who follow their teachings, under an eternal anathema.[39] Thus, the early church viewed this doctrine not as the pious expression of the faith of the faithful but as a heretical doctrine that probably originated from gnostic sources. Discoveries such as these only underlined my growing awareness that Rome did *not* accurately represent the historic doctrine of the early church, much less what I saw in the New Testament.

Rome teaches that Mary is a mediatrix and even a co-redemptrix with Christ and that grace cannot be applied to man except through her.[40] This teaching is also false. It not only contradicts the scriptural teaching of the unique and exclusive mediatorial role of Christ[41] but there is not one word found in Scripture of Mary functioning in the role of mediatrix or co-redemptrix. Nor is there one word of this kind of teaching in the writings of the Fathers.

The Roman Catholic Church teaches that Mary has been given the title Queen of Heaven and that she rules over the church along with her son Jesus Christ. This is also false. There is absolutely nothing in Scripture of such a title or role being assigned to Mary. There is no Queen of heaven and earth. There is only one sovereign Lord and ruler over the church, and He is the God-man Christ Jesus. There is not a word of this Marian doctrine in the patristic writings. What is really surprising is that it actually originated, as with the assumption teaching, with the heretical *Transitus* literature.[42]

CONCLUSION

In light of these facts what can we conclude? Many Roman Catholics, like me for a number of years, are genuinely sincere in their belief that the Roman Catholic Church is the *one true* church, the "infallible" authority established by Jesus Christ, which has preserved inviolate the apostolic tradition handed down from Christ to the apostles. But, sadly, the foundation upon which my presuppositions rested during those years was historically and biblically erroneous. The teaching of Keating, Hahn, Matatics, and others of like mind is not faithful to the facts of history. Scores of Catholics implicitly and uncritically accept what these men teach without serious study on their own simply because their arguments sound plausible. These apologists play on widespread ignorance within both Roman Catholicism and Protestantism, and many are being misled.

An example of my point came home to me recently when I heard Scott Hahn make the unbelievable statement (on tape) before a predominantly Roman Catholic audience that no bishop of Rome has ever been accused of heresy. Most Catholics will hear that without recognizing it as an outright falsehood, thus settling into convictions that are rooted in error. This is just one of many examples that could be used from the teaching of these apologists. I am compelled to conclude that they are guilty of seriously misrepresenting the facts of history and of true Protestantism.

The claims for Roman Catholic authority cannot be supported by the facts of history or the truth of Scripture. In reality the Roman Catholic Church has departed from the teaching of the historic catholic church and can no longer be rightly described as catholic, but as Roman. The supposed two-thousand-year consensus for the teaching of its tradition is nonexistent. Even knowledgeable Roman Catholic authorities admit this to be the case. Patrologist Boniface Ramsey states:

Sometimes, then, the Fathers speak and write in a way that would eventually be seen as unorthodox. But this is not the only difficulty with respect to the criterion of orthodoxy. The other great one is that we look in vain in many of the Fathers for references to things that many Christians might believe in today. We do not find, for instance, some teachings on Mary or the papacy that were developed in medieval and modern times.[43]

It is not that the Church of Rome does not affirm any truths that are truly catholic and apostolic. There is a body of doctrine that Roman Catholic, Protestant, and Orthodox churches all share in common, as Tom Nettles has shown in chapter 1. The problem is with the teachings that are *added to* this common consensus, those that were introduced many centuries after the apostolic age. These added doctrines are a departure from the faith of the early church *and* the truth of Scripture. It is not the Reformation that introduced novel doctrines but the evolving Roman Catholic Church. The facts reveal that the Reformers' teachings can be validated both by Scripture and by the teaching of the Fathers. Therefore, historic Protestantism stands in the genuine tradition of historic Christianity, and those Roman Catholics who, like me, have left their church can be assured that, on the basis of the truth of history and Scripture, they have followed the biblical course, aligning themselves with the historic Christian truth and, thus, a biblical church.

History testifies that the Roman church is not an infallible interpreter of Scripture, that its popes are not infallible, that it did not establish the canon for the church, and that much of the teaching of its tradition was either completely unknown or explicitly repudiated by the Fathers of the early church.

Roman Catholic apologists justify the church's tradition on the basis of a theory of development—that is, that church tradition is a development of doctrine that was implicitly accepted in the early church and became more explicit over time. This is not supported by the facts. The teachings of Roman Catholic tradition were, in reality, repudiated by the early church. They are not supported, furthermore, by the principle of unanimous consent, and they plainly contradict Scripture. What we discover is not a *development* of truth but a *departure* from it. Roman Catholic teaching in its exaltation of tradition, the papacy, and the church is a depreciation of the authority of Scripture and the supreme authority of Jesus Christ. In the end, the Roman church has displaced divine authority with human authority. The Reformers' accusations still stand, supported by both Scripture and history.

What is so tragic in this controversy is not simply that men and women have embraced error regarding church history but that, in so doing, many have implicitly accepted Roman Catholic teaching on salvation, which, as we have seen throughout the volume, is a perversion of the true gospel. This perversion is the same "gospel" in principle that the apostle Paul denounces in his epistle to the Galatians. The sad result is that multitudes of Roman

Catholics have a zealous love for and confidence in their church, without understanding biblical salvation. I was one such Catholic, struggling on in my darkness until God in His sovereign grace opened my eyes to the righteousness that is in Christ alone. I fear that many Roman Catholics have been inoculated against the truth of the gospel because they have been misinformed about the facts of history. Consequently they do not take seriously the salvation teachings of the Reformation, dismissing them as heresies that have emanated from men who have rebelled against the "infallible" church. But what they do not realize is that just as the Reformers were right on the issues of history they were also right on the doctrine of salvation. The gospel they proclaimed of faith alone, grace alone, and Christ alone *is* the biblical gospel, the message of saving truth.

I conclude this chapter by making an appeal to Roman Catholics to "come out from them and be separate" (2 Corinthians 6:17). Why do I say that? Am I being impolitic in this counsel, especially when many evangelicals are saying we should *not* call upon Catholics to leave their communion? Let me begin with an illustration. Döllinger was one of the most celebrated Roman Catholic historians of the last century. Just before Vatican I, which convened to discuss the issues of papal rule and infallibility, he coauthored a book under the pseudonym, Janus, titled *The Pope and the Council*. In it he appealed to this council, in light of the facts of history, not to pass decrees that would contradict the truth. His plea fell on deaf ears. He refused to recant his position and was later excommunicated from the church he loved. His commitment to truth exacted an enormous price. When asked why he would not repudiate his intellect and reason for the sake of communion with Rome he stated,

> Because . . . if I did so in a question which is for the historical eye perfectly clear and unambiguous, there would then be no longer for me any such thing as historical truth and certainty; I should then have to suppose that my whole life long I had been in a world of dizzy illusion, and that in historical matters I am altogether incapable of distinguishing truth from fable and falsehood.[44]

I stand, a former Roman Catholic, with thousands whose conscience has compelled them to leave the church they once loved. So I reiterate the counsel of Catholic apologist Karl Keating: we have a *solemn responsibility* to seek and respond to truth. That will be costly. I believe that a Roman Catholic who is sincerely committed to following truth will eventually leave the Roman Catholic Church, realizing as the Reformers taught that it is not *the* historic, biblical, holy, catholic church. Keating and Hahn feel no qualms about urging men and women to forsake evangelical Christianity for Roman Catholicism. I appeal to you, then, on the basis of the truth of history and Scripture, to leave your Catholic heritage. I give you the following reasons.

First, the *ultimate commitment* the Scriptures call us to is the person of Christ, *not* a church. We are called to trust, love, worship, and follow Christ *exclusively*. Inherent in that commitment is full acceptance of all that Scripture teaches regarding salvation and, in particular, the truth of the gospel. Paul states in Galatians 1:6–8 that any who embrace a perverted gospel actually deserts Christ. If a Roman Catholic *obeys* the salvation teachings of the Roman Catholic Church, it must logically result in disobedience to God and a desertion of Christ because these selfsame teachings invalidate God's Word. The Scriptures point us to the person of Christ, not a church, as the source of our eternal salvation.

The "gospel" promulgated by the Church of Rome is a perversion of the gospel of grace. Therefore, to stay within Roman Catholicism is to be identified with a system that fundamentally denies the sufficiency of the work of Christ alone. Christ lays the issue squarely before us in uncompromising terms when He says, "If anyone would come after me, he must deny himself and take up his cross and follow me. For whoever wants to save his life will lose it, but whoever loses his life for me and for the gospel will save it" (Mark 8:34–35). There is no mention of the church as a *means* of salvation here or anywhere else in Scripture. To follow Christ means a life of denying self to live for His sake and the gospel's. This means we must be openly identified with Him and His truth and be willing to suffer the rejection, the ostracism, the criticism, and even loss of life that such identification can bring. Centuries of faithful evangelical Christians have learned these truths by sailing through such troubled waters. Can we do less, if necessary? There is a cross at the very center of our identification with Christ and His gospel. Jesus makes clear that we cannot seek peace and unity at any cost. Truth divides. Much of the ecumenical movement of the last fifty years or so would have us downplay the importance of truth for the sake of unity. But the ultimate issue is not unity; it is commitment to Christ. And that means a commitment to truth. The whole basis for church unity and for following and worshiping Christ is the truth of the gospel (cf. John 4:23–24; Galatians 1:6–8; Ephesians 1:13; Philippians 1:27–28; 3:2–11; Colossians 2:6–15.). If we forsake truth for a man-made unity, we actually forsake Christ!

Finally, I appeal to Roman Catholics to come out because the Church of Rome is moving farther and farther away from truth (as we saw in Robert Strimple's chapter). The church has historically demonstrated a terrible resistance to correction and reform. By the anathemas of Trent and Vatican I and the papal decrees on Mary we have seen a continued and progressive departure from truth and a hardening of the Roman Church theologically against the gospel. On the other hand, there is a disturbing trend developing, a growing tolerance of pagan religions in the name of unity and peace. In 1986, when the pope stood with the representatives of the major religions of the world on a public platform to pray for peace, he did something that would have been unthinkable for a bishop of the catholic church in the early centuries of Christianity. Can you imagine a bishop of the second century standing on a public platform with the representatives of Gnosticism, Roman deities, and other pagan religions to pray for peace? Such a person would have been condemned for apostasy. Christ's gospel proclaims the fact that He alone is the answer to the sin of the world and that He alone can bring peace to men's hearts. I ask you, can one be true to Christ and remain in a system that so fundamentally denies Him in teaching and practice? Ponder your answer carefully.

The issues that separate Protestants and Roman Catholics are not minor. They are major. They have to do with the eternal destinies of men and women. They hit right at the heart of truth, both biblical and historical. The defining issue is truth. The Reformation was not unnecessary, unjustified, or a tragedy. The tragedy lies in the fact that it was necessary. It was, in fact, one of the greatest revivals ever witnessed in the history of the church, and it restored the church to the truth of the true gospel that had become obscured and perverted through the traditions of men.

NOTES

1. Karl Keating, *Catholicism and Fundamentalism* (San Francisco: Ignatius, 1988), 10.

2. *The Catholic Encyclopedia* (New York: Universal Knowledge Foundation, 1912) gives the following background and definition for the term anathema:

   To understand the word anathema . . . we should first go back to the real meaning of *herem* of which it is the equivalent. *Herem* comes from the word *haram*, to cut off, to separate, to curse, and indicates that which is cursed and condemned to be cut off and exterminated. . . . In the New Testament anathema no longer entails death, but the loss of goods or exclusion from the society of the faithful. . . . But he who is separated from God is united to the devil, which explains why St. Paul, instead of anathematizing, sometimes delivers a person over to Satan (1 Tim. i,20; 1 Cor., v,5). . . . Anathema remains a major excommunication which is to be promulgated with great solemnity. . . . In passing this sentence the pontiff takes his seat in front of the altar or in some other suitable place, and pronounces the formula of anathema which ends with these words: "Wherefore in the name of God the All-powerful, Father, Son, and Holy Ghost, of the Blessed Peter, Prince of the Apostles, and of all the Saints, in virtue of the power which has been given to us of binding and loosing in Heaven and on earth, we deprive N— himself and all his accomplices and all his abettors of the Communion of the Body and Blood of Our Lord, we separate him from the society of all Christians, we exclude him from the bosom of our Holy Mother the Church in Heaven and on earth, we declare him excommunicated and anathematized and we judge him condemned to eternal fire with Satan and his angels and all the reprobate, so long as he will not burst the fetters of the demon, do penance and satisfy the Church; we deliver him to Satan to mortify his body, that his soul may be saved on the day of judgment." (1:455–56)

3. Irenaeus expresses the principle of universality, antiquity, and consent: (1) *Universality*: "The universal church, moreover, through the whole world, has received this tradition from the apostles" (*Against Heresies* II.9.1); (2) *Antiquity*: "True knowledge is that which consists in the doctrine of the apostles and the ancient constitution of the church throughout all the world, and the distinctive manifestation of the body of Christ according to the succession of bishops by which they have handed down that church which exists in every place, and has come even unto us, being guarded and preserved without any forging of Scriptures, by a very complete system of doctrine, and neither receiving addition, nor suffering curtailment in the truths which she believes" (*Against Heresies* IV.33.8); (3) *Consent*: "The preaching of the church is everywhere consistent and continues in an even course and receives testimony from the prophets, the apostles, and all the disciples" (*Against Heresies* III.24.1).

4. Philip Schaff and Henry Wace, *Vincent of Lerins, A Commonitory* II.4–III.7, Series Two, vol. XI, of *Nicene and Post-Nicene Fathers* (Grand Rapids: Eerdmans, 1955).

5. The Council of Trent states:

> No one relying on his own judgment shall, in matters of faith and morals pertaining to the edification of Christian doctrine, distorting the Holy Scriptures in accordance with his own conceptions, presume to interpret them contrary to that sense which holy mother Church, to whom it belongs to judge their true sense and interpretation, has held and holds, or even contrary to the unanimous consent of the Fathers, even though such interpretations should never at any time be published. (See The Council of Trent [Rockford: Tan, 1978], 18–19)

This decree was reaffirmed by Vatican I.

6. Scripture is described as being pure, perfect, eternal, sure, truth, forever settled in heaven; it sanctifies, causes spiritual growth, is God-breathed, authoritative, it gives wisdom unto salvation, makes wise the simple, is living and active, is a guide, a fire, a hammer, a seed, the sword of the Spirit; it gives knowledge of God, is a lamp to our feet, a light to our path, produces reverence for God, heals, makes free, illuminates, produces faith, regenerates, converts the soul, brings conviction of sin, restrains from sin, is spiritual food, is infallible, inerrant, irrevocable, searches the heart and mind, produces life, defeats Satan, proves truth, refutes error, is holy, equips for every good work, is the final judge of all tradition, is the Word of God (Heb. 4:12, Pss. 119: 9–11, 38, 105, 130, 133, 160; 19:7–11; 111:7–8; Is. 40:8; Eph. 5:26; 2 Tim. 3:15–17; Jer. 5:14; 23:29; Matt. 13:18–23; Eph. 6:17; Ps. 107:20; Titus 2:5; 1 Peter 1:23; 2:2; Acts 20:32; John 8:32, 10:35, 17:17; Matt. 15:2–9). Where are we told these things about tradition?

7. *The Catechetical Lectures* IV.17, V.12, XII.5, in *A Library of the Fathers of the Holy Catholic Church* (Oxford: Parker, 1845).

8. J. N. D. Kelly, *Early Christian Doctrines* (San Francisco: Harper & Row, 1978), 46.

9. "See to it that no one takes you captive through hollow and deceptive philosophy, which depends on human tradition and the basic principles of this world rather than on Christ" (Col. 2:8); "Thus you nullify the word of God for the sake of your tradition. . . . They worship me in vain; their teachings are but rules taught by men.'" (Matt. 15:6, 9; cf. Mark 7:3–13; Gal. 1:14; Col. 2:22; 1 Peter 1:18).

10. Irenaeus, *Against Heresies* III.1.1, in Alexander Roberts and W. H. Rambaugh, trans., in *The Writings of Irenaeus* (Edinburgh: T & T Clark, 1874).

11. Ellen Flesseman-Van Leer, *Tradition and Scripture in the Early Church* (Assen: Van Gorcum, 1953), 133.

12. "Now, brothers, I want to remind you of the gospel I preached to you, which you received and on which you have taken your stand.By this gospel you are saved, if

289

you hold firmly to the word I preached to you. Otherwise, you have believed in vain. For what I received I passed on to you as of first importance: that Christ died for our sins according to the Scriptures, that he was buried, that he was raised on the third day according to the Scriptures" (1 Cor. 15:1–4).

13. Brian Tierney, *Origins of Papal Infallibility* 1150–1350 (Leiden: Brill, 1972), 16–17.

14. St. Jerome, *Prefaces to Jerome's Works, Proverbs, Ecclesiastes and the Song of Songs, Daniel,* Series Two, vol. VI, of Schaff and Wace, *Nicene and Post-Nicene Fathers,* 492–93.

15. *New Catholic Encyclopedia* (Washington, D.C.: Catholic Univ., 1967), III:29.

16. Gregory the Great, *Morals on the Book of Job,* vol. II, parts III and IV, Book XIX.34, in *A Library of the Fathers of the Holy Catholic Church,* 424. The *New Catholic Encyclopedia* confirms that Pope Gregory did not accept a canonical status for the Apocrypha (II:390).

17. Taken from his comments on the final chapter of Esther, in *Commentary on All the Authentic Historical Books of the Old Testament;* cited in William Whitaker, *A Disputation on Holy Scripture* (Cambridge: University Press, 1849), 48. Cf. John Cosin, *A Scholastical History of the Canon* (Oxford: Parker, 1849), III:257–58, and B. F. Westcott, *A General Survey of the Canon of the New Testament* (New York: Macmillan, 1889), 475.

18. *New Catholic Encyclopedia,* II:390, III:29.

19. "If anyone does not accept as sacred and canonical the aforesaid books in their entirety and with all their parts, as they have been accustomed to be read in the Catholic Church and as they are contained in the Old Latin Vulgate Edition, and knowingly and deliberately rejects the aforesaid traditions, let him be anathema" (Fourth Session, *Decree Concerning the Canonical Scriptures,* of *The Canons and Decrees of the Council of Trent* [Rockford: Tan, 1978], 18).

20. Cited in Henry Bettenson, ed., *Documents of the Christian Church* (London: Oxford Univ., 1963), 116. Vatican I, after affirming that the bishops of Rome are the rightful rulers over the church to whom all Christians must submit in matters of faith and morals and discipline states, "This is the teaching of Catholic truth, from which no one can deviate without loss of faith and salvation"; cited by Philip Schaff, *The Creeds of Christendom* (New York: Harper, 1877), II:263.

21. Oscar Cullmann, *Peter: Disciple, Apostle, Martyr* (Philadelphia: Westminster, 1953), 207, 236.

22. St. Augustine, *Sermon XXVI.1–2,* Series Two, vol. VI, of Schaff and Wace, *Nicene and Post-Nicene Fathers,* 340.

23. *Homilies of S. John Chrysostom on the Gospel of St. Matthew,* Homily 54.3, in *A Library of the Fathers of the Holy Catholic Church.*

24. Johann Joseph Ignaz von Döllinger, *The Pope and the Council* (Boston: Roberts, 1869), 74.

25. Cullmann, *Peter: Disciple, Apostle, Martyr,* 162.

26. Karlfried Froehlich, *St. Peter, Papal Primacy and the Exegetical Tradition 1151–1350.* Found in Christopher Ryan, ed., *The Religious Roles of the Papacy: Ideals and Realities 1150–1300* (Toronto: Pontifical Institute, 1989), 42, 4.

27. The Council of Constance (A.D. 1414–1418) passed the following decree regarding the supreme authority of General Councils over popes: "This holy Council of Constance . . . declares, first that it is lawfully assembled in the Holy Spirit, that it constitutes a General Council, representing the Catholic Church, and that therefore it has its authority immediately from Christ; and that all men, of every rank and condition, including the Pope himself, is bound to obey it in matters concerning the Faith,

the abolition of the schism, and the reformation of the Church of God in its head and its members. Secondly, it declares that any one, of any rank or condition, who shall contumaciously refuse to obey the orders, decrees, statutes or instructions, made or to be made by this holy Council, or by any other lawfully assembled council. . . . shall, unless he comes to a right frame of mind, be subjected to a fitting penance and punished appropriately: and, if need be, recourse shall be had to the other sanctions of the law" (Decree: *Sacrosancta* [A.D. 1415]; taken from Henry Bettenson, ed., *Documents of the Christian Church* [London: Oxford Univ., 1963], 135). The decrees of this council were officially approved by Pope Martin V (A.D. 1417–1431) and by Pope Eugenius IV (A.D. 1431–1447)

28. *Epistles of St. Gregory the Great*, Book VII, Epistle 33, and Book V, Epistle 18, Series Two, vol. XII, of Schaff and Wace, *Nicene and Post-Nicene Fathers*, 226, 167.

29. Vatican I states: "We teach and define that it is a dogma divinely revealed: that the Roman Pontiff, when he speaks *ex cathedra*, that is, when in discharge of the office of pastor and doctor of all Christians, by virtue of his supreme Apostolic authority, he defines a doctrine regarding faith and morals to be held by the universal Church, by the divine assistance promised him in blessed Peter, is possessed of that infallibility with which the divine Redeemer willed that his Church should be endowed for defining doctrine regarding faith or morals; and that therefore such definitions of the Roman Pontiff are irreformable of themselves, and not from the consent of the Church. But if any one—which may God avert—presume to contradict this our definition: let him be anathema" (*Dogmatic Decrees of the Vatican Council, Concerning the Infallible Teaching of the Roman Pontiff*, Chapter IV; cited by Philip Schaff, The Creeds of Christendom [New York: Harper & Brothers, 1877], 2:270–71).

30. Tierney, *Origins of Papal Infallibility*, 12–13.

31. The exact words of condemnation by the sixth ecumenical council are as follows:

> After we had reconsidered . . . the doctrinal letters of Sergius . . . to Honorius some time Pope of Old Rome, as well as the letter of the latter to the same Sergius, we find that these documents are quite foreign to the apostolic dogmas, to the declarations of the holy Councils, and to all the accepted Fathers, and that they follow the false teachings of the heretics; therefore we entirely reject them, and execrate them as hurtful to the soul. But the names of those men whose doctrines we execrate must also be thrust forth from the holy Church of God. . . . We define that there shall be expelled from the holy Church of God and anathematized Honorius who was some time Pope of Old Rome, because of what was written by him to Sergius, that in all respects he followed his view and confirmed his impious doctrines. . . . But as the author of evil . . . having found suitable instruments for working out his will (we mean Theodorus . . . Sergius . . . Honorius who was Pope of elder Rome) . . . has actively employed them in raising up for the whole Church the stumbling blocks of one will and one operation in Christ our true God, one of the Holy Trinity; thus disseminating, in novel terms, amongst the orthodox people, an heresy similar to the mad and wicked doctrine of the impious Apollinaris . . . To Honorius, the heretic, anathema! (*The Seven Ecumenical Councils*, Second Series, vol. XIV, of Schaff and Wace, ed., *Nicene and Post-Nicene Fathers*, 342–44)

32. Tierney, *Origins of Papal Infallibility*, 11. See also Charles Joseph Hefele, *A History of the Councils of the Church* (Edinburgh: T. & T. Clark, 1896), V:180.

33. These are the words of Pope Pius IX relative to the teaching of the Immaculate Conception: "Therefore, if some should presume to think in their hearts otherwise than we have defined (which God forbid), they shall know and thoroughly understand that they are by their own judgment condemned, have made shipwreck concerning the faith, and fallen away from the unity of the Church; and, moreover, that they, by this very act, subject themselves to the penalties ordained by law if, by word or writ-

ing, or any other external means, they dare to signify what they think in their heart" (*The Decree of Pope Pius IX on the Immaculate Conception of the Blessed Virgin Mary*, From the Bull *Ineffabilis Deus* [A.D. 1854]. Taken from Schaff, *The Creeds of Christendom*, 2:212).

34. Pelagius and Celestius used Mary, the mother of Jesus, as an example of one born free of original sin. Vincent of Lerins points out the origin of the teaching of the Immaculate Conception with these words: "Who ever originated a heresy that did not first dissever himself from the consentient agreement of the universality and antiquity of the Catholic Church? That this is so is demonstrated in the clearest way by examples. For who ever before the profane Pelagius attributed so much antecedent strength to Free-will, as to deny the necessity of God's grace to aid it towards every good in every single act? Who ever before his monstrous disciple Celestius denied that the whole human race is involved in the guilt of Adam's sin?" (Vincent of Lerins, *A Commonitory* 24.62, Series Two, vol. XI, of Schaff and Wace, ed., *Nicene and Post-Nicene Fathers*, 149–50).

35. Juniper Carol, ed., *Mariology* (Milwaukee: Bruce, 1955), 1:146.

36. "For all have sinned and fall short of the glory of God" (Rom. 3:23). "There is none righteous, not even one" (Rom. 3:10).

37. Pope Pius XII affirms this in these words:

   We pronounce, declare, and define it to be a divinely revealed dogma: that the Immaculate Mother of God, the ever Virgin Mary, having completed the course of her earthly life, was assumed body and soul into heavenly glory. Hence, if anyone, which God forbid, should dare wilfully to deny or call into doubt that which we have defined, let him know that he has completely fallen from the divine and Catholic faith. . . . It is forbidden to any man to change this, Our declaration, pronouncement, and definition or, by rash attempt, to oppose and counter it. If any man should presume to make such an attempt, let him know that he will incur the wrath of Almighty God and of the Blessed Apostles Peter and Paul. (*Munificentissimus Deus* [A.D. 1950], 44–45, 47; taken from *Selected Documents of Pope Pius XII* [Washington: National Catholic Welfare Conference])

38. This fact is affirmed by the Roman Catholic historian and Mariologist Juniper Carol (*Mariology*, 1:149) in these comments: "The first express witness in the West to a genuine assumption comes to us in an apocryphal Gospel, the *Transitus beatae Mariae* of Pseudo-Melito."

39. In his decree, *Decretum de Libris Canonicis Ecclesiasticis et Apocrypha*, which was later affirmed by Pope Hormisdas, Gelasius lists the Transitus teaching by the following title: *Liber qui apellatur Transitus, id est Assumptio Sanctae Mariae* under the following condemnation: "These and writings similar to these, which . . . all the heresiarchs and their disciples, or the schismatics have taught or written . . . we confess have not only been rejected but also banished from the whole Roman and Apostolic Church and with their authors and followers of their authors have been condemned forever under the indissoluble bond of anathema" (St. Gelasius I, Epistle 42; taken from Henry Denzinger, *The Sources of Catholic Dogma* [London: Herder, 1954], 69–70). Cf. Migne P.L., vol. 59, col. 162, 164.

40. Popes Leo XIII and Benedict XV make these statements:

   When Mary offered herself completely to God together with her Son in the temple, she was already sharing with him the painful atonement on behalf of the human race . . . (at the foot of the cross) she was a co-worker with Christ in His expiation for mankind and she offered up her Son to the divine justice dying with him in her heart (*Jucunda semper*). . . . Thus she (Mary) suffered and all but died along with her Son suffering and dying—thus for the salvation of men she abdicated the rights of a mother toward her son, and insofar as it was hers to do, she immolated the Son to placate God's justice, so that she herself may justly be said to have redeemed together with Christ the human race. (*De Corredemptione*; cited by Carol, ed., *Mariology,* 1:383, 37)

41. "For there is one God, and one mediator also between God and men, the man Christ Jesus" (1 Tim. 2:5).

42. "Since explicit testimonies to Mary as Queen date from the fifth century and are linked closely with her divine Maternity, the richest source of this doctrine is the *Transitus Mariae* literature. In proclaiming the glories of the Mother of God and in describing her triumphant entrance into paradise, they hail her as a glorious queen" (Carol, ed., *Mariology,* 1:177).

43. Boniface Ramsey, *Beginning to Read the Fathers* (London: Darton, Longman & Todd, 1986), 6.

44. Cited by W. J. Sparrow Simpson, *Roman Catholic Opposition to Papal Infallibility* (London: John Murray, 1909), 324.

Where have evangelicals and Catholics come in relationship with each other? How did they are at this point, and what effect has Vatican II had on Catholicism? What has changed? How should evangelicals understand post-Vatican II Catholicism? The present changes offer some new opportunities for dialogue that should be entered into cautiously, for Rome is really no closer to the major concerns of the Reformation than she was five centuries ago. Indeed, she is much further away when we consider the effects of modernity and liberal theology.

Millions of Catholics and Protestants are in need of the grace of God revealed only in the gospel. Evangelicals, who may very well be at a great moment in their history, have lost knowledge of, and confidence in, the gospel. The answers are not to be found in a new revivalism, which, in fact, is more Roman Catholic than genuinely evangelical. What is needed is a widespread doctrinal reformation coupled with the power of the Word and Spirit in preaching.

ESSAY
13

THE EVANGELICAL MOMENT?

John H. Armstrong

Much has changed on the religious scene in recent decades. Certain individual Roman Catholics increasingly sound more and more like evangelicals, while certain evangelicals sound more and more like Roman Catholics. Older stereotypes don't seem to fit any more.

As we have already seen, especially in Part 3, there is a growing common ground being found between Protestant evangelicals and Roman Catholics, especially in the public arena of moral and ethical concerns. This alone has caused scores of priests and evangelical ministers, along with committed church members from both traditions, to "find one another." The publication of "Evangelicals & Catholics Together: The Christian Mission in the Third Millennium" (April 1994) is the most obvious example of a growing evangelical desire to work more closely with Roman Catholics. The response to all of this ranges from excitement over our common faith and message to open skepticism that any good thing can come from this relationship. Evangelical excitement, for example, can be observed in the highly respected writings of Charles Colson: "When Catholic priests and Protestant lay people stand together peacefully praying, in front of abortion clinics, it is a powerful witness. Many have been arrested, but I doubt that they've sat around in those bleak jail cells debating the Council of Trent."[1]

Critical reaction to Colson and to contemporary Catholic-evangelical discussion in general, ranges from gasps of horror and passionate outrage to careful and helpful criticism. Texe Marrs, author of numerous popular titles, asks Chuck Colson, "Will You Sell Your Soul to the Devil for a Million Dollars?" (because of the gift of a million dollars to Prison Fellowship associated with his accepting the John S. Templeton Prize for Progress in Religion).[2] From a different theological front, John Robbins writes: "The issue is the counterfeit gospel Colson teaches while on Earth, which is misleading many souls besides his own. Colson—and anyone else—will make it to heaven only if he believes the Gospel of Jesus Christ, which is not the gospel Colson preaches."[3]

In the book, *Evangelical Catholics*, Charles Colson writes in the fore-word: "It's high time that all of us who are Christians come together regard-less of the difference of our confessions and our traditions and make common cause to bring Christian values to bear in our society. When the barbarians are scaling the walls, there is no time for petty quarreling in the camp."[4]

Statements like these add fuel to a growing controversy. It is only fair to observe that Colson, for all the attack that has been leveled against him, does not specifically urge the overt surrender of evangelical doctrine. His words, taken in their plain sense, do not directly touch important categories of Protestant belief. He seems quite plainly to be speaking of a *common cause* that we can share in the "public square," as Richard J. Neuhaus has referred to it. But a growing concern has been felt by many evangelicals when they read these kinds of statements. They seem unwise. They seem to say, since (certain) doctrines divide us, let's find our cause together wherev-er possible and leave off the thorny issues that have separated us for more than four centuries. When several notable evangelical ministers and authors have gone over to Roman Catholicism in recent years (as we saw in Kim Riddlebarger's essay in chapter 10), is it any wonder that thoughtful evan-gelical readers are concerned? Paul G. Schrotenboer, writing an introduc-tion to published papers on Roman Catholicism prepared by the Theological Commission of the World Evangelical Fellowship, sums up this instinctive and proper concern by saying,

> There is much to give [evangelicals] hope for reformation according to the Word of God in the Church of Rome. There is also much in the recent reaffirma-tions of Roman Catholicism to give us pause in believing that all basic differ-ences will soon have been removed.
>
> The challenge is to bear witness to the faith once for all entrusted to the peo-ple of God (Jude 3) and to be honest and open in recognizing both agreements and departures from this faith.[5]

The landscape is definitely changing. But is this change something we should applaud without significant reservation? I think not. When Colson refers to the differences between evangelicals and Roman Catholics as "pet-ty quarreling in the camp," I think we need to ask some serious questions that might be hard to address clearly in the present atmosphere. Though many evangelicals seem genuinely delighted to put aside the old attitudes and Catholic bashing of an earlier century, are we not in danger of denying the very doctrinal concerns that have seriously divided us for 450 years? R. C. Sproul sums up my concern well when he places himself in the category of "a small minority of Protestants who take very seriously those lines of demarcation." Sproul expresses the fear that this overall change in attitude reflects doctrinal apathy more than genuine theological unity when he adds, "One of the reasons we don't fight about truth anymore is that we don't care about truth as much."[6]

These differing responses of evangelicals to Roman Catholicism could be seen in August 1993 when Pope John Paul II addressed Catholic young people at World Youth Day (1993) in Denver, Colorado. Concern was evident among many Catholic leaders that because so many young people were being lost to the Roman Catholic Church, and many of them particularly to evangelical churches, something needed to be done to address these and other concerns. Several aggressively evangelistic ministries sought to challenge Roman Catholic youth to turn to Christ and leave their church, while other high-profile evangelical leaders expressed publicly their sympathy with the event. The International Bible Society provided a commemorative leaflet, based on the gospel of John, with funding for this coming from several sources, including the Catholic Diocese of Colorado Springs. Prominent musicians, generally associated with evangelicals and their ministries, performed at Youth Day concerts.[7]

This new kind of cooperation has grown remarkably in recent years. Truly old hostilities are dying. Much in this can be praised, but many of the old questions still remain relevant for those of us who are committed to the centrality and sole authority of Scripture as well as to the priority of grace alone received through faith alone. With R. C. Sproul I am concerned that the real problem for both Roman Catholics and evangelicals, as several essays in this volume have sought to demonstrate, is that we don't care very deeply about the truth any more. Evangelicals must be willing to dialogue regarding twentieth-century issues and concerns, but one begins to wonder if we are willing to give away the farm in the process.

HOW DID WE ARRIVE AT THIS MOMENT?

As has been shown by Robert Strimple (chapter 4), we didn't come to this moment in our history overnight. Vatican Council II was convened on October 11, 1962, by Pope John XXIII (who died in June 1963). It was this pontiff who desired to "open the windows and let in some fresh air." The council was concluded with a fourth major session on December 8, 1965. Pope Paul VI presided over the last three sessions, leading the council in the production of sixteen major documents that now fill two large volumes.

Roman Catholicism has always had divisions within its ranks, but one thing was always quite clear—if you were a Roman Catholic you knew what your priest, your bishop, and your church *really* believed. Catholicism looked much the same in almost every place it took root, and Catholics, with few exceptions, generally believed and practiced the same faith, at least publicly. Since Vatican II, all that has changed. Michael Howard, Regius

Professor of Modern History at Oxford, has aptly referred to this Vatican Council as the "second great revolution" of our century. (The first was the Bolshevik Revolution of 1917, which makes me wonder if we have seen a third great revolution in the recent overthrow of communist governments in the former Soviet Union and in Eastern Europe.) Why? George Weigel, a Roman Catholic, has answered, "[because of] the transformation of the world's oldest continuous institution from an instrument of the status quo into an instrument of change." Weigel asserts, furthermore, that "Vatican II was not a serendipitous upheaval; a generation of Catholic philosophical, theological, biblical, and liturgical scholarship paved the way."[8] What kind of revolution did Vatican II cause? Weigel suggests there were five aspects to it, or, to be even more precise, "five revolutions in Rome."

The first is *modernity*. A break came from "Apologetic Catholicism," by which Weigel means that the church opened itself up to the fruit of modern scholarship and began to abandon neoscholastic forms of expression, which it had treated as virtually immutable for centuries. It changed, almost overnight, from its centuries-old defensive posture toward new insights. John XXIII spoke of "prophets of gloom . . . (who) behave as though they had learned nothing from history, which is, nonetheless, the teacher of life." And as Weigel notes, the pope urged the view that "authentic doctrine should be studied and expounded through the methods of research and through the literary forms of modern thought . . . [for] the substance of the . . . deposit of faith is one thing, and the way in which it is presented is another."[9]

It is important for evangelicals to understand this change. Building on the thinking of theologians like Jacques Maritain, Henri de Lubac, Yves Congar, Karl Rahner, and John Courtney Murray, Vatican II officially opened the doors for a new way of thinking about the world, about history, and about the Christian faith in particular. Sometimes Protestants are prone to argue that since Rome cannot and does not change—*semper idem* ("always the same")—nothing was really changed by Vatican II. This kind of argument was advanced by Lorraine Boettner in 1965:

> The Roman Church has now been frozen into a definite pattern from which she cannot change and which is basically the same today as it was in the days of the Inquisition. What sometimes looks like a change is merely a policy of caution which she has been forced to adopt because of public opinion. She changes her methods, but not her spirit.[10]

David Wells, an evangelical scholar who has given considerable attention to the actual documents of Vatican II, wrote more than twenty years ago, "the truth is, Boettner notwithstanding, that both the spirit and the doctrine of Catholicism *are* changing" (italics added).[11] Wells properly concludes: "the myth of an unchanging Catholicism has now been exploded."[12]

Weigel notes that the second revolution sparked by Vatican II was *self-understanding*. By this he means that the church, with its hierarchical concept of leadership that can be viewed much like a pyramid, took a new approach to the laity. To be a "lay" Catholic was now a "calling," not simply the absence of a "religious vocation."[13] This ongoing revolution in Rome can be seen in numerous lay organizations for church and personal renewal that spring up regularly.

The third revolution was *liturgical*. This is the change most Protestants have seen if they have been awake during the last thirty years. It is often said by well meaning evangelicals that the only thing changed by Vatican II was that the Latin Mass can now be heard in English and meat can be eaten on Fridays! Such a response is far too simplistic.[14]

Fourth, *the council radically altered the relationship Roman Catholicism has to other churches, to Judaism, and ultimately to all non-Christian religions*. Plunging into the liberal Protestant stream of ecumenism, Rome entered into interfaith dialogue. One must say upon reading the theology that has come out in the ensuing years, that the results have generally led to religious syncretism.[15]

Finally, and this was no small concession of change for Rome, Vatican II

taught that religious liberty was the most fundamental human right: a revolutionary "extension" for a Church that had long seen altar-and-throne arrangements, like those in pre-reformation England and, later in Franco's Spain, as the desirable norm. The Declaration on Religious Freedom was the particular gift of the American Church to Vatican II: its principal author was John Courtney Murray, and the Declaration reflected the distinctive experience of American Catholicism in a natively pluralistic religious environment.[16]

The Protestant Reformers did not begin their protest with the intention of dividing the church of their time. Their clear intention was to call the church back to her historic foundations and to the gospel of the New Testament. They challenged Rome's teaching authority on the basis of the gospel. They were patristic scholars, using the Fathers of the church to establish most of what they argued. Their burden was to show that what they believed was established in Scripture and confirmed in historical faith and practice. They did not argue, as do modern restorationists, that after the close of the Canon the church had been almost immediately lost. Rome's response, twenty-five years after the challenge had begun, was to convene a council in the northern Italian city of Trent (1545). On three different occasions this council met, finishing its work in 1563. The decrees of this council became the definitive and authoritative answers of the Roman Catholic Church against the teachings of the Protestant Reformers. The meaning of grace, the Scripture's authority, the sacraments, and the role of the papacy were all determined with a kind of harsh finality! Anathemas were pronounced upon all the *distinctive* evangelical doctrinal elements taught by the Reformers.

A good summation of the effect of Trent on Roman Catholic faith and life is provided by Robert A. Burns, a Roman Catholic professor of religion at the University of Arizona:

> The Council of Trent was held to present the authoritative answers of the Catholic Church to the objections of the Protestant reformers. In order to promote Catholic unity, clear definitions were given concerning Catholic dogma. For example, a definition of the Church's role emerged that stressed its visible institutional structures and identified the Church with the kingdom of God on earth. Because of the narrowness of this definition, Catholicism tended to become exclusivistic in its thinking and static in its world view. The Council of Trent also issued a number of regulations to promote unity. . . . The liturgy of the Mass was standardized and the Index of Forbidden Books was issued. These edicts helped maintain Catholic uniformity for the four hundred years after Trent. Great stress was placed on Church authority to maintain this post-Tridentine Catholic oneness.[17]

All of this led to what Burns and other modern Catholic academicians freely refer to as a "fortress" mentality. Two significant movements affected the church in the eighteenth and nineteenth centuries—the Enlightenment and the French Revolution. The Enlightenment undermined belief in the supernatural in general and the Bible in particular. Human reason was deified. The French Revolution (1789–99) introduced these ideas into the realm of political thought and brought about the downfall of the old order in Europe. Christianity was bitterly attacked in France, and the effects extended far beyond. Burns is helpful once again when he writes, "In order to understand why the Catholic Church reacted so negatively to the French Revolution and the idea of political democracy, one need only recall that the Church favored monarchy as the ideal and advocated the notion that Catholicism should be the official religion of every nation."[18]

There arose in France two distinctly different movements that would affect Roman Catholic thought into the twentieth century, and the divisions would only be settled officially at Vatican II. One movement reasserted the authority of the church, and in particular the papacy, as a bulwark against encroaching rationalism and post-Kantian thought. This conservative movement has been called ultramontanism (which meant literally "beyond the Alps"). This name was given because the papacy was located across the Alps in Italy. The other movement, which was obviously more liberal, sought to incorporate the newer ideas of freedom in thought and the separation of church and state.[19]

It was out of this post-Enlightenment thinking, mixed into a century-plus of papal authority virtually unchecked by other forces in the church, that Rome entered the twentieth century. By the time Vatican II was convened it was inevitable that the forces that had been at work for some time to bring Roman Catholic thought and practice into line with modern worldviews were going to win the day.

It is here that most evangelicals are confused about modern Catholic theology and practice. The new Catholic position—and again we must realize that it is *new*—reinterprets the old concepts, dogmas, and life in *terms* of the new. Wells wisely expresses the essence of my argument:

> On the level of cognition—what man can know—the old Catholic was confident and affirmative. The new Catholic by contrast, tends to be agnostic in some respects and uncertain in others. He is the child of the existential, not the classical, world. For him, the object of religious knowledge, in this case Christ, is often obscure. The sharp lines of distinction in matters of truth are not untenable, perhaps even desirable. The concern has shifted from objective definition to subjective experience. It is not what you believe which is important but that you believe, not what you believe in but the quality of your commitment as you believe.[20]

All doctrinal formulations, in this way of thinking, are subject to revision, precisely because truth, which may be perspicuous to God, is blurred and unclear to us. As Protestant Wells notes, the close relationship between Christ and the church, which had always been a part of Roman Catholic reality, was now broken. Amazingly, it was Pope John XXIII who helped break this relationship when he said at the initial session of Vatican II, "the substance of the ancient doctrine of the deposit of faith is one thing, and the way in which it is presented is another." This statement means more than saying that truth is objective and final; we must learn to put it in new words and forms for differing cultures. Wells says that John XXIII's "single sentence was a pithy, if deceptively simple, summary of the new ideas: There is a distinction to be drawn between truth in itself ('the deposit of faith is one thing') and truth as it is comprehended by the Church and taught to the world ('the way in which it is presented is another')."[21]

Radical theologians like Hans Küng, Leonardo Boff, and Charles Curran, who were eventually marginalized by the Catholic hierarchy, simply developed this kind of thinking, whether or not the church was ready for it. Theology has a wax nose with this approach. What kind of Catholicism do you want? You are working with "the deposit of faith" just like the other person, but what you see in it can be different; indeed it probably will be.

That is precisely why the present pope, John Paul II, can appear to be so very traditional in certain areas and at the same time embrace non-Christian religions and speak of salvation for non-Christians. This confuses evangelicals and not a few traditional Catholics who don't understand what has happened. When the *Constitution on the Church* says, "at all times and among every people, God has given welcome to whosoever fears Him and does what is right,"[22] then I can only conclude that B. C. Butler has understood Roman Catholic thought correctly when he writes, "Salvation is, for the individual, radically dependent on subjective good intention [rather] than on external ecclesiastical allegiance."[23]

For centuries the magisterium had insisted that there was no salvation outside the church (*extra ecclesiam nulla salus*), which meant, of course, the Roman Catholic Church. This sometimes caused a decidedly uncharitable response to Protestant evangelicals, who were considered lost outside of Rome and her sacramental system. What changed? Did Rome officially retract the old doctrines of the Council of Trent, admitting that they had been in error in teaching them previously? Of course not. What Rome did was add a new formula, or a new way of thinking about these matters. Doctrines could now be taken up in an unrelated manner, just as had been done for decades in liberal Protestant schools and churches. This has effectively caused a completely new understanding of the old confessions of faith in much of Protestantism, changing the meaning of received truth entirely. It is doing the same in modern Catholicism. The result is an understanding of man and salvation that pictures God's salvific activity to be like concentric circles. Christ is at the center, with the closest circle being the Roman Catholic Church. The next circle, farther from the center, but still in relationship with it, consists of non-Catholic Christians, or "separated brethren." The next circle would include the non-Christian religions. Even here there is relationship to Christ and to His church; that is, you can begin to talk about a Hindu who is really in fellowship with the Roman Catholic Church, and thus with Christ, even though he doesn't realize it. (This has, of course, redefined the missionary calling of the church so that Rome often does not seek to bring members of non-Christian religions into her communion as she did in previous centuries.) Wells helps us see the thinking behind this missiology more clearly:

> The Council was not saying that all religions are equally true. Rather, it was trying to combine the old idea that Christ is to be found only in the Roman Catholic Church with the newer idea that something of the divine can be seen in all men. . . . The outstanding problem which has been posed, but hardly answered, by the new concept is how much of a Christward orientation is needed to establish membership in the People of God. Some theologians, building on the Council's teaching, have argued that one day the People of God will become coextensive with the human race. Are all, then, members of God's kingdom even now?[24]

But what about atheists and infidels? Well, even atheists are not without hope in the theology of prominent Roman Catholic theologian Karl Rahner, who calls them, amazingly, "anonymous Christians."[25]

Roman Catholics and evangelicals cannot afford to ignore each other. In a world like the one we live in, building walls of strict isolation will be increasingly impossible for all Christian traditions. An *Index of Forbidden Books* will no longer serve to keep the faithful in line, whether issued by Rome or by a fundamentalist school or fellowship determined to keep their youth in the faith. Davis Duggins, senior editor of *Moody* magazine, perceptively sums up our present situation: "Changes in society and in the Catholic Church are forcing evangelicals to reexamine their relationships with Catholics. While the previous generation of evangelicals and Catholics generally avoided any contact, such isolation has become much less feasible. Today the questions concern what kind of cooperation and how much is appropriate?"[26]

Protestant and Catholic theology have been converging in our time but, as John W. Montgomery has aptly noted, "not at a recognizable, articulated, and firmly established juncture, but in a mystic cloud of unknowing."[27] This "cloud of unknowing" seems to surround many of the recent attempts at agreement addressed in this volume.

As we have seen in Part 3, there is room for carefully defined common ground between us. I believe that this type of common ground is likely to increase, precisely because the culture seems hell-bent on turning away from its Western moral foundation that was grounded in the Christian tradition, socially and ethically. In those areas where spiritual communion could bring us together around the central truths of the gospel, I believe we already see evidence that the door is closing and that conservative Catholics increasingly desire to stress again the doctrines of Trent, which can never be accepted by evangelicals who maintain a truth base for fellowship in Christ and the visible church. Wells, writing some fifteen years after his fuller analysis of Vatican II was published, notes:

> If Catholicism is to become more Catholic in the future, which is what I expect under the present pope, then theological differences with evangelicals will become sharper but our alliances with Catholics against the secular culture can become deeper. I, for one, am ready for that tradeoff. Evangelicals have far less to gain from dialogue with Rome than they do in using a common Christian arsenal with Catholics to protect life and values in the midst of an exceedingly crooked generation.[28]

WHERE ARE WE AT THIS TIME IN HISTORY?

The type of thinking that has developed since Vatican II, which is representative of serious Catholic theologizing in the last decade of the twentieth century, tends to cast a different light upon where we are today and how we got there. If evangelicals are to be wise, and remain faithful to the gospel, they must be extremely careful in navigating these presently uncharted waters.

Whereas certain evangelicals are attacking popular spokespersons such as Charles Colson, with some basis due to his lack of theological clarity in areas where caution and clearer thinking might have served his cause better, others are almost unquestioningly following Colson, along with several other popular evangelical writers. More than thirty years of cooperative non-theologically based mass evangelism has prepared a generation for a new way. Many are thinking, *We agree on so much, why not work together and forget our old hostilities?* They may have a friend who displays love for Christ and the Scriptures who has remained in the Roman Catholic Church. Their neighbor seems to be genuinely evangelical in every way and just as concerned for biblical Christianity as they are, if not more so. Their Bible study group might include Roman Catholics who have come, through their study of the Word, to openly confess their love for Christ. They have displayed open excitement about knowing the Scriptures. Or perhaps they have served on the community evangelistic planning team and worked alongside a Catholic, seeing their evident zeal for reaching others with the gospel. They use our tracts and methods in witnessing, respect our best-known evangelist and spokesman, Billy Graham, as much as we do, and they now even sing our songs. Who can forget, if they were in attendance or watching on television, seeing Pope John Paul II joining the throngs who sang "Amazing Grace" in Chicago's Grant Park during a huge outdoor celebration of the Mass? I recall the enthusiastic comments of some evangelicals: "He is one of us, a true evangelical. Did you see him? Did you hear him quote from the Bible?"

It serves no good purpose to question the pope as a person or to offer judgment about his ultimate standing before God. He is a fallen man and therefore must stand before God as any other mortal in need of divine grace and reconciliation through Christ. Even his own doctrine does not attribute infallibility to him, except when he speaks *ex cathedra* ("from the chair"), which has been done only a few times in the past several centuries. It serves no real purpose to argue with other evangelicals about what we should call Roman Catholicism. (A debate swirls around this constantly, with some insisting that we must label Roman Catholicism a "cult" in order to be faithful to the teaching of the Bible.) My purpose, rather, is to question the growing response by evangelicals that no longer shows discerning love for the truth and clear understanding of the essential issues of the gospel of Christ. My purpose is to address the questions of life and death, the ultimate issues that must be addressed by all to take seriously the historic Christ and His message.

What this comes back to is truth. What is truth? Where is it to be found? Must truth be embraced by faith for one to know Christ savingly? Is it vitally important to know what is our ultimate source of truth? (In the present concern, as we have seen already, we might even begin by asking, "Can we even know the truth at all, and is there any *objective* source of truth to be found?")

We must begin by realizing that Roman Catholicism is much more than another evangelical church with a few minor doctrines added to the gospel. This kind of approach is both naive and reductionistic in the extreme. Because the Spirit of God is breaking through obstacles of spiritual blindness and regenerating individuals by granting them the gifts of faith and repentance does not mean that the Roman Catholic Church is undergoing a powerful new awakening in our day, much less a biblical reformation process. We must become more realistic about the gains that have been experienced since Vatican II. Contrary to the sometimes cheerful evangelical evaluation of a biblical Roman Catholic movement, the opposite is in fact taking place. Harold O. J. Brown, author of chapter 7, has written elsewhere,

> Many points of Catholicism contain sound biblical teaching. But the system is so overlaid and interwoven with non-biblical and even unbiblical ideas and practices that it seems to resemble what Paul called "a different gospel" (Gal. 1:6). When Catholics are saved, it is because they have received the grace to sort out the wheat from the chaff. Sometimes it seems to be as much despite the church as thanks to it.[29]

There are, in reality, two Catholicisms at work in the present church. One is progressive, deeply influenced by Vatican II and what we have seen already (in chapter 4). The other is traditional, very desirous of defending the papacy and the old doctrines peculiar to Catholicism, particularly since the few centuries prior to and after the Protestant Reformation (chapters 2 and 3). Vatican II progressive thinking, reflected almost universally in the prolific writing of theologians of this century and in the universities of American Catholicism, sees authority arising from the church itself, that is, from the laity as the people of God. The other, the more traditional Catholicism developed over centuries of reacting against the gospel message of the Reformers and the divisions of the sixteenth century, sees authority as descending from the papacy and magisterium down to the people. In the progressive view, salvation, as I have shown, is broad, inclusive, and grounded in intentions and subjective response to divine light available to all, even those without the church.

The older view still maintains that salvation is grounded in the sacraments and visible relationship to the Catholic Church. The progressive view is at work in the church quite widely, but the present pope, on the whole, is turning it back in several areas as he asserts the more traditional position in crucial moral and theological areas. Examples of this direction can be seen in the papacy's response to liberation theology and modern sexual and reproductive concerns. This conservative response can also be seen in the attention given in recent years to the place of Mary, the saints, and the magisterium. Catholic spirituality and preoccupation with mysticism as the means of living the Christian life are undergoing a virtual revival in many quarters. Witness the writings of Thomas Merton and Henri Nouwen who have had a great fascination for some evangelicals at the mystical end of the Protestant spectrum. This does not encourage me to believe that the more biblically correct approach of Spirit and Word (chapter 5) is central to these movements of piety presently at work in many Protestant and Roman Catholic communities. Some of the excitement over new spiritual life sounds more like New Age thinking covered with old Catholic dress. Evangelicalism has a "weak underbelly" here and may suffer extensive damage in this dialogue if it continues to drift doctrinally. The mood of Western culture is much more likely to climb on this wagon than on one that calls believers to the written Word and the Spirit's great work through preaching and teaching.

As we saw in chapter 12, many Catholics have never heard, much less understood, the gospel of grace. Catholic apologists such as Scott Hahn, Karl Keating, and others aside, the experience of almost every well-taught evangelical Christian is that it is a rarity to meet a faithful Roman Catholic who can articulate plainly the essential doctrines of the gospel, doctrines that are openly and aggressively opposed by the new conservative Catholics like Hahn, Matatics, and Keating. Some Catholics give evidence of "trusting Christ *alone*" for right standing with God, but most, it must sadly be observed, still equate being a baptized Roman Catholic with being rightly related to Jesus Christ. It should be added that multitudes of Protestants have this same sandy basis of hope for eternal life.

I remember the first time, as a college freshman, that I began to talk directly to other students about their relationship with Christ and their hope of eternal life. I remember using a survey to break the ice and start discussion. When I asked Catholics, "When did you become a Christian?" the universal answer was, "When I was baptized." Then I would ask them, "Do you believe that you will go to heaven when you die?" The almost universal answer was, "I hope so!" And then, following the provided discussion starter, I asked, "On what basis should God allow you into heaven?" The answer time after time was, "Because I have been a good Catholic, sought to obey God's laws, and taken the communion regularly." I can never remember hearing the answer of the gospel of free and sovereign grace, which believingly replies, "I expect to be accepted in heaven solely on the basis of God's grace received by faith, which itself is God's gift to me!" And I will never forget the first time I led a young man into a decision, not realizing then that such evangelistic methodology is more Roman Catholic than genuinely evangelical, only to ask him the so-called follow-up question, "Where is Christ right now?" He answered happily, "I have received Him into my heart in prayer with you, just as I receive Him into my heart every time I take the Mass."

When I heard the young man's answer that evening on the ocean front I determined there and then to understand his answer better, and that was in fact the beginning of a life-long desire to understand Catholic faith and practice. It has led me to attend Catholic conferences, groups, and gatherings. It has led me into dialogue with some lovely people who I have every reason to believe genuinely trust Christ alone to save them, in spite of what they have or have not been taught in their parishes. It has prompted me to watch a good bit of the programming of EWTN, the Catholic cable network. It has taken me into Catholic libraries and bookshops, where I have bought numerous books and teaching tapes. In all of this I keep encountering the same thing I have referred to above. Wherever one turns he will inevitably find either traditional Catholic concepts, with all the old misunderstandings about grace and faith evident in the anathemas of Trent and its attack on "the righteousness which is of faith," or he will find modern interpretations placed upon these old doctrines that sound much more like the old liberalism of an earlier Protestant era.

Often scholars, aware of debates waged over the centuries, will seek to be careful in how they position themselves on these critical issues, but in the end they are unwilling, or perhaps honestly unable, to assert the straightforward message of justification by faith *alone*. If, as Luther said, "this is the article of a standing or falling church," and if he was correct as evangelicals for centuries have believed, then we cannot think of Rome as a church standing on the gospel and the grace of God. She has fallen and has thus lost the marks of the church (cf. chapters 3 and 11).

Furthermore, when one speaks of being a Roman Catholic today the evangelical needs to understand that this statement in itself doesn't tell much about what the person really believes. (Again, the same is true often with those who refer to themselves as "born again" evangelicals.) John R. W. Stott, writing in *Christianity Today* in 1977, said, "For what exactly is the church of Rome that one can relate to it? The old illusion of a monolithic structure has been shattered. Today it appears almost as pluriform as Protestantism. What does it believe and teach? Has it really changed? Or is its old boast of changelessness and irreformability true?"[30]

When Protestants and Catholics discussed theological concerns prior to our generation, the discussion always arrived at the question of religious authority. Further discussion only made it increasingly plain that Rome believed in a church that interpreted the Scripture, while Protestantism affirmed a perspicuous, self-interpreting Bible that had final authority over the institution of the church. Now the ground underneath both traditions has suffered the opening of massive fault lines. In the words of one Protestant, "Prior to the pontificate of John XXIII, Protestant relations with Roman Catholicism could be characterized as negative but clean-cut."[31] The foreseeable future offers no reason to believe that things will go back to the way they were when they were "clean-cut."

Various modern factions can be observed within a pluriform and often pluralistic Roman Catholicism:

1 Liberals, who, as we've previously noted, are at the forefront of Catholic higher education and written philosophy and theology.

2 Extreme syncretists, who mix all kinds of religious practice with Christian symbols and teaching. This form of Catholicism is often seen in Third World countries like Papua New Guinea, Haiti, among Brazilian Indians, and so on, where multitudes of baptized Catholics are voodoo worshipers, believing in magic more than in the confessed essentials of historic Christianity.

3 Nominal Catholics, by far the largest number worldwide in the Roman Church. In America only a little more than one in four Catholics now attend the Mass weekly. Among these are the vast numbers who practice birth control, and who often believe in "abortion on demand." They remain members only because the church does not remove them or they do not take steps to remove themselves, a step almost never taken by even the most radical ex-Catholic.

4 Conservative (moderate) Catholics, who are those who seek to maintain a kind of halfway position, defending the magisterium and the historic councils and creeds, yet identifying with the changes of Vatican II and accepting the modernizations and theological shifts, albeit with some reservations.

5 Archconservatives, or old traditionalists, like the late Marcel Lefebvre of France, who along with many others who did not necessarily follow him publicly, wanted to maintain the old Latin Mass. These are the few remaining antiecumenical Catholics. Lefebvre, who supported the papacy and its traditional dogmas, was expelled from the church by the very papacy he defended. These are Catholics who often feel that Pope John XXIII and Pope Paul VI developed suicidal policies that must be resisted.

6 Charismatics, a group that draws much attention from evangelicals, but which seems no longer to be growing as rapidly as in the 1970s and 1980s. Charismatics were initially a disruptive force to the Catholic establishment, but now they have been quieted and absorbed into the larger stream of the church, a phenomenon that is common in Roman Catholic history.[32]

It is for this reason that evangelicals must be concerned by much of the discussion of our time that speaks of the two traditions coming together. On what basis are we coming together? This question must be honestly asked. George Carey, the present Archbishop of Canterbury, underscores my very concern when he observes positively regarding the charismatic renewal among Catholics and Protestants, "It is the only revival in history which has united evangelicals on the one hand, with their strong emphasis on the death of Christ and full atonement, and Roman Catholics on the other, with their emphasis on the sacraments. Somehow charismatic experiences have brought together people who on the face of it have little in common theologically."[33]

This strange observation, written by an Anglican leader who considers himself an evangelical, sends up warning flares that trouble serious Protestant evangelicals who have not abandoned the gospel insights of Luther and the Reformers. If we have a unity with "little in common theologically," one must be troubled over what kind of unity we really have come to. It is clearly not the unity Christ prayed for in John 17.

As one committed to the power of the gospel to save those who believe, through faith alone, I am still moved with profound sadness and deep soul anguish when I see the practice of *old* Romanism the world over. On a recent journey to Brazil I made a trip to the Catholic shrine at Aparecida. Here millions of Brazilians have come to pray and worship before a small, unimpressive wood carving that stands about eighteen inches tall. The story is that in 1717 two fishermen found this statue in the Paraiba River. Was it an idol, or simply a piece of Indian artwork? We do not know for sure. As has been typical of Catholicism, miraculous powers were soon attributed to this statue and she (?) was soon elevated before the masses of superstitious worshipers who came to pray and adore her. Today this statue is the patron saint of Brazil!

As I watched I saw people praying, weeping, bowing, giving money, and laying aside their braces and crutches in claiming a miracle at Aparecida. I was witnessing the type of Catholicism that still grips millions of souls the world over. Built around this phenomenon is the second largest basilica in the world. Only St. Peter's is larger. A booming tourist business has developed, and the Brazilian government has a vested interest in the site.

Walking through this huge basilica one can see rooms where the bodies of former spiritual leaders are buried. People are touching and praying over the tombs of the deceased. "The Miracle Room," where photographs and letters by the thousands hang, all giving testimony to the power of the lady of Aparecida and the miracles she has granted, is a place of amazement. Vast amounts of money are collected from the faithful, and Mass is said regularly at various hours of the day.

I could not help but wonder what some of my Roman Catholic friends in the U.S. would make of all this. Perhaps they would decry it in much the same way I decry the hucksterism of evangelical televangelism and the promise of cures for the faithful who pray and give their money.

What lingers with me even now is Pope John Paul II's visit to Aparecida. Did he condemn this whole business as "old Catholicism" of the sort that needed to be cleaned up by a great sweeping biblical reformation? Quite the contrary; he blessed the statue and thereby endorsed the superstition and idolatry by lending his profound weight to the whole business.

Can the reader not understand why those who love the Lord Jesus and are genuinely jealous for His glory and worship are deeply distressed by places like Aparecida? In a country where there is an even more desperate need for hearing the gospel, due to centuries of superstition and spiritual ignorance, is it any wonder that evangelicals still experience great soul trouble over this type of Catholicism?

Kenneth Kantzer observed in 1986 that Rome is a church on the move. He stated that the most exciting change is a new freedom for the gospel in our time. Openness among many to read, study, and hear the Bible's teaching is a sign of better things if the trend continues. It is this that many Protestant evangelicals have experienced positively with their friends who are in the Roman Catholic Church.

> Where, then, is the Roman Catholic church today, and where is it going? Part of it is rigorously defending its traditions, changing only enough to survive. Other segments, particularly its lay members [primarily in North America, it should be noted], are becoming evangelical. Much of its leadership is moving in the direction of liberal Protestantism. Pope John Paul II has noticed his theologians' leaning toward liberalism and has firmly asked them to stand by the content of the traditional faith. His own ecumenical efforts have turned toward the Eastern Orthodox churches. At the same time, he has fostered dialogue with the World Council of Churches.[34]

If this observation be true, how does this movement among Roman Catholics affect evangelicals?

It is my conviction that we are at a critical crossroads in Christian history, especially in the West. As the new paganism threatens us at every turn, so the church is in danger of continually surrendering its truth claims to the relativistic thought of our age. As Roman Catholicism has opened the door to us in Vatican II we must be careful that we know how to respond to this "open door." We must understand the real direction of Roman Catholic thought, and we must be vigilant for the truth of Scripture. We must avoid negative criticism that is unfounded, but we must also guard against naive assumptions of new agreements. The writings of a converted conservative Presbyterian minister like Scott Hahn, considered by Kim Riddlebarger (chapter 10), and conversions to Rome by former evangelicals like Tom Howard should give us pause when we are inclined to think there is no remaining appeal left in old Catholic dogma and in the lure of an authoritative papacy and church tradition. We must understand what it means to be truly evangelical in our age and how to stand for the gospel in thought and deed, powerfully and clearly. My concern, theologically, is that we are losing the gospel in evangelicalism, and thus we can easily enter into all kinds of discussion and agreements that ultimately lead us into the sacrifice of the very message from which we get our identity—the Evangel.

What does all of this mean for us in coming years?

WHERE DO WE GO FROM HERE?

A few years ago, one of this century's most highly regarded liberal scholars, Paul Tillich, observed that the Protestant era was ending. He said, in essence, that America stood much closer to the non-Reformation tradition than it did to the Reformation tradition.[35] I was shocked by this observation when I first read it. I assumed Tillich didn't understand, since he was *not* an evangelical. I now believe he was correct in his analysis of the American religious scene. Modern evangelicalism is, in reality, more Catholic than Protestant.

Louis Bouyer, a French Protestant scholar who converted to Roman Catholicism in the 1950s, points out in his apologia for conversion to Rome, that evangelical revivals, particularly in America, often unintentionally brought the Protestant movement much closer to Rome.[36] What does Bouyer mean? Simply that Catholic spirituality makes the inward work of grace *central* to its understanding of salvation. Modern revivalism has done exactly the same thing.

The Protestant Reformers (as seen in chapter 5) certainly made room for the internal work of the Holy Spirit, but the good news was what God did for sinful man outside of his heart. He gives an alien righteousness, He saves a man based solely on what Christ did objectively at the Cross. If the human sinner looks anywhere else, he ultimately looks away from the objective gospel and thus away from the righteousness of God. Faith, created in the heart by the active work of the Holy Spirit, produces fruit in repentance, good works, and outward service to God and man. The believer, we can say properly in this way of thinking, is truly saved by works—the works of Christ alone! The works the believer produces, by the Spirit's inward work, are the *response* of the believer to the grace of God; thus they have no part in creating faith or in making the sinner right with God in any sense of the word. As Protestantism has moved further and further into mysticism and subjectivism since the nineteenth century, it has proportionately moved away from its evangelical foundation. This move into subjectivism, combined in recent years with post-Enlightenment relativism, undermines our confidence that truth can be truly known and understood. It has virtually destroyed the foundation upon which the whole Protestant evangelical movement was established.

Harold Bloom, a contemporary critic of religion in the United States, writes of our present civil religion and its radical departure from confessional Christian Protestantism in *The American Religion: The Emergence of a Post-Christian Nation*. His important book should trouble many evangelicals because it points out the present state of religion in a manner that ought to awaken us to the national religion we have created in our own image. He adds to our understanding of this present hour when he adroitly writes:

> Religion, in the ostensibly Protestant United States, is something subtly other than Christianity, though to say that we are a post-Christian country is misleading. Rather, we are post-Protestant, and we live a persuasive redefinition of Christianity. It is so persuasive that we refuse to admit that we have revised the traditional religion into a faith that better fits our national temperament, aspirations, and anxieties. A blend of ancient heresies and nineteenth-century stresses, the American Religion moves towards the twenty-first century with an unrestrained triumphalism, easily convertible into our political vagaries.[37]

What then is the answer?

We need a new biblical reformation as we enter the twenty-first century—a reformation that is like the old one in certain areas. This is true precisely because we have lost our understanding of the gospel and its objective essence. We also need a reformation unlike the old one in that this one needs to challenge the total abandonment of truth in our day. It must be a reformation that challenges the revivalism of American church life for the past 150 years. It must be a reformation that affirms doctrinal recovery and denies present idolatries—e.g., materialism and the power that corrupts us, ministerial moral breakdown that has devastated our credibility, therapeutic models of ministry that have completely reinterpreted the theology of the Scriptures into a man-centered message, and public worship services that are aimed directly at fulfilling man's felt needs at the expense of the transcendent holiness of a sovereign God who is feared and reverenced.

In *No Place for Truth* David Wells writes, "At moments like this the customary response to the sense of Christian inadequacy, whether in relation to God or some aspect of the Christian message, has been to call for revival."[38] This call has usually been associated with a Finneyesque type of idea that sees the church as rejuvenated through its own efforts, albeit joined with the Spirit's work. What is needed is more than a recovery of excitement and spiritual interest. We can have that, and not one thing will substantially change. Revival, as conceived of in the era prior to Finney (1792–1875), was always understood to be a sovereign visitation of God upon the church *when* the gospel was preached and the Scriptures were firmly established as central in the life and method of the church. Such a true awakening in our time must be joined with a wholesale reformation, or any genuine spiritual rain that may be given will undoubtedly fall upon a setting where it will be quickly lost on a people unprepared to establish it in the clearest biblical categories of grace and truth.

In the 1992 Public Broadcast System television miniseries, *Mine Eyes Have Seen the Glory,* author and narrator Randall Balmer portrays twentieth-century evangelical Christianity in America as a subculture that insulates itself from society and retreats from intellectual pursuit in the marketplace of modern ideas. He shows how the last decade has seen an emergence of this very same subculture into mainstream America, but with one problem—it is still the same antirational, anticultural movement, but now bolstered by the display of newly discovered political and social muscle. Balmer may overstate his thesis, and surely certain parts of his series can be faulted, but on the whole I fear he has spoken the truth, albeit too painfully and prophetically for most evangelicals to accept his point until they reject much of what they are presently doing in the culture.

It was painful for this writer to hear Balmer speaking of how he never "got it" while worshiping among evangelicals—by which he apparently meant the great emotional experience that many evangelicals refer to as conversion. I wondered: *Did Balmer begin to think, as I did in my college days, that evangelical Christianity had little to do with critical analysis, the use of reason, and commitment to creativity? Did he get the message so many of us have gotten—just surrender and believe, that is, do not doubt?* This kind of evangelicalism is a blanket denial of the historic Protestant Reformation and the truths it so firmly rediscovered in the Scriptures.

What we need, quite obviously, is a deep, intellectual, doctrinal, moral reformation grounded in Christ alone, grace alone, faith alone, and Scripture alone. What we need is a sweeping, true, great awakening in our generation, one grounded in the objective gospel and the complete authority of Scripture. It is precisely because of this great need, perceived so plainly by critics like Bloom and Balmer, that this book has been written. This present volume has been written not only to help evangelicals and Catholics understand one another better, which is good in itself, but to foster the kind of understanding that will create a new climate for true reformation and revival in our time. The desire of each author has been to explain some of the important forces that were at work in our history and are at work in the present age to shape contemporary Catholicism, both its faith and its practice. We have sought to understand as well the Protestant evangelical response to Roman Catholicism, both historic and current. We have seen that evangelicals in some areas agree, while in others we must voice dissent that is based on our loyalty to the Word of God and the gospel. This is what ultimately keeps us apart in this present hour and will undoubtedly keep us divided unless God does something we cannot presently see or humanly forecast.

There was a time when evangelicals were universally convinced, as John W. Montgomery wrote in the 1960s, "that considerations of truth must precede considerations of union, unity, worship, or fellowship."[39] I fear that such time is no more and the dangers of present discussion with Catholicism are problematic in many cases precisely because both sides of the discussion are unsure of what they actually believe and what they are genuinely committed to as believers.

Make no mistake about it: the legacy of Vatican II seems to be one of change and tension. Comments evangelical theologian James I. Packer:

> More than at any time since the Reformation, Catholics and Protestants are now divided in the same way, into conservatives, radicals, and those who can only be called compromisers, and who battle constantly within their own communities on the same set of issues—Scripture as revelation; Christian supernaturalism; the Christian mission; the meaning of worship and piety.[40]

Change is desirable, but we must not be naive about the nature of such change, or the purpose of it. Change for the sake of change is clearly not always healthy.

As long as Rome maintains a two-source view of authority (the idea that God's authority comes to us through the Bible and the traditions of the church), we will not be able to solve our serious disagreements. And as long as Rome insists on an understanding of justification by faith that undermines the Pauline doctrine of grace as explained in the epistles to the Galatians and the Romans, we shall remain divided.

At the same time many evangelicals get quite shaky when they read a book like this one. They will see only the potential for compromise written everywhere. Why? The mere mention of working together in any arena sounds so, well, *so liberal!*

Most evangelicals do not realize that the concern for finding and preserving Christian unity in the post-Reformation era was birthed out of the evangelical missions movement of the nineteenth century, not the liberal social agenda of the twentieth century. It was almost always the burden of earlier evangelical missionary efforts to preserve the unity of believers wherever possible, especially in alien cultures hostile to the gospel. Further, how can we read the New Testament and not sense the concern of the Epistles for preserving unity in the gospel. Heresy itself is independent belief and willful action that separates one from the church.

Furthermore, it is extremely important to realize (as we observed in chapter 12) that evangelicals have always understood their practice and faith as that of historic Christianity and not a modern departure from apostolic, catholic, Christian faith. As we have previously seen, it was Luther's view that the Roman Catholic Church had left the gospel and the Scriptures, and thus, in reality, *it had left the church* of Jesus Christ. Much polemic flowed from both sides in this debate, but let it be understood that Protestant evangelicalism is not, *inherently,* schismatic. Let Wells again have a word to guide us here:

> The New Testament writers are unequivocally in favor of Christian unity provided it is established on a Christian basis. That is to say, Christians must find their unity in the same truth which they profess rather than in some common project in which they participate. Furthermore, the truth they profess must reiterate the truth . . . the apostles taught. This is the apostolic succession . . . the New Testament teaches.[41]

What we stand for as historic evangelicals is not anti-Catholicism. Luther was not an anti-Catholic. He was a Catholic initially, and many of those who tutored him in the faith were Catholics whom he dearly loved. He longed for the church of his day to return to the apostolic gospel. He labored for her recovery and left the church of his birth only when he was forced to by the events that culminated in Rome's refusal to hear the gospel. There were many in Luther's day who did hear the gospel. Some did not leave the Roman Catholic Church with him. Political and social reasons, as well as personal concerns that are beyond our ability to analyze, all came to play in these choices. The point is this: though Luther attacked the papacy as an institution that perpetrated awful confusion and abuse of power, he still counted people on both sides of the divide as brothers. He was concerned, very early on in his own context, that many souls had followed the evangelical Reformation in Germany, yet without new life in Christ through the gospel. It is for much more of this kind of *genuine* evangelical spirit that this book has appealed. What needs to be analyzed is not who we talk to, why we talk, or where, but rather, "What is the basis for fellowship (of any kind) and what is the nature of it?" I fear that many conservative evangelicals, myself included, have often tended to judge by *appearances* and not by *truth* in a context of love.

This is the appeal the apostle makes to us in Ephesians 4:15 when he charges us to labor at "speaking the truth in love." We must keep both ends of this in balance. Biblical truth must not be compromised, under any circumstances. Christian character and action must never be compromised either. We must speak the truth, but we can only do so, if we are to be truly Christian, in love. There is enough error on both sides of this injunction to bring shame to all who have concerned themselves with these great doctrinal issues that have divided us for more than four centuries. Wells adds, "Love must direct us to the point where the biblical Christ is confronted, for truth will only be found here. And it is the truth question alone which must absorb our attention. This is, after all, what theology is all about."[42]

The more I have studied Roman Catholicism the more I realize how shades of meaning and thought behind certain Catholic doctrines have been both misunderstood and misrepresented by many evangelicals, including myself. I have resolved to work honestly at fuller understanding of these teachings so that I might speak the truth. I have also realized the pride of place and position that often characterizes Christian doctrinal disputes. Frankly, a part of my mind and spirit thrives on a good debate, especially when I am thoroughly convinced that I am right and the other person is clearly wrong. I don't always debate a point with a mind "open" to learn and grow, but with resolute determination to give up nothing of the truth as it is revealed in Scripture. I confess, because of my firm belief in God's sovereignty, that only the Spirit of God can truly give a truth, any Christian truth, to any person. My problem is this: though truth itself is not relative and is never up for negotiation, I am not always ready to respond to the truth. I have defenses of all kinds, made in my sinful self, to keep me from being radically altered by the gospel. But truth can be known. Essential truth is not hidden and made known only to a magisterium, whether it be that of Rome or fundamentalism. As the evangelicals of Luther's day were wont to say, essential truth is perspicuous, or plain, and it is found only in the written Scripture. Yet I can be so dull, so slow of heart to believe. I do wonder about both Catholics and evangelicals who cannot come to the table of discussion with this much readiness to be humbled before God and His Holy Word.

As I am troubled by certain Protestant misunderstanding and misrepresentation, ı am increasingly aware that this street has two sides. When the National Conference of Catholic Bishops in the United States met in 1987 and issued a document on "fundamentalism," it concerns me that they got a good bit wrong.

Responding to the recent surge of converts into evangelical churches the bishops felt constrained to do something to stop the exodus. They described fundamentalism as a "general approach to life that is typified by unyielding adherence to rigid doctrinal and ideological positions." They add, further, that fundamentalists "present the Bible, God's inspired Word, as the only necessary source for teaching about Christ and Christian living." The bishops went on to link the teaching that "the Bible alone is sufficient" and that there is in such churches no place "for creeds and other doctrinal formulations" (meaning Rome's, of course) with the belief "that the Bible is always without error." Even though one of the theologians involved said the document was aimed at small sects and television evangelists, conservative evangelicals must, by all conscientious commitment to the truth of their faith, be troubled by a response like this. Carl F. H. Henry commented at the time by saying that, while fundamentalism deserves criticism on certain points, the bishops' statement takes a swipe at the Protestant Reformation.

This kind of response, noted Henry, is "another way of saying that fundamentalists don't accept the legitimacy of the papacy and don't accept the finality of the Roman Catholic Church." He added, "if Rome wants to fight the battle of the Reformation all over again, that is its prerogative."[43]

The same type of concern has surfaced once again in the recently published document "The Interpretation of the Bible in the Church" issued by the Pontifical Biblical Commission in Rome. The highly technical 125 page study not only supports the use of questionable conclusions from historical-critical methodology but blames the fundamentalist approach to the Bible on the Reformers. It significantly distorts a Protestant view of inerrancy and attacks the evangelical doctrine of Scripture aggressively. When this kind of attack on the Word of God continues, how can any biblical theological discussion advance meaningfully?

Finally, if we are to see the much needed new reformation that I have written of, we must be about the work of "*speaking the truth* in love" more obviously. Nothing is gained in the consideration of Roman Catholic doctrine, by either Catholics or evangelicals, when we avoid those doctrines that divide us. I have learned to appreciate Mary for her loving faithfulness to God. Reading Catholic material has stimulated some of this appreciation, but I am still convinced, with S. Lewis Johnson in chapter 5, that Marian theological formulations in the Roman tradition are harmful and potentially fatal to true faith in Christ alone. Should I keep quiet about this when I consider the teaching of the Word of God with my Catholic neighbor? Not if I love him and am still convinced that he hasn't gotten this right yet. I don't have to put labels and aspersions on him that hurt and wound, but I owe it to God and to my friend to "speak the truth." I also owe it to him to do it "in love."

I am convinced that with rare exception, and that in opposition to the official creeds of the church and the writings of major Catholic theologians, Roman Catholic theology still does not believe or understand justification by faith alone. Avery Dulles, a Jesuit theologian who is considered somewhat of a moderate, was asked about this important doctrine by Donald Bloesch in an interview published in *Christianity Today* in 1986. Dulles said, "We do not greatly disagree on the way in which the individual comes to justification: through the grace of Christ accepted in faith." Bloesch, wisely knowing the history of this debate and the nuances of important differences, asked Dulles to elaborate, to which he added, "The response to Luther was made official at the Council of Trent [1545–63]. In its 'Decree on Justification,' the council described the process of justification and insisted that it is through faith that one is justified."[44]

You might well ask, "What then is wrong with Dulles's statement?" Bloesch asked Dulles if it is the word *process* that is the key difference. For

Rome justification is a process inside of me, a process whereby I am being saved and made right with God. For Luther, and for a true evangelical, justification is not a *process*, it is a *finished work* done outside of me by Christ. When I am justified I am accepted into fellowship with God freely. I can say with Paul, "There is therefore, now, no condemnation" (Romans 8:1). Upon this crucial hinge Luther defended his entire understanding of a vital and radically different gospel message. If I "speak the truth in love," then I must not leave this doctrine aside in the relationship, as almost all modern Catholic-evangelical discussions seem to do.

And when my Roman Catholic friend wishes to define the issue of authority in terms of a church that gave us the Scriptures and that interprets them properly, giving me a source of authority that is ultimately above, or over, the written Scriptures, I cannot remain silent. My conscience bears witness to this truth taught by the church Fathers and restored in practice by Luther and Calvin in the sixteenth century. Truth demands that I press this matter forward in any discussion where the truth is under attack, either explicitly or implicitly.

Our present conciliatory atmosphere has allowed a new level of discussion. It is my hope that a book such as this one displays something of that good spirit. Having said this, however, I concur with G. C. Berkouwer: "The Reformation did not break with the church. . . . On the contrary the church rejected it." The Reformers, to use Berkouwer's words again, "knocked on the door, but the Council of Trent shut out the *sola fide, sola gratia, sola scriptura* of the Reformation." This leads Berkouwer to deduce—properly, I think—that "eventually the men of conciliatory temper will have to face quite seriously the question, Why did Rome reject the Reformation?"[45]

In 1987, then-Lutheran Richard John Neuhaus wrote a book by the intriguing title *The Catholic Moment*. I was fascinated by his thought. He considered what he called the paradox of the church in the postmodern world.[46] This is similar to the question Wells raises in his more recent book *No Place for Truth*. Since writing that book, Neuhaus, whose writings I find almost always useful, has converted to Roman Catholicism. As I have thought about this subject for some months I continue to think, *What if this were to become, as in the sixteenth century, the evangelical moment?*

The true Protestant spirit has great force; it has great meaning. It is the spirit of life that flows out of the proper view of God's authority and God's glory—it is not simply a spirit of protest against Rome, or any other fallen institution. It is a strength that has great recovering and healing power. As Berkouwer has said, "The power of the Reformation was not the strength of man, but the strength which manifested itself in weakness. 'I can do all things through Christ which strengtheneth me.' That was the power of the Reformation."[47]

That is my prayer and has been for a number of years now. My hope is not that we might defend or prop up a sectarian movement known as "evangelicalism," or "Protestantism," but rather that we might see another great era for the gospel like that which the Spirit began when He powerfully opened the eyes of an Augustinian monk in the early sixteenth century, and through him broke open much of Europe, launching the greatest "recovery" movement in the history of the church. Luther did not get it all right, as no reformer or theologian ever does. But he got two vitally important things right—the doctrine of Scripture and the doctrine of the gospel. Precisely here the modern evangelical church gropes about in weakness like a giant without sight. Precisely here we must seize the present moment and recover the spirit of the older, truer, sounder evangelicalism.

Will we see another great reformation? Will there be another revival like that which broke out through the recovery of the Scriptures and the gospel in the sixteenth century? God alone knows, but we who love Him must labor for it and pray that He might be gracious to His people even in these dark times. *This could be the evangelical moment.* Let us pray that it will be and that revival mercies might flow again across Western nations.

Notes

1. Charles E. Colson, *The Body* (Dallas: Word, 1992), 114.
2. Texe Marrs, "Texe Marrs Asks Chuck Colson: Will You Sell Your Soul to the Devil for a Million Dollars," *Flashpoint: A Newsletter Ministry of Texe Marrs* (June 1993), 1.
3. John Robbins, "The Counterfeit Gospel of Charles Colson, Part 2," *The Trinity Review* (February 1994): 4.
4. Keith A. Fournier, *Evangelical Catholics* (Nashville: Nelson, 1990), vi.
5. Paul G. Schrotenboer, ed., *Roman Catholicism: A Contemporary Evangelical Perspective* (Grand Rapids: Baker, 1987), 12.
6. David Duggins, "Across the Divide," *Moody* (November 1993), 14.
7. Ibid., 14–15.
8. George Weigel, "Post Vatican II," *Eternity* (October 1986), 21. Weigel is a Roman Catholic theologian who has worked alongside many traditions in dealing with ethics and public policy issues.
9. Ibid.
10. Lorraine Boettner, *Roman Catholicism* (Philadelphia: Presb. & Ref., 1965), 447. Boettner is typical of older evangelical writers in that he seeks to show what is wrong with Roman Catholicism by treating the doctrines of Trent as normative in all cases. His quote here displays an approach often taken by conservatives that is neither accurate nor helpful.
11. David F. Wells, *Revolution in Rome* (Downers Grove, Ill.: InterVarsity, 1972), 19. This volume, which I quote quite heavily in my response to conciliar post Vatican II Catholicism, is the wisest and most cogently and compactly argued commen-

tary written by an evangelical that I know. I am sorry that it is out of print and wish that a revised edition might be done in the light of nearly twenty-five years of history.

12. Wells, *Revolution in Rome*, 24.

13. Weigel, "Post Vatican II," 24.

14. Ibid.

15. Ibid., 26.

16. Ibid.

17. Robert A. Burns, *Roman Catholicism: Yesterday and Today* (Chicago: Loyola Univ. Press, 1992), 8.

18. Ibid., 13.

19. Ibid., 13–18.

20. Wells, *Revolution in Rome*, 83.

21. Ibid., 86.

22. *Constitution on the Church*, 9; cited in Wells, *Revolution in Rome*, 87.

23. B. C. Butler, *The Theology of Vatican II*, 167; cited in Wells, *Revolution in Rome*, 88.

24. Wells, *Revolution in Rome*, 90.

25. Ibid., 90–94.

26. David Duggins, "Across the Divide," *Moody* (November 1993), 17.

27. John Warwick Montgomery, *Ecumenicity, Evangelicals, and Rome* (Grand Rapids: Zondervan, 1969), 39.

28. David Wells, "Catholicism at the Crossroads," *Eternity* (September 1987), 14.

29. Harold O. J. Brown, "What Do Catholics Believe?" *Moody* (November 1993), 21.

30. John R. W. Stott, "Evangelicals and Roman Catholics," *Christianity Today*, 12 August 1977, 30.

31. Montgomery, *Ecumenicity, Evangelicals, and Rome*, 33.

32. Malachi Martin, *The Final Conclave* (New York: Stein & Day, 1978). Martin is always an interesting read for those who would like to read a popular Roman Catholic author who is often critical of his church while remaining faithful to her.

33. George Carey, *A Tale of Two Churches: Can Protestants and Catholics Get Together?* (Downers Grove, Ill.: InterVarsity, 1985), 17.

34. Kenneth Kantzer, "Church on the Move," *Christianity Today*, 7 November 1986, 17.

35. Paul Tillich, *A History of Christian Thought* (New York: Harper & Row, 1968), 225–26, 239.

36. Louis Bouyer, *The Spirit and Forms of Protestantism* (Westminster, Md.: Newman, 1957), 186–97. This is a very interesting and impressive apologia for a Protestant who converted to Rome in the 1950s.

37. Harold Bloom, *The American Religion: The Emergence of a Post-Christian Nation* (New York: Simon & Schuster, 1992), 45.

38. David F. Wells, *No Place for Truth: Or Whatever Happened to Evangelical Theology?* (Grand Rapids: Eerdmans,1993), 296. This is perhaps the most important call to a new reformation in the evangelical churches that we have in our time. Professor Wells knows Catholicism, and he knows evangelicalism. Highly recommended for all serious evangelicals.

39. Montgomery, *Ecumenicity, Evangelicals, and Rome*, 21.

40. James I. Packer, "Counterpoint: A Protestant Assessment," *Eternity* (October 1986), 25.

41. Wells, *Revolution in Rome*, 122–23.

42. Ibid., 126.

43. "Catholic Bishops Address Protestant Fundamentalism," *Christianity Today,* 11 December 1987, 54.

44. "America's Catholics: What They Believe—Catholic Doctrine According to Jesuit Theologian Avery Dulles," an interview with Avery Dulles conducted by Donald Bloesch, *Christianity Today,* 7 November 1986, 26–27.

45. G. C. Berkouwer, *Recent Developments in Roman Catholic Thought* (Grand Rapids: Eerdmans, 1958), 31.

46. Richard John Neuhaus, *The Catholic Moment: The Paradox of the Church in the Postmodern World* (San Francisco: Harper & Row, 1987).

47. Berkouwer, *Recent Developments in Roman Catholic Thought,* 74–75.

GLOSSARY

absolution The forgiveness of sins. Derived from a Latin term meaning "to set free," it came to refer to the remission granted by the Roman Catholic Church.

actus purus A description of God as a fully actualized being.

aggiornamento The modern effort to present Roman Catholic teaching and practice so that people will better understand and accept them. New approaches in ecumenical dialogue.

Albigensians A medieval French heretical sect that denied Christ's true humanity, crucifixion, and resurrection believing that salvation was attainable through liberation from physical matter.

Anabaptist(s) Sometimes referred to as "the left wing" of the Protestant Reformation, the name is used to describe most of those groups that were not a part of the Lutheran or Reformed movements. Embraced the baptism of those who professed faith, rejecting infant baptism. Upheld the separation of church and state and the authority of scripture alone. Many were pacifists, and quite a number were executed by other Protestants and Roman Catholics. Ranged from radicals who were mystics and prophets of divine revelation to those who were much more akin to modern baptistic practice.

Anselm (1033–1109) A medieval monk who became Archbishop of Canterbury. His theology was Augustinian, following Plato's philosophy in building his thought. He asserted that Jesus satisfied the honor and justice of God by atoning for human sin and insisted that faith must precede reason. He also developed the popular ontological argument for God's existence. His theology has influenced numerous later theologians, including Karl Barth.

anthropomorphism The act or practice of attributing human form or qualities to gods, animals, or things. Used in Christian theology to describe various biblical terms referring human features and qualities to the divine person.

anti-Nicene Against the Council of Nicea and its dogmas (*see* Nicea).

Apocrypha Literally, "the hidden things" (Greek), and in reference to the Bible the books that some in the early church received as part of the Greek version of the Old Testament but were not included in the Hebrew Bible. They were included in the Latin translation of the Old Testament known as the Vulgate and thus have been included in the Roman Catholic versions of the Bible.

Aquinas, Thomas (1225–1274) The greatest theologian and philosopher of medieval Christianity. who is best known for his two great summaries of human knowledge. One defended the truth of the Catholic faith against the pagans by clearly distinguishing between reason and faith, and the other summarized all that was known about God and man.

ARCIC II An Anglican–Roman Catholic Consultation that included dialogue aimed at a common understanding of Christian faith. Reviewed critically by Alister McGrath in chapter 10.

Arians (Arius, d. 336) Those who followed the teaching of Arius, a presbyter of the Alexandrian church, believing that the person of Christ is the highest of the created beings and is thus appropriately referred to as god, but not *the* God.

Aristotle (384–322 B.C.) A Greek philosopher who, though a student of Plato, developed an empirical system of philosophy quite contrary to Plato's ideas. His philosophy became quite influential on Christian thought in the Middle Ages, leading to the development of a Christian scholasticism.

Aristotelian causality That which is effected by, or caused by, the philosophical influence of Aristotle.

Aristotelian empiricism The teaching, taken from the influence of Aristotle, that all human knowledge is rooted in experience; thus an empirical theology is one built on the observation of religious experience, not on theoretical principles.

Arius's reductionistic Christology The doctrine of Christ's person that is reduced from the observations made by Arius (*see* Arianism above).

Athanasius (293–373) The bishop of Alexandria, who became the chief defender of orthodox Christianity against Arianism. Through his faithful teaching, steadfast character, significant writings, and commitment to God's truth, he contributed much toward the confessional triumph of historic orthodoxy at the Council of Constantinople eight years after his death.

Bernard A Cistercian abbot (1090–1153) who founded a monastery at Clairvaux. A solitary person of austere habits who sought to combine worship with the service of humanity. He opposed the heretical teaching of Abelard and the teaching of Arnold of Brescia.

catechesis Literally, "to resound" (Greek). Came to be used of written and spoken words, plus visual and audio aids, to pass down the gospel of Christ; thus a catechism is a teaching tool that uses questions and answers to teach the faith.

catechumens Literally, "instruction" (Greek); came to refer, in the early church, to the people who were being given catechesis with the specific, ecclesiastical meaning of someone who is receiving formal instruction in the Faith, with a view to reception into the church and full participation in her sacramental life.

Cathari A term applied to several different groups in church history that have emphasized purity of life.

Chalcedonian Christology (doctrine) A Christology, or doctrine of Christ, that accords with the orthodox definition prescribed by the fourth general council of the historic church, the Council of Chalcedon (451): Jesus Christ as fully God and fully man, two distinct natures in one person.

Chemnitz, Martin An important Lutheran theologian (1522–1586) who wrote the most important Protestant critique of the Council of Trent, as well as numerous other evangelical works. A friend of Melanchthon, he helped to reunite the divided Lutheran Church in the Formula of Concord (1577).

conciliarism A fifteenth-century reform movement in the Roman Catholic Church that asserted the authority of general councils over the popes.

concupiscence The tendency or inclination of human nature toward sin arising from the disobedience of Adam and Eve. All persons, except Jesus and Mary (according to Roman Catholic dogma), possess concupiscence, or the desire for bodily pleasure. Concupiscence is not evil, per se, but leads to sin when unchecked.

Constantinopolitan (denouement) Referring to the solutions reached by the Councils of Constantinople (381, 553, and 680–81), which addressed a number of heresies surrounding the doctrine of Christ, including Arianism, Nestorianism, and Monphysitism.

consubstantiation The idea, characteristic of Lutheran theology, that in the Lord's Supper the bread and the wine are *not* transformed into the body and blood of Christ but that the molecules of the flesh and blood are present "in, with, and under" the molecules of the bread and wine.

conventicles A conventicle is a religious group or a meeting for worship outside of, and to some degree in protest against, the established church.

Curia A medieval council, or law court, that became the Roman Curia, or the total organization that assists the bishops in their performance of duties for the church. In it are ten congregations in the modern church including education, evangelism, worship, and so on. Reformed extensively in the post-Vatican II church since 1967.

deification The idea that there is a process by which we are transfigured in the likeness of God.

denouement The solution, clarification, or unraveling of a plot; the outcome or final solution of a sequence of events.

dialectical theology A synonym for neoorthodoxy, a twentieth century reaction against European liberal theology. This term was used especially in the earlier years of neoorthodoxy.

Dionysius A Pope from 259 who was Greek by birth. His was the task of reorganizing the church after the persecution during which his predecessor Sixtus II had been martyred. He sent help to beleaguered Christians in Capadocia and helped to further the concept of the primacy of Rome by resolving a charge of heresy against Bishop Dionysius of Alexandria.

Docetic heresy Docetism is the belief that the humanity of Jesus was not genuine; i.e., He merely appeared to be human.

Dominican A Roman Catholic order of "The Preachers." From its inception this order stressed the study of the Scriptures and theology.

Donatists A movement of those who followed Donatus, a North African bishop (d. 355), and became a separatist movement that objected to the reinstatement of Christians, especially clergymen, who surrendered the Scriptures under persecution. They sought refuge in views of the end of the age, and the more extreme courted martyrdom.

ecclesiastical Of or having to do with the church or the clergy; i.e., not laypeople.

encyclical A circular letter, especially a papal document in modern times.

Episcopal See An Episcopal diocese or archdiocese.

Erasmus, Desiderius (of Rotterdam) A Dutch humanist (1466–1536) whose work helped to spur the Reformers on in study of the text of Scripture by pointing back to the Fathers and earlier sources and away from scholasticism. Appointed a professor at Cambridge, he would not leave the Roman Catholic Church and was opposed by Luther in his major work, *The Bondage of the Will*. His writings were banned by two popes.

eschatological prophet Eschatological refers to the study of the last things or of the future generally; thus, Jesus was a prophet of the final age as the term is used in chapter 5.

esoteric theology Esoteric means understood only by a select few; intended for an inner circle as of disciples or scholars.

ex cathedra A term that means, "from the throne" (Latin); used by Roman Catholicism to describe the most solemn and authoritative infallible statements of the church.

existentiell Modern German theologians use two terms, *existentiell* and *existential*. *Existentiell* is used as an adjective in a general sesne to refer to one's individual, concrete, "life-out" experience. In English this would commonly be the same thing as that meant by the word *existential*.

existential A philosophy that emphasizes existence over essence; thus, the question "Does it exist" is more important than "What is it?" It is used in chapter 5 either as an adjective or as a noun to speak of a particular tenet of Heidegger's philosophy or in reference to the characteristic qualities of human existence.

expiations Refers to the cancellation or covering of sin. Expiation contrasts with propitiation, which is appeasing divine wrath.

forensic act of God An act that is legal in form or argument; generally used in referring to justification by faith alone as a forensic action on God's part in crediting righteousness to the believing sinner based solely on faith.

Gnostic (Gnosticism) Gnosticism was a movement in early Christianity, begun at least as early as the first century, that (1) emphasized a special higher truth that only the more enlightened receive from God, (2) taught that matter is evil, and (3) denied the humanity of Jesus. Several theories of the origins of the movement have been advanced, but most agree that several portions of the New Testament were written to counteract incipient Gnosticism in the church.

hagiography A collection of sacred writings or, more particularly, the writing of saints' lives.

Hegel, Georg Wilhelm Friedrich German idealistic philosopher (1770–1831) whose views inspired both absolute realism, which is the theory that all of reality is mental and organic in nature, as well as dialectical materialism, the Marxian interpretation of reality that sees all change as the result of constant conflict between opposites arising from internal conflicts in all events, ideas, and movements.

Hegelian nature With reference to the philosopher noted above, the idea that the world was created by a philosophical evolution, with the meaning of life discernible in the history of the human race.

Heidegger, Martin A German existentialist philosopher (1889–1976), who studied at a Jesuit school for a short period. A follower of Sartre's thought, his writing influenced radical liberal theologians like Bultmann, Tillich, and Macquarrie, as well as Karl Barth. His concept of the "existential" moment when man responds to God by choosing "authentic" existence is perhaps his most prominent contribution to theological thought.

Hellenism (Hellenistic) Various ideas, ideals, and practices associated with ancient, classical Greece that became part of the culture of the Roman Empire. Hellenism became an important factor in the way in which the church expressed its faith.

Hus, John Bohemian reformer (1373–1415) who studied Wycliffe's works and sought to call the church back to important biblical doctrines. He was burned at the stake by the civil authorities as a heretic when he would not recant his views even though he had been promised "safe conduct" by the emperor in 1414.

hypostasis From the Greek word for "substance" or "nature," the real or essential nature of something as distinguished from its attributes. In Christian thought the term is used in reference to any one of the three distinct persons of the Trinity, and especially Christ, the second person of the Trinity, in His divine and human natures.

hypostatic union Referring to he union of Jesus' divine and human natures in one person.

Ignatius Bishop of Antioch and martyr who died at Rome in 107 A.D. during Trajan's reign. All we know about him comes from seven of his letters that tell how he was tried and condemned at Antioch by the governor and was escorted across Asia Minor by ten guards and thrown to wild beasts in Rome.

imputed righteousness God's act of crediting the righteousness of Christ to sinners who believe and accept his gift.

infused righteousness The Holy Spirit's work in pouring divine grace into the heart and soul of a sinner so that he may have eternal life and divine forgiveness; i.e., the Roman Catholic doctrine of salvation inside the believing person, not outside, as taught by Luther and the Reformers. In Roman Catholic teaching this process begins with regeneration and continues in justification and sanctification.

Irenaeus Bishop of Lyons (130–200). His defense of orthodoxy, *Against Heresies,* took issue with Gnosticism and Montanism and underlined his claim to be the first great Western theologian. He contributed significantly toward the development of the canon of Scripture.

Justin Christian apologist (100–165) who first brought together the claims of faith and reason. His writings emphasize that Christians are the heirs of God's promises to Israel.

justification The act by which we are declared righteous through faith alone, by grace alone, in Christ alone.

Kant, Immanuel German philosopher (1724–1804) who sought to unite philosophical rationalism, a strong emphasis upon reason that went beyond Scripture and historic theology, and empiricism, the idea that all knowledge comes through sensory perception or experience.

kenoticism A theology that emphasizes the self-limitation of Christ or His giving up of divine prerogatives and attributes, often based on improper exegesis of Philippians 2:5–11.

Lydian stone Lydian is (1) of Lydia (an ancient country in western Asia Minor famous for its wealth and luxury), its people, or their language; (2) of the Lydian mode; soft; gentle; effeminate.

Magisterium The Roman Catholic Church's teaching authority, believed to be instituted by Christ and guided by the Holy Spirit, which seeks to safeguard and explain the truths of the faith.

Manichaeans Those who believed the dualistic philosophy that became a major religion in the ancient world. There was a strong emphasis upon asceticism as a means of salvation.

Mediatrx A title once given to Mary, mother of Jesus. Vatican II declared that Mary may be called by this title as long as it is understood in such a way that it does not take away from or add to the role of Christ as sole Mediator.

medieval synthesis The combination of parts or elements into a whole produced by the medieval developments in church history.

Meritum de condigno Latin, meaning "condign merit." Merit that is deserving of our own power.

Meritum de congruo Latin, meaning "congruous merit." Merit that is based on God's generosity after we have done all that we are able through our own power.

Molinist (view) The theological doctrine proposed by Luis Molina that emphasized human freedom and diminished the efficacy and power of grace. He held that God possesses Sovereign authority in regard to human freedom and contended that without compromising human freedom, God can direct it as it pleases Him because of His knowledge of future conditions.

monasticism The movement within the development of the church's life that sought withdrawal from society into private groups that practice asceticism and other forms of spiritual discipline.

monergism The view that conversion is accomplished totally by the working of God.

Monophysites Those who believed the doctrine that Jesus had only one nature rather than two. It usually takes the form that the humanity of Jesus was absorbed into his deity.

Montanists Those who believe the teachings of Montanus, a Phrygian Christian who fell into a trance and began to "prophesy under the influence of the Spirit." It came to refer to those with the view that the Holy Spirit continues to speak through prophecy.

neonomian Neonomianism is a movement that arose in the early eighteenth-century Church of Scotland during a controversy over the relationship between law and gospel in salvation. The Neonomians maintained that the gospel is a new law replacing the Old Testament law: the legal conditions of faith and repentance must be met before salvation can be offered.

neoorthodox theology A system of theology associated particularly with Karl Barth, Emil Brunner, and Reinhold Niebuhr. While accepting biblical criticism and a certain amount of existential thought, the movement emphasized divine transcendence as well as human sinfulness and need. It represented a return to modified forms of orthodox doctrines as contrasted with the earlier liberal abandonment of such doctrines.

neoplatonism The recasting of the philosophy of Plato by Plotinus and others. Some Christian theologians used it to expand the truths of Christianity, and its influence lasted into the medieval period.

Neo-Thomist *See* Thomism.

nonprimatial Refers to a primateship; thus, it has the meaning of the position or rank of a church primate.

omega point One of four points (of a evolutionary theory holding that there are four stages of development in the universe) of French Jesuit Pierre Teilhard de Chardin (1881–1955) that says, "evolution from individual rational beings to a society with Christ as Lord."

ontological Ontology is the philosophical study of the nature of being. What is real? What is ultimate reality beyond everything that seems to be real?

ontological argument A way of reasoning concerning God's existence. It was first advanced by Anselm of Canterbury (1109). God is said to be a being such that a greater being cannot be thought of. Anyone having such an idea of God and accepting what it means cannot deny that God truly and necessarily exists.

Orphism A religion or philosophical system based on the mysteries and verses attributed to Orpheus.

pantheistic Pantheism is the belief that everything in nature is divine.

Pantokrator From the Greek, meaning ruler of all, Pantocrator is the title given in the Eastern Church to Christ as the Ruler of Heaven and Earth.

patristic age "Patristic" refers to the age during which the Fathers of the church of the first seven or eight centuries wrote—i.e., their lives, doctrines, and writings.

Pelagianism, Pelagians (Pelagius) The view of man embraced through influence of the beliefs of Pelagius, who emphasized human ability and free will rather than depravity and sinfulness. In the view of most Pelagians, it is possible to live without sin. The effect of Adam's sin upon his descendants was simply that of a bad example. Condemned as heresy by the church.

philosophical paradigm The pattern or example of a view or way of thinking.

pietism A historical movement in the church that stressed the need for faith to be fulfilled in Christian practice, particularly through personal study, prayer, holiness, seriousness, and faithful fulfillment of duties associated with faith.

Plato A Greek philosopher (427–347 B.C.) active in Athens. A disciple of Socrates, he emphasized the reality of the ideal rather than the empirical. Plato has had a profound influence upon Western philosophy and also upon much Christian theology.

Platonic idealism Plato's confidence in the human mind to find absolute truth; also a longing for a better world and encouragement for a high view of morality.

Plotinus The most noted exponent of neoplatonism (205–270) who held that the material world is unreal. Reality lies beyond life in the union of the soul with the mystical source of all truth, goodness, and beauty. He emphasized that all things have emanated from God.

Polycarp Bishop of Smyrna (70–155). According to Irenaeus, Polycarp was a disciple of the apostle John, and thus his long life was a significant link with the earliest days of the church. A champion of orthodoxy against heresy, notably against Gnosticism, he was burned to death for refusing to recant his faith.

postconciliar After the conciliar movement (*see* above).

post-Kantian Referring to thought that comes after the influence of Immanuel Kant, referred to above.

post-Nicene Thought that developed after the Councils of Nicea (325).

prereflexive Before thinking or meditating.

prevenient grace The work of the Holy Spirit in preparing a sinner to receive divine illumination and grace.

Rahner, Karl The best-known writing theologian of the Roman Catholic Church in our century (1904–1984). Chapter 5 devotes considerable attention to his thought because it is so important to understanding academic Roman Catholic theology today. He is strongly influenced by Thomism, but his theology is not that of orthodoxy.

rationalism A philosophical stance assigning reason to a determinative role in coming to truth.

Ritschlian liberalism The system of thought attached to the name of Albrecht Ritschl, a German Protestant theologian (1822–1889). It emphasized value judgments rather that theoretical doctrines.

sacerdotalism The teaching that the act of ordination to certain religious offices conveys the ability to administer the sacraments and thus dispense grace to those who take the sacraments.

sacramental grace The idea that a sacrament imparts grace in virtue of the right itself.

sanctification The process by which we are made righteous through faith and the works of love.

sanctifying grace In Roman Catholic theology the grace conveyed by the sacraments, combining both justification and sanctification as defined above.

See In Latin, "chair, or throne"; it thus became a name for a diocese or archdiocese

semi-Pelagianism A doctrinal position developed during the fifth and sixth centuries by theologians who did not wish to adopt the views of Pelagius or Augustine. This term was coined in the sixteenth century to describe Arminianism, which was semi-Pelagian, or a kind of "halfway" position between the two views debated earlier by the church.

sola fide Faith alone.

sola gratia Grace alone.

sola Scriptura The Scripture alone, meaning the written Scriptures of the Old and New Testaments are the sole source of authority for all faith and practice.

Soli Deo gloria Glory to God alone.

solus Christus Christ alone.

soteriological Of or pertaining to salvation.

synergistic The idea that man works together with God in certain aspects of salvation, for example, faith or regeneration.

Tertullian African Christian apologist (160–220) who was the first great writer of Christian material in Latin. By 210, disillusioned by the low quality of Christian practice, he had become a Montanist, but even the Montanists fell short of his expectations and he reportedly founded his own sect.

Theotokos Literally, "God-bearing," an expression used of Mary, the mother of Jesus. *Theotokos* can be used either as an affirmation of the deity of Jesus Christ or as a form of Mariolatry.

Thomistic The system of thought inspired by Thomas Aquinas's synthesis of Christian doctrine and the philosophy of Aristotle. It includes an emphasis on rational evidences for the existence of God.

Thomistic Aristotelianism A Christian use of Aristotle's philosophy and ethics, which relied on the thought of Thomas Aquinas (*see* above).

Traducianism The belief that the human soul is received by transmission from one's own parents.

Trallians Members of the ancient church (Asia Minor) to whom Ignatius wrote an epistle.

transcendence The transcendence of God is God's otherness or separateness from the creation and the human race.

Transcendental Thomism The Thomism that desires to be in tune with that which is contemporary.

transubstantiation The Roman Catholic doctrine that the bread and the wine in the Mass actually change into the substance of Christ's body and blood.

Tridentine That which originated at or developed from the Council of Trent.

unclimatable An unfriendly environment.

via media A Latin word for "a middle way"; thus, a mediate course (especially applied to the Anglican Church as standing halfway between the Roman Catholic and Protestant beliefs).

Vincent of Lerins A French monk and theologian (d. 445) who was a leader of the semi-Pelagian party who opposed Augustine's views. Upheld Scripture as final arbiter in faith and conduct and offered a threefold test for tradition: "What has been believed everywhere, always, and by all?"

viva voce Latin, "live voice," thus, a living person.

Waldo, Peter Founded a reform movement in France known as the Waldensians. His followers were known as "the poor men" because of the stress on living simply. Placed under papal ban in 1184. Rejected doctrines such as purgatory, prayers for the dead, and civil oaths. By the time of the Protestant Reformation most Waldensians, persecuted for centuries, were found in certain Alpine valleys. Today, Waldensianism is still the most prominent representative of Protestantism in Italy.

Whitehead, Alfred North A mathematician and philosopher (1861–1947) whose views have become the fountainhead of process philosophy, which emphasizes progress and evolution, and process theology, which builds theological ideas on the philosophy. Thus, God is in some way evolving, or changing and developing. The influence of this thought is impacting theology very significantly in our time.

Wycliffe, John English Reformer (1329–1384) who became widely known as rector of Lutterworth in Leicestershire. He was critical of the church's acquisitive attitude to property and questioned it openly. Led in translation of the Bible into English and sought to make right doctrine and practice correspond. Properly called "the morning star of the Reformation."

GENERAL INDEX

SCRIPTURE INDEX

Moody Press, a ministry of the Moody Bible Institute,
is designed for education, evangelization, and edification.
If we may assist you in knowing more about Christ
and the Christian life, please write us without obligation:
Moody Press, c/o MLM, Chicago, Illinois 60610.